1974

American Society and Black Revolution

American Society and Black Revolution

Frank Hercules

New York

Harcourt Brace Jovanovich, Inc.

First edition
ISBN 0-15-106180-7
Library of Congress Catalog Card Number: 72-78458
Printed in the United States of America
B C D E

The author wishes to thank the following for permission to quote from the works listed: Bantam Books, Inc. and Julian Bach Literary Agency, Inc., for *Soledad Brother: The Prison Letters of George Jackson,* copyright © 1970 by World Entertainers Limited, published by Coward, McCann, Geoghagen, Inc. and Bantam Books, Inc., all rights reserved; Basic Books, Inc., Publishers, New York, for *Black Rage* by William H. Grier and Price M. Cobbs, editors, 1968; Beacon Press, for *Negations* by Herbert Marcuse, copyright © 1968 by Herbert Marcuse; Harcourt Brace Jovanovich, Inc., for *Dusk of Dawn* by W. E. B. Du Bois; and for *The American Quest 1790–1860* by Clinton Rossiter, copyright © 1971 by Mary Crane Rossiter; Harper & Row, Publishers, Inc., for "For a Lady I Know" from *On These I Stand* by Countee Cullen, copyright 1925 by Harper & Row, Publishers, Inc., renewed 1953 by Ida M. Cullen; Humanities Press, Inc., for *Reason and Revolution* by Herbert Marcuse; International Publishers Co., Inc., for *The World and Africa* by W. E. B. Du Bois, copyright © 1965; and for *The Autobiography of W. E. B. Du Bois* by W. E. B. Du Bois, copyright © 1968; Alfred A. Knopf, Inc., for *American Violence: A Documentary History* by Richard Hofstadter and Michael Wallace; McGraw-Hill Book Company, for *Soul on Ice* by Eldridge Cleaver, copyright © 1968 by Eldridge Cleaver; Harold Ober Associates Incorporated, for "Silent One" by Langston Hughes, copyright © 1962 by The New York Times Company; Random House, Inc., for *The End of Empire* by John Strachey, copyright © 1959 by John Strachey; Russell & Russell, for *Black Reconstruction in America, 1860–1880* by W. E. B. Du Bois, © 1935, 1963; Tangerine Music Corporation, for "You're in for a Big Surprise," © 1965 by Tangerine Music Corporation.

For Dellora,
because our marriage has been a
constant symposium of ideas, cre-
ating the world anew each morn-
ing, even on the seventh day;

and for Eric:

This little silent one—
He's all the atoms from the sun
And all the grass blades
From the earth
And all the songs
The heart gives birth
To when the throat
Stops singing—
He's my son—
This little
Silent
One.

> —Langston Hughes, "Silent One"

Nations, people, the human race are living now in a new world, though their thoughts remain in the old: therein lie humanity's hopes as well as humanity's misfortunes.

—Milovan Djilas, *The Unperfect Society*

Acknowledgments

WHATEVER TRUTHS this book may have succeeded in expressing, or such other virtues as it may perhaps here and there be thought to possess, are due solely to the editorship of Mr. James Milholland, Jr.

I should be gravely remiss if I did not also recall here, and in this way commemorate, the friendship shown me by Mr. Julian Muller, Editor in Chief. My gratitude to him reaches beyond this book into all the years of his steady interest in my work.

There are others to whom, as well, I owe appreciation: Mr. William Goodman, with whom I early explored the idea of a book such as this; Mr. Don Buckner, formerly of the Division of Urban Education of Harcourt Brace Jovanovich, whose enthusiasm for the book was contagious in the highest degree; and if it chances that she is last to be mentioned, she is certainly not least to be thanked, Miss Regina Shannon, assistant to Mr. Milholland, and of generous, heart-warming aid to me.

American
Society
and
Black
Revolution

Prologue

I call you "Mister"
    I shine your shoes
You go 'way laughing
    While I sing the blues.
You think I'm funny
    And you're so wise
But, a-a-a-ah, baby,
    You're in for a big surprise.

—"You're in for a Big Surprise"

I SUPPOSE that if one were to find and incapsulate the essential spirit of a black revolution against the American society, those lines would come as close as anything to complete discovery. They also bring into lyric relief the contours of a drama in which, patiently and with implacable purpose, the victim stalks the oppressor. The only question is the intention of the victim. To what end, ultimately, does he aim to consign the oppressor? If it were anything so prosaic as revenge, it would not be interesting. It would even be trite. So, what is the real object of this centuries-long stalking, this inexhaustible patience, this measureless enduring? What impulse animates it? What dream sustains it? What architecture prescribes its shape?

When, over a quarter of a century ago, I first came to the United

3

States of America, I carried with me several letters of introduction. Although I am a black West Indian and now a citizen of the United States, I traveled at that time from England, where I had been studying for the Bar at the Honourable Society of the Middle Temple in London. One evening at dinner at Grosvenor House, I was introduced to Lord and Lady Simon, who invited me to call on them. When I did accept their invitation, I was about to leave England for the United States, and Lord Simon had meanwhile become Chancellor of the Exchequer. He had held other great offices of state, among them the Foreign Secretaryship of Great Britain. There were those, however, who thought that he was a better lawyer than a statesman. He was a very great lawyer indeed. I had the deepest admiration for his legal learning and acumen. At No. 11 Downing Street, I had tea with Lady Simon, to whom I announced my intention to go to the United States. She herself was American, having been born in, I think, Tennessee. At any rate, she gave me letters of introduction to friends of hers in America. Among them were W. E. B. Du Bois and Walter White. In due course I met them both and presented my letters.

So began my odyssey in a strange land. The beginning was unorthodox. I had left the ship on a Saturday afternoon with a distinguished English writer and his wife, who, because they were in transit to Japan, the destination of the vessel, were not required to undergo customs examination. I was not in similar case. But I was so eager to see New York that I decided there was no need for me to be personally present at the examination of my luggage. Except for a small overnight bag, I left my luggage behind to be dealt with by the customs inspectors at their leisure and mine.

The following Monday, after an exhilarating introduction to America, I returned to collect my luggage. The customs inspector, a white man, to whom I was directed, greeted me: "So you're the guy who walked off and left your luggage." I objected to his use of the term "guy" in reference to me. After all, I was a member of the Honourable Society of the Middle Temple of the Inns of Court, and other things besides. The inspector did not conceal his astonishment at my attitude. He laughed, however, with unaffected heartiness. This further offended me.

When he had concluded his examination of my luggage, I bade him in a haughty and peremptory tone to "get me a cab." I can still see his head as it jerked backward and the genuine mystification in his eyes. Then he recovered himself and laughed again, more heartily even than before. "Okay," he said. "Okay." There was infinite kindliness in his voice, and infinite understanding. Assisted by a porter, he carried my luggage for me as he escorted me to a cab. When I was about to get in, he gave me a friendly pat on the arm. And with the same kindliness, the same understanding, he said to me, "You'll learn, buddy. You'll learn."

I am not at all certain that I have learned very much. But I am sure that I shall never forget that customs inspector as long as I live. If he should chance to read this book, I should like him to know how much I have cherished his memory. For me, he will always remain a glowing proof of that finer, generous America that my yearning celebrates, however sharply many actualities may contradict it.

The taxicab conveyed me to Harlem.

The lives of black Americans are mirror images, more pellucid than any, of American society. They refract, to an unparalleled degree, and with unmediated clearness, the social actualities that plummet from the surface to the inmost depths. Precisely as the condition of the Jews in Germany under Hitler defined the meaning of the German society, and the condition of the blacks in South Africa defines the meaning of the South African society, just so does the condition of the blacks in America define the meaning of the American society. From 1619 to 1972, from the first black slave who was brought to North America to the black insurrectionists who, now, would impose their will to redress that original evil and its consequences, from the Middle Passage to the Freedom Marches, the blacks have served, collectively, as the moral gauge of the American society. I do not mean that they have been exemplars, but that their treatment at the hands of their white fellow inhabitants of this continent has always been exemplary of the fundamental state of American society at any given moment. Not even the condition of the decimated Indians, which has never been anything but pitiable, has had quite this effect. More than any other ethnic group or social circumstance, the blacks and their well- or ill-being have measured the validity of the moral professions of America. There is poetic irony, perhaps poetic retribution, too, in this situation. The tyrant must always be made to accuse and condemn himself. He must then be brought to erect his own gallows and, having kicked himself off into eternity, be left to dangle there as a warning to the

5

like-minded. At least, this is a possible inference from the no doubt unconscious design of black Americans toward their oppressors. The Black Panthers demand that their courtroom judges accuse themselves, and that their relative roles be reversed, in all historical honesty. It is the first explicit sign to emerge of what may be a latent urge on the part of the whole collectivity of black Americans to judge their oppressors rather than be judged by them. The Nazis should have been tried at Nuremberg by Jews, and Jews alone. Belated recognition of this fact by the Israelis resulted in the Eichmann trial.

The cardinal defect of black writing is that it shrieks as victim instead of constructing its own artistic forum and, having brought the oppressor to trial under dispassionate indictment, calmly presiding over the trial and lucidly rendering judgment. I mean judgment against the background of history, and not simply of local circumstance. And by history I mean that of the human species and not only of the African slave trade, with its despoliation of Africa and debouchment of countless black chattels upon the shores of the Americas. This is tragedy, yes, of undeniable magnitude. But it is only a fragment of history. What is the grand design as opposed to the secondary plot? Who will write the black American *War and Peace?* For only on such a canvas will the necessary perspective be achieved. Perspective: it is not easy to maintain this habit of mind on even a minor scale. The emotional strain is severe. So black writers tend either to cry or laugh. So far, we seem to be incapable of intellectual austerity. Much more familiar to us, and much easier, is hysteria at opposite ends of the scale.

What do I wish to say about the American society and black revolution? I wish to say in measured language, and without raising my voice, three things above all. One, that, over the vast continuum of history, the American society differs from, say, the Sumerian society only in point of location in time and certain surface manifestations like technology. Two, that the moral progress of mankind over the past 7,000 years has been negligible. Slavery, for instance, continually repeats itself. Three, that the black revolution—if it exists—is simply another uprising on the part of a helot class. Now, how shall I say these things (as well as others) without seeming smug rather than judicious, desiccated of human feeling rather than dispassionate, intoxicated by my own mind rather than sobered by its exercise? How shall I attain serenity of judgment amidst the horror of the human

6

record? How shall I vindicate the faint smoke drift of a black revolution without invalidating the whole laboring, stumbling, groaning effort of the American society to lift itself to the level of its aspirations? I cannot pretend to deny the moral necessity of revolution *in certain circumstances*. But I must neither prejudge nor appear to prejudge the present constituents of American life that would affirm or deny the necessity of black revolution. I must not merely keep what is called an open mind. I must retain a balanced mind—a much more difficult feat. An open mind may be little else than a depository for rubbish; a balanced mind imports discriminating exercise of the intellect. This is what I need and must bring to bear upon my theme. Yet to do so in the face of the vast human tragedy implicit in the context of the American society, to make my mind the tranquil, undisturbed center of a vast hurricane of human struggle, will be far from easy. For one thing, I am deeply involved. I am black. Which is to say, I am, willy-nilly, counsel for the prosecution at the very time that I presume to carry out the function of judge. How, then, shall I reconcile these roles? There is only one way. I shall have to abdicate my position as prosecutor. Let History take my place.

History as prosecutor will be W. E. B. Du Bois, Booker T. Washington, Frederick Douglass, Monroe Trotter, Martin Luther King, Paul Robeson, Malcolm X, John Brown, Marcus Garvey, Charles Sumner, Wendell Phillips, William Lloyd Garrison, Adam Clayton Powell, among others.

But will not History itself be playing an ambiguous role? For who shall defend the American society, if not History? And who shall judge the American society, if not History? Can History, then, be counsel for both prosecution and defense, and at the same time occupy the judgment seat? Is this possible? In a formal, legal sense, no; artistically, yes.

I must be clear, first of all, as to exactly what I mean by History. I begin by saying what I do not mean. I do not mean the partisan record of events and personalities that is inspired, for example, by nationalism and other human aberrations manifesting self-interest. I do not mean emotional or intellectual bias in any form whatever. The Gospel according to Matthew is flawed by the same defect that characterizes the Gospel according to Marx: an insufficient regard for evidence. Both were clever men, these two, but both were actuated in supreme degree by the ambition to advance an apostolate

7

leading, in the former instance, to the subversion of the kingdom of this world and its supplanting by the kingdom of heaven; and, in the latter, to the subversion of the kingdom of capitalism and its supplanting by the kingdom of socialism. I do not regard Jesus Christ as a Christian. He seems to me to have been Manichaean. His apostles were much abler men, who, in relation to Christ, sought to be king-makers. What they did not reckon with was the Saviour's predilection for half-baked revolution. But they did the best they could with him, and when, inevitably, he overplayed his hand into martyrdom, they saw their chance and took it. They made a mystique out of him. The consequences continue to bedevil the world and, in particular, have borne disastrously upon his fellow Jews. In the light of what actually occurred, is Judas Iscariot, rather than Jesus Christ, the real founder of Christianity?

So what I mean by History is neither Tacitus, Matthew, nor Marx, Josephus nor Mommsen, Herodotus nor Geyl, Gibbon nor Spengler, nor, least of all, that Christian apologist in the guise of an ecumenical historian, Arnold Toynbee.

Who, then—and what—is History? Perhaps the Greek Zeus in the form of the Roman *Deus ex machina,* a presiding but nonintervening intelligence dispassionately concerned with human affairs and content to consider with detachment, though not with disinterest, the inter-play of human character with human destiny.

That is the ideal function of the historian, and the result of the process is history.

The Hindu godhead, for example, is too meddlesome and officious. Siva is a bloodthirsty villain, with a delight in carnage much like the Christian God of Battles, and forever interposing himself into the human concerns of his adherents. He lacks dignity. His passion, like Jehovah's, caricatures the conduct of a god and circumscribes his influence. He has no sense of human necessity; he *must* interfere. The Buddha comes closer to Greek detachment. Unfortunately, he exhibits from time to time an infantile tendency to play with his feces.

Some time ago, in a conversation with a great classical scholar at the University of Hamburg, I raised the subject of the German notion of *Schicksal* and its affinity, if any, to the ancient Greek concept of fate. Without attributing to him a particular view, there seems to me to be some warrant for the conclusion that this is an ethnographic matter. The gods of the Teutonic cosmogony are primitive creatures

8

alongside the sophisticated occupants of Mount Olympus. The notion of *Schicksal* imports resignation to necessity. *Ich kann nicht anders.* But the Greek concept of fate is replete with striving against necessity. This is the central drama of the Greek character as opposed to the will-bereft automatism of the Teuton confronted with fate. Faust did not choose; he was seduced by the blandishments of Mephistopheles. But Paris chose, even if by so doing he gave great offense, in the train of which followed those "dire events" of which Homer sings. It is choice, the brute existential necessity, that I mean when I speak of fate.

To limit myself to the compass of the American society and black revolution, I shall distinguish crucial choices in the long and complex interweaving of these strands: for instance, the complicity—and attendant complacency—of the Founding Fathers of the republic toward the institution of human slavery. Their exclusion of blacks from the dubious thesis that "all men are created equal" contributed its own horrible fuel to the fires of the Civil War less than a century later. For they had ratified, rather than repudiated, slavery. Black Spartacists like Denmark Vesey and Nat Turner ascended to their definitive places in history as a consequence of this choice on the part of the Founding Fathers. And what if Lincoln had proclaimed the emancipation of the slaves as an objective of the Union from the outset, instead of subordinating the issue of their freedom to political considerations? He would today have been a genuine hero of black Americans rather than a bad joke perpetrated by white-racist historians.

Without slavery, however, there would have been no abolition movement—and no Frederick Douglass. Yet it would be pointless and in the worst possible taste to suggest that the epiphany of Frederick Douglass offset and countervailed the measureless agony of black slaves in the two preceding centuries. Or that the moral righteousness of the abolitionists redeemed the collective virtue of the republic.

No. My point, and it is one of paramount importance, is that human choice has human consequences that are sometimes incarnated as Frederick Douglass, perhaps, or W. E. B. Du Bois or Malcolm X. In short, to what extent and how did choice exercised in the circumstances of American history create the phenomena known as Douglass, Du Bois, Malcolm X, and others? And without imputing a rigid automatism to the process by which a society creates its own denizens, are such men products as indigenous to the American society as the "cherry pie" employed by H. Rap Brown as a metaphor for American violence?

Does a society create its outcasts in its own image?

In 1972, is the Nixon administration, with its "Southern strategy," on the way to another compromise like that of 1876? There is no dearth of symptoms: legislative retrenchments of political gains by blacks, painfully achieved during the past two decades; a new alliance between Big Business, embodied by the Nixon administration, and the South; promises to "guarantee peace, good order, protection of the law to whites and blacks." These are only a random sampling of the signs. What, then, should blacks do in the face of these warnings from history? Revert to the Christian meekness, sacrifice, and humility by which they have been consistently betrayed? In a word, shall it be Martin Luther King or Malcolm X? The resignation and submission of the Christian faith or the resolution and defiance of the Black Panthers?

When, on coming to America, I met Dr. W. E. B. Du Bois and talked with him, the impression I derived was of an aristocrat for whom the sound of an approaching tumbrel held no terrors. He had been hearing it all his life, and it could produce in him no fear; only contempt. He invited me to join him in his work. I have at length done so in my own way and on my own terms.

10

1

In so far as black-white relations are concerned, it is the whites who hold the power of crucial decision. The blacks are not powerless, but they are much less powerful than their opponents. They may take decisions, yet they are unlikely to be able to enforce them against the superior power of the whites. The predominant term in the whole conflict is white power. It would be silly to suppose, however, that this either implies or prescribes black impotence. For this is clearly not the case. In any civil struggle between the two groups, on whatever level it is waged, while without the slightest question the whites will be the victors, the blacks are in a position to do incalculable damage.

But this presupposes a struggle in which the two sides are more or less starkly defined: the blacks, on one side, the whites, on the other. This, however, is unlikely to be the case. In the actual event, there would be no such simple division of the contending parties. It is not even certain that the blacks, as a group, would come together in a solid alliance, unbroken in its ranks, undivided in its opposition to the whites. Nor is it certain that the latter themselves would achieve complete cohesion. Indeed, it is far from fanciful to assume that there would be blacks fighting on the side of the whites, and whites on the side of the blacks. To be sure, the racial struggle in America is, in a primary sense, one in which blacks are pitted against whites. There

11

are, however, secondary, tertiary, and other levels of emotional loyalty and intellectual conviction that combine to make skin color in some instances a treasonous uniform. As intermarriage between the two groups increases, it will become so much the more difficult to predict with certainty the side of the barricades on which a black or a white will fight. Such a conflict, if it should come to that, would split families, black and white, into mutually destructive factions. It would be a war of brother against brother and sister against sister, children against parents and parents against each other. At this very moment, the course of social evolution in this country already makes it impossible to distinguish with assurance over a considerable range of the population exactly who are white and who are black. The late Senator and sometime Governor of the State of Louisiana Huey Long is reported to have said of his state that he "could take a single loaf of bread and feed all the genuinely white people in it." A similar statement might be made with equal accuracy about a significant number of other segments of the population of the United States. Precisely how, in this vast, centuries-long admixture, individuals will react when forced to choose sides is a matter that not even they themselves can predict with invariable certainty. Their conscious inclination may be contradicted by subconscious predisposition; in some cases, they may be paralyzed in their effort to decide. Still others may choose against the grain of their actual sympathy, seeking instead what they may conceive to be their true self-interest. And there will be others, too, who, evading the compulsion of choices that they cannot make, may be swept up and eddied along on the current of the swifter stream, the more powerful cataract, the mightier wave, or simply the trend in their immediate vicinity. For many, it will be a monstrous nightmare of involuntary choice. For most, however—and this is the prospect to be confronted—the choice will have already been made by the arbitrament of skin color.

It seems odd that a civilization not wholly lacking in the cultural ingredients of greatness should be menaced in its existence by so trivial a circumstance as the light or dark of human skin. Yet this is where the matter stands at present. The reason, or unreason, of choice or inability to choose in the contemplated event is, however, not exhausted by the consequences flowing from racial admixture. There is the element of class interest. This is, of course, one of the classic tools of Marxist historical analysis. But it is not necessary to regard it, as Marxists do, as a magic key to the secrets of the universe, in order to realize that within its conceptual and practical limitations it can yield illuminating results. The thesis that people tend in general to be bound together by an identity of economic interest is clearly demonstrable. But that they will act invariably in consonance with their economic interest is much less certain. Human behavior a good deal of the time is a paradox. As a whole, people are more creatures of appetite than devotees of reason, capricious rather than rational. Marx, when drunk, sometimes attempted to climb lampposts at Highgate in North London, where he resided. This was not a reasonable thing to do, since he was an economic theorist and a political analyst and not a lamplighter. It was a drunken caprice. He tried to do much the same sort of thing with his theory of class conflict. A useful insight was perverted theoretically, and strained pragmatically, by its application to circumstances well beyond the range of its relevancy. It fossilized into dogma and became an article of faith of the Marxist persuasion. In less doctrinaire hands, it might have been developed instead into a dialectical instrument, free of political tendentiousness, superbly adapted to the search for the enshrouded sources of human motivation. Even now, despite all the accretions of mystique, it still remains an insight of immense value into the dynamics of human activity. If only Marx had not been so deficient in his knowledge of psychology, or so unimaginative in his use of it as a social scientist, the theory of class conflict might indeed have come to fruition as a cardinal enterprise of the human intellect.

Yet there are, in gross fact, those occasions when men and women do combine on the basis of some interest that they identify as common to themselves exclusively, and as having that order of value in which the sum is greater than the parts. Hence their class interest. Ordinarily, where the given class of persons is more or less undifferentiated in its composition, and there are no latent and mutually contradictory bundles of interest, the theory works with a certain precision; as, for instance, in the case of a class of shareholders in a corporation, all intent on extracting a larger dividend than the board of directors deems it prudent to declare. But as the possible examples of class interest grow more elaborate, more complex, more ramifying, the probability of internal contradiction is increased. As—to take a further instance—in the case of the owners of a co-operative apartment building, some of whom are black and some white, these latter being in the majority by a substantial margin. They were, as it chanced, the original co-operators and, as such, they arrived at an unwritten agreement among themselves to establish a tenant quota for blacks. The white co-operators, obviously, conceive it to be in their interest to limit the number of black tenants. The blacks, on the other hand, consider it to be to their advantage to increase their number. True economic self-interest on both sides would dictate that the co-operative be equally open to both groups, conditioned only by such factors as personal character and financial ability. But racial prejudice enters into the situation and confuses and complicates it. Economic self-interest is sacrificed to sociological unreason. Class interest is contradicted and canceled out by group caprice. Human psychology is largely an uncharted realm of the irrational. Here the unpredictable is sovereign. This fact makes arrant nonsense of the materialistic view of history in its doctrinaire extension to the whole range of human behavior.

Yet the assumption of class interest remains tenable in certain circumstances. One such may come to be the identity of economic interest, on a class basis, between the black and white segments of the American society. The signs are already visible in the case of the black and white middle class. This is the meaning of the black middle-class thrust for integration and its support and acceptance by the liberal vanguard of the white middle class. These subcultures have identified between themselves a coincidence of class interest. They earn comparably the same incomes, wear uniformly the same clothes, live quietly or conspicuously in the same type of housing, send their children to the same schools, interchange visits to each other's homes for social purposes, wrestle with the same order of mortgage indebtedness, and experience the same frustrations with the servant shortage.

They are, in fact, a single class differentiated, superficially, by the sole incidence of skin color. They recognize this and they have resolved to ignore it. The decision was not a simple one to take; a high degree of social courage was involved. Nor has it proved easy to put into effect. Social custom in America is dead against it. Large numbers of white Americans of all classes disapprove of it, and similar numbers of black Americans view it with apathy, cynicism, derision, or outright hostility.

The movement toward black separation, as opposed to integration, is gathering momemtum, and the likelihood is that its pace will become more rapid during the next decade. Disenchantment with white America is deepening throughout black America, and the store of faith in the national profession of equal opportunity for all dwindles near disappearance. In these circumstances, integration has not flourished and, granted their continuance, is unlikely to do so. From the integrationist standpoint, accordingly, the future lies in the answer—yes or no—to the question whether there will be a profitable market in America for the commodity called integration and whether, that being the case, the irrational in the American expression of the human psyche will permit the degree of free play in the market that will in turn permit integration to establish its own price level. Given, then, the assurance of supply, the market will indicate the quantity of demand. How much demand will there be in the next decade or two for integration in America?

So far, as has already been pointed out, it has been a limited demand confined to subgroups of the black and white middle class. And if the white demand should become more widespread and insistent, would the black supply in the face of increasing black separatism be commensurate? This latter question, now, is hardly less pivotal than the former regarding the quantity of white demand for integration. For it is at this time, and it will be for all the foreseeable future, no longer simply a question of what white America wants: what black America wishes will have to be taken equally into account. And what black America wishes now, and will continue to demand during the next decades, is black separatism on self-respecting terms rather than integration on humiliating conditions, such as the black middle class in its undignified craving for white acceptance conceded with a complacency that was contemptible.

Integration without equal economic opportunity is a mockery. And equal economic opportunity cannot be achieved without equal education—"education" being defined as what happens not merely in a place called school, but also in the place called home. In other words, housing and its attendant circumstances.

The head, back, and front of the problem is decent housing, adequate education, and remunerative jobs. It should not be impossible, or even inordinately difficult, for America to solve this problem. If it does not, if it will not, if it cannot, then the future of America will be revolutionary chaos, seesawing violently from repression to anarchy to national extinction.

At the heart of this problem is the black demand for equal access to the resources of the American society on all the various levels: in particular, housing, education, and jobs. It is plainly evident that the conditions in which the preponderant mass of black people live in America contain all the classic ingredients of revolution. The marvel is that the blacks have on the whole been so quietly enduring. Whether they will continue to exercise this unparalleled restraint—if it is not imposed upon them by official repression—is the question for the future. Growing numbers of blacks, although not yet perhaps, on a realistic basis, a significant nucleus of the whole ethnic group, have moved from constitutional protest to extraconstitutional activity. To construe this blandly as a marginal development, an aberrancy restricted to the fringes of the group, would be a serious delusion. On the other hand, to see it as smoke rising from a house completely on fire would be a wild exaggeration. It can, however, indeed must, be regarded as a portent of far worse things to come—unless white America mends its ways.

The established practice in the past was to place the onus upon the blacks to be patient. The whites, as lords and masters of the land, never even felt called upon to consider with sustained care and attention the precise circumstances in which the blacks were expected to be patient. "Tell the puppy I never look at my footman's face," said one English lordling in a message to a fellow aristocrat with whom he was at odds. In the same spirit, although in this instance the social levels were unequal, white America did not deign to look at the face of black America and so preserved itself against seeing the suffering there slowly losing its aspect of patience and becoming a hostile sneer, which is the black face of America that any white who chooses to look at his "footman's face" may recognize today and recoil, if not retreat, from tomorrow. For that black face, after so many centuries, is the face of Strindberg's footman who has seduced Miss Julie and finds her no more exciting than his usual quarry, the scullery maid. There is contempt on the footman's face.

Blacks in America were once not so long ago ruled by fear. The future may bring a recurrence of this type of despotism. The attitudes of certain public officials and sections of the police already reveal this tendency. So do legislative enactments on federal and local levels. As the country grows less certain of its "Manifest Destiny" to police the world and remold it nearer to the lineaments of the American dream, as internal pressures mount in the wake of a host of unsolved domestic problems, and as white racism enlarges the contribution of its irrational mystique to the reinforcement of white power, the blacks of America will come more and more to occupy the position of the Jews under Hitler. White power is the problem of the future, as it is the problem of today. Whites will, of course, play their traditional game of shifting the onus, at which long practice has made them quite expert. It will not therefore be they who are unjust, but the others who are impatient; not they who are gluttonous, but the others who have acquired "rising expectations"; not they who are white racists, but the others who are wrong to oppose their white racism by resorting to black or brown or yellow racism.

The United States, constituting 6 per cent of the world's population, consumes 40 per cent of the world's resources. Irritatingly, the other 94 per cent of the world's population will not content themselves with the remaining 60 per cent of the world's resources. This land has never known foreign invasion (except the one so successfully carried out by the European intruders against the North American Indians). Yet it does not scruple to intervene by military incursions in the domestic quarrels of other lands. And with classic great-power cynicism it deems these latter guilty of quarreling in the first place.

We Americans litter the world with the shoddy artifacts of a money-mad culture, then accuse the recipients of possessing an indiscriminate taste for these worthless things. Across the face of the earth we carry the leprous contagion of our white racism and marvel that others become contaminated by it. On a scale that defies the imagination we contrive the means of mass destruction. Our justification is a plea of self-defense. Although ours is the richest country in the world, as we never tire of boasting, we yet permit degrading poverty to flourish on our very doorstep. Then we lecture the victims of our callous regard, because, we assert, they cling out of laziness and inertia to their poverty.

When we pollute earth, air, and water with our chemical pestilences, we assail those who do not understand that a price has to be paid for progress. We make a vast human holocaust of Japanese cities by a method revolting in its sheer fiendishness, then blame this horror upon the Japanese for having started the war. We ignore the fate of Dresden but point to Coventry; thrust aside the memory of Hamburg and recall London. It was not the fault of Hitler but that of the Jews who permitted this monster to exterminate them. Nor was it the moral responsibility of the white slavers who brought their black human cargo to the Americas. The ethical burden was that of the black slavers who sold their fellow blacks into slavery. Thereafter throughout three centuries of enslavement the happy slaves refused to free themselves. Of very little account is it that for four centuries and more the white racists have ground their jack boots into the faces of heavily outnumbered and unarmed blacks. The fact is that the blacks have always had a peculiar fondness for being at the receiving end of boot leather. And, of course, it goes without saying that they are not to be trusted with guns.

The lynching of black men and the raping of black women, the starving to death and the outright murder of black children, are their own fault. Everyone knows that black men lust for white women, and black women yearn for white men. And if the black children were allowed to reach adulthood, they would simply become bad, uppity niggers.

The question the cynicism of white racism poses for blacks is how, first of all, to survive and, next, to surmount the formidable menace of white power.

As we have seen—as indeed we witness at the present time—some blacks, although relatively few, return the answer to that question in the form of revolution. Other blacks essay other responses, more moderate, less incendiary. It is simply accurate to assert that these latter, in their forbearance and tempered restraint, represent beyond all question the great majority of blacks in America. Of all the ethnic groupings of the American population, the blacks probably are the most conservative. The reasons for this are not far to seek. To begin with, they were uprooted from an African tribal system that, in its observance of custom and deference to tradition, was essentially conservative. On the North American continent to which they were transported, and especially in the Southern region, they found themselves in a social environment that was not dissimilar from their country of origin in its emphasis upon the past and its hostility to innovation. Their inbred conservatism was to this extent, accordingly, reinforced by this social characteristic of their new surroundings.

They were then given, and they accepted, a system of religious belief and practice, namely, Christianity, which encouraged them to refrain from disturbing the *status quo* in return for the assurance of a transfigured life in the hereafter. Their terrible sufferings were to be

18

patiently, and even passively, endured as the necessary precondition on earth of this heavenly future. As Christ preached it, Christianity was a revolutionary doctrine. But Christ was not a Christian; he was an Essenian mystic. When, however, his insights, as developed into a handbook for social revolution and given intellectual substance and authority by Saint Paul and others, fell into the hands of the clever men surrounding Constantine at a time of considerable turmoil in the Roman Empire, something happened. As Edward Gibbon observes in his *The Decline and Fall of the Roman Empire:*

Personal interest is often the standard of our belief, as well as of our practice; and the same motives of temporal advantage which might influence the public conduct and professions of Constantine would insensibly dispose his mind to embrace a religion so propitious to his fame and fortunes. His vanity was gratified by the flattering assurance that *he* had been chosen by Heaven to reign over the earth: success had justified his divine title to the throne, and that title was founded on the truth of the Christian revelation. . . . Lactantius, who has adorned the precepts of the Gospel with the eloquence of Cicero, and Eusebius, who has consecrated the learning and philosophy of the Greeks to the service of religion, were both received into the friendship and familiarity of their sovereign; and those able masters of controversy could patiently watch the soft and yielding moments of persuasion, and dexterously apply the arguments which were the best adapted to his character and understanding.

These men saw at once that whereas the pagan gods were forever enjoining war and fomenting strife through their priestly representatives, who were ambitious for secular power, this new creed, for all its rhetorical fervor, really stopped short of promulgating revolution. "My kingdom is not of this world." Here, then, were men, these followers of Christ, who were expressly removing themselves from the competition for secular power. They proposed no rivalry with the established regimes. Indeed, on the very authority of their founder, they had gone so far as to prescribe in explicit terms deference to the state. For had he not said, "Render unto Caesar the things that are Caesar's. . . ."? For the rest, they set great store by meekness. "Blessed are the meek. . . ." By love. "Love ye one another." By peace. "Blessed are the peacemakers. . . ." Far from being subversives, these new people— these followers of some obscure Essenian hermit—were actually (or could easily become) a stabilizing element in a volatile empire that was even then flying apart. It would not at all be difficult (after, of course, some unpleasantness with power-hungry priests and misguided fanatics) to make use of these people and their ludicrous doctrine as an impulse to conservatism, a pacific queller of unrest in this turbulent empire.

Gibbon also remarks:

The passive and unresisting obedience which bows under the yoke of authority, or even of oppression, must have appeared in the eyes of an absolute monarch the most conspicuous and useful of the evangelic virtues . . . the humble Christians were sent into the world as sheep among wolves; and since they were not permitted to employ force even in the defence of their religion, they should be still more criminal if they were tempted to shed the blood of their fellow-creatures in disputing the vain privileges or the sordid possessions of this transitory life. . . . While they experienced the rigour of persecution, they were never provoked either to meet their tyrants in the field, or indignantly to withdraw themselves into some remote and sequestered corner of the globe. . . . But the Christians, when they deprecated the wrath of Diocletian, or solicited the favour of Constantine, could allege, with truth and confidence, that they held the principle of passive obedience, and that, in the space of three centuries, their conduct had always been conformable to their principles. They might add that the throne of the emperors would be established on a fixed and permanent basis if all their subjects, embracing the Christian doctrine, should learn to suffer and to obey.

Christianity was gradually debauched into a drug valued mainly for its opiate effect. It was in this spirit, and to this purpose, that it was administered to the African slaves in North America. No link in the fetters that bind black souls in America has been harder to break than this Christian shackle. The late Dr. Martin Luther King, Jr. understood this very well. In this he was at one with the plantation squirearchy. So was the long white-polled and black-suited line of black preachers who did not sell their brothers' bodies into slavery but did what was far worse: betrayed their souls to a Christian god. Their defense—admissible in the circumstances—was ignorance, or might be. What was Dr. King's defense? A dream—of brotherly love. It is true that in the early Christian communities, which were Eastern, group homosexuality was an acceptable social usage. Why Dr. King should have contemplated this, even unconsciously, as a solution to endemic group hostility among human beings is a matter into which it is really not necessary to enter. More interesting and pertinent is the fact that,

20

within the human species, brothers are notoriously incapable of harmonious relations with one another. "Brotherly love" is a poetic fancy quite unrelated in actuality to the ambivalence that is typical of the emotional attitudes that human siblings display in their mutual relations. What could have led Dr. King to suppose that whites, who are so clearly deficient in "brotherly love" among themselves, would somehow be able to bestow this feeling upon blacks? The kindest judgment upon Dr. King in this regard would hover indeterminately between the conclusion that he was a simpleton and the suspicion that he was a charlatan.

In human affairs, there is no illusion so disastrous as that of a nonexistent human "goodness." Human beings, like all other organisms, are neither good nor evil. They are creatures of necessity; they merely do what they must. These terms, "good" and "evil," are labels of convenience. They possess a certain limited usefulness in enabling us to pass moral judgments, a certain expedient usefulness. That is all. Organisms—human beings, if you like—are moral neuters. We find it socially advantageous to construct a moral universe for them in which we invest them with a positive and negative potentiality that we label good and evil.

The Black Muslims in the American society habitually describe whites as "evil." Quite wrong. As a group, whites are ruthless predators. There are individual exceptions, of course; many. But we speak of them as a group—the most successful, because the most ruthless, of all the groups of mankind. In this sense, it is also the most primitive of all human groups, because more than any other its members remain creatures of necessity. But evil? No. That is a romantic view that is quite as false as would be the opposite attempt to describe them, or any other human group, as "good."

It is not necessary to contemplate organisms—human beings—as moral entities in order to arrive at their actual nature. In fact, the introduction of a "moral" perspective operates to obscure, where it does not distort, the relevant evidence. So let us say once more what is a simple matter of concrete observation: the white groups of mankind are powerful, ruthless, ingenious, and resourceful predators. Let us repeat, too, that within those groups, as in all other groups, there are exceptions: individual exceptions. Let us, finally, remove from our consideration of them those assumptions of a "moral character" that we fancifully suppose to inhere in them. Let us see them as they really are, as all of us really are: let us see them as moral neuters, differing from other human groups only in their relative freedom from moral trammels. Let us see them in Nietzschean terms, if you prefer, as "beyond good and evil"; for that is where they are. And let us now deal with them accordingly. Let us now for the first time be rational about white people. This attitude must in future replace the seething, unsteady compound of love and hate with which whites are regarded by blacks in America. And not only in America. In the British—the former British—West Indies, one of the most startling of sociological facts to be observed is the impassioned love of black middle-class West Indians for white people.

The black middle-class West Indian is God's original Uncle Tom—or Aunt Jemima. There is not a black American on the face of this continent who can compete with a black middle-class West Indian when it comes to worshiping white people. You have only to express a mildly unfavorable view of white people to a black middle-class West Indian in order to become at once an object of cold suspicion as a "radical." Political analysts of the West Indian migration to the United States of America and of the "trouble making" that some of the immigrants engage in here miss, in general, a supremely important point concerning the class structure of that migration. It is, on the whole, the lower-middle-class and working-class West Indians who uproot themselves and come over to the Land of Promise. The middle-class West Indians stay at home. Why should they leave? They do all right there; they have always done all right in their native islands. They have held the best jobs, drunk the best rum, eaten the best food, worn the best clothes, made whatever money the British colonial predators would allow them to make. In this last sense, they were the hyenas skulking on the fringe of the lions' feast for the remnants of the carcass. That was the economic role of the black middle class in the West Indies. They were hyenas watching the colonial beasts of prey feasting on the exploitation of the black masses and silently, sometimes snarlingly, awaiting the departure of the engorged preda- tors. For the rest, they learned—and this is the important thing—to play the sociological game by the white masters' rules. The more skill- fully they played that game, the more rapidly they ascended the lad- ders reserved to them. Some of them played it very skillfully indeed, even better than their masters. With all this they had still another role, as black Janissaries of empire. Here, too, their performance was of a very useful order. For such services their white colonial masters rewarded them with knighthoods and such other minor distinctions, all nevertheless badges of black servitude. One outstanding black athlete, who excelled at cricket, even became a member of that decaying institution, the British House of Lords. A black scholar of distinction, who also engages in politics, was made a Companion of Honour. What these blacks could not bring themselves to see, for the realization would have shattered their carefully class-structured universe, was that the acceptance of these "honors," these "distinctions," these rewards proclaimed of the recipients: *"I am an Uncle Tom!"*

From this colonial level of a master-servant relationship in the West Indies, however, the black lower middle class and the black working class were excluded; except where, by academic success, since they were otherwise penniless, they got a chance to go to England to further their studies, as the phrase went, and become doctors, lawyers, or something of the sort; then to return to the islands in due course with their new status as accredited members of the black middle class. But in general they either languished in their impoverished condition in the West Indies or managed to emigrate to the United States. These people were never apathetic about their economic situation in their island homelands. They did what they could, organizing protest against the British raj, originating political activity designed to lead to freedom from colonial subjection, impeaching the black middle class for selling them down the river. They were never complacent, these black lower-middle-class and working-class West Indians; the black middle-class West Indians were, and they had reason to be. They were the masters' favorite servants: house niggers.

So it is not true to say, as has been said, of these black lower- and working-class West Indian immigrants to the United States that they were silent and supine in the face of their disadvantaged circumstances in the West Indies, but that as soon as they came here and encountered the American version of the racial problem, they became militant. That is untrue. Its untruth derives from ignorance of the internal class structure of West Indian society. These black, West Indian immigrants simply found here, in America, freer, larger scope not only for their personal ambitions but for the expression of their grievances. The possibilities of effective organization were greater; their voices were more audible: they could be heard, since there was no black middle class in America, as in the West Indies, with interests in the *status quo* so deeply vested that they switched off the microphones every time the black West Indian immigrants got up to speak. They were not more militant here than they were in the West Indies: they were simply more effective. The objective conditions were better.

Marcus Garvey, it is no exaggeration to say, shook the United States of America from top to bottom with his shrewd and powerful appeals to the racial pride of black America. He had come here from Jamaica, where, the record is clear, he had been anything but apathetic. He was a lower-middle-class black. When the American government finally broke him and got rid of him (with the assistance of prominent middle-class American blacks) and sent him back to Jamaica, he became virtually a cipher in his native island. The white colonial masters never laid a finger on him themselves; they simply sicked their black middle-class retainers on him. Within a short time, Garvey was reduced to ludicrous impotence. His flamboyant preachments, which were not without a core of solid good sense, became windier and windier, wilder and wilder, more and more the ravings of an embittered fanatic under the mocking contempt and unconcealed derision of the black Jamaican middle class, the loyal servants of the British colonial masters. And—irony of ironies (the British have a genius for arranging this sort of denouement)—Garvey went off to England to die in frustration and chagrin, politely ignored by the British.

The British never kick a man when he's down, but they don't as a rule help him up, either. The Americans may put the boot to him in a similar situation, depending on the angle of his backside (the temptation may be irresistible, which is perfectly human); but they are also pretty sure then to turn around, pick the man up, brush his clothes off, and give him a job. That is a national difference not lightly to be discounted.

Just as the Japanese have been made honorary whites by the South Africans, some black middle- and upper-class West Indians were accorded similar status, implied rather than expressed, by the British in the Caribbean colonies. This had the effect of further detaching them from the struggle of their fellow blacks of the lower middle and working classes for economic redress and political emancipation. They were allowed into white clubs and might exchange social visits and conduct other forms of superficial intercourse with whites. They had more than arrived; at this point they were transfigured. A chromatic miracle had been performed: black was white.

Were these black men and women (and to the extent that they still engage in this degrading activity, are they) wicked? Not necessarily. Most of them were merely foolish. In most cases, they did not have even the shady distinction of being dishonorable. They were and are as badly off as that; they are to be pitied. Yet it must be said, more in sorrow than in anger, that the tragic consequence of their being used in this way was that it permitted the stark actuality of British racism in the West Indies to clothe itself in a decent-seeming suit of black accommodation. That was what it did, and it was a terrible thing when expressed in terms of the generations-long suppression and exploitation of the black lower middle and working classes.

In America there has been little or no concealment in any guise on the part of white racism, except here and there among Northern and other regional liberals with restive social consciences. The result is that black Americans of all classes, although shackled in many ways, have at least been free, on the whole, of the illusion of white racial decency that the British successfully imposed upon their colonial subjects of the black West Indian middle class. Perhaps a further consequence is that while black America has produced a number of people of world stature, not one such individual has emerged in the former British West Indies since Alexander Hamilton. Certainly not in politics; certainly not in literature or the arts; certainly not in science, pure or applied; certainly not in the social sciences; certainly not in any other field of human endeavor.

It is an arid retrospect indeed. This is not to say that there are not able black men in the former British West Indies, clever men, ambitious, dedicated. But they are all involved in one way or another, on one level or another, in the soul-destroying commerce of trading for white British recognition; which means, as it must in any run, long or short, the sacrifice of their people's well-being on this squalid altar of neocolonial aspiration. Since, for example, to win and retain for as long as possible high political office means there, as it does elsewhere, to have and keep a hand on the fulcrum of power, West Indian politicians (like their counterparts everywhere) value freedom much less than they do power. With one or two exceptions, they will make any deal, stoop to any trick, consort with any bedfellow, for the sake of power.

While this sort of thing is normal enough among politicians, it does have peculiar consequences in the West Indies. For the rewards are much greater there than they are for black politicians in America who are similarly successful. Here, in America, such persons become Congressmen, which is by no means an undistinguished office, or mayors, and so forth. But in the West Indies, these people become prime ministers and heads of state. They exercise real power, and because they are, materially, still in many instances dependent on the former colonial master, and, for the rest, bound to him by his ability to enhance their careers with "honors" and "distinctions," there is always the real danger that the point will presently be reached when they will be unable, or unwilling, to perceive any conflict, however visible to observers, between their personal ambitions and their people's welfare. In the former British West Indies political power is acquired on a scale considerably more lavish than is the comparable case among black Americans and, perhaps for this reason, if for no other, corrupts more deeply.

The failure of the West Indies to produce figures of world stature cannot be explained, then, simply on the basis of a population factor. The social quality of West Indian life must also be held to account for this defect. And salient in the fabric of West Indian society, like a master in bas-relief against a frieze of servants, is the delusive personality of the British raj dissembling his racism before the uncritical, adoring gaze of the black middle class. These blacks have been so busy imitating the British that they have had too little time for evaluative scrutiny. In the system of academic education that the British foisted on them, West Indians became excellent rote learners, trained to ingest and then, upon demand, regurgitate information for reward. The system aborted their creative impulse.

The genius of the black West Indian has lain in the fidelity with which he has succeeded in adapting himself to the cultural patterns of the British master. The genius of the black American has lain in his superhuman effort to transcend the limitations imposed upon him by the white American overlord. People who aim at transcendence are always likelier to reach a surpassing level of self-expression than those who only aim at adaptation. Hence the largely sterile black West Indians; hence the powerfully creative black Americans.

Yet it is precisely this combination of black West Indian immigrants and native-born black Americans that now confronts white power in America. These are the forces from which black revolution draws its recruits. They constitute the foundation on which the future of blacks in America will either collapse in chaotic ruin or tower in triumph to the sky.

The infusion of lower-middle-class West Indian drive into black American leadership on the racial issue has been of vital consequence

26

in the struggle. But at no time whatever were the black Americans deficient in their own militant leadership. They have constantly thrown up such individuals from their own ranks on all levels, local as well as national. The fact that so many black leaders who have come to prominence in America have been of West Indian, or partly West Indian, origin might even be explained, to some extent at least, by the fact that the native-born black Americans were more clearly aware of the tremendous magnitude of the problem and thus constrained to greater caution in their approach. They knew, as the immigrant black West Indians did not, that the monster whose head reared in sinister menace from the sea was even more formidable in the potent destructiveness of its massive body coiling and uncoiling in the depths below. Theirs, the immigrant black West Indians', was the bold, foolhardy assault of raw troops against a heavily fortified enemy entrenchment, whose defenses they had not reconnoitered and whose firepower they had disastrously underestimated. That they were not massacred was due in large part to the self-protective strategy of the seasoned black Americans, skilled and patient campaigners in the centuries-long struggle against vastly superior forces.

The boldness of the black West Indians was the result of their relative freedom from the terror, psychological no less than physical, to which the black Americans were subjected by white power. The black West Indians experienced that terror when they arrived in America, and it was the very unfamiliarity of the experience that shocked and stung them into instant, reckless retaliation. On the other side, white power, expert at containing the sober tactics of the suppressed blacks, was astonished and confused to the point of partial paralysis by this unexpected irruption of suicidal black West Indians upon the racial scene. White power was unaccustomed to frontal assault by blacks. Had it occurred in the South, however, these blacks would have been exterminated. But it took place in the North, where the traditional white ambiguities that passed for racial tolerance recoiled upon themselves and rendered white power incompetent to deal decisively with the situation. So the black West Indian immigrants became shock troops whose effectiveness largely was the ironic fruit of the regional hypocrisy of white power in its Northern bastion. In time these black West Indians fanned out across the country, even penetrating into the South and proving that there, too, surprise was a potent tactic.

The black West Indian immigrants became the shock troops of the black revolution not as a consequence of any conscious strategy. They carried out this role because of their cultural preconditioning by less blatant, though not less poisonous, racial usages in their native islands; and also because they lacked that intimate knowledge of the overwhelming might of white power which would have urged them to proceed toward the vindication of their manhood with more "deliberate speed."

The future relationship between whites and blacks in America will therefore reflect the British colonial experience of the Caribbean blacks, but predominantly in its lower-middle- and working-class aspects. And as the position of the blacks of the United States becomes increasingly a matter of world attention across the whole range of the problem, good and ill together, other black influences and associations will manifest themselves. The African influence, already evident in black hair styles and modes of dress, is likely to derive repeated renewals of inspiration from the ascent of divisions of sub-Sahara Africa among the nation-states of the world. The sheer circumstance of an emergent Africa has, in fact, been a significant source of pressure on the United States of America to mend its manners toward black people. As, and if, Africa grows stronger, achieves greater cohesion, redefines its traditional concepts of collective power by moving away from smaller to larger social units as the basis of its national organization, appropriates and develops its own economic resources—in the first phase, for the benefit of its own people, and, in the next, as co-trustees of the welfare of all mankind—further improvements will occur in the situation of black Americans. Add to this, Russian mistrust of and hostility to the United States and the latter country's reciprocal attitude, with its pathological fear of Communism, and black Americans will be better off still.

Few factors have so deeply affected the plight of black Americans for the better as the conflict between these two countries, which so far has stopped just short of open warfare. More than any other segment of the American population, blacks have been the beneficiaries of American involvement in foreign wars, their disproportionate casualty rate in the Vietnam war to the contrary notwithstanding. The First World War, in which the United States made a belated entrance, opened a breach in the wall for black Americans; the Second World War enlarged it; and a third World War will probably demolish the wall completely.

It is, tragically, to the interest of black Americans that this country embark on foreign military adventures until the last chain has been struck off the legs, and the last manacle removed from the hands, of the last unemancipated black American. White America's wars are black America's heralds of freedom. A cynical realism perversely conducive to the blacks' self-interest would dictate for them the slogan: "Make war, not love!" In the obscene conditions of the contemporary world, black Americans stand to reap a harvest of improvements in their civil status by successfully addressing this appeal to white Americans. Nothing should be the occasion of such delight for black America as when white America goes to war; and this even in the face of the higher rate of casualties that black troops will sustain by comparison with their white comrades.

Nor is it untenable as argument that in a number of instances sufficient to establish the tendency as characteristic, American intervention abroad has exhibited a racist motivation both in the fact of the intervention itself and in the military quality of that intervention. White America typically intervenes in the domestic affairs of nonwhite nations. The diplomatic pretexts are always ready to hand, or they are conveniently manufactured, but they are never lacking. A Communist threat is the most serviceable. And since, in any case, the Communists are opportunistic enough to batten upon the absence of social justice, which an arrogant, unheeding capitalism has either contrived or connived at, this mare's nest of a Communist menace is easily identified or fabricated. Moreover, white technological ascendancy in the present-day world has had the effect of leaving the nonwhite sections of mankind far behind. As apprentices to the sorcerer technology, the white nations have grown rich.

Under cover of foreign aid, however, and the employment of other forms of economic and political righteousness, the United States of America has effectively controlled and, where such control has proved unattainable, ruthlessly subverted the governments of the poorer (that is to say, nonwhite) countries. Neither has it shrunk from outright military intervention in consistency with its declared mission of policing the world. The fact that Lebanon, Korea, Guatemala, the Dominican Republic, Vietnam, Laos, Cambodia, and Thailand are all nonwhite countries cannot exactly be described as a meaningless series of coincidences. The fact that white America expended so egregious an amount of time and energy keeping the People's Republic of China out of the United Nations cannot so be described, either. And when it is recollected that the people of Japan, whom white America subjected to the ultimate horror of the atomic bomb, are nonwhite people, the evidence in support of the indictment of American foreign policy as actuated to a measurable degree by racism becomes irresistible.

This racism, which, from the standpoint of black people, is such a salient feature of American foreign policy, is also one of the chief contributory factors to the deepening rift in the world between blacks and whites, or whites and nonwhites. It is quite impossible for any nonwhite person with the slightest pretension to conscience to be unaware of the essentially prowhite and antihuman attitudes and practices that, on balance, typify the United States of America; and this despite its very considerable economic assistance to nonwhite countries. For such assistance is always implicitly conditioned upon acceptance or tolerance of American racist ideology. So that for an African country to receive economic aid from America with anything like an easy conscience, it must turn a blind eye to the treatment of blacks in America, as well as to the quite probable circumstance that the disbursing agents of American assistance personally subscribe to the theory and practice of white racism. The recipient nonwhite countries are thus obliged to compromise with American racism as the price of relief for their economic necessities.

The intangible constraint involved in such an arrangement enlarges the self-contempt of the recipient and doubles its disesteem for the benefactor. This explains in part why, together with its unparalleled generosity, the United States continues to be the object of so much contempt and hatred the world over. Naturally, envy is not absent from this reaction, although it is perhaps more significant as a factor in the relations of America with other white countries. There is a level of poverty that deprives the poor even of the faculty of envy. Beyond the satisfaction of their primary necessities, they are capable only of being greedy. Most of the nonwhite countries are in this position.

In a world, then, in which the United States of America is a predominant power, its racist outlook is a necessary ingredient of any forecast encompassing its relations with the nonwhite groups of mankind. There is little question, as matters now stand, that the racial issue divides humanity more deeply than any other and that it will continue to do so well into the next century, provided the whites in the course of the coming decade have not accelerated the drift from universal pollution to the violent extinction of human life by nuclear weapons; in which case they will have solved the racial issue in the only way they seem capable of doing so: by violent means and the brute abandonment of intelligence.

For this culmination, if and when it should occur, white America will bear a primary responsibility. At present, no major incident of any conceivable future seems likelier; none less avoidable; none so unnecessary.

It is the grimmest, and also the sorriest, axiom of contemporary import that, in general, the white groups of mankind would rather be white than human. They see themselves, on the whole, as a superior abstraction from the swarming mass of the human species. While this conviction persists among the preponderant majority of them, and while they fabricate and monopolize the prepotent means of world destruction, what hope can there be for the nonwhite people of the earth?

This is the question the nonwhite world now faces with profoundly disquieting urgency, and will face in the coming decade with an immediacy swiftly, insistently catastrophic, patently, palpably involving no lesser stake than the continuance of life on this planet.

Inevitably, this will lead to the further questions: how are these antihuman groups of whites to be disarmed? How are these weapons to be taken from them, since it is clear that they will never surrender them of their own free will? For these weapons are the ultimate guarantee of the triumphant persistence of their white racism. While they retain their existing monopoly of these instruments of destruction, they will remain able to blackmail the rest of mankind with more or less impunity. They will maintain their present capability of imposing their racist will on the remainder of the species. They are aware of this; they know that their group power is directly linked to their group monopoly of devastating weapons, that when all is said and done, this is—for them—the last and surest hope of all. Small wonder, then, that they dragoon their fittest youth into standing armies and marshal their finest brains and amplest resources for the production of destructive weapons. These weapons are at least as much for the final defense of the white groups of mankind as they are for the extermination of Communism; more indeed for the former than for the latter, in view of the growing *rapprochement*, the increasing *détente*, between the United States of America and the Soviet Union.

From an international point of view, the most formidable threat to the hopes of black Americans for complete equality with their white fellow Americans will arise from the prospect or actuality of reconciliation between the Soviet Union and the United States. The pressures of the cold war on the United States have been of crucial assistance to black Americans in their domestic struggle. As a matter of "cruel necessity," in the Cromwellian sense, it will be no more than enlightened self-interest on the part of black Americans to regard the maintenance of these pressures as desirable. Every lesson of the past validates this view, and every survey of the future suggests its soundness as prediction.

Black Americans will become increasingly aware of the moral sensitivity of white America to any attempt to make the internal status of blacks in America an international issue. This sensitivity has so far been expressed negatively, on official levels, by explicit condemnation and various forms of reprisal against persons associated with such efforts. The final chapter in the tragic career of Paul Robeson is testament to this disapproval. The late Malcolm X was an acute internal irritant to the United States, but he became intolerable when he began to use foreign countries as platforms for the airing of the domestic grievances of black Americans. There are those who believe that his violent death was not unconnected with this development in his activities. It seems likely, however, that the continued denial of redress will lead increasing numbers of black people to appeal to the conscience of the world from forums outside the United States. One consequence will certainly be a strengthening of the bonds of common cause, already faintly intimated in the outlines of the so-called Third World, against the white racist oppressor. Blacks and other nonwhite people will have abundant opportunities of appreciating, in this regard, the deep, underlying truth of François Mauriac's statement that "it is not what separates the United States from the Soviet Union that should frighten us, but what they have in common. . . ."

The Soviet Union, in the evolution of its statecraft, has shown a marked preference for pragmatism to ideology. In this respect it is no different from any other nation-state. Long before Machiavelli set down his observations, and most clearly after him, the power of the prince has always been acquired, as well as maintained, by successful manipulation of the objective circumstances instead of by academic exercises in abstract theory. Black Americans have nothing to hope for from the Soviet Union, China, India, or the newly fledged nations of Africa on ideological grounds importing humane concern with their inferior status in their native country. They may hope only that the fact of their unequal condition may coincide with some vital national interest of a major foreign power. The latter may then, in the traditional spirit of political opportunism, utilize this coincidence in an attempt to gain some tactical end or strategic advantage against the United States. Ideology, still less idealism, plays no part in such matters. Nation-states cannot afford to be moral; their very nature obliges them to act at all times in cold detachment from ethical imperatives. The power of the prince operates beyond the ethical boundaries of a moral universe.

Black Americans will have to realize, as now they do not, that only a disastrous naïveté will continue to mislead them into the expectation of help in their struggle from any nonwhite nation-state or any nation-state at all, unless the latter's political calculations indicate some advantage, outweighing the inherent risk, as likely to accrue to itself from espousing in limited terms the cause of the black Americans against the United States.

Realpolitik is the essential basis of survival of a nation-state, black, white, or nonwhite. It seems that this is a difficult lesson for dissident blacks to learn. But they will have to learn it. Otherwise they will persist in their fatuous error of looking to foreign nation-states for help because of ideological considerations. They will have to realize that even a common language in relations with nation-states cannot be permitted to supplant a common identity of interest, with its amoral calculation of the ratio between risk and advantage.

In practical effect, what this means is that black Americans will have to rely solely upon themselves in their struggle to achieve equality in America. They cannot much longer evade the brute fact that aid from any foreign quarter, notably that of the Third World, will not be extended for humanitarian reasons. Any such aid will strictly be contingent upon the self-interest of the foreign nation-state, black, white, or nonwhite.

At present and for a generation to come, armed revolutionary struggle by black Americans to bring about the necessary complex of changes in this country can have only one outcome: catastrophic defeat at the hands of white power. Not all the heroics of Huey Newton or Bobby Seale, the rhetoric of H. Rap Brown or Eldridge Cleaver, or the indoctrination of black revolutionary cadres in the technique and practice of guerrilla warfare could alter this consequence by as much as the weight of a single hair from an Afro or a solitary thread from a dashiki. Black revolution is not at the present time, nor will it be for at least a generation to come, the slightest match for white power. Which does not mean, of course, that it is absolutely contraindicated; it simply means that it is of severely limited usefullness and that its potential cost in terms of the lives of black Americans, together with its probable retardation of the prospects of achieving black equality, makes it impractical now and for a generation or more to come.

Yet, the faith in white American promise and performance on the score of more decent attitudes that should sustain black Americans in peaceful protest has little foundation except in black middle-class wishfulness. White America appears on the whole to be beyond rehabilitation. Making all due allowance for exceptions, white America, in its relations with blacks, can be described only as a hardened, incorrigible criminal.

The black American is like a sick man in unspeakable agony whose physician is treating him by a process so slow in its curative effect that the patient, driven by unbearable pain, is tempted to commit suicide. This is precisely the situation of the black revolutionaries. The middle-class blacks in general are not revolutionaries only because they have succeeded in obtaining opiate drugs (success and the external trappings of the American middle class) for partial relief of their suffering. At the same time, these opiates have tended to reduce their sensitivity to the wretched state of their fellowblacks of the lower classes. Alienation has set in between these two subgroups, and the black middle-class American is as much an object of loathing and contempt as the white American in the eyes of the lower-class black. A corrective trend is slowly being established, however, by the desire of the black middle class to identify itself with the current vogue of Afro-American symbolism; and also, to a much more important degree, by the racial pride and assertiveness of the younger generation of the black middle class. A chasm that had been in danger of widening beyond passage has now begun to narrow again. The probability is that this deepening cohesiveness of black Americans will be further cemented by the necessity to make common cause for survival's sake against white America.

The principal success of the marginal black revolutionary movement during the next ten or twenty years will be in producing new types of leadership to meet the tactical demands of the struggle of all black people for complete freedom and equality. This incipient revolutionary movement has already made obsolete the black leadership of the accommodationist type. The accommodationist leader has no future in black America.

It is not that black accommodationists have been of no value; on the contrary, they have been quite useful and even now are serviceable. But they are, essentially, reformists pretending to leadership in a revolutionary conflict. They are Kerenskys. They must be either eliminated or liquidated, according to the logic of revolutionary struggle. Youthful blacks, in general, are hostile to accommodationists; they consider them "irrelevant." This is a glib and superficial judgment, which underestimates the continuing capacity of such men to be useful in the struggle. But it also indicates the nature of the criteria by which fitness for black leadership in America is being evaluated by the younger generation of blacks. Accommodationism is a fatal disqualification. White approval in any form is another. When, for example, the New York *Times* confers an accolade on any black, this is a kiss of death from the standpoint of the black community. That black, in the framework of this reasoning, at once becomes suspect. If the New York *Times* approves of him, then there must be sound reasons why the black community should distrust him.

Another disqualification for black leadership (and this goes almost without saying) is selection by whites. That was the way it used to be done: the whites said, "Here is your leader. Follow him." And the blacks fell in line.

Still another disqualification arises from the black version of the Horatio Alger fairy tale. Black man, by dint of patient endurance, steady ambition, and unremitting industry, makes it in white man's world. Whites automatically bestow on him the status of black leader. But no more. The very fact of his success in a white man's world renders him suspect, hints at compromises of his racial integrity, of deals in furtherance of his career made at the expense of his fellow blacks, gives him the doubtful standing of a cryptic Uncle Tom.

Crypto-Toms (or "Oreo cookies"—black outside, white inside) were the typical products of the striving by black people for "integration." They were inevitable in a process that subordinated ethnic self-respect to the benefits that, it was argued by a cloud of experts, would follow from legislated association on various levels of American life with whites. Black children would read better, learn more quickly, and acquire greater competitive confidence. No reason was advanced why these same benefits could not be equally attained in a black environment, provided only that black fathers were allowed access to employment equally with white fathers, that black housing was, as a whole, at least no worse than white housing, that the teaching in black schools was as good as that in white schools, that textbooks and technical aids to education, laboratory facilities, and the like were made available to blacks as abundantly as they were to whites, and that health services were as unstinted for blacks as for whites.

In a word, the experts on the side of integration produced no evidence that once the black environment, independently, was enabled to attain equality with the white environment, it would not produce people who were in every measurable respect the equals of those produced in the white environment. The only objection of anything like substance was that, from a financial standpoint, such a dual system might be too expensive. So these experts proceeded to belabor their thesis of integration, of enforced social admixture, because that has long been the black middle-class dream. And then their intellectuals, spearheaded by black experts on education, who were aided by their white liberal counterparts, contrived all manner of fallacious proofs to make their dream come true. But the dream dried up like a "raisin in the sun," because it was a false dream.

The true dream is that of equal access to economic opportunity based upon equal access to educational opportunity based upon equal access to decent housing and health services.

This, then, is the vital pyramid: health services and housing, education, jobs. The black middle class had achieved all of these, or were well on the way to doing so, and were now in a position, as they saw it, to enter the Promised Land. But the great mass of blacks in America were in no such position. They were without adequate health services, decent housing, useful education, and unemployment was chronic among them. In these circumstances, to talk to them of integration was simply a coarse species of class mockery. Their reaction has been to shift from a counterproposal of desegregation, instead of integration, to their present advocacy of separatism. This last proposal is likeliest of all to be the deliberate policy of the future for black Americans during the next two or three decades. They will not by then have come abreast of white Americans in enjoyment of the essentials of a tolerable existence. Quite to the contrary, the gap between the two groups in this respect may have grown wider. But the situation of black lower-class Americans, as compared with their former position, will have undergone a revolutionary change for the better. Best of all, from a psychological point of view, through their insistence upon separatism rather than integration, and even though the former is no more practicable than the latter, they will have recaptured their self-respect and regained their souls. For nothing is so destructive of the dignity of an individual or of a group as a craving, on no matter what pretext, for the society of someone who spurns you. The future of blacks in America will acquire increased dignity in proportion to their resolve to discard the notion of white acceptance. They have only to accept themselves.

It will also be necessary for them to reject the concept and value structure of "white liberalism." The whole burden of tolerance, benevolence, and high-mindedness, which this sociological device has enabled whites to impose upon blacks, must be thrown overboard. Blacks can no longer allow themselves to be regarded as the objects of sympathetic concern implicit in the notion of the "white liberal." Few developments in the future will so decontaminate relations between blacks and whites as the dispensing with this major source of racial pollution. White liberalism has spawned more hypocrisy and given birth to more Uncle Toms than any other social incident in the history of the two races in America. This is not to suggest that decent, well-meaning white men and women do not answer to the description of "white liberal." They do; so no mere exercise in ingratitude is being attempted here. Rather, this is an effort to distinguish where the true emphasis of enlightened racial interest and action should lie. Whatever warrant there may have been in the past for the existence of the white liberal and the institution of white liberalism, it is plain that it can have no place in the probable circumstances of the future.

The present generation of blacks and those immediately to come will not be content to subject their demands for freedom and equality to the moral restraints of the Judeo-Christian system of religious belief and inspiration, out of which white liberalism and the white liberal have traditionally emerged.

Black Americans see now more clearly than ever that, given the unregenerate nature of white racism, Christianity offers no path to salvation for the black race. What it offers is a masochistic road to genocide. It is a road signposted with the Sermon on the Mount and other pietistic guides to heaven by way of concentration camps, gas ovens, and incineration chambers. Thanks to Malcolm X, this present generation of blacks and those to come will not go down that road. There will be stray sheep from Martin Luther King's vanishing herd to whom this pacific highway will make an irresistible appeal. They will be lured to destruction by the name of the street: Brotherly Love. But there is an excellent story, which should provide a useful warning to these misguided people, that the best whorehouse in hell is called Saint Peter's Girls' Home. There is a moral in this for blacks, who, as a group, are easily seduced by the sound of words. This may not be unconnected with their African origins and the drum as an instrument of communication. As a matter of fact, infatuation with sheer sound is a principal weakness of blacks. It explains their tendency to confuse language with action, their inclination to mistake the former for the latter. Revolutionary fervor among blacks expresses itself not in planning but in proclamation. They tell the enemy what they are going to do, when they are going to do it, and how. Then, and only then, do they concern themselves with preparation. But since preparation involves planning, and planning is a dull occupation compared with the heady delights of irresponsible language, they soon abandon any pretense of doing anything so drab as making well-considered plans. They resort instead to the more agreeable exercise of saturating the air with sound and fury, signifying—alas!—nothing but words.

The American republic is in no danger from revolutionary planning on the part of its black citizens. Nor is it ever likely to be. Where the danger lies is in the increasing prospect of the sudden eruption of unmarshaled black discontent that acquires concert and cohesion under the pressure of the event, improvising organization, tactics, and strategy in response to the practical demands of the objective situation. Organization in the classic sense of precedent concert is not essential to the outbreak of revolution. As Régis Debray puts it in his *Revolution in the Revolution?*:

Once again, and in spite of all previous experience, institutions are taking priority over actions. Even before going into action, fledgling revolutionary movements or small groups of men numbering a few dozen are working out tables of organization more complex and unintelligible than those of a ministry, replete with Orders, Directives, Commissions—as if a revolutionary movement were to be measured by the number of its subsidiary units. Forms of organization precede the content, while content itself remains unorganized. Why? Because such people are not liberated from the old obsession; they believe that revolutionary awareness and organization must and can in every case precede revolutionary action.

Black revolution—such as it is—in the United States is the direct outcome of white racism. The counterrevolution—what is called the white backlash—is white racism defending itself through its official, institutional, private vigilante agencies and individual supporters. The cancer rotting away the vitals of American life is white racism. The traitors to the American Republic are the white racists. The forfeiture of the moral leadership of the world by the United States is solely attributable to white American racism. The evil ambassadors who, in their millions, disfigure the likeness of America abroad and diminish its stature among nations are the white American racists. They are the germ carriers of the American sickness, the focal point of the disease that is destroying America. It is they who have brought America to the pass where this country is devoid of moral influence in the councils of mankind; who have debased America so that its professions of national decency mock the country with their emptiness and make it an object of widespread derision, whose only rejoinders are blackmail by brute force and massive corruption through its power to expend vast sums of money.

White racism is a greater menace to America than "red" Communism. It is this—white racism—that in very large part obliges America to spend $200 million a day for "national defense"; that involves the major nations of the world (America foremost among them) in spending $200 billion a year on military activities and—by comparison—$7 billion in foreign aid. The former Secretary of Defense of the United States, Robert McNamara (now President of the World Bank) is reported to have said at a joint meeting of the World Bank and International Monetary Fund that the United States must decide whether it is to "funnel national resources into an endlessly spiraling consumer economy—with its by-products of waste and pollution—or to dedicate a more reasonable share of these same resources to improving the fundamental quality of life both at home and abroad."

No one who witnesses the mindless stampede of this country to ever larger and ever deadlier armaments, to more and more diabolical systems of destruction, can doubt what that decision will be. White racism leaves it no alternative.

The United States does not intervene, hardly indeed stirs a little finger, to protect the black inhabitants of South Africa from the white minority that oppresses them with a despotism of scarcely paralleled barbarism. The United States does not intervene to help the black inhabitants of Rhodesia against a white minority that visits a similar despotism upon them. But the United States intervenes in Vietnam to "protect" Vietnamese against one another; in Korea to "protect" Koreans against one another; in Cambodia to "protect" Cambodians against one another; in Laos, in Thailand; and would latterly have intervened in Jordan under the usual imperialistic pretext—to protect the lives of American citizens—if only the Arab-Israeli impasse had not so firmly implanted Russian power in the Middle East. It is, however, illuminating to note that in all these instances of intervention by the United States of America, the countries concerned are nonwhite. Is it possible to doubt that this is merely the old colonial story under the aegis of the Pax Americana?

The British were refreshingly frank about their reason for abstaining from direct action against the white Rhodesians. They could not shoot at their own "kith and kin." Or, to paraphrase for the enlightenment of the innocent: "White racists cannot be expected to kill one another." Quite true. They reserve their antipersonnel weapons and napalm bombs for nonwhites only.

There is at present no prospect that the whites will cure themselves of this antihuman sickness. In medical terms, the prognosis is hopeless. The future will disclose for blacks and other nonwhites the ineluctable necessity, for sheer survival's sake, to organize themselves, wherever possible, into collective resistance against the mass paranoia of the white group of mankind. In the world at large, to employ a historical parallel from German history, the whites constitute a Prussian state, geographically dispersed but nevertheless a unitary imperium in its single-minded drive, its ruthless ambition for dominance. The only difference—and this merely on the surface—is the explicit ethnic motivation that characterizes the white group impulse. The Prussian state was overtly political in its objectives and militaristic in its methods. It aimed to subject its neighbors to the grand design of a Greater Germany. The whites of the world, utilizing Prussian methods, intend to subject the rest of mankind to the overlordship of a racial elite comprised of themselves. They are employing technology for this purpose; in this they have placed their faith.

The problem for blacks and other nonwhite peoples is how to turn the whites away from their antihuman activities by persuading them to abandon the idolatrous worship of their god, technology.

In the specific context of the struggle of black against white Americans, however, this problem will be less urgent than one that will increasingly preoccupy blacks during the coming two or three decades: the necessity to avoid overreacting to white racist provocation; for if they fail to do so, they may be decimated.

The critical problem, therefore, for black Americans in the coming thirty years or so is how to escape the diminution of their numbers by massacre and other forms of near-extermination designed to reduce the chance of their further dilution of the ethnic composition of white America. The American dream is of a lily-white America closer to the Australian model than the present size of the black population of the country would allow. White America does not want its black population; but, as yet, it is undecided what to do about it. There are a number of choices open. The following list is not exhaustive; it suggests only some of the main lines of approach to the problem:

—Assimilate the blacks unconditionally.

—Assimilate them subject to conditions.

—Isolate them.

—Resettle them, as in the case of the European Jews, outside the territory of the United States—perhaps in Africa, on the basis of their having there a historic homeland.

—Expel them by a steadily mounting campaign of official discrimination—as in the case of Hitler Germany—using such methods as confiscation of their property, deprivation of their civil rights, and the terrorization of concentration camps.

—Exterminate them.

—Tolerate them within roughly defined limits, as is more or less the present case.

—Tolerate them in conditions of equal freedom.

—Encourage them, subject to restrictions.

—Encourage them without restrictions.

—Treat them as a special group to be conceded for a specified period compensatory advantages in order to enable them to come abreast of the mass of the general population of the country.

—Treat them just as every other group in the population.

Obviously, some of these processes are already taking place, compatibly as well as contradictorily. The main questions are which, in the long or short run, will assert itself—or themselves—as the solution, whether "final" or interim; and whether it might be deliberately chosen by some exercise of the general will or permitted by some popular abstention through apathy or complicity.

Concern with the future, however, necessarily involves the potential of white America for choosing, or permitting the choice of, one or another procedure or combination of them.

It would be idle to pretend that white America has no stomach for the mass extermination of black people on the well-known lines laid down by Hitler in his treatment of the European Jews. There would clearly be no lack of camp commandants, crematorium and gas-oven technicians, and dispensers of Cyclon B available from the ranks of white America. The slogan "Black is beautiful" would acquire a touching significance in the form of black skin processed into lamp-shades and the fatty deposits of black bodies converted into soap. Moreover, the idolatrous regard of white America for science and technology would furnish adequate moral justification for any cryo-genic, high-temperature, implantation, or other medical experiments that sadism might suggest for white America to carry out.

The central point is that the potential for Nazism in America is just as high as it was in pre-Hitler Germany. And just as there were Jews in Hitler Germany—Nazi Germany—to truckle to the oppressors and make terms with them, so will there be blacks in America to truckle to the oppressors and make terms with them. Just as there were Jews who on the very brink of the concentration camp were able to find something good in the Nazi system, so will there be blacks who on the very brink of the concentration camp will find something good in American Nazism.

Without necessarily implying that the present situation in America bears anything other than a remote resemblance to the circumstances that typified Nazi Germany, a recent incident involving two prominent blacks in the two leading black middle-class organizations in America is instructive. The first black described the Nixon administration as the most hostile to "Negro" rights and progress of any national administration since Woodrow Wilson's. Now this statement was remarkable— indeed it was unique—coming from a quarter so conservative as the Chairman of the Board of Directors of the National Association for the Advancement of Colored People. That fact alone invested it with a quality of moderation attested to by a long history of tactical compromises with the racist usages of white America. It was as if the High Priest of Accommodationism had spoken. The statement had all the thunderous impact of the totally unexpected. It was still reverberant, and the Nixon administration still reeling from the shock of this harmless worm turned venomous snake, when white racism found, as it so often does, a black defender. This time it was the Executive Director of the National Urban League, who presented himself as an apologist for the Nixon administration, whittling away at the forthright statement of the Chairman of the Board of the NAACP, diminishing its force and diluting its content with a typical black infusion of trust, after all, in "Massa."

In the wake of this performance, it turned out that the Executive Director was taking the position that he could not rule himself out of consideration for a job in the Nixon administration. This is the type of leadership that black Americans have had to endure for much of their 400 years in this hemisphere. Their future cannot any longer be entrusted to temporizing, though well-meaning, hands. But neither can it be confided into the undisciplined hands of self-styled "revolutionaries." The stakes are too high, the cause too precious. For black Americans are the vanguard of the world-wide struggle of blacks against white racism. There is a direct relationship between the black struggle for freedom and equality in America and the black struggle for freedom and equality elsewhere in the world. In this sense the black struggle against white racism in America has already been internationalized, despite the determination of white America to suppress this effort and destroy all blacks who would denounce white racism in America from international forums.

A principal concern of the future, then, must be the quality of black leadership in America. The essential prerequisite of such leadership is the capacity and determination to see the black struggle in America as one that is not against whites, but against white racism. It is, of course, true that without whites there would be no white racism. Not all whites, however, are racists. It will therefore be necessary for black leadership to make careful common-sense distinctions between whiteness as skin color and whiteness as racism. In tactical terms, this will mean that black leadership of the future will adopt from the very outset the position eventually reached at the end of his life by Malcolm X, when he recognized nonracist whites as necessary allies in the struggle. The difference between Malcolm X's position in this respect and that, say, of the National Urban League or the National Association for the Advancement of Colored People was that to Malcolm X these nonracist whites were equal allies; while to the National Urban League and the NAACP they were patrons. Malcolm X prefigured black leadership and will remain for a long time to come the fountainhead of black revolutionary inspiration in America and a heroic prototype.

His acceptance of nonracist whites was a dramatic reversal of his preceding attitude. Yet it did not mean that he had made either a philosophical or a pragmatic departure from separatism to integration. To the end of his life he continued to be aware that for another generation or two, the self-respect of black people could be achieved and maintained only in psychological dissociation from white America. He knew that black people needed time and psychic withdrawal from whites in order to regain and re-establish an integral sense of group identity, as far as possible in independence of white values. Malcolm X knew that a separate state for black people within the existing federal arrangement was an opium dream of street-corner oratory. But he also realized that the symbolism of the demand was useful in itself as an antidote to the sickness of the black middle-class disease of integration. Malcolm X was a person of the most extraordinary intelligence, and he knew as well as anyone that from an economic standpoint alone, black separatism was infeasible. But he was also aware of what the black middle class has never been able to get through its collective head: that integration in the present dominance of American life by white racism could only be a deadly trap for black people. The process of integration is a bringing together of separate parts to make a whole. When completed, however, the process leaves undisturbed the intrinsic inequality of such parts as were unequal, for it is a process of substitution rather than of transmutation. An integer takes the place of fractions; yet these component fractions, in so far as they were unequal, remain unequal within the integer. This precisely would be the situation of black Americans at the present time and for decades hence in the event of integration. They would merely continue to be, as historically they have been, a helot class with imperfect rights and truncated privileges: with, however, the full burden of obligations incident to citizenship. Stokely Carmichael's "Hell, no! We won't go!" with reference to the war in Vietnam was explicit recognition of this fact. So is the cardinal tenet of the program of the

Black Panthers, which requires its members to refuse service in the armed forces of the United States of America, among others (except in the Black Liberation Army).

The experience of Brazil as an integrated society is instructive. There class distinction was substituted for racial discrimination. But since social class is determined mainly by economic categories, and the mass of the blacks who were enslaved until late in the nineteenth century occupied the lowest of these categories, the blacks as a whole were correspondingly in the lowest social classes. All that integration had done for them was to supply the chance of racial assimilation. It had not made them better off in any quantifiable respect; it had only given them the illusion that they were free and equal citizens of Brazil against whom no official policy of racial discrimination was in effect.

Yet the coarse fact is that no such policy is necessary, since what it would accomplish is already performed efficiently by the institution of social class. With the exception of the so-called primitive Indians, blacks are at the bottom of the sociological heap in Brazil. Given the chaotic circumstances of life in that country and its chronic economic malaise, they are likely to remain just where they are for a long time to come. Their situation as integrated Brazilians is even more infuriating than that of blacks in the United States as segregated Americans. For the latter are under no delusion that they are free and equal citizens. Their position as an underclass considered unassimilable denudes for them the racist policies of white America of that false disguise of ethnic toleration in which the Brazilian situation masquerades. At least black Americans know where they stand; black Brazilians do not. But this also has the effect of making the black American middle class's yearning for integration in present circumstances a still more curious exercise in sociological folly. By their inversion of cause and effect, integration is translated into a cure, when, in fact, it is the disease itself. Black Americans have always been integrated into American society, but as unequals, which explains their historic as well as their contemporary plight. This is why separatism, in default of integration as equals, seems to many blacks the logical and necessitated remedy.

As Sir Winston Churchill said, in effect, when out of power before the Second World War and on declining at that time and on that footing an invitation to visit Hitler: "Either as an equal or not at all." Despite the white racism that marred his greatness, Churchill was a

45

self-respecting man. Black Americans—in particular, black middle-class Americans—are deeply lacking in this quality in their relations with whites. But the younger generation of black Americans is well on its way toward redemption. The resolution of the struggle into its opposite aspects is clear in its future cast. It will be not a conflict of choice between integration in the black middle-class sense and separatism in the sense of the black nationalists. These are not the true alternatives. Instead of integration as though it had never existed before (that is, the black middle-class attitude), it will be integration as unequals (which, absurdly, is what the black middle class wants, because, actually, that is all they can get from white racism), as against integration as equals (which, juridically, is what all blacks ought to have, and which, both vociferously and silently, the great mass of black Americans want). Then there is separatism, and if the choice is between this and integration as unequals, why, then, it will be separatism; but if the choice is between separatism and integration as equals, it will be integration as equals. The decisive revolutionary movement in America will be the passage of the black millions, not from unequal integration (which is where they stand at present) to separatism as a political end in itself, but from unequal integration by way of a transient psychological separatism to equal integration as the major synthesis of their American citizenship.

Any black revolutionary movement in America is justly to be assessed by two predominating criteria: as a response to white racism; and as a black drive for group self-respect.

One of the first casualties of a revolutionary situation is national loyalty on the part of the disaffected group. Black Americans, as such a group, have remained more loyal than might have reasonably been hoped, than might have realistically been expected. But if they continue to occupy their present position of helot underclass, then the future is certain to see a dramatic lessening of their deep, traditional loyalty. Then black traitors will become as numerous as white traitors. Racial dissidence among black and white troops in Indochina, racial unrest among black and white troops in Germany, and resistance on racial grounds to the draft in America—all these symptoms of disaffection and others will multiply manyfold and will be either met with Hitlerian repression or accorded statesmanlike amelioration. Upon this single circumstance, the racial struggle, depends the future of America and, for the foreseeable morrow, the future of the world.

When a British foreign secretary, Sir Alec Douglas-Home, proposes on various pretexts to sell arms to white South Africa, his attitude is well understood among growing numbers of black and nonwhite people the world over. It should occasion no surprise and produce no shock. Douglas-Home is simply acting in character. He is a white racist. For him, and others like him, it is "Christian" not to isolate white South Africa even while that country pursues a remorseless policy of segregation against the black majority of its inhabitants. Douglas-Home's attitude is: Let's not be beastly to the white South Africans; let's sell them arms, especially since Britain's safety is involved. There is the Cape route to defend, and South Africa is ideally positioned to do it. Aside from this, there is a treaty between us covering this matter. And we mustn't forget, either, that the white South Africans are our best trading partners. Just consider our tremendous financial investment in that country. We simply can't afford to be sentimental about the blacks.

This myth of the highly civilized English that has taken in so much of the world for such a long time is gradually being dispelled by the pressure of nonwhite immigration on the complacent hypocrisy of English society. England is being stripped bare of its racial pretenses and is being shown to be just as racist as white America except for a single difference, which should not be underestimated. That is the operation of the English law. Here reposes a vestige of proof of the vaunted tolerance and fair-mindedness of English society. No one, certifiably sane, would claim that the American legal system functions with impartiality where black people are concerned. But it is possible, in all sanity, to make this claim in general on behalf of the English system. So far, with some exceptions, justice in England has shown itself, in the best sense of the abstract symbolism, not only blind in pragmatic fact but also color-blind.

Not so, however, in white America. Here, as a general rule, justice has traditionally been perverted wherever black people are involved. And while there is evidence here and there throughout the country of changes of practice in this regard, the custom of withholding justice from black people in the courts of the land remains a predominant feature of American jurisprudence. What assurance there is at the present time that this misuse of the law will cease in the discernible future is mainly to be derived from the growing contempt and disrepute into which the administration of justice in America has fallen.

The law in America will redeem itself in the future by becoming less class-dominated and more demotic. The evolution of the law has hitherto been in the direction of institutional aloofness from society. Its future direction, measuring the future as the next thirty or forty years, will be toward the expression of its major purpose as a social instrument rather than a sovereign institution. The doctrine of the "sovereignty of law" has grown juridically untenable and socially obsolete. It was, in its origin, an outgrowth of an English class struggle for whose resolution it was employed as a compromise acceptable to both parties. Neither the king and his faction—the aristocratic party—nor Parliament and its adherents—the middle-class party—but the law, was sovereign. As a principle, it was imported into the American colonies, where it was put to use in its function of supreme social arbiter without incurring any particular odium until the colonists decided that they had had enough of colonialism and embarked upon revolution. The Stamp Act was the law of the land, and the law was sovereign, but this did not prevent the theorists of the Revolution from establishing a co-sovereign in the form of the popular will. Conflict between these two sovereignties, the law and the popular will, is a prime cause of revolution.

So it was in the case of the American Revolution. Depending upon whose side is taken by the big battalions, one or the other of these sovereignities usually goes into abeyance for the duration. Superior force may insure that the sovereignty of the law is upheld against the popular will, or conversely. It is, in gross fact, power that is truly sovereign in any society. The law (and its manifestation as justice) is simply an index to the location of power within the society. Where the power resides, there is the law. If the power resides in the popular will, then there is the law. If the power resides elsewhere than in the popular will, then again, there is the law. *Cuius potestas, eius lex,* to parody the ancient maxim.

The "supremacy of law" is political dogma descriptive of the ambition of the class in power to maintain its dominant position by a rigid insistence upon legitimacy. This principle will be asserted by the members of the class in power as long as it promotes their vital interests. Thus the welfare of the society as a whole is subordinated to the well-being of a component class. And the theoretical instrument employed for this purpose is the notion of the "supremacy of law." What it amounts to is this: the rules of the game favor our side; therefore they must be heeded by everyone.

So when we talk about the future of law in America, what we are really discussing is the probable location of the effective state power in the future. In other words, in whose hands—in the hands of which group within the society—will the greatest quantum of the national power reside?

If it should continue to repose where it does now, then social change will come at a pace calculated to leave largely undisturbed these repositories of the sovereign power. So long as this arrangement has either the express or tacit approval that is conferred in institutional and customary forms by the popular will, revolution or the threat of revolution will be no more than a mainfestation of minority discontent. This is currently the case in the United States. The popular will does not challenge or otherwise call into question the present repositories of power. It does not follow that they are right not to do so, that the popular will affords the proof of its own wisdom by its abstention from issuing such a challenge. Rightness and wisdom are matters of intelligence and not of numbers. Majorities are not necessarily more right or more wise than minorities. In normal circumstances, majorities simply tend to be more powerful. That is all. The more essential it is, then, to bear in mind that there can be circumstances where minorities, in contradistinction, are more powerful than majorities. Once more, however, no automatic accession to rightness or wisdom is to be deduced from this circumstance. Power always provides its own validation in complete independence of either rightness or wisdom. It is a law unto itself. And, finally, it is the law. But the converse is not true, that law is power. Law is merely an aspect of power. So law will go as power goes and will do as power dictates, since it is the creature of power—in America, white power.

Law in its current social manifestation is under increasing attack from several diverse quarters of the national community. Yet this is not, in fact, a threat to dislodge and discard the present repositories of power. It is, rather, a demand to refashion this social instrument and so make it of more efficient service to current needs.

The existing attack on the law is insurrectionary and not revolutionary. The strategic scope of an insurrection is more limited than that of a revolution. It may expand into revolution, but it is not yet revolution.

There is need to make this distinction clear so as to emphasize what is actually taking place in certain white sectors of the American society and also among relatively small numbers of black people. In both instances, something in the nature of an insurrection is in progress, yet with little informal concert and apparently nothing like an organized alliance between the two groups.

Black insurrection is a marginal phenomenon even within the black group. By this very fact it is devoid of the support of the black community and, by logical extension, of the national purpose. It thus confronts, with whatever allies it can muster from other disaffected sectors of the society, white American power in its entrenched repositories fortified by popular sanction. And the challenge it throws down is to this consecrated sovereign that embodies and exercises after a fashion and to an effect deemed despotic by the whole of the black minority the general will of the white majority.

The attack on the part of the black minority ranges accordingly from insurrection to constitutional agitation for reform. It assaults the entire encampment of American institutions, usages, and law, and will continue to do so until it either forces the white defenders to yield the required changes or is itself thrown back, defeated, and rendered incapable of further such attacks. Thus the battle has been joined, and the only question for the future is its outcome.

Will American law, through the courts of the land, persist in denying justice to black people?

Will the jury system remain in the future, as it is today, a legal device that, in its actual operation, denies blacks the right of trial by their peers?

Will justice continue to be a concept of disjunctive import, meaning one thing for blacks and quite another for whites?

Will the black people of America, making up as they do some 12 per cent of the population, continue to constitute a disproportionate percentage of those confined in state and federal prisons throughout the land?

Will bail continue to be set at larger sums for blacks than for whites, thereby putting into effect the practice of preventive detention of blacks without trial?

Will justice, by being inordinately delayed, continue to be denied to blacks?

These are only a few of the relevant questions on this issue. Whatever the nature of the answers returned by white power, the fact that these questions are being posed by blacks will not be without influence in the shaping of the American future.

The forms in which these questions are being put by blacks are many and various, not all of them by any means revolutionary. But from whichever black quarter they come, they all proclaim one thing in common: an outcry for social justice. At the best of times, it is far from easy to determine the concrete application of justice. As a concept, it is not quite so slippery in apprehension and may, roughly, be defined as the impartial apportionment of right and wrong. Clearly, however, these terms involve philosophical difficulties of the most complex order. "Right" and "wrong," unless construed in a social context, quickly degenerate into unrestrained subjectivism. The most any of us can hope for, even in the most favorable circumstances, is an approximation to justice.

In the administration of the law, judges are engaged for the most part in quantifying the resolution of issues that come to them for decision. Their activity is not qualitative in the sense that there are values of justice to which, contingent upon their own character and ability, they may give perfect expression. Nothing of the sort. They are, in fact, to adapt Edmund Burke's celebrated lament on the execution of Marie Antoinette, "economists and calculators." They quantify justice on a legal scale calibrated by the dominant forces in the society as expressed in the decisions of higher courts, customary law, or enactments of the legislature. Theirs is an essay in social measurement, guided by rules of law, and aimed at achieving a tolerable degree of approximation to justice. Its motive spring is empiricism, not idealism.

When black people complain of white injustice perpetrated against them by the courts of the land, they are saying, in effect, one thing above all: whatever the fine professions of the organic law of the United States, otherwise known as the Constitution, law is as law does. And it is precisely for this reason, the law being a practical application of social ethics, that they consider the Constitution to be worth a great deal less than the paper it is written on.

There is nothing sacred about a written constitution. The British, for example, have done quite well, on the whole, with an unwritten one. If any appeal is to be made to an enhallowed principle in a society, it must be to the precept of social justice. And if this principle is to retain its sacrosanct position, it must command an allegiance throughout the society that is based upon its impartial translation from principle into equal practice. The American Constitution is a signal failure in this regard where the black citizens of the country are concerned. Thus, paradoxically, the best justification for black

51

revolution in the United States is the Constitution itself. No black person who reads this document can deduce from it, in the present circumstances, anything other than a warrant for revolution.

It is often said in defense of Christianity that it is a sublime corpus of religious inspiration betrayed in practice by self-professed Christians. By analogy, the only trouble with the Constitution of the United States is its nonobservance by white racist America.

Yet, since the effective state power, the sovereign exercise of the national will, is within the grip precisely of this element in the country, blacks are excluded in principle and practice from the application of social justice. It is axiomatic that social justice is part and parcel of the patronage of power.

In times of social crisis, demands for law and order always issue from the repositories of power. And to the question Whose law? or Whose order? their answer, naturally, is: ours.

Their law and their order; which simply is another way of saying, "We are sovereign: we possess the power, and we mean to keep it." The inherent concern of power is not with social justice, but with its self-perpetuation. Where social justice should be the great end of society, power substitutes itself as that end and subordinates social justice to the status of a means. Social justice itself would be meaningless, within a human context, in the absence of human society. Human beings constitute the great end of human society and are each, as individuals, an end in themselves. In the calculation of power, however, which is impersonal in its intrinsic nature, human beings are merely means to the greater end that is power itself. There is, accordingly, an irreconcilable opposition between power and social justice. The sovereign is compelled by its own animating principle, power, to be hostile to social justice.

In the United States of America, the sovereign is white, hence white power. The deep alarm that the specter of black power conjures up in the imagination of the white sovereign derives from the knowledge of the antiblack use to which white power is put. If the tables were turned, would not whites be relegated to the position now occupied by blacks? That is the nightmare of white power, the succubus-haunted dream of white America. And it is why the appeal of the blacks for social justice is met with a stony-faced insistence on law and order by the white racists. Hitler also demanded his own law and order, and in circumstances not inherently dissimilar from those that at the present time characterize American society.

52

The future of social justice for blacks in America is, therefore, dependent upon the future cast and quality of power. To put it otherwise: into whose exercise will power in the United States devolve? If, as now, it remains in the hands of white racists, black revolution for liberty or death will be the only alternative to repression. But if it should come into the hands of enlightened whites—and, of course, blacks—who, on balance, command the support of the popular will, social change by peaceful evolution could be the consequence. The immediate, though not the long-term, prospect is that power will continue in the possession of the white racists. The immediate prospect, correspondingly, is black revolution.

It would be gross oversimplification, however, to suggest a purely mechanical relationship between white power and black revolution, for these two are not isolated phenomena in the American society, sealed off from contact with other factors. They are in constant interaction with the rest of the life of the society and subject to its influence. Yet this does not render the situation so indeterminate in its essentials as to give warrant to a prediction that anything may happen. Anything does of course happen in human affairs, but not necessarily as a rule. There are a number of crucial conditions involved in the conflict between white racism and black revolution, any of which may at any time prove decisive. Some of these conditions may, together, be described as mediatory, in the sense that they tend to conciliate; others, taken together, may be described as inflammatory, in the sense that they tend to exacerbate. From the general welter, one condition of salient importance may be extracted without the slightest hesitancy: leadership. And since the quality of white leadership will be racist for some time to come, what will the quality of black leadership be? What, in short, is the most intelligent, and, therefore, the most effective, response on the part of black leadership to white racism? For this is what it comes down to: intelligence.

The brute, abysmal folly of white racism has already been established beyond all question. Yet it remains, equally beyond all question, the paramount fact of American life and society. America is a land peopled, predominantly, by white racists. America is a land governed, pre-eminently, in accordance with the theory and practice of white racism.

What, then, should be the intelligent—not the militant, not the moderate—response by blacks to this state of affairs?

Obviously, there can be no doctrinaire rejoinder to this question.

Any dogmatic approach to the immensely complicated problem posed by white racism in America would inevitably fail to illuminate the matter, let alone provide a constructive solution. For this reason, Frantz Fanon's historical analysis is almost entirely irrelevant to the objective circumstances of the American society. While many of the incidents characteristic of colonialism typify the situation of blacks in this country, blacks nevertheless are not a colonial people in the classical sense. To view them as though they were is to commit a fundamental error of analysis that converts all related statements into pointless diatribe—picturesque diatribe, no doubt; interesting polemic; but pointless. Fanon's tortuous ratiocinations all have one thing in common: a feverish dialectic that owes at least as much to the assumptions of psychopathology as to the class fundamentalism of Karl Marx. No general theory of historical development will suffice to cover the black-white situation in the United States of America. This situation is *sui generis,* unique in itself.

The antecedent conditions that led to the Algerian struggle for independence against the French bear, at best, only a superficial resemblance to American conditions. In the former instance, there was a colonial power in the form of a metropolitan country, and there was an indigenous people, the Algerians, who were being subjected to the classic incidents of colonial exploitation in their native land. In the latter—the American—instance, there is no metropolitan power, and neither is there a native people, as such (except the Indians), although, as has been said before, certain of the incidents common to colonial exploitation do attach to the blacks. Nonetheless, black Americans clearly do not constitute a colony, nor can white racist Americans be regarded in this connection as a metropolitan power. Imprecise language is often a reflection of imprecise thinking, and there is a good deal of both on this subject. A historical analysis that would, even by implication, assimilate the black-white experience in America to the French-Algerian in North Africa is wrong in its premises and false in its conclusions.

The revolution in Algeria had, it was distinctly enunciated, a territorial objective: to drive the French out; to expel the metropolitan power, and thus put an end to the colonial servitude of Algerians.

With the Indian revolution, too, the objective was territorial: to drive the British out (the British being, of course, the metropolitan power), and thus put an end to the colonial servitude of Indians.

As for the middle-class revolution in Germany in 1848, that revolution had no territorial objective. It was a revolution of ideas. The aim was, essentially, to replace a ruling set of ideas by another whose values would mirror the type of society deemed more desirable by the bourgeois revolutionists. It failed. There is nothing so impotent as an idea whose hour has not yet come. But the point to be borne in mind is that, by contrast with the Algerian and Indian revolutions, it was a revolution of ideas, without a territorial objective.

Such, too, was the English middle-class revolution of the mid-seventeenth century to secure the supremacy of Parliament against royal absolutism.

The French revolution in the latter half of the eighteenth century —the Age of Reason—and the Russian revolution in the first quarter of the twentieth were different; they were both examples of revolutions of ideas, but they also possessed something in the nature of a territorial objective, though not the same kind as that of the Algerian and Indian revolutions. The territorial objective here was the redistribution of the great landed estates. The element of the extrusion of a foreign power was absent (although in the case of the Russian revolution it eventually became necessary for the new Russian rulers to defend their accession to power against the intervention of foreign countries, among them the United States).

The central point to be garnered from these examples is that revolutions are either ideological, territorial, or a combination of both, and that their dominant objective is the seizure of power.

A further point, of scarcely less importance, is that they derive their character in general, especially when they are successful, from the pragmatic conditions they confront and are ambitious to change. A successful revolution never superimposes a governing ideology alien to the actual conditions. That would be to make theory of superior consequence to fact, which could only be disastrous.

In contemplating the prospect of revolution in the United States, how are the essential preconditions to be assessed?

First, it must be clear exactly what is meant by revolution. A revolution is a process, typically involving the use of armed force, by which the power that confers effective control of the state is seized by a dissident group which thereupon supplants the previous holders of power.

The strategic goal of any revolution by armed force is always the seizure of power. This does not preclude the fact that an armed revolution may have a more limited objective. It may aim merely to force desired changes in the *status quo*. The microscopic black revolution (or, more accurately, insurrection) will be of the second category. It will be only partly an armed revolution, and it will also be a revolution of ideas.

It will be an armed revolution to the extent that some black revolutionaries either carry arms or advocate the use of arms; and it will be a revolution of ideas to the extent that some black revolutionaries engage in the commerce of disseminating opinions and beliefs with a view to inducing desired changes through persuasion. Both of these processes are under way at one and the same time in the United States.

Behind these armed and ideological revolutionaries are massed from 25 to 30 million black Americans, in a multitudinous diversity of attitudes ranging from impassioned concern and support without active participation to perfunctory interest and apathetic indifference. There are also blacks who oppose revolution in any form. They may or may not be content with the established order, but even if they see change as necessary, they would rather leave it to the chance of time. These 25 to 30 million black Americans constitute a "silent majority." Yet a courteous demurrer must be entered here to President Nixon's strict construction of that term to the effect that "silence means assent." If a man holds a knife to another's throat and then relieves him of his wallet, the latter's silence cannot reasonably be interpreted to have meant assent. President Nixon has given insufficient thought to all the implications of this innocent-seeming aphorism, from which he draws tacit sanction for the conduct of his office, however dubious this may be in some respects. For silence, far from signifying assent, may simply mean, among other things, a choking sense of outrage; and, in the instance of the well-nigh 30 million black Americans, a choking sense of black outrage.

Thus it may be asked: is revolution in the United States necessary, interpreting "necessary" to mean "intelligent," and if so, which type of revolution is warranted by the existing circumstances: a revolution of ideas, a territorial revolution, or a combination of both? These are only two of the teeming questions that the future will address to white as well as black Americans. They will be answered by the evolution of the American society.

2

THE BLACK PEOPLE of America have a knife at their throat. It is held there by an American thug known as white racism. With this knife at their throat, the black people have had to submit to being robbed of their liberties, their material resources, their social development, their dignity, their self-respect. They have had to endure being called lazy, dirty, shiftless, stupid, childish, backward, inferior—to cite only a few of the milder epithets traditionally hurled at them. They have had to endure the rape of their womenfolk, the torture and lynching of their menfolk. They have been called upon to "serve their country," to endure, to be patient, understanding, tolerant, to be accommodating in their own humiliation by white racism.

In this way have the Black Codes operated from the time of their inception as the repressive agency of white racist reaction in the slave period and during the post-Reconstruction era. The Black Codes have undergone many changes of outward form. They appeared after Reconstruction as enactments by state legislatures in the conquered South making discrimination against people of black skin a matter of public policy and official practice. They appeared subsequently as regional customs invested with quasi-legal standing by ancient prescription. And even when the statutory law expressly forbade an antisocial act, the commission of such an act against a black person did not give rise to legal redress. For example, murder was legally prohibited by all the Southern states. In practice, however, the murder of a black person by

57

a white mob, otherwise known as a lynching, did not result in accountability to the law. For most purposes, blacks were outside the law in their dealings with whites.

The notorious decision in the *Dred Scott* case, to the effect that a black man had no rights that a white man need respect, possessed a cultural significance quite apart from its juridical aspect, far antecedent and long consequent to the date of its pronouncement. It was merely a judicial expression of the sociological attitude of white America, as a whole, toward black people. Where the attitude differed from one region of the country to another, the difference was not so much qualitative as a matter of degree. As recently as forty-five years ago, a black physician in Detroit, in the act of protecting his home against an attacking white mob, shot and killed a member of that mob in self-defense. It was only after two trials (the first ended in a hung jury) and with the assistance of the greatest criminal lawyer in the United States, supported by the National Association for the Advancement of Colored People and other interested organizations and individuals, that he was acquitted. The atmosphere surrounding the trial, the testimony adduced by the prosecution, the attitude of the white mob against whom the black physician had invoked and exercised his right of self-defense—all gave contemporary point to the historic thesis of white racists that a black man has no rights that a white man need respect. Whether it is a black physician in Detroit, or the Scottsboro boys in Alabama, Emmett Till in Mississippi, or the Black Panthers who, asleep in their beds, were shot to death by Chicago police officers—no matter who, provided only that he is black, and no matter where in the United States, this white-racist thesis comes either expressly or inarticulately into operation against him.

The roots of the matter are buried deep in the institution of slavery. Black men, women, and children were sold from their African homeland by black and Arab slave traders to Europeans engaged in the same trade, who then transported them to the Americas. This transatlantic trade in black slaves uprooted countless millions of Africans from their homes and forced those who survived into servitude of the most barbaric description abroad. It is impossible to arrive at an accurate count of the Africans who were thus enslaved. Estimates vary widely, ranging from tens of millions to scores of millions. But all accounts agree that the circumstances of their uprooting and, in particular, the conditions of their transportation from Africa to the

Americas represent a degree of cruelty scarcely paralleled in the history of the human species. About this there is no question whatever.

But what manner of people were these—these Africans — who sold one another—brothers, sisters, friends, fathers, and mothers—into slavery to white traders in black human beings?

Granted the precedent that all peoples have engaged in this infamous activity (the Russian Caucasus, for instance, was regularly raided to obtain supplies of white slaves for Arab markets, and whites have never scrupled to sell one another into slavery); granted this, as well as the fact that the Europeans were backed by superior military might in their penetration of Africa, it remains nevertheless something of an enigma that any people could be so basely venal as these Africans showed themselves to be.

So their betrayed compatriots were brought here and also taken elsewhere in the Americas, and reduced to desolating and complete deprivation of freedom.

Much has been made of purported distinctions between slave systems. In the Arab system, for instance, blacks, though slaves, might hope to rise to positions of eminence, contingent upon demonstrated ability, in their master's service. In essence, nevertheless, they remained chattels at their master's disposal, their lives and persons the playthings of his whim and in absolute subjection to his will. Otherwise, the social incidents attached to their status were in general less restrictive than was the case with transatlantic slavery. Despite their Moslem faith, the Arabs were not devoid of racial consciousness, which, however, seemed to express itself in aesthetic terms, although not by any means exclusively. For they also saw "stupidity" as an attribute of "blackness," as much Arabic literature makes abundantly clear. But simultaneously with this attitude, they also practiced a considerable degree of tolerance toward their slaves, by which the latter were enabled to gain a measure of social mobility. Professor Bernard Lewis, the distinguished historian of the Near and Middle East at the University of London, and an authority on Arabic literature, has devoted an article in *Encounter* to the racial attitude of Arabs toward blacks. He discloses the racist attribution by Arabs of derogatory qualities to the black slaves because of their blackness, as well as the social latitude existing within the rigid boundaries of the Arab slave system. It is a study of the utmost penetration by a scholar whose massive learning illuminates an historic subject that has hitherto been replete with obscure and ambiguous recesses.

The late Frank Tannenbaum, Professor Emeritus of the History of Latin America at Columbia University, in his celebrated work *Slave and Citizen: The Negro in the Americas,* differentiates slavery in Latin America from slavery in North America by asserting of the former that it conceded to the enslaved African a soul for the religious purpose of conversion to the Catholic church and thus permitted him to remain a person, though unfree. The North American system, by contrast, completely divested the slave of personality and regarded him as a soulless chattel.

The differences between these various systems of enslavement, whose victims were in huge preponderance Africans, reflected cultural ideologies modified or otherwise emphasized by economic imperialism. Racism is not a modern phenomenon in the sense that it was completely unknown in theory and in practice before the appearance of the Comte de Gobineau's *Essai sur l'inégalité des races humaines* (*The Inequality of Human Races*) in the middle of the nineteenth century. It can be considered modern only to the extent that with the rise of the European nation-state and the discovery of the New World, its rationale was no longer based exclusively on cultural differences.

Economic motive now asserted the validity of slavery as a human institution and produced its warrant in the form of Christian theology. This development is peculiar to the history of the Western world. While slavery is an institution almost coeval with human culture, this was the first time in recorded history that any of the groups of mankind had attempted to rationalize it, employing a system of dialectical supernaturalism expounded in the name of a Christian God. Strange have been the uses of Christianity, and this, one of the strangest of all. Its direct inspiration was in no way theological but owed its world-transforming impulse and its unparalleled release of the collective energies of a single human group—namely, the white group—to the quest for the material wealth that they saw as the Golden Fleece of the New World. Impelled by their lust for gold, they did not scruple to defile their God, let alone exterminate Indians and enslave Africans. They were not argonauts, but merely a greedy, murderous scum. Economic imperialism was the historical development that followed upon the discovery of the New World, and racism was its principal support for the consequent debasement of human values. As Hannah Arendt observes in *The Origins of Totalitarianism:*

The fact that racism is the main ideological weapon of imperialistic politics is so obvious that it seems as though many students prefer to avoid the beaten track of truism.

African slaves had begun to arrive in the New World ten years after its discovery by Christopher Columbus in 1492. But this simply represented the transatlantic extension of the trade in African slaves that was already in vigorous and profitable commerce between Portugal and Africa. The immediate occasions for the enlargement of the slave trade from Europe to the New World were the economic demands asserted by the Spanish settlers in Hispaniola, together with a plea by Bartolomeo de las Casas, "Protector of the Indians," for African slaves to replace the Indians, who lacked the physical stamina to withstand the savage rigors of the murderous toil imposed upon them by the conquerors. The latter was a curious instance of inverted humanitarianism, with consequences of far-reaching portent for the future of the Americas. The introduction of African slaves as a source of replacement for the nearly exterminated Indians followed.

For all those who think that the Nazi treatment of the Jews decreed by Hitler was without precedent and is without parallel in human history, Las Casas' appeal to Charles V of Spain on behalf of the Indians of the New World against the Spanish colonizers would be instructive. It is not in order to minimize the sufferings of the Jewish people and others in Nazi concentration camps that the record of the human species as a whole, good and ill together, should be borne in mind. Rather is it to acquire the perspective essential to the comprehensive portrait of mankind, as of all sentient creatures, the supreme exponent of calculated evil. It is quite certain that, from a moral point of view, the species man is by no means the best of all living things. Indeed, it is beyond question that he is the vilest.

According to Las Casas' account, *The Tears of the Indians,* more than 50 million Indians were massacred by the Spaniards in circumstances of such fiendish barbarity that those sixteenth-century European adherents of the Christian faith would have nothing to learn from the Nazis except modern technology. On the contrary, the Nazis might have picked up a thing or two from them.

The Spaniards which are among the Indians do breed up a sort of fierce dogs, which they teach and instruct to fall upon the Indians and devour them. Now let all men, judge whether Christians or Turks, in this it much imports not, whether so much cruelty ever pierc'd their ears before. These dogs they take along with them in all their expeditions, carrying also divers Indians in chains for the sustenance of those dogs. And it was a common thing for them to say to one another: "Give me a quarter of your Indian for my dogs, and tomorrow when I kill one I will pay it you again." As if they were no more to be accounted of than the offals of a hog or sheep. Others were wont to go a-hunting in the morning, and being asked how they had sped: "Oh, very well," replied the other, "my dogs have killed fifteen or sixteen Indians this morning."

The recital of horrors would exhaust the most sadistic imagination.

Neither would their cruelty pity women with child, whose bellies they would rip up, taking out the infant to hew it in pieces. They would lay wagers who should with most dexterity either cleave or cut a man in the middle, or who could at one blow soonest cut off his head. The children they would take by the feet and dash their innocent heads against the rocks, and when they were fallen into the water, with a strange and cruel derision they would call upon them to swim. Sometimes they would run both Mother and Infant, being in her belly quite through at one thrust.

Nothing that the debauched whim of depraved and diseased European whites could inflict upon these hapless Indians was spared them. They drank the cup of white cruelty to its hideous lees.

It was now the turn of the Africans. "I cannot understand why so many Negroes die," wrote the Spainsh King to a correspondent in Hispaniola in the year 1511. He would have had no difficulty understanding why if he had undertaken a royal progress on a slave ship bound for the New World and, having arrived there, had inspected their conditions of employment. Later on, with the development of the trade in slaves from Africa, chiefly by England, Portugual, France, Spain, and Holland (although other European nations also participated), the Middle Passage to the Americas became a classic synonym for inconceivable horror.

The late W. E. B. Du Bois, in *The World and Africa,* cites a committee of the House of Commons as follows on the Middle Passage:

The Negroes were chained to each other hand and foot, and stowed so close that they were not allowed above a foot and a half for each in breadth. Thus rammed together like herrings in a barrel, they contracted putrid and fatal disorders; so that they who came to inspect them in a morning had occasionally to pick dead slaves out of their rows, and to unchain their carcasses from the bodies of their wretched fellow-sufferers to whom they had been fastened.

Other commentators consider that the conditions in which African slaves were transported to the Americas were no worse, in general, than the standards of the age tolerated. One of these, the West Indian historian Eric Williams, adduces the comparable case of indentured servants and even, indeed, of passengers in transit on the ocean-going vessels of those days. Williams would also minimize the horrors of the Middle Passage by asserting the sufferings of white indentured servants in vile, overcrowded conditions on ships plying between Britain and the North American colonies. Nor, he says, were conditions for free passengers much better. He omits to make a distinction, however, between the abominable circumstances in which free passengers, as well as indentured servants, traveled by ship and those in which black Africans were transported. The black Africans were enslaved, and they went in chains. From the standpoint of an academic historian, this is perhaps a trifling distinction; yet it is worth making. As Williams himself points out in *Capitalism and Slavery:*

The sole aim of the slave merchants was to have their decks "well covered with black ones." It is not uncommon to read of a vessel of 90 tons carrying 390 slaves or one of 100 tons carrying 414. Clarkson's investigations in Bristol revealed a sloop of twenty-five tons destined for seventy human beings, and another of a mere eleven tons for thirty slaves. The space alloted to each slave on the Atlantic crossing measured five and a half feet in length by sixteen inches in breadth. Packed like "rows of books on shelves," as Clarkson said, chained two by two, right leg and left leg, right hand and left hand, each slave had less room than a man in a coffin. It was like the transportation of black cattle, and where sufficient Negroes were not available cattle were taken on.

But it is as though one were to discount the terror and misery of the Nazi concentration camps by reference to the working conditions of coal miners in Wales or Pennsylvania. By any standards imaginable, the conditions in which African slaves were carried to the Americas reveal the abysmal depths to which human beings are capable of descending in their gluttonous search for material wealth.

Tannenbaum cites Rev. R. Walsh (*Notices of Brazil,* 1831) as follows:

The height, sometimes, between decks, was only eighteen inches; so that the unfortunate human beings could not turn round, or even on their sides, the elevation being less than the breadth of their shoulders; and here they are usually chained to the decks by the neck and legs. In such a place the sense of misery and suffocation is so great, that the Negroes, like the English in the black-hole at Calcutta, are driven to frenzy. They had on one occasion, taken a slave vessel in the river Bonny: the slaves were stowed in the narrow space between decks, and chained together. They heard a horrid din and tumult among them, and could not imagine from what cause it proceeded. They opened the hatches and turned them up on deck. They were manacled together, in twos and threes. Their horror may well be conceived, when they found a number of them in different stages of suffocation; many of them were foaming at the mouth, and in the last agonies—many were dead. The tumult they had heard, was the frenzy of those suffocating wretches in the last stage of fury and desperation, struggling to extricate themselves. When they were all dragged up, nineteen were irrecoverably dead. Many destroyed one another, in the hopes of procuring room to breathe; men strangled those next them, and women drove nails into each other's brains. Many unfortunate creatures, on other occasions, took the first opportunity of leaping overboard, and getting rid, in this way, of an intolerable life.

Tannenbaum also quotes from Lawrence F. Hill (*Diplomatic Relations Between the United States and Brazil*):

The stench below was so great that it was impossible to stand more than a few minutes near the hatchways. Our men who went below from curiosity, were forced up sick in a few minutes; then all the hatches were off. What must have been the sufferings of those poor wretches, when the hatches were closed! I am informed that very often in these cases, the stronger will strangle the weaker; and this was probably the reason so many died, or rather were found dead the morning after the capture. None but an eye witness can form a conception of the horrors these poor creatures must endure in their transit across the ocean.

The enslaved Africans were dragooned from every part of sub-Sahara Africa, but chiefly from the coastal area. The historical evidence makes it clear that all the tribes of this vast region were affected. The Western assertion that they were "savages" is of a piece with the whole tissue of lies fabricated in an attempt to justify this revolting episode. Aimé Césaire, in his introduction to *Esclavage et colonisation* (*Slavery and Colonization*), by Victor Schoelcher, writes:

What sort of men were these, then, who had been torn away from their families, their countries, their religions, with a savagery unparalleled in history? Gentle men, polite, considerate, unquestionably superior to those

64

who tortured them—that collection of adventurers who slashed and violated and spat on Africa to make the stripping of her the easier. The men they took away knew how to build houses, govern empires, erect cities, cultivate fields, mine for metals, weave cotton, forge steel. Their religion had its own beauty, based on mystical connections with the founder of the city. Their customs were pleasing, built on unity, kindness, respect for age. No coercion, only mutual assistance, the joy of living, a free acceptance of discipline. Order—Earnestness—Poetry and Freedom. From the untroubled private citizen to the almost fabulous leader there was an unbroken chain of understanding and trust. No science? Indeed yes; but also, to protect them from fear, they possessed great myths in which the most subtle observation and the most daring imagination were balanced and blended. No art? They had their magnificent sculpture, in which human feeling erupted so unrestrained yet always followed the obsessive laws of rhythm in its organization of the major elements of a material called upon to capture, in order to redistribute, the most secret forces of the universe.

And exactly what was the level of civilization from which they came? The answer is supplied by the great ethnologist Leo Frobenius, in his *Histoire de la civilisation africaine:*

What was revealed by the navigators of the fifteenth to the seventeenth centuries furnishes an absolute proof that Negro Africa, which extended south of the desert zone of the Sahara, was in full efflorescence, in all the splendour of harmonious and well-formed civilizations, an efflorescence which the European conquistadors annihilated as far as they progressed. For the new country of America needed slaves, and Africa had them to offer, hundreds, thousands, whole cargoes of slaves. However, the slave trade was never an affair which meant a perfectly easy conscience, and it exacted a justification; hence one made of the Negro a half-animal, an article of merchandise. And in the same way the notion of fetish (Portuguese, *feticeiro*) was invented as a symbol of African religion. As for me, I have seen in no part of Africa the Negroes worship a fetish. The idea of the "barbarous Negro" is a European invention which has consequently prevailed in Europe until the beginning of this century.

Lest it be supposed that only in the case of the Africans did the Europeans exhibit not the slightest particle of moral scruple, or that by contrast with Césaire's "gentle" Africans the Indians of the New World were "bloodthirsty savages," listen again to Las Casas:

This infinite multitude of people [the Indians] was so created by God, as that they were without fraud, without subtlety or malice, to their natural Governors most faithful and obedient. Toward the Spaniards whom they serve, patient, meek, and peaceful, and who laying all contentious and tumultuous thoughts aside, live without any hatred or desire of revenge; the people are most delicate and tender, enjoying such a feeble constitution of body as does not permit them to endure labor, so that the children of Princes and great patrons here [in Spain] are not more nice and delicate than the children of the meanest countryman in that place. . . . They are of a very apprehensive and docile wit, and capable of all good learning, and very apt to receive our religion, which when they have but once tasted, they are carried on with a very ardent and zealous desire to make a further progress in it; so that I have heard divers Spaniards confess that they had nothing else to hinder them from enjoying heaven, but their ignorance of the true God. To these quiet Lambs, endued with such blessed qualities, came the Spaniards like most cruel Tigers, Wolves, and Lions, enraged with a sharp and tedious hunger; for these forty years past, minding nothing else but the slaughter of these unfortunate wretches, whom with divers kinds of torments neither seen nor heard of before, they have so cruelly and inhumanely butchered, that of three millions of people which Hispaniola itself did contain, there are left remaining alive scarce three hundred persons.

To listen to latter-day expositors of the human record, one would get the impression that Adolf Hitler and his Nazi followers invented the crime of genocide. People like these find it convenient to forget what the Belgians—another group of European whites—did to the inhabitants of the Congo when, under the royal and Christian sponsorship of Leopold II, they reduced the population of that region of Africa from between 20 and 40 million to something like 8 million by systematic and sadistic murder. They forget Karl Peters in German Southwest Africa. The following quotation in reference to Leopold II's decimation of the Congo is from John Harris's *Dawn in Darkest Africa:*

Europe was staggered at the Leopoldian atrocities, and they were terrible indeed; but what we, who were behind the scenes, felt most keenly was the fact that the real catastrophe in the Congo was desolation and murder in the larger sense. The invasion of family life, the ruthless destruction of every social barrier, the shattering of every tribal law, the introduction of criminal practices which struck the chiefs of the people dumb with horror —in a word, a veritable avalanche of filth and immorality overwhelmed the Congo tribes.

It is people like Leopold II and his Belgian subjects, white Christian Europeans, who haughtily refer to Africans and other nonwhite peoples as "savages." The mass murder to the point of near extermination of the North American Indians at the hands of another gang of white European invaders is yet another story of the same kind.

In so far as all these campaigns of large-scale murder, fiendish torture, and moral and physical degradation were conceived and carried out by white Christian Europeans, they were not only actuated by economic considerations but they had a racial motive as well. From a purely materialistic point of view, it would have hardly been worth the while of the white Christian Europeans to mount campaigns of invasion and massacre against the inhabitants of foreign lands unless there was an attractive prospect of economic gain. White European Christians have seldom been motivated simply by ideology; most, if not all, of the time the conduct deemed desirable for entry into the kingdom of heaven has been postponed to the conduct considered necessary for the conquest of the kingdom of this world. While the ritual language prescribed for admission to the kingdom of heaven has often been retained, its injunctive content has more often been cast aside.

In the moral conflict thus engendered between the rival claims of the divine hereafter and the Caesarean now, Christianity compromised fatally. The white Christian Europeans were, from a dialectical standpoint, not unlike the founder of their belief, Jesus Christ himself, whose sophistical expedient in rendering "unto Caesar the things that are Caesar's, and unto God the things that are God's" has inspired much of the subsequent conduct of his followers. This moral flaw at the very heart of the Christian doctrine predisposed its eventual employment as a convenient dogma and temporizing instrument in the hands of white European imperialism. To these imperialists of the sixteenth century and after, the ritualistic profession of devotion to God under the aegis of the Christian faith was a sufficient performance of the scriptural duty, as laid down by the founder, to "render unto God the things that are God's." Caesar's due, equally to be rendered, could then legitimately be accomplished on Caesar's terms.

Christ did not intend this dualistic consequence in its abhorrent implications, but he did not reckon with the retarded moral evolution of the human species. His years of ascetic isolation, necessitated by his prophetic calling, had deprived him of adequate firsthand knowledge of his fellow men. So he tended to see them not as they actually were in all their genetic deficiencies and neurological imbalances.

Instead he saw them in his autohypnotic state as children of his Father—of whom he was, of course, the Son—as candidates for heaven contingent only upon their good behavior. It was a tragic error. In his innocence, he denounced "scribes and Pharisees," with whom he differed on ideological grounds. He regarded them as symbols of evil, of which "hypocrisy" was the expression most to be abominated. With the then Roman occupation he had some contact. Apparently, however, he did not find it morally intolerable, and indeed as these things go, it could not be accounted an unmitigated despotism.

But if he thought so little of "scribes and Pharisees," how would he have regarded Spanish conquistadors; English, Portuguese, Spanish, French, and Dutch slave traders; European exterminators of the North American Indians, Belgian mass murderers of the Congolese people of Africa, Australian (that is to say, European) mass murderers of aborigines, German mass murderers of Jews, or American (once more, derivatively, European) mass murderers of Vietnamese?

So the economic aspect of white European Christianity in its political expression as imperialism validated itself, first of all, as social ideology by making an absolute distinction between Christian and heathen, according a complete moral sanction to the former. This was at once the unifying, as well as the impelling, spirit of the Crusades for the recovery of the Holy Land. And since the geographical path of the Christian faith had been charted by its original promulgators through Asia Minor into Europe, itself a peninsula of Asia, it was not chance precisely that made Europe under the pristine leadership of Rome the religious executor of the last will and testament of the Galilean thaumaturgist—to employ Anatole France's celebrated phrase. Yet historical accident played its own unpredictable role, too. The whole issue of the religious successor to paganism as an official creed might have been resolved in favor of Mithras as against Jesus if Julian the Apostate had not come to an untimely end at the early age of thirty-two. *Vicisti, Galilaee!*

Christianity in the course of the succeeding centuries devolved in its status of official religion from one secular ruler of the kingdoms of Europe to another. These all derived their legitimacy, until the rise of European nationalism, from the representative of Christ on earth, His Holiness the Pope.

Nationalism achieved, in the first place, consolidation as a domestic force. It adhered tenaciously in all instances to the Christian doctrine

68

as official religious policy, and it employed this doctrine against its internal and external foes with the same self-righteous zeal and ruthlessness that it later exhibited toward the alien heathen; but now, however, with a difference. For while white Europeans might be heretics, they were seldom, if ever, heathen, no matter in how profound a cultural abyss they might wallow. They were Christians. And because Christianity in the Near and Middle East had made, by comparison with its phenomenal success in Europe, little headway, Europe had come by the end of the Dark Ages to occupy a position which was virtually that of a lone outpost of the Christian communion. Its historic fount and origin was located in the Near East, but its active existence as the official religious ideology of states, with the professed allegiance of the inhabitants of those states, was largely being conducted in Europe. Beyond Europe there were, in the mass and main, the heathen; inside Europe the Christians. In terms of this geographical division, the heathen were nonwhite; and the Christians, white. From this physical circumstance, it was not difficult to deduce a divine intention. Skin color ascended to crucial importance as a determinant factor in the revelation of God's favor. To be white was to be on God's side; to be nonwhite was to be against Him. Modern science would supply in time dubious credentials for the rationalization of skin color into "race." At that moment, however—when Christianity identified itself as a practitioner of the skin-color test for eligibility as a member of God's party—it condemned itself to ideological extinction.

It had, meanwhile, important services to render to white European nationalism in its expansionist phase as imperialism. For this purpose it made a pact with the new technology, by which, in return for the forcible conversion or seduction under various guises to Christianity of heathen souls, it would give its blessing to the white European despoilers of their lands, pray for the success of their brutal undertakings, and share in their depredations, adorning Christian churches with their ill-gotten gains, and, where Judas Iscariot had asked only for silver, demanding gold as the price of Christ's betrayal. The Christian church played the role of harlot to European imperialism.

With skin color firmly established as a geographical guide to the Christian communion, the next step in this monstrous paralogism could occur. It would be doing the "will of God" to extirpate the nonwhite heathen wherever it was unprofitable or obnoxious to keep them alive, and, as a matter of fanatical principle, to subject them to every cruelty and indignity that human ingenuity could devise—in the name of God. The enslavement of Indians (Columbus himself sent the first batch of these hapless people to Seville) and the enslavement of Africans followed with a terrible consistency.

It is pointless to assert, as some writers do, that there was no racial impulse in white European imperialism, that its motive force was purely economic. Commercial advantage and (in the case of Great Britain, for example, before the passage of the Reform Act of 1832) the initial demands of the new industrialism, coupled with territorial aggrandizement, were certainly factors of decisive importance. But to exclude altogether the ideological drive generated by racism based up to then on skin color is to fail to take into account one of the prime sources of the cultural attitude of white Europeans (and now, by necessary extension, the white group of mankind) toward nonwhite peoples. This aspect of the white ethos should not be exaggerated, but neither should it be completely discounted. That would be to miss entirely the significance of the part undertaken and carried out by Christianity in the conception and development of the theory and practice of white racism. While the role of Christianity, from an institutional standpoint, was always dualistic and replete with surface contradictions, its actual influence operated to permit, where it did not actively instigate, the insemination and growth of this atrocious social deformity.

Christianity did not give rise to nationalism, any more than it did to imperialism. It was neither cause nor effect. But it did furnish vital ideological support in the form of moral sanction—if only, for the most part, of a passive kind—for the barbarous excesses of its adherents. Institutional Christianity is guilty of the basest complicity.

From nationalism to imperialism to racism; from Europe to Africa to the Americas; these twin paths, the one ideological, the other geographical, converged and intersected in the near extermination of the Indians and the enslavement, centuries-long, of countless Africans.

It was with this sinister heritage and cultural prospect that the Pilgrim Fathers came to North America in December, 1620.

These early English settlers also brought with them an impassioned attachment to individual liberty and an ardent profession of religious tolerance. They were idealists in the visionary sense of the seventeenth century, and they conceived of a human community

70

emancipated from traditionalism and, in philosophic essence, subject only to the governance of individual consciences orchestrated into a general will. The emphasis was upon the supreme worth of every human being expressed in terms of freedom and tolerance upon the basis of an explicit social contract. It is the attempt to develop and apply this notion in response to the successively enlarging demands of community, colony, and nation over three and one-half centuries that is implied by reference to the American society.

The attempt in its institutional form, viewed from a political stand-point, has been chiefly remarkable for its ambition to determine and effectuate the popular will through a civil magistracy divested of royal privilege and a representative body answerable only to an electorate, with a system of justice functioning, like the other two, in complete independence.

No human community has ever been conceived on nobler lines or striven with so much resourcefulness, supplemented by such vast material wealth, to translate a great ideal into living, organic reality. But the dream and the waking effort have mainly been denied realization because of one obstacle intractable above all others, namely, white racism.

The original community of settlers was Christian, as was the successor coalition of colonies, which, together with other geographical units, evolved through war and peace into the federal republic of the United States of America. It was, and is, in social practice, though not in legal theory, a Christian state.

This fact has had consequences of an external, as well as an internal, nature, and all of them in precise symmetry with the Christian doctrine, yet at the same time directly contradictory of its central precepts.

Christianity is, paradoxically, a collateral ancestor of white racism, for by remote historical chance it supplied a set of ethical values from which it was possible to deduce a doctrinaire division of men into Christians and infidels. Geography facilitated the transmission of this idea from the Middle East to Asia Minor and into Europe. The rest followed with a fateful automatism. Europe (by which is meant the white Western world) assumed in the course of the centuries the role of defender of the Christian faith against the non-European, nonwhite world beyond the West.

With this cultural heritage, the early American settlers saw themselves as the divinely appointed guardians of an orthodoxy bound together by faith and, no less important, by race. It was no accident that their iconography, their entire scheme of color values, and their noumenal projection of a supreme deity all reflected, as their European models had done, a besetting conviction that whiteness was the sign of the Chosen. Race and religion had become inextricably intertwined. Whiteness was the outward and visible sign of orthodoxy, and non-whiteness of heresy. In the name of God—white God—no mercy should be shown to heretics. The fact that heretics were, fortuitously, in large numbers nonwhite extended the possible area of missionary activity for the redemption of the heathen. But conversion to Christianity, while indispensable to salvation in the hereafter, was of lesser account from the standpoint of economic necessity in the here and now. At the onset of the Christian hegemony over Europe, whites were enslaved as impartially as nonwhites. Conversion to Christianity might sanctify their souls but did not necessarily liberate their bodies. The demand for abundant supplies of cheap labor, wherever required, did not discriminate in favor of Christians. It was only as the mystique of race became part and parcel of the rationale of slavery that this form of discrimination arose. By then, of course, Christians were, in the main, white. A holy alliance was contracted between Christianity and white racism.

The early European arrivals in North America were therefore able to have as little compunction in massacring Indians as their counterparts displayed against these hapless people in South and Central America and the Caribbean. The intervention of economic necessity is always more effective than the intrusion of God in such matters. The North American Indians were superfluous from an economic point of view. They were simply a redundant population in possession of desirable land. And since they were neither Christian nor white, they could be exterminated in the name of God.

The Europeans in South and Central America and the Caribbean were, similarly, covetous of the wealth of the Indians. They massacred them and expropriated their lands. But because they also considered them to be of economic utility, they enslaved them and set them to work in mines, fields, and cities. However, the Indians proved un-profitable as a source of cheap labor, for they grew enfeebled too quickly and died under the stress of their working conditions. The conjunction of economic necessity and the pleas on behalf of the

72

Indians by Las Casas induced the introduction of African slaves to supplement and replace the debilitated and dying Indians.

This was the principal distinction between the attitude of the European invaders of North America toward the indigenous Indians and that of the European invaders of South and Central America and the Caribbean. The former had no economic use for the Indians; the latter did. But in both cases, indifferently, the Christian God was invoked to sanction mass murder and brutal outrage. He was called upon to bless and prosper His worshipers as they dealt at will with nonwhite, non-Christian peoples for whom they had no economic use. In the same spirit, He was besought to bless and prosper His other European worshipers as they went about murdering, maiming, plundering, and enslaving in His name for the sake of economic necessity. All groups of mankind have exploited their gods for base purposes. Few have gone to such lengths to fabricate false rationalizations as the white Christians of the Western world. Perhaps this is a sign of progress. At least they have felt impelled to offer, in however cynical a spirit, some semblance of moral justification to their god.

As the mass murder of North American Indians was beginning, shiploads of enslaved Africans were arriving. The twin circumstances would ride abreast of each other in the generations that lay ahead in a blood-soaked and ominous procession. The fate of the Indians, for whom there was no economic use, and that of the Africans, for whom there was, were indissolubly bound together.

Frank Tannenbaum makes much of the "idea of the moral value of the individual [which] outlasted slavery and became the chief source of its undoing." This view is unacceptable. It was slavery that outlasted the economic value of the individual. When the individual as a unit of production became less profitable than machines from the standpoint of cost efficiency, slavery as an institution also became more vulnerable to moral strictures. While it remained profitable, its moral critics continued to be impotent. When it grew unprofitable, they came into their own. In the whole record of human affairs, morality has seldom flourished unless the economic circumstances were favorable. Tannenbaum says further:

Just as the favoring of manumission is perhaps the most characteristic and significant feature of the Latin-American slave system, so opposition to manumission and denial of opportunities for it are the primary aspect of slavery in the British West Indies and in the United States.

The late distinguished professor was a great scholar and a magnificent human being. But his thesis of a "moral" distinction, based upon the personality of the slave in the Latin-American system, in contradistinction to the slave's chattel status in the North American and British West Indian systems, is unwarrantable. He overlooked, in the case of the Latin-American system, economic considerations which tended to make that system less onerous, on the whole, but which had nothing whatever to do with moral idealism. When economic necessity demanded it, the Latin-American system never hesitated to divest the slave of all vestiges of personality and reduce him remorselessly to the chattel status characteristic of the North American and British West Indian systems.

Tannenbaum's view honors him as an illustrious historian of Latin America in the great humanist tradition. It does not, however, take sufficiently into account one of the gross motivations of human behavior constituted by economic necessity. When economic necessity holds sway, human morality pays court. The relative ease with which manumission could be achieved by a slave in the Latin-American system merely reflected a less exigent demand for his labor on the part of that system, as contrasted with the corresponding state of affairs in North America and the British West Indies, where an economic response of a different order had to be made to the requirements of the world market. It was so massive and compelling in its nature that little room was left for humanitarian sentiments. That was why the average life expectancy of a slave in the British West Indies was seven years. It was not that his owners worked him to death in this short period out of spite or racial prejudice, purely as such, but that, first, the market demanded the maximization of his utility in the shortest possible time and, second, his owners had calculated on a cost-efficiency basis that it was cheaper to work him to death in seven years and then replace him than prolong his life span beyond that limit and be faced with assuming the extra expense of feeding and caring for him when his economic usefulness was at an end.

Tannenbaum cites Thomas R. R. Cobb:

[In the United States], in every slaveholding state . . . restrictions . . . have been placed upon the manumission of Negro slaves. . . . In several of the states domestic manumission, that is, manumission to take effect within the state, is prohibited.

74

This was not done because slaves were hated in the United States, but because they were valuable property. Their value was a function of the extremely profitable prices fetched by tobacco and cotton in the world market; and their cheap slave labor was the prime coefficient of that value. They were also valuable property in Latin America, of course, yet they did not in general play a role of such pivotal importance in the economy of that region in relation to the world market. When the importance of their labor increased, their conditions of servitude became quite as burdensome and inhibiting as those existing to the north. It was at all times an economic matter, with moral impulses becoming effective only as the prospect of economic profit declined.

In so far as the Christian church was concerned, its conduct in this matter was in keeping with its established character. It compromised with domestic actualities wherever it encountered them, accepting local institutions of slavery while inveighing against the whole degrading business. Between the fifteenth and nineteenth centuries the slave trade was condemned by several of the heads of the church of Rome. It flourished undisturbed by such moral homilies, sensitive for the most part only to fluctuations of commodity prices in the market. The abolition of the slave trade by Britain and the United States in 1807 had a good deal more to do with the decline of mercantilism than with the rise of humanitarianism. While the mercantile system lasted, one of its principal requirements was an abundant supply of cheap labor. Slavery met this requirement. It is not a meaningless coincidence that the slave trade and the mercantile system can be plotted into a graph of almost identical curves, outlining economic developments in the Western world between the end of the Middle Ages and the American War of Independence. There is, in fact, a clear causal connection between the system and the trade. One of its ironical aspects is the rough conjunction of the mercantile system and the slave trade with the inception of the historical period known as the Renaissance.

North America was a small, primitive society of trading posts when the first African slaves were imported into the British colonies. By 1787, when the Constitutional Convention sat in Philadelphia to draft a constitution, there were thirteen states, with a total population of nearly 4 million. Of this population, about 18 or 19 per cent were blacks, and of these blacks more than 90 per cent were slaves. Maine

75

and Massachusetts alone had no slaves. There were a few in Vermont, rather more in New Hampshire, and less than 1,000 in Rhode Island. The greatest concentration was in the Southern states. In Virginia, they constituted about 40 per cent, in South Carolina about 42 per cent, and in Georgia about 35 per cent of the population. The more than 100,000 in Maryland made up roughly 35 per cent of its population. In Delaware they made up 20 per cent, in North Carolina more than 25 per cent, in Kentucky 16 per cent, and in Tennessee 10 per cent of the population. New York had more than 20,000 slaves, and New Jersey more than 11,000, in each case representing some 7 per cent of the population. In Pennsylvania there were less than 4,000, or less than 1 per cent of the population. Taken all together, there were approximately 700,000 slaves distributed among the states, with about 60,000 free blacks. The evolution of the country from a sparse number of trading posts dealing in peltry to an agricultural economy based on tobacco and cotton had, in large part, been made possible by the slave system.

It must in fairness be said that there was at all times opposition in various quarters of the loosely settled country to the institution of slavery. The fact that such opposition was notoriously ineffective should not be taken to imply a lack of Christian fervor. Quite the contrary. While in its doctrinal essence Christianity distilled the principle of freedom for all men, it incurred no abatement of zeal by recommending that the heathen slaves be converted. The reluctance of the owners was overcome by the assurance of the Christian ministry that it did not aim to free these black slaves, but only to render them more tractable to servitude. And that is precisely what it did. The major contribution of Christianity to the plight of the slaves was to administer to them a spiritual narcotic against their mental and physical misery. It enjoined love and meekness, patient enduring and humble obedience, and it held out the prospect of heavenly redress in the hereafter for present wretchedness. Christianity welded the shackles of the slave system more firmly about the slaves. To the bondage of slavery it added the bondage of spiritual fetters. It confused the slaves and divided and paralyzed their wills. However doubtful the chance of a successful mass revolt against slavery, Christianity whittled away even that slender possibility. Its principal service was to spawn large numbers of black converts throughout successive generations of enslavement and thereafter, all hopelessly addicted to the spiritual drug of its narcotic doctrine. For leaders, it created Uncle Toms, and as followers, docile masses of black hymn singers and babblers of the Western-appropriated folklore of a fanatical religious sect, with its origins in the Middle East. While this was going on, the white Christian church and its white Christian followers steadily grew richer, and the land they had stolen by brutal force from the Indians became more prosperous, through the unfree, unpaid labor of the deluded black Christian slaves.

Nowadays—and especially during the Colonial era—some Africans say wryly that the white Christian missionaries came to Africa, gave them the Christian Bible, and in exchange took away their lands. In North America the black slaves were given the Christian Bible and their manhood and their womanhood were taken away. It was a bad bargain, and it can be defended by the black victims only on the ground that it was made under duress.

Surrounding these thousands of black victims of European greed and racism abetted by African tribal rapacity was a bustling, vigorous society of adventurers and parvenus, in whose eyes they were as despised and degraded as their labor was valuable and vital to the growth and enrichment of the society itself. These black slaves had seen the economy on which this society founded its affluence grow apace with their own numbers. When they were but a handful, the society was but a scattering of trading posts. As they were disembarked in larger and larger numbers on the shores of North America, they could see the society knit itself together into incipient nationhood, and they could see the trading posts supplanted by an agricultural economy, which, in turn, would yield to commerce before the last-named itself gave the superior place to industry. Indigo, rice, cotton, tobacco, sugar cane: it was upon the backs of black slaves that these major structures of the country's wealth were erected. It was by their toil, their degradation and wretchedness, that millions of European immigrants could lay claim to North America as a "Land of Promise." Behind the ceaseless extension of the frontiers of the land lay the ceaseless labor of the black slaves.

Within this vast unfolding of economic expansion by the North American colonists was contained the cultural germ of white racism clearly evidenced by black slavery. Eric Williams argues, however: "Here, then, is the origin of Negro slavery. The reason was economic, not racial; it had to do not with the color of the laborer, but the cheapness of the labor." Williams selects economic factors and cites other circumstances in an attempt to prove his assertion. Along the way he announces that "slavery was not born of racism: rather, racism was the consequence of slavery." Then, finally, "Slavery in no way implied, in any scientific sense, the inferiority of the Negro." With the last of these pronouncements, no serious-minded person will quarrel. But even in the restricted context of the history of the Caribbean, the second will not hold water; it leaks at the historical seams. As regards the first of the statements, it can only be said that it is a plain instance of a plausible oversimplification drafted into the service of an inadequate historical theory. For in order to be at liberty to make so complacent a statement, this historian dismisses by implication the whole racial ethos of the then contemporary white Christian culture. He closes his mind to the literature of that age, to the social thought of Europe at the time of the first Portuguese contact with the west coast of Africa, which was roughly coincident with the invention of printing. He overlooks the white Christian complex of cultural symbolism, in which black has immemorially stood for foulness and the devil, and white for purity and God. No one would deny the compelling economic reasons that actuated the enslavement of Africans. On the other hand, it is an affront to historical evidence to suggest that the black skin of the African furnished merely ex post facto rationalization. Anyone whose vision was not impaired by a doctrinaire allegiance to economic determinism would recognize at once the psychological conditioning in color values that predisposed the white Europeans and their transplanted counterparts, the North American colonists, to the enslavement of black Africans. In the pragmatic context of economic necessity, the racial factor may have played a secondary role, but it was not absent.

When this eminent historian announces that "racism was the consequence of slavery," he offers only a fragmentary statement of the relevant facts. He neglects to take into account such factors as religion, nationalism, and aesthetics, which were conspicuously racist in their European expression. These factors antedated Caribbean slavery. By comparison with its immediate economic causes they were, arguably, less compelling. But they predisposed toward it. Theirs had been the work of creating a European mentality in whose world outlook race was dominant. To this racist mentality the alleged economic necessity of black slavery was in no sense repugnant. And so it aided and abetted the process. Having first of all generated a malign psychological impulse, the evil trinity of religion, nationalism, and aesthetics provided a systematic philosophy of racism to lend respectability to the impulse and endow with virtue the barbarous horror of slavery and the brutal excesses of economic necessity. But so obsessed is Williams with economics as the "origin of Negro slavery" that his view of other causal factors is obscured. His attention riveted on a single tree, he fails to see the forest.

The Middle Passage was only the beginning of the slaves' sufferings. Upon their arrival in the New World, the survivors were subjected to a process known as seasoning. This was a brutal method of physical and psychological conditioning for the indescribable severities of toil as plantation slaves. In addition to the overseer's whip, merciless labor, and unutterably squalid housing, there was the callous destruction of the slave family. William Goodell, in *The American Slave Code in Theory and Practice*, adduces the following instances, among others:

NEGROES FOR SALE.—A negro woman, 24 years of age, and her two children, one eight and the other three years old. Said negroes will be sold SEPARATELY or together, as desired. The woman is a good seamsstress. She will be sold low for cash, or EXCHANGED FOR GROCERIES. For terms, apply to MATTHEW BLISS & CO., 1 Front Levee.

I WILL GIVE THE HIGHEST CASH PRICE for likely Negroes, from 10 to 25 years of age.   GEORGE KEPHART.

ONE HUNDRED AND TWENTY NEGROES FOR SALE.—The subscriber has just arrived from Petersburg, Virginia, with one hundred and twenty likely young negroes of both sexes and every description, which he offers for sale on the most reasonable terms. The lot now on hand consists of ploughboys, several likely and well-qualified house servants of both sexes, several women with children, small girls suitable for nurses, and SEVERAL SMALL BOYS WITHOUT THEIR MOTHERS. Planters and traders are earnestly requested to give the subscriber a call previously to making purchases elsewhere, as he is enabled to sell them as cheap or cheaper than can be sold by any other person in the trade.   BENJAMIN DAVIS
(Hamburg, S.C., September 28, 1838).

Frederic C. Bancroft, in *Slave-Trading in the Old South*, writes as follows of four cargoes of slaves transported to New Orleans in 1834 and 1835:

Of the four cargoes making a total of 646 slaves, 396 were apparently owned by Franklin & Armfield. Among these there were only two full families: the fathers were 21 and 22 years of age, the mothers 19 and 20, and the children 1 and 1½. There were 20 husbandless mothers with 33 children, of whom one was 2 weeks old, 4 others were less than 1 year old, 19 were from 1 to 4 years old, and 9 were from 5 to 12 years of age. The remaining 337 were single and may be grouped thus:

> 5 were from   6 to   9 years old, both inclusive
> 68   ”   ”   10 ” 15   ”   ”   ”   ”
> 145   ”   ”   16 ” 21   ”   ”   ”   ”
> 101   ”   ”   22 ” 30   ”   ”   ”   ”
> 9   ”   ”   31 ” 39   ”   ”   ”   ”
> 8   ”   ”   40 ” 50   ”   ”   ”   ”
> 1 above 50, a man of 60

93 per cent of these 337 were from 10 to 30 years of age.

A slave who purchased his freedom, in his *Interesting Narrative of the Life of Oloudah Equiano, or Gustavus Vassa,* published in 1789, had this to say about the remorseless breakup of the black slave families at the hands of white owners and traders:

O, ye nominal Christians! might not an African ask you—Learned you this from your God, who says unto you, Do unto all men as you would men should do unto you? Is it not enough that we are torn from our country and friends, to toil for your luxury and lust of gain? Must every tender feeling be likewise sacrificed to your avarice? . . . Why are parents to lose their children, brothers their sisters, or husbands their wives? Surely, this is a new refinement in cruelty, which, while it has no advantage to atone for it, thus aggravates distress, and adds fresh horrors even to the wretchedness of slavery.

At about the same time, Thomas Jefferson, reflecting upon the enslavement of blacks in *Notes on the State of Virginia,* trembled to think that God is just.

Despite the efforts of apologists for the system, such as Ulrich B. Phillips, to minimize the terrible squalor of slavery, it remains a ghastly record of barbarous cruelties. The black historian John Hope Franklin writes in *From Slavery to Freedom: A History of Negro Americans:*

Housing for slaves was especially poor. The small, rude huts were usually inadequate as well as uncomfortable. Windows and floors were almost unheard of. Frederick Olmsted was shocked when he viewed the slave cabins on some of the plantations he visited. He described them as small and dilapidated with no windows, unchinked walls, and practically without furnishings.

A Polish visitor to George Washington's plantation commented in a similar vein on the living conditions in which the Father of His Country kept his black slaves.

Yet housing was almost, as it were, a minor inconvenience alongside the great white Southern sport of nigger hunting. For this purpose, dogs (known as nigger dogs) were especially trained. According to Frederick Olmsted in *The Cotton Kingdom:*

Dogs were trained, when pups, to follow a nigger—not allowed to catch one, however, unless they were quite young, so that they couldn't hurt him much, and they were always taught to hate a negro, never being permitted to see one except to be put in chase of him. . . . No particular breed of dogs is needed for hunting negroes: blood-hounds, fox-hounds, bull-dogs, and curs were used, and one white man told me how they were trained for it, as if it were a common or notorious practice. They are shut up when puppies, and never allowed to see a negro except while training to catch him. A negro is made to run from them, and they are encouraged to follow him until he gets into a tree, when meat is given them. Afterwards they learn to follow any particular negro by scent, and then a shoe or a piece of clothing is taken off a negro, and they learn to find who it belongs to, and to tree him, etc.

There are accounts of black runaway slaves being pursued and, when caught by these dogs, being torn virtually to pieces without the least quiver of compunction on the part of the hunters. For some of these slave owners and slave catchers, it was a sport altogether more satisfying than fox hunting.

Nor was this all.

If a nigger ran away, when he [a certain slave owner] caught him, he would bind his knee over a log, and fasten him so he couldn't stir; then he'd take a pair of pincers and pull one of his toe-nails out by the roots; and tell him that if he ever run away again, he would pull out two of them, and if he run away again after that, he told them he'd pull out four of them, and so on, doubling each time. He never had to do it more than twice—it always cured them. [Olmsted.]

The catalogue of horrors is endless.

"That won't do," said he [the overseer to a female slave]. "Get down." The girl knelt on the ground; he got off his horse, and holding him with his left hand, struck her thirty or forty blows across the shoulders with his tough, flexible, "rawhide" whip (a terrible instrument for the purpose). They were well laid on, at arm's length, but with no appearance of angry excitement on the part of the overseer. At every stroke the girl winced and exclaimed, "Yes, sir!" or "Ah, sir!" or "Please, sir!" not groaning or screaming. At length he stopped and said, "Now tell me the truth." The girl repeated the same story. "You have not got enough yet," said he; "pull up your clothes—lie down." The girl without any hesitation, without a look of remonstrance or entreaty, drew closely all her garments under her shoulders, and lay down upon the ground with her face toward the overseer, who continued to flog her with the rawhide, across her naked loins and thighs, with as much strength as before. She now shrunk away from him, not rising, but writhing, grovelling, and screaming. "Oh, don't sir! oh, please stop, master! please, sir! please, sir! oh, that's enough, master! oh, Lord! oh, master, master! oh, God, master, do stop! oh, God, master! oh, God, master!" [Olmsted.]

Blacks were burned alive, hanged, castrated, shot, and tortured with impunity. It was all done as casually—or as premeditatedly, when occasion served—as spitting out a wad of chewing tobacco.

The high-minded lamentations of Jefferson and others, decrying this iniquitous institution, occasionally rose above the din of sophistry issuing in a thunderous cataract from the defenders of the system. Although himself a slaver owner, Jefferson could write, as he did in *Notes on the State of Virginia:*

When arguing for ourselves, we lay it down as fundamental, that laws, to be just, must give a reciprocation of right; that without this, they are mere arbitrary rules, founded in force, and not in conscience; and it is a problem which I give to the master to solve, whether the religious precepts against the violation of property were not framed for him as well as his slave? and whether the slave may not as justifiably take a little from one who has taken all from him, as he may slay one who would slay him? That a change of the relations in which a man is placed should change his ideas of moral right and wrong, is neither new, nor peculiar to the colour of the blacks. Homer tells us it was so, 2,600 years ago:

> Jove fixed it certain, that whatever day
> Makes man a slave, takes half his worth away.

But the point of view held by Jefferson and shared by other men of enlightenment, North and South, would be long in prevailing. A civil war would be fought and, with the threat of secession as its political

82

catalyst, slavery elevated to a place among the issues of overriding national consequence. The controversy over the abolition of slavery thus came to be one of the most important incidents of the Civil War. It had previously made a lavish contribution to the friction between the two regions of the country, the Northern and Southern states. The abolitionists gained the day as a result of the Civil War. Yet it was the development of Northern *laissez faire* and its concerted attack upon Southern monopoly that dealt the fatal blow to slavery. The war was fought, in paramount essence, over the cotton monopoly of the slaveholding states. On March 4, 1858, Governor James H. Hammond of South Carolina addressed himself to the Senate of the United States as follows:

The institution of African slavery is a means more effective than any yet devised, for relieving a large body of men from the necessity of labour; consequently, states which possess it must be stronger in statesmanship and in war, than those which do not; especially must they be stronger than states in which there is absolutely no privileged class, but all men are held to be equal before the law.

The civilized world is dependent upon the Slave States of America for a supply of cotton. The demand for this commodity has, during many years, increased faster than the supply. Sales are made of it, now, to the amount of two hundred millions of dollars in a year, yet they have a vast area of soil suitable for its production which has never been broken. With an enormous income, then, upon a steadily rising market, they hold a vast idle capital yet to be employed. Such a monopoly under such circumstances must constitute those who possess it the richest and most powerful people on earth. The world must have cotton, and the world depends on them for it. Whatever they demand, that must be conceded them; whatever they want, they have but to stretch forth their hands and take it.

No! you dare not make war upon cotton; no power on earth dares to make war upon it. Cotton is king; until lately the Bank of England was king; but she tried to put her screws, as usual, the fall before the last, on the cotton crop, and was utterly vanquished. The last power has been conquered: who can doubt, that has looked at recent events, that cotton is supreme?

There was, in fact, some concrete warrant for this effusion. Between the years immediately succeeding the American Revolution and those immediately preceding the Civil War, American exports of cotton to Great Britain increased by more than 1,000 per cent. This was accomplished, however, as Ulrich B. Phillips makes clear in his *American*

Negro Slavery by the slaveholding regime keeping "money scarce, population sparse and land values accordingly low; it restricted the opportunities of men of both races, and it kept many of the natural resources of the Southern country neglected." This view is supported by Eugene D. Genovese in *The Political Economy of Slavery*. He argues, in substance, that slavery was a hindrance to the growth of capitalism in the South. It was the Age of Industrialism, and while slavery had been an economic instrumentality highly adaptable to the mercantilist system that had preceded the new age, it was much less useful to the latter. The invention of the cotton gin stimulated the need for slaves and made them more valuable. But while machinery did not by any means supplant slave labor, it did make considerable numbers of them outside the cotton industry redundant where hitherto they had been essential. In the year 1860, 2.25 million blacks, representing more than 35 per cent of the inhabitants of the region, lived in the South. The overwhelming mass of them were slaves. This constituted a tremendous economic investment on the part of the South. To preserve this investment, the South exhausted the soil by negligent crop rotation and, despite the overseer's whip, low productivity of labor. Further, it curtailed the extension of profitable markets and impeded the expansion of technology. The economy of the South, wedded to slave labor, had grown backward and obsolete. It was now an inefficient and wasteful monopoly standing athwart the path of development of the Industrial Revolution, whose presiding genius was the capitalistic ideal of free competition. Adam Smith, rather than Abraham Lincoln, emancipated the slaves. Capitalist enterprise, operating on the principle of *laissez faire* and fanning out from the North in the train of the new mechanical inventions—the cotton gin, the steam engine, the puddling process for the smelting of iron, and others —encountered the outmoded monopoly of the South and in a bloody conflict destroyed it. As an incident of the struggle, not quite by chance, yet not quite by design, the black slaves were freed.

Abraham Lincoln himself, in a reply to an editorial of 1862 by Horace Greeley, was explicit on the point.

My paramount object in this struggle is to save the Union, and not either to save or to destroy slavery. If I could save the Union without freeing *any* slaves, I would do it; and if I could save it by freeing *all* the slaves, I would do it; and if I could do it by freeing some and leaving others alone, I would also do that.

In the preceding year, Jefferson Davis, who by then had become the President of the Confederate States of America, declared in his Inaugural Address that slavery was "necessary to self-preservation"—meaning, of course, the "self-preservation" of the South. Alexander Stephens, the Vice-President of the Confederacy, asserted that the Confederate government

rests upon the great truth that the Negro is not equal to the white man, that slavery, subordination to the superior race, is a natural and normal condition. . . . Our new Goverment is the first in the history of the world, based upon this great physical, philosophical, and moral truth. [Cited by Peter M. Bergman and Mort N. Bergman in *The Chronological History of the Negro in America*.]

Lincoln's attitude toward blacks was not free from ambiguities. He could say, as he did in the course of a debate with Stephen Douglas, that "we [the Republican Party] think it is a moral, a social and a political wrong. . . . On the other hand . . . there is a sentiment which treats it as not being wrong. That is the Democratic sentiment of this day." But at the same time, he did not wish blacks to have the vote, he objected to the appointment of black political officials, he was hostile to intermarriage, and he said that "there is a physical difference between the . . . races which I believe will forever forbid the two races living together on terms of . . . equality."

H. Ford Douglass, a prominent black from Illinois, said in the course of a speech on the Fourth of July, 1860 (James M. McPherson, *The Negro's Civil War*): "I care nothing about that anti-slavery which wants to make the territories free, while it is unwilling to extend to me, as a man, in the free states, all the rights of a man." And while Abraham Lincoln and Stephen Douglas were debating with each other and electioneering, John Brown was rescuing slaves and shepherding them to freedom in Canada. In 1859 came Harpers Ferry.

The abolitionists, however, had long been at work. In the year 1700, Boston was the principal port of the slave trade in North America. It was the center of supply for all the New England colonies. In that very year, the Boston Committee, with Judge Samuel Sewall at its head, agitated for the imposition of a large excise tax on the importation of slaves. The move was defeated. Still earlier, in 1696, the Quakers pronounced a ban on their members from participating in the trade. The Boston Committee's activity was an attempt to make the trade uneconomic for the New England colonies and thereby reduce and eventually bring it to a halt. Sewall was a Quaker who took part in the notorious witchcraft trials at Salem. He did so as a member of the special commission appointed to try persons accused of witchcraft. The commission sentenced nineteen such persons to be hanged and one to be "pressed to death." Some indication of the level of moral enlightenment at its apex in the New England colonies toward the end of the seventeenth century may be derived from his character. He was an ardent and active opponent of slavery. He was the author of *The Selling of Joseph,* in which he rejected the misuse of the Christian text of the Bible to rationalize slavery. He considered the enslavement of the blacks to be illegal. His diary and his letter book are among the most illuminating records of the private and public life of his times. Yet he was capable of accepting the testimony of hysterical young females and their neurotic accomplices as conclusive proof of allegations of witchcraft against social scapegoats; such, for example, as Tituba, the West Indian slave of a local minister. There was, then, this contradiction existing even in the most enlightened minds of the time between the moral imperative of universal human freedom, which, as in Sewall's case, they recognized and conceded, and the benighted claims of superstitious belief, which, equally, divested them of their reason. Sewall, to be sure, was not a representative man of the late seventeenth century. He was more: he was an instance of its finest efflorescence. In his very atypicalness, however, resided the hope and portent of a harbinger of some higher humanity in the form of a man just, reflective, and compassionate. In January, 1697, he admitted in open meeting his fault as a member of a commission that put people to death on nebulous charges of an unsubstantiated character. Every year for the rest of his life he devoted a day to fasting and repentance for his offense.

The later abolitionists, both black and white, were people of the most diverse characters and circumstances. They ranged from David Walker, a free black born in North Carolina and an impassioned advocate of violent revolution, to Frederick Douglass, the great statesman and orator in the cause of black liberation; Charles Remond, a free man from Massachusetts, who at first was an apostle of nonviolence and who later became a protagonist of violent revolt; Henry Highland Garnet, born a slave in Maryland and, like his predecessor David Walker, persuaded of the necessity of armed revolution by the slaves to free themselves; Samuel Ringgold Ward, an escaped slave and a torrential orator; Martin R. Delany, author and traveler; William Wells Brown, historian. Among the women were Harriet Tubman and Sojourner Truth. There were other blacks, innumerable, men and women, who, in John Brown's classification, were either "talking abolitionists" or "acting abolitionists." And there were the whites, ranging from Samuel Sewall to Levi Coffin, William Lloyd Garrison, Wendell Phillips, John Brown, Thomas Garrett, Theodore Weld, and William Ellery Channing. Large numbers of other whites were also sympathetic or participants or both. And behind the thunderous rhetoric of the public platform, the fire and fury of the pamphleteers, the quiet appeals, the anxious councils, were the perilous stealth and triumphant surprise of the Underground Railroad.

The central point to be established is that all this ferment did not lead directly to the Civil War, did not precipitate it, was not decisive in its occurrence, except in combination with secession. The Civil War was not fought over the issue of freedom for the slaves. "With the single exception of the question of slavery extension," said Frederick Douglass, "Mr. Lincoln proposes no measure which can bring him into antagonistic collision with the traffickers in human flesh." The Civil War facilitated the freeing of the slaves. It was simply another instance of the manner in which black Americans, in their struggle for freedom, have always benefited from white America's going to war. Nor would the Civil War have been fought had the South been more adaptable to the economic demands of the new Age of Industrialism and less mired in the plantation economy of the vanished era of mercantilism. The consciences of the abolitionists would have bled to death if the Industrial Revolution had not made its appearance on the economic scene. Social idealism is always of lesser account in such matters than economic necessity. The British abolitionists began to prosper in their efforts when the plantation economy of the West Indies began to be less profitable. The abolitionist cause in Britain was impotent so long as sugar was profitable. Cotton freed the West Indian slaves, as sugar had enchained them.

The American Revolution of 1776 was fought at least as much against mercantilism as for freedom from colonialism—the old colonialism, of which mercantilist theory and practice were merely economic manifestations. Beyond all question, freedom was involved in the struggle. But it was not conceptual freedom as a great social ideal, despite all the impassioned protestations of Patrick Henry and other "patriots." It was freedom to choose between monopoly and *laissez faire,* mercantilism and industrial capitalism. The "patriots" of the American Revolution, in their transformation on the heels of success into "Founding Fathers," were not liberal social philosophers; they were pragmatic businessmen. Having to choose between a king and country whose adherence to the practices of monopoly threatened their "sacred fortunes" and the prospect of a republic that, by acceptance of the economic principle of *laissez faire,* would enhance those fortunes, they transferred their allegiance to the latter. Had they been actuated by some abstract ideal of individual liberty, they would long since have put their fortunes to the hazard on behalf of the slaves in their midst.

In the year 1776, there were more than 500,000 slaves in the colonies. Of these, about 13,500 were in New England. The leading revolutionary patriots owned a number of them. Idealism would have begun at home if only it had not, as is usually the case, been restrained by economic interest. Slavery was profitable. The slaves were useful and their ownership a considerable source of domestic convenience to the middle and upper levels of colonial society. Their servitude was indispensable to the prosperity of the colonies until the Industrial Revolution.

One of the principal objectives of the Civil War a century later would be to force the South into awareness of the fact that an industrial revolution had occurred. The American Revolution was indeed a political consequence of the Industrial Revolution. Adam Smith's *Inquiry into the Nature and Causes of the Wealth of Nations* was very much more the philosophical inspiration of the former than were the abstractions of the liberal social thinkers in Britain and the Encyclopedists in France. The economic realities propounded in his book shaped and gave revolutionary content to the substantial issues of the struggle of the North American colonies against mercantilism and monopoly.

Though the encouragement of exportation and the discouragement of importation are the two great engines by which the mercantile system proposes to enrich every country, yet with regard to some particular commodities it seems to follow an opposite plan: to discourage exportation and to encourage importation. Its ultimate object, however, is always the same, to enrich the country by an advantageous balance of trade. . . . To hurt in any degree the interest of any one order of citizens, for no other purpose but to promote that of some other, is evidently contrary to that justice and equality of treatment which the sovereign owes to all the different orders of his subjects. . . . It is unnecessary, I imagine, to observe how contrary such regulations are to the boasted liberty of the subject, of which we affect to be so very jealous; but which, in this case, is so plainly sacrificed to the futile interests of our merchants and manufacturers.

Adam Smith continues:

But in the system of laws which has been established for the management of our American and West Indian colonies, the interest of the home consumer has been sacrificed to that of the producer with a more extravagant profusion than in all our other commercial regulations. A great empire has been established for the sole purpose of raising up a nation of customers who should be obliged to buy from the shops of our different producers all the goods with which these could supply them. For the sake of that little enhancement of price which this monopoly might afford our producers, the home consumers have been burdened with the whole expense of maintaining and defending that empire. For this purpose, and for this purpose only, in the two last wars, more than two hundred millions have been spent, and a new debt of more than a hundred and seventy millions has been contracted over and above all that had been expended for the same purpose in former wars. . . . It cannot be very difficult to determine who have been the contrivers of this whole mercantile system: not the consumers, we may believe, whose interest has been entirely neglected; but the producers, whose interest has been so carefully attended to; and among this latter class our merchants and manufacturers have been by far the principal architects.

The principle of universal human freedom, therefore, was not the grand motivation of the leaders of the American Revolution. They were concerned with freedom from the monopolistic practices of the mercantile system. Their new economic deity was *laissez faire,* and Adam Smith was the high priest of the temple. The Revolutionary War was not fought for ideological reasons but for practical considerations. Pragmatism, not ideology, brought on the struggle. So little was the question of slavery involved as a determinant in the onset of that conflict that George Washington refused to allow slaves to serve in the Continental Army. He objected to arming them for fear they might revolt against their masters. That was the military aspect of the matter. Evaluating slavery from an economic standpoint, Adam Smith had this to say about the "peculiar institution":

It appears, accordingly, from the experience of all ages and nations, I believe, that the work done by freemen comes cheaper in the end than that performed by slaves. It is found to do so even at Boston, New York, and Philadelphia, where the wages of common labour are so very high.

By contrast, slaves of course earned no wages, and the cost of their maintenance was as low as was consistent with the owners' interest in keeping them alive so long as they were productive and a source of profit to them.

Wilbur J. Cash, in *The Mind of the South*, makes the point that the plantation system was "based on Negro slavery which was a vastly wasteful system and could be made to pay only on rich soils." This view is generally supported by Ulrich B. Phillips and, latterly, by Eugene D. Genovese. But Kenneth M. Stampp, in *The Peculiar Institution*, takes a more qualified view.

If the employment of slaves was unprofitable (or nearly so), it must somehow be explained why slaves brought high prices in the market and why masters continued to use them. To say that no other form of labor was available hardly answers the question, for slave labor could have been converted into free labor by emancipation. And would not an employer use no labor at all in preference to a kind that gave him no return on his investment? Perhaps it was the mere expectation of profit, though seldom or never realized, that kept him going from year to year. Perhaps the slaveholder did not keep careful and accurate business records and therefore did not realize that he was on an economic treadmill. Or perhaps slavery, having been profitable in the past, survived now only because of custom and habit—because of a kind of economic lethargy. These are possible explanations, or partial explanations, why an unprofitable labor system might survive for a considerable length of time.

They are indeed only "partial explanations." As Stampp himself suggests, "slavery in the ante-bellum South was not purely or exclusively an economic institution: it was also part of a social pattern made venerable by long tradition and much philosophizing."

Any attempt to discover a valid answer to the question why slavery persisted in the South long after it became unprofitable must be sought in the less tangible areas of the peculiar institution. One exception must be noted to the general unprofitability of slavery. Cotton continued to generate large fortunes for plantation owners and to be the major factor making for prosperity in the economy of the South, despite the economic wastefulness of the slave system. The invention of the cotton gin by Eli Whitney in 1793 gave unprecedented stimulus to the growth of the cotton industry. Toward the end of the eighteenth century slave prices had fallen off considerably. But, says Ulrich B. Phillips, in his *Slave Economy of the Old South:*

90

The developments following Whitney's invention of the cotton gin revolutionized the situation. Slave prices entered upon a steady advance, which was quickened by the prohibition of the African trade in 1808. They were then held stationary by the restrictions upon commerce, and were thrown backward by the outbreak of war in 1812. But with the peace of Ghent the results of the new cotton industry and of the cessation of African imports became strikingly manifest. The inland fields of the lower South proved to be peculiarly adapted for the production of cotton. The simplicity of the work and the even distribution of the tasks through the seasons made negro slave labor peculiarly available. With the increasing demand of the world for cotton, there was built up in the South perhaps the greatest staple monopoly the world has ever seen. The result was an enormous demand for slaves in the cotton belt. American ports, however, were now closed to the foreign slave trade. The number of slaves available in America was now fixed, the rate of increase was limited, and the old "tobacco South" had a monopoly of the only supply which could meet the demand of the new "cotton South."

Here was one of the chief economic causes of the American Civil War. Ostensibly, the war was fought on the political issue of secession. The social question of slavery, whether it was justifiable or not within a society professing freedom and equality for all men, was ancillary to the political issue. But dominating both was the economic imperative of the huge vested interest of the South in slavery. Between 1800, less than a decade after the invention of the cotton gin, and 1860, on the brink of the Civil War, the average price of a prime field hand had increased from $450 to $1,800. By the end of the decade immediately preceding the Civil War, Britain was being supplied with 80 per cent of its cotton imports by the United States.

A pamphlet by Samuel DuBose, reproduced in the *History of the Huguenots in South Carolina* by T. G. Thomas, provided evidence of the rapidity with which substantial profits were extracted from cotton.

With the improvement of the gins, the cotton culture increased and was extended, until 1799, when Capt. James Sinkler planted three hundred acres at his plantation Belvidere, on Eutaw Creek, and reaped from each acre two hundred and sixteen pounds, which he sold for from fifty to seventy-five cents per pound.

At the comparable period in Georgia, the average New York price of upland cotton was thirty cents per pound.

Underlying the whole conflict between North and South was an economic clash between mercantilism, with monopoly at its core, and *laissez faire,* with free trade as its governing principle. The American Revolution had been fought, in essence, against the mercantilism of the colonial power Great Britain and its strangulating system of monopoly. Slavery had not then been in issue between the protagonists, except indirectly and as fuel for moral indignation, such, for example, as Thomas Jefferson expressed against George III in his original draft of the Declaration of Independence:

He has waged cruel war against human nature itself, violating its most sacred rights of life and liberty in the persons of a distant people who never offended him, captivating them and carrying them into slavery in another hemisphere, or to incur miserable death in their transportation thither. This piratical warfare, the opprobrium of infidel powers, is the warfare of the Christian King of Great Britain. Determined to keep open a market where MEN should be bought and sold, he has prostituted his negative for suppressing every legislative attempt to prohibit or to restrain this execrable commerce; and that this assemblage of horrors might want no fact of distinguished die, he is now exciting these very people to rise in arms among us, and to purchase that liberty of which he deprived them, by murdering the people on whom he also obtruded them; thus paying off the former crimes committed against the liberties of one people, with crimes he urges them to commit against the lives of another.

Despite his moral outrage and his frequent reprobation of slavery, Jefferson was never able to muster the resolution to free his own slaves during his lifetime. Moreover, he deleted from his draft of the Declaration the passage quoted above, though this was done at the insistence of some of the representatives from the other colonies, among them South Carolina, Georgia, and New England states holding slaves.

Yet it must be emphasized once more that in the year 1776 the paramount issue was economic freedom. And since the flag follows trade, rather than the other way around, economic principles were soon reinforced by political concepts deployed by the aggrieved colonists in their support.

Nearly a century later, the American Civil War was fought to vindicate the same principle of economic freedom. Again the political issue was thrust into the forefront. In the struggle with Great Britain it was freedom from tyranny; now it was secession. Then it was the death struggle of mercantilism against victorious *laissez faire.* And now, curiously, the same struggle was being repeated between the North and the South of the United States of America; for the South, through its retention and large-scale exploitation of the institution of human slavery, had also retained as the animating principle of its economy the monopolistic ethos of the mercantile system. In the context of the Age of Industrialism at the midpoint of the nineteenth century, the economy of the South was anachronistic. The North, on the other hand, had evolved from the standpoint of its economic practices consonantly with the ideology of free trade, whose shield-bearer had been the War of Independence of 1776. It was the old struggle all over again. The difference was that now it would be waged not against a colonial power but between two regions of the United States, the North and the South.

Monopoly dictated the misguided economic reliance of the South upon slavery. It did so in allegiance to King Cotton. But there were other reasons, as well, of a less ponderable nature, and perhaps they were articulated as explicitly by Thomas Lynch, of South Carolina, as by anyone else. On July 30, 1775, he declared in the course of a debate during a session of the Continental Congress:

If it is debated, whether their slaves are their property, there is an end of the confederation. Our slaves being our property, why should they be taxed more than the land, sheep, cattle, horses, etc.? Freemen cannot go to work in our Colonies; it is not the ability or inclination of freemen to do the work that the Negroes do. [Cited by Bergman and Bergman.]

The concluding sentence is the operative element in the passage. Time and again this sentiment recurs in the expressions of proslavery opinion in the South. It assumes a multitude of guises. It might be cloaked in appeals to the precedent of the slave system that existed in classical Greece, or in invocations of a postulated law of natural inferiority of the black slaves, or in the assertion of the superior welfare of the white inhabitants of the South as a matter of civilized necessity. Always, of course, there was the power of entrenchment dominating the higher reason and distorting the imagination, perverting the judgment and paralyzing the moral will of the foremost representatives of the South. Even when it was clear in numerous instances of economic failure and collapse that slavery was a wasteful system of labor to the point of being counterproductive, the South still attached itself to this most tragic and most inhuman of its legion of lost causes. Psychological delusions undermined a sense of economic reality, so that the white Southerners were finally unable to make pragmatic judgments of the economic cost of slavery. They could not see that even their sovereign staple, cotton, would be more efficiently produced by free labor, because slavery had invested them with a higher regard for comfort than for profit.

In some measure this was the slaves' revenge. The South abandoned itself to its imperial visions, to the "purple dream," in Stephen Vincent Benét's phrase, of extension of slavery to the West. In November, 1860, R. B. Rhett made a speech before the Assembly of South Carolina. He forecast that by the year 2000 the South would have extended "their Empire . . . down through Mexico to the other side of the great Gulf" (Samuel Eliot Morison, *The Oxford History of the American People*). They would have established, he said, "a civilization teeming with orators, poets, philosophers, statesmen and historians, equal to those of Greece and Rome." This civilization would be founded on African slavery. "The whole trade of South America with Europe," said a Virginian, Lucius H. Minor, would be dominated by such a Southern Confederacy, as well as the "transit trade," in Morison's interpretation, "between Atlantic and Pacific." Also, according to Morison, citing Henry Timrod, the "Southern Confederacy would not only extend from sea to sea, but would solve the problem of poverty throughout the world." Morison cites a Virginia Congressman who indicted the North, in the following passage:

The free suffrage and free labor of the North . . . has so shattered the framework of society, that society itself exists only in an inverted order. African slavery furnishes the only basis upon which republican liberty can be preserved. There is more humanity, there is more unalloyed contentment and happiness, among the slaves of the South, than any laboring population on the globe. For every master who cruelly treats his slave, there are two white men at the North who torture and murder their wives.

This type of claptrap was what betrayed the South. But meanwhile the "purple dream" had cast its hallucinatory spell over the South. The Missouri Compromise was abrogated by the Kansas-Nebraska Act in 1854 and, in 1857, pronounced unconstitutional by the decision in *Dred Scott* v. *Sanford*. The West lay open to slavery and the fulfillment of the Southern Confederacy's "purple dream."

In concrete terms, a cotton monopoly, based on slavery, would be extended to the West. Other economic ambitions consistent with Southern mercantilism would also be realized. Whatever their commercial and industrial character, slavery would be their indispensable economic foundation. Ulrich B. Phillips writes, in *The Slave Economy of the Old South:*

Negro slavery was established in the South, as elsewhere, because the white people were seeking their own welfare and comfort. It was maintained for the same economic reason.

Thus the issue was joined between North and South: between Northern *laissez faire,* which saw Southern mercantilism based on slavery as the main impediment to a "more perfect Union," and Southern monopoly, which saw Northern free trade as the chief antagonist, masked in a politics of human freedom, threatening its enormous capital investment in human chattels and the Southern way of life thereby made possible. It is not altogether an oversimplification to summarize the essential terms of the struggle as a contest between the addicts of the "purple dream" and the adherents of the "American dream."

The economic unreality of the Southern position, to the extent, at any rate, that it sought to establish itself both then and thereafter on slavery, has been pointed out by Paul M. Gaston in *The New South Creed:*

The striking and enduring contrast between Southern poverty and American opulence dates most obviously from the devastation of the Civil War era. But even before the War the peculiar structure of the Southern economy had put the South at a disadvantage within the union. Plantation slavery made fortunes for many men, of course, but, as Douglas C. North points out, the income received in the South from the export of staple crops had "little local multiplier effect, but flowed directly to the North and West for imports of services, manufactures and foodstuffs." Whether or not Eugene D. Genovese is correct in characterizing plantation slavery as technologically backward, self-defeating, incapable of reform, and incompatible with genuine industrialism, there is no doubt that Southerners became increasingly aware of their dependence on—and inferiority to—the North. This awareness was revealed in the frantic and abortive campaigns to achieve economic independence and in the bitter denunciation of special economic legislation presumed to favor Northern interests at the expense of the South. As Thomas Prentice Kettell correctly saw, Southern wealth was systematically converted into Northern profits.

The Southern cotton monopolists were simply repeating the experience of the West Indian sugar planters in the previous century when the latter were obliged to confront economic actualities. The consequence was a link in the chain of events that led to the American War of Independence. Now, in so far as the cotton monopolists of the South were concerned, secession was the only solvent for the increasing bankruptcy of their economic, as well as moral, position; secession—

and the "purple dream" of a tropical empire of the Southern Confederacy. It led to war.

"One of the purposes of secession," Paul Gaston asserts:

was to invigorate Southern economic growth and destroy the colonial dependence on the North. Not only, of course, were these objectives not realized, but the smashing victories of the Union troops seemed to symbolize the hopelessness of the venture in the first place. Concentrating on the development of their own strength, Union leaders greatly expanded productive capacity and appeared almost to ignore manpower losses, instead of playing cautiously on their enemy's weaknesses. In many ways it seemed to be a story of the rich beating the poor; or so it appeared, in any case, to many disillusioned Southerners in 1865.

The fact that the South was the defender of slavery enhanced the moral position of the North in the conflict, even as the institution of slavery itself debilitated the economy of the South and cut it off from regenerating sources of moral strength. It was not that many enlightened Southerners did not oppose slavery. They did, precisely like their Northern counterparts. And the Southern Baptists were diligent on the side of the abolitionists in the aid they gave to fugitive slaves. Neither was it the case that all Northerners were opposed to slavery. And hardly less that Northerners of light and leading were in some instances by no means enthusiastic about the cause of abolition, especially when, as it happened, abolition and the preservation of the Union seemed to be in diametrical opposition. There was no difference between the attitude in this matter of, say, Francis Parkman, the historian, and that of President Lincoln.

In 1859, Charles O'Conor, a prominent New York lawyer who was also president of the local bar association, declared in a speech:

Now, gentlemen, to that condition of bondage the Negro is assigned by nature. . . . He has strength, and has the power to labor; but the hand which created him denied to him either the intellect to govern, or willingness to work. Both were denied to him. And that nature which deprived him of the will to labor, gave him a master to coerce that will, and to make him a useful and valuable servant . . . useful for himself and for the master who governs him. . . . I maintain that it is not injustice to leave the Negro in the condition in which nature placed him, to leave him in a state of bondage, and the master to govern him . . . nor is it depriving him of any of his rights to compel him to labor in return, and afford to that master just compensation for the labor and talent employed in governing him and rendering him useful to himself and to the society around him.

Jefferson Davis was at least less sophistical and no more benighted. He said quite simply that slavery was "necessary to self-preservation." Nevertheless the South took the road that ran through havoc to shattering defeat.

For itself, the North could not countenance the obstruction placed in the path of the development of the country, as a whole, by the outmoded monopolistic practices of the South. It was enough that Northerners were forced to resort to legislative ingenuity to circumvent the obstacles posed by Southern economic backwardness. But when the Missouri Compromise was rescinded and subsequently declared unconstitutional, the time had come for the North to take an uncompromising stand. What it faced was not monopoly based on slavery south of the 36° 30′ line; it was eye to eye with the threat of monopoly based on slavery in the vast Western area of the United States, a mercantilistic empire of the Southern Confederacy extending from the Atlantic to the Pacific. Laissez-faire capitalism could have none of this. Saving the Union was not a mere exercise in political idealism. It was Francis Parkman who wrote: "I would see every slave knocked on the head before I would see the Union go to pieces, and would include in the sacrifice as many abolitionists as could conveniently be brought together" (Morison). Yet it is clear beyond all question that, on the part of the South, the war was fought in order to have a free hand to extend its monopolistic area to the Western territories, with African slavery as its essential economic underpinning, and thus to achieve a vast aggrandizement of the Southern Confederacy. In the light of such vaulting ambition, the dissolution of the Union must have seemed a trivial price to pay. On the part of the North, the war was fought in order to enlarge the national area of free trade, to facilitate the free movement of goods and the natural interplay of markets, to strike off the shackles of monopoly, and to win vast new territories of staggering potential for free capitalist enterprise.

When the Southerners decided on secession, they fell into the trap the Northerners had set for them. They presented the latter with a political issue whose virtue was a self-evident truth. When to this was added the flagrant injustice of slavery, there was a landslide of moral ground from beneath the feet of the South. But the primary issue was economic, whatever the self-righteous protestations of the North.

3

THE CIVIL WAR occurred as a revolution precipitated by the political issue of secession. But its overriding impulse was economic. An important generator of that impulse was the chattel slavery of blacks. Yet it was not the only matter in controversy, nor even the crucial source of conflict. If this can be located with historical precision, then it must be recognized as the clash between Southern mercantilism, with its attachment to the preindustrial concept of monopoly, and Northern *laissez faire,* whose essential dynamic was uninhibited freedom of enterprise. The conflict was aggravated, and its inevitability sharpened, by the "purple dream" of the South, which involved nothing less than the annexation of the new territories of the West and their incorporation into the obsolete mercantile system of the South based on slavery. Moral factors deriving from sentiments hostile to slavery obtruded at all times but were never of decisive import. They did not tip the scales in favor of conflict; nor did they restrain the combatants from armed encounter. The latter circumstance would have imported some consciousness on the part of the South of the inferior moral position in which their exploitation of human slaves had placed them. But this was not the case. The Union and the Confederacy were protagonists of capitalism in its preindustrial and industrial phases. The Union was the representative of the Industrial Revolution; the Confederacy was the knight-errant of an antiquated system that the American Revolution

98

of 1776 had effectively discarded. In a sense, therefore, the Confederacy had lagged for almost a century behind the economic developments of the age that had succeeded the Renaissance and its effulgent climax in the Enlightenment.

But it must also be pointed out that in so far as the specific issue of slavery was concerned, some of the choicer spirits of those remarkable centuries of material and intellectual expansion in Western Europe and North America, ranging from the invention of printing to the French Revolution, still clung to the classical Greek and Roman concept of slavery as consistent with civilization. The diametrical opposition between, say, David Hume and Benjamin Franklin typified the state of higher opinion on this point. While Hume regarded blacks as subhuman, Franklin declared of slavery that it was "an atrocious debasement of human nature"; and, on another occasion, that "slaves rather weaken than strengthen the state." These opposing attitudes, and a complex scheme of gradations between them, were characteristic of the South, so that there was nothing even remotely resembling unanimity on this question. Moreover, less than 30 per cent of the whole Southern population of 7 million persons owned slaves. Of these, less than half a million owned 75 per cent of the 4 million slaves.

The value of a slave bore a direct relationship, not to the price, but to the production of cotton. Ulrich B. Phillips misses this point. He remarks, in *The Slave Economy of the Old South:* "The change which took place in the relative slave and cotton prices was really astonishing." And, he further remarks, from 1800 to 1860 "there was an advance of some 1,000 or 1,200 per cent in the price of slaves as measured in cotton." He also realizes that one of the factors making for "overproduction," as he terms it, was inefficiency. But he overlooks the fact that by 1850 Britain was importing 80 per cent of its cotton requirements from the United States, as compared with less than 1 per cent immediately preceding the invention of the cotton gin.

There was a world-wide demand for cotton. The fall in the market price of the commodity reflected increased competition, and not simply "overproduction." For this term—"overproduction"—is to be construed strictly in relation to demand. It is beyond argument that there was no lack of demand for cotton in the domestic as well as the foreign market. To isolate overproduction, as Phillips tends to do, is to give insufficient attention to other influences, such, for example, as the inability of the monopolistic system of the South to respond to the commercial challenge of the Industrial Revolution. In 1860, when the country as a whole produced some 5 million bales of cotton, the average price of a prime field hand in Georgia was about $1,800. Earlier in the same decade, when the national production of cotton was around 3 million bales, a similar type of slave fetched $600 less in Georgia. The correlation is clear. Cotton was king, but its sovereignty was impaired by mercantilist inefficiency.

And now the South wished to extend its obsolete, wasteful economic system to the nation's newly acquired Western territories. Maintaining such a system in the South alone in the face of the superior efficiency of Northern *laissez faire* was backward enough. To be ambitious to extend its moribund structure to the vast reaches of the West, with all the stupendous wealth to be extracted from this region, was, from the standpoint of the North, intolerable. The extension of slavery to the West meant, quite simply, the territorial extension of the South as against the North. It meant the reduction of the North to the status of a junior partner in the federal enterprise. And slavery was the instrument by which this grandiose scheme was to be effected. For wherever the South might succeed in implanting the "peculiar institution" would become, by that fact, a part of the South. So even when slavery was well advanced toward outliving its economic usefulness, the South found a geopolitical use for it.

Meanwhile every demonstration in the concrete terms of actual experience that made plain the superiority of free to slave labor by the test of cost efficiency was rejected by the psychological dependency of the South upon the institution of slavery. Not only was the moral life of the South corrupted and its economic competence diminished, but its ability to defend itself against Northern military organization, when the time came, was also undermined by slavery. The South fought the Civil War with the threat of a potential fifth column in the form of its slave population always implicit in its consciousness. Never can there have been wholly absent from the minds of the military planners of the South the possibility, however remote, of a slave uprising to stab them in the back as they turned to face the Northern foe. Their concentration on strategic ends was fatally split by the necessity, even if it arose more out of impalpable fear than from any tangible reality, to guard their rear against the chance of surprise attack by their slaves. In the words of General Patrick R. Cleburne, of the Confederate Army of the Tennessee (cited by James M. McPherson in *The Negro's Civil War*):

Apart from the assistance that home and foreign prejudice against slavery has given to the North, slavery is a source of great strength to the enemy in a purely military point of view, by supplying him with an army from our granaries; but it is our most vulnerable point, a continued embarrassment, and in some respects an insidious weakness. . . . All along the lines slavery is comparatively valueless to us for labor, but of great and increasing worth to the enemy for information. It is an omnipresent spy system, pointing out our valuable men to the enemy, revealing our positions, purposes, and resources.

General Cleburne proposed recruiting slaves into the armies of the Confederacy

to enable us to have armies numerically superior to those of the North, and a reserve of any size we might think necessary; to enable us to take the offensive, move forward, and forage on the enemy. . . . It would instantly remove all the vulnerability, embarrassment, and inherent weakness which result from slavery. The approach of the enemy would no longer find every household surrounded by spies. . . . There would be no recruits awaiting the enemy with open arms, no complete history of every neighborhood with ready guides, no fear of insurrection in the rear.

While there appears to have been no mass uprising of the slaves during the Civil War, there is abundant evidence of sporadic guerrilla action in various parts of the South by fugitive slaves. Yet, in Abraham Lincoln's assessment of the situation on November 24, 1863, "the society of the Southern States is now constituted on a basis entirely military. It would be easier now than formerly to repress a rising of unarmed and uneducated slaves." That was the sober truth. But it did not mean that the black slaves were apathetic in the face of an opportunity, such as the Civil War, to free themselves by armed revolt. Scores of thousands managed to infiltrate the Union lines in order to offer their services in the struggle. As Herbert Aptheker puts it, in *American Negro Slave Revolts:*

Hourly its encampments [the Union Army's] were reached by scores of fugitives, and even early spurning could not stop the flow which soon reached flood proportions. From this came two hundred thousand workers for the Union Army—to fell trees and dig trenches and cook food and drive wagons. Regularly came offers to serve in the ranks, and finally these were accepted. . . . And as spies, scouts, and pilots they served as eyes and ears for the advancing strangers. Added to this wholesale flight were all the other means by which, for generations, the Negro people had fought back against enslavement—sabotage, strikes, "insubordination," individual acts of violence, and conspiracy and rebellion.

Accounts such as this must be balanced against those that portray the black slaves as acquiescent in their servitude and supinely loyal to their white Southern enslavers during the Civil War. Some 500,000 of these contented slaves escaped from Confederate into Union territory in the course of the conflict. Emancipation, when it came by Lincoln's proclamation, on September 22, 1862, of freedom for all slaves in rebellious states by January 1, 1863, was the unexpected outcome of an expedient pattern of temporizing and compromise. Less than three months before, on July 4, Frederick Douglass had declared:

I feel quite sure that this country will yet come to the conclusion that Geo. B. McClellan is either a cold blooded Traitor, or that he is an unmitigated military Impostor. He has shown no heart in his conduct, except when doing something directly in favor of the rebels, such as guarding their persons and property and offering his services to suppress with an iron hand any attempt on the part of the slaves against their rebel masters.

I come now to the policy of President Lincoln in reference to slavery. . . . I do not hesitate to say, that whatever may have been his intentions, the action of President Lincoln has been calculated in a marked and decided way to shield and protect it from the very blows which its horrible crimes have loudly and persistently invited. . . . He has steadily refused to proclaim, as he had the constitutional and moral right to proclaim, complete emancipation to all the slaves of rebels who should make their way into the lines of our army. He has repeatedly interfered with and arrested the anti-slavery policy of some of his most earnest and reliable generals. . . . It is from such action as this, that we must infer the policy of the Administration. To my mind that policy is simply and solely to reconstruct the union on the old and corrupting basis of compromise, by which slavery shall retain all the power that it ever had, with the full assurance of gaining more, according to its future necessities. [McPherson.]

Douglass was neither incorrect nor unfair. The Civil War was not a moral crusade, with the abolition of slavery as its grand humanitarian end. Lincoln had never scrupled to make this unmistakably clear. His manipulation of the slavery issue to serve, as he conceived it, the greater cause of preservation of the Union was consistent with the position he had taken in the matter from the beginning: the Union first, last, and always, with or without slavery. He had never been guilty of dissembling on this point. He may have been wrong; he may have been unwise; but he could not be accused of either vacillation or dishonesty. He addressed himself, and directed the attention of the nation, to the question of the emancipation of the slaves as a political and not a moral problem. His pragmatism did not so much counterpoise as outweigh his idealism. There was no working balance, exquisitely struck, between the one and the other.

At all times where slavery was concerned, there was little difference in concrete effect between the attitude of Governor James Hammond, of South Carolina, for instance, and of Lincoln. The former wrote, in *Letters on Slavery: 1845,* and in direct reference to the moral ardor of the abolitionists, and in open expression to them of his own views:

But if your course was wholly different [meaning, the course of the abolitionists]—if you distilled nectar from your lips, and discoursed sweetest music, could you reasonably indulge the hope of accomplishing your object by such means? Nay, supposing that we were all convinced, and thought of Slavery precisely as you do, at what era of "moral suasion" do you imagine you could prevail on us to give up a thousand millions of dollars in the value of our slaves, and a thousand millions of dollars more in the depreciation of our lands, in consequence of the want of laborers to cultivate them?

Hammond was simply putting on an economic plane what Lincoln preferred to deal with as a political issue. But in the end it was one and the same thing: slavery was not a moral question. Frederick Douglass might well have spared his breath. Nevertheless, he returned to the attack later in July of 1862.

ABRAHAM LINCOLN is no more fit for the place he holds than was JAMES BUCHANAN, and the latter was no more the miserable tool of traitors and rebels than the former is allowing himself to be. As to McClellan he still leaves us in doubt as to whether he is a military impostor, or a deliberate traitor. The country is destined to become sick of both McClellan and Lincoln, and the sooner the better. [McPherson.]

Lincoln moved, meanwhile, with infuriating pragmatism, from compensation to confiscation, taking in the process a backward, intermediate step by way of a letter altering General John C. Frémont's proclamation of August 30, 1862, "instituting martial law in Missouri and freeing the slaves of every rebel in the state."

Then came the sudden leap to full-scale emancipation, from the

Battle of Bull Run, in its desolating outcome, to the glory and redemption of Antietam. Yet the question remains: What if the North had won the Battle of Bull Run? Would the issue of slavery have acquired the military consequence which, when imported into the political context of the struggle, made abolition an expedient tactic against the South? It is not cynical to speculate that Bull Run may have provided the opportune occasion for the emancipation of the slaves, and Antietam the convenient pretext. For the racism of the North was conspicuous in the manner in which it exploited slavery for military advantage. Once the political issue of secession had been joined, slavery was relegated to a purely tactical status. Before the issue was joined, it was a subject of national debate, tedious or absorbing according to the geographical location or economic interest of the debaters. The moral fervor of the abolitionists was counterpoised by the capitalistic ardor of the slaveholders. And in between were the crafty Laodiceans, of whom Lincoln was a prime example, who were neither hot nor cold but lukewarm, and who tended to spew both sides out of their mouths. Whatever moral convictions Lincoln held on the question of slavery were dissipated, in practice, by their subordination to, first of all, political and, next, to military expediency. He spoke often of the repatriation of the African slaves and their colonization somewhere in their ancestral homeland. During the war, some time in August, 1862, he told a delegation of blacks: "There is an unwillingness on the part of our people, harsh as it may be, for you free colored people to remain with us. . . . It is better for us both, therefore, to be separated" (McPherson). To which Frederick Douglass replied: "The President of the United States seems to possess an ever increasing passion for making himself appear silly and ridiculous, if nothing worse."

A prominent black abolitionist, Robert Purvis, also expressed himself on the subject of colonization:

The President has said, "Whether it is right or wrong, I need not now discuss it." Great God! is justice nothing? Is honor nothing? Is even pecuniary interest to be sacrificed to this insane and vulgar hate? . . . Sir, we were born here and here we choose to remain. . . . Don't advise me to leave, and don't add insult to injury by telling me it's for my own good. Of that I am to be the judge. It is in vain you talk to me about "two races" and their "mutual antagonism." In the matter of rights, there is but one race, and that is the *human* race. . . . Sir, this is our country as much as it is yours, and we will not leave it. [McPherson.]

Another black man, A. P. Smith, of New Jersey, responded to Lincoln:

Pray tell us, is our right to a home in this country less than your own, Mr. Lincoln? . . . Are you an American? So are we. Are you a patriot? So are we. Would you spurn all absurd, meddlesome, impudent propositions for your colonization in a foreign country? So do we. [McPherson.]

Lincoln had proposed the resettlement of a colony of blacks in Central America, where they might find employment in coal mining. To this proposal A. P. Smith replied: "But say, good Mr. President, why we, why anybody should swelter, digging coal, if there be any in Central America?" Lincoln had declared that "coal land is the best thing I know of to begin an enterprise." A. P. Smith exclaimed:

Astounding discovery! Worthy to be recorded in golden letters, like the Lunar Cycle in the temple of Minerva. "Coal land, sir!" Pardon, Mr. President, if my African risibilities get the better of me, if I do show my ivories whenever I read that sentence! Coal land, sir! If you please, sir, give McClellan some, give Halleck some, and by all means, save a little strip for yourself. [McPherson.]

In Newtown, on Long Island, there was a large public meeting in August, 1862, to discuss Lincoln's proposal for the repatriation or recolonization of black Americans in some foreign country in the midst of an internal American war. The following is a portion of the statement issued by the convenors at the close of that meeting:

This is our country by birth. . . . This is our native country; we have as strong attachment naturally to our native hills, valleys, plains, luxuriant forests, flowing streams, mighty rivers, and lofty mountains, as any other people. . . . This is the country of our choice, being our fathers' country. We love this land, and have contributed our share to its prosperity and wealth. . . .

We have the right to have applied to ourselves those rights named in the Declaration of Independence. . . . When our country is struggling for life, and one million freemen are believed to be scarcely sufficient to meet the foe, we are called upon by the President of the United States to leave this land. . . . But at this crisis, we feel disposed to refuse the offers of the President since the call of our suffering country is too loud and imperative to be unheeded. [McPherson.]

There was no inconsistency in Lincoln's attitude and pronouncements on the subject of Negro deportation from America. That had always been his position. The only questions were its moral justice in the period before the Civil War and its practical wisdom in the midst of the war. It was not that he departed significantly from the main tenor of American opinion on this matter of black repatriation or colonization outside the country. Men as enlightened as he—Jefferson, Madison, and Franklin, among others—had held the same view. Jefferson wrote in his *Autobiography:*

Nothing is more certain in the book of fate, than that these people are to be free; nor is it less certain that the two races, equally free, cannot live in the same government. Nature, habit, opinion have drawn indelible lines of distinction between them. It is still in our power to direct the process of emancipation and deportation, peaceably, and in slow degree; as that the evil will wear off insensibly.

James Madison wrote: "If an asylum could be found in Africa, that would be the appropriate destination for the unhappy race among us." He was, however, doubtful of the prospect of success in this effort by the American Colonization Society. He wrote further:

Some other region must be found for them as they become free and willing to emigrate. The repugnance of the whites to their continuance among them is founded on prejudices, themselves founded upon physical distinctions, which are not likely soon, if ever, to be eradicated. [Cited by Bergman and Bergman.]

While Benjamin Franklin observed:

Why increase the sons of Africa, by planting them in America, where we have so fair an opportunity, by excluding all blacks and tawnys, of increasing the lovely white and red? [Cited by Stanley Feldstein, ed., in *The Poisoned Tongue.*]

The late Marcus Garvey's Back to Africa Movement and its contemporary successors would receive, as indeed they have, the enthusiastic endorsement of some of the leading white public figures of America, the dead were they able to bestow it, as well as the living. But the fact that Lincoln could still concern himself with a project of this nature during the course of a civil war when the very existence of the nation hung in the balance was evidence, mainly, of two things: first, the depth of his white racism; and, secondly, his desire to reassure the South—in particular, his Southern friends—that he no more than they contemplated the permanent presence of blacks in this country, which he regarded as a necessary evil to be tolerated only so long as national convenience required it. He had no moral sympathy for the slaves that was not far outweighed by his white racism. Slavery generated in Lincoln no moral conflict, but only a dervish dance of racist expedients whirling around a shifting center of political and military calculations. Whatever the reality of his log-cabin nobility or his rail-splitting honesty, on which white Americans in general preen themselves in historical reflection, there is another reality that Lincoln presented to black Americans—the reality of a deeply persuaded white racist.

Bull Run was not the occasion to emancipate the slaves, since the connection between Northern defeat in battle and the abolition of slavery, so obviously asserted, would have stripped the last shred of moral pretense from Lincoln's calculated teeterings to and fro on the issue. It would have given an indelible association to the freeing of the slaves, in the popular mind, with Northern defeat. Worse, it would have made plain to the slaves themselves, and indeed to all blacks, the amoral opportunism of the Lincoln administration. As nothing else could so clearly have done, it would have demonstrated to the black people that slavery had exchanged its role of a political gambit for that of a counter in the military strategy of the North. William H. Seward, Lincoln's Secretary of State, persuaded him to withhold the Emancipation Proclamation he would have issued after Bull Run. It was decided to await a significant Northern victory. When Antietam occurred, the deed was done.

The need to rehabilitate American society as a whole was plainly manifest long before Appomattox. With victory, however, the North could deflect its attention to the reconstruction of the Southern segment of the national society in the dawn of the abolition of slavery. Yet racism was no less rampant in the North, and while slavery had never acquired there the large-scale institutional character it had gained in the South, antiabolitionist sentiment among significant numbers of Northerners had scarcely been less impassioned and vociferous than in the South. This fact must be set against the considerable agitation for the freeing of the slaves that was at all times in active ferment in many parts of the North. It is no exaggeration to encompass the attitudes of enlightened Northerners in the words of Abigail Adams:

I wish most sincerely there was not a slave in the province. It always appeared a most iniquitous scheme to me—fight ourselfs for what we are daily robbing and plundering from those who have as good a right to freedom as we have. [Cited by Bergman and Bergman.]

But it is, equally, no exaggeration to apply to the North what John Randolph said of Edward Livingston: "He is a man of splendid abilities, but utterly corrupt. He shines and stinks like rotten mackerel by moonlight." As a cultural summary of the North, this stricture would have been precisely in point.

A careful distinction must be drawn between attitudes which, in explicit essence, reconciled a moral duty to free the slaves with a philosophic belief in racism, and those attitudes which attempted no such reconciliation, since, to these latter, slavery and racism each independently furnished its own self-evident justification. Of the first outlook, Washington, Jefferson, Madison, and many of their contemporaries may be taken as exemplars; the second outlook was generalized widely throughout the country, North and South. There were those, of course, who rejected both slavery and racism, but they were not among the Founding Fathers. Yet wherever the teeming variety of protagonists stood on these seminal issues of the fledgling American state, they all shared one thing in common: the spirit and the intent of revolution to remold the national society, by persuasion if possible, but by force if necessary. Revolution was, from the beginning, the political axis upon which all vital changes turned in the function and structure of American life. From its inception, America has been in a state of permanent revolution; from Plymouth to Yorktown to Appomattox, Reconstruction, and the continuing beyond.

When the last shot of the Civil War was fired and every slave stood free, when the "purple dream" of the South was ended and Northern capitalism, with its dynamic of unrestricted trade, had triumphed over Southern capitalism and its static principle of monopoly, the revolution yet went on. Redemption and Reconstruction were its themes, twin, tormented, irreconcilable.

The single dominant aspect of Reconstruction is its revanchist theme. Revenge, despite Lincoln's plea to "bind up our wounds," suffused both North and South. In the outcome, the emancipated blacks were the chief sufferers. The story is a familiar one. The North quartered an army of occupation upon the South in the wake of victory. A train of Northern speculators and all the ragtag of commercial greed and avarice descended on the prostrate South. The bitterness of defeat was borne in upon the vanquished with myriad

108

humiliations. This was not Lincoln's intent or that of his administration, but the exploiters of Northern victory were not high-minded men, and in their quest for financial profit they trampled into the mud every consideration of magnanimity. With small exception, they were a numerous gang of gluttonous scoundrels. Nor were their counterparts lacking in the South itself, even though these were, oftener than not, actuated by different motives, tending toward objectives that were the opposite of those pursued by the Northern camp followers. The white Southerners conceived it important to resume possession of their lands, to recover ownership of their property, to re-establish their control of the region. But most important of all, they were determined to put the Negro back in his place. Nothing else mattered quite so much as this, for without it, life for white Southerners would continue to be insufferable. The whole ethos of the South had been constructed on the institution of slavery. It had come to be its indispensable resource of psychic energy, as it was the essential component of its anachronistic economy, now shattered and brought to irretrievable ruin. Slavery and the slaves were for the South a narcotic addiction from which they had been forcibly withdrawn by the North. The symptoms of their violent remission were manifold, but the most conspicuous and also the most intractable of them was their incurable craving for black slavery.

A single statistic will suffice to show what, in economic terms, happened to the South in consequence of the Civil War. In 1861, the year of the outbreak of the war, the cotton crop amounted to more than 5 million bales; in 1866, a year after its ending, the cotton crop comprised 1 million bales. Gutted mansions, abandoned plantations, a decimated population, and everywhere waste and desolation: this was the face of the South after the Civil War. And in the eyes of the white Southerners the most hideous scar upon its collective visage had been inflicted by the Northern conquerors' assertion of equal rights for blacks. Accommodation was sought, and in many instances achieved, by the white South in negotiation with the North. But on this point—this point of no return for the South, black slavery—white Southerners in the main went from obduracy to intransigence. The record of Reconstruction in the South is the attempt, largely successful, on the part of the white Southerners to reimpose at least the essential incidents of slavery, even if the system was given the name of freedom.

All the lies and vicious inventions of apologists for the slaveholding South, the cruel, distorted allegations of Negro ineptitude and coxcombry in the decade following the Civil War, are attributable solely to the desire to return the manumitted blacks to their former status of chattel slavery. No lie was left untold, no slander or libel unuttered, no baseless caricature undrawn. When the time came for Joseph Goebbels, the Nazi archpropagandist, to provide spurious warrants for the mistreatment of Jews, he could have found an inexhaustible repository of precedents in the denigration of Negroes by the white South and its collaborators. The Redeemers of the South, like their successors and present-day counterparts the Ku Klux Klan, came into existence out of the pathology of the white Southern obsession with black slavery, and not to "defend the South" from anything but the clumsy, halfhearted, ill-organized effort of the North to cure the white South of this psychotic addiction. There was no altruism about the motives of the North, for, excepting only the institution of slavery, the North was quite as racist as the South. The Civil War had been fought ostensibly to prevent the extension of slavery to the West, but in actuality to capture for the North, as against the South, the vast potential wealth of the new territories. The South coveted the West for cotton; the North, for the Industrial Revolution. The two capitalisms, old and new, the South and the North, contested this issue primarily—and only secondarily any other —on the field of battle. Racism or its extirpation was not a factor in the struggle, and, after all, slavery is, in a modern concept at any rate, merely an extreme instance of racism.

The Civil War was, first and foremost, a territorial struggle. Its economic objectives, beneath and beyond the political issue, were paramount. Moral considerations performed, as in any large-scale human conflict, their customary role of a propaganda device to conceal the real aims of the opposing forces. The South was not more racist than the North, only more attached to black slavery than was warranted by economic common sense. The vengeance that the black slaves exacted against the white South was the Civil War. Not because this conflict was waged on the former's behalf—it wasn't—but for a different reason: this being, that the black slaves had infected the white South with a psychological addiction to slavery which neither empirical reason nor economic actuality could cure. So the South went headlong to its destruction, urged along by slavery, the incubus of its "purple dream" that turned into a nightmare. Dimly here, more lucidly there, the South came eventually to realize this

110

fact. But it did not make the South less addicted to slavery, only more vengeful against its former slaves, on whose account, it reasoned with its habitual self-deception, the South had been "betrayed." This delusion set the temper and directed the tenor of Reconstruction. The one was inveterately hostile; the other blindly misguided.

The Civil War had been a revolution. Reconstruction was the counterrevolution. The revolution had had the unintended result of emancipating the slaves. Reconstruction involved a deliberate attempt, bitterly opposed by the vanquished South, to give legal form and political content to the newly won freedom of the slaves. Behind this attempt was the presence of the Northern army of occupation.

The freed blacks plunged into the postwar surge of Southern politics. Perhaps, in view of all the circumstances, their entry might have been more carefully prepared. The presence of blacks in Southern legislatures and their outright dominance of certain constituencies, once they had begun to exercise the right of suffrage, were not circumstances calculated to reconcile the South to its defeat. The problem at all times was to effectuate the civil liberties of the freed blacks, without exposing this largely unorganized mass of bewildered people to the unrelenting hostility of their former enslavers and to the risk of destructive reprisals. But the North was feckless of the central social issue inevitably arising between the freedmen and their erstwhile masters. There could have been no humiliation for the South in the admission of human beings to the equal enjoyment of freedom. Neither did the North design any such punishment for the conquered South. Yet it is at least arguable that the former was as unwise in its abrupt and arbitrary imposition of counterrevolutionary institutions upon the South as the latter was intemperate and unstatesmanlike in its circumvention and eventual rejection of them. Nor was the North a model of devoted constancy to its own democratic innovations. The time came, at no greater distance than the end of a decade, when the North abjured its wardship of the liberated slaves for the dubious advantage of political expediency, withdrawing its army of occupation, whose presence alone had guaranteed the course of the counterrevolution, and leaving the recently liberated blacks to the implacable vengeance of the white racists of the unreconstructed South.

W. E. B. Du Bois has described the betrayal of the blacks by their Northern protectors in *Black Reconstruction in America, 1860–1880:*

In 1876 came the bargain between Big Business and the South. . . . The Republicans guaranteed that Mr. Hayes, when he became President, would by non-interference and the withdrawal of troops allow the planter-capitalists, under the name of Democrats, to control South Carolina and Louisiana. They also agreed to induce President Grant to adopt the same policy before the end of his term. This meant that Southern landholders and capitalists would be put in complete control of disfranchised black labor. The Democrats promised to "guarantee peace, good order, protection of the law to whites and blacks"; or, in other words, exploitation should be so quiet, orderly and legal, as to assure regular profit to Southern owners and Northern investors. . . . The last act was to appoint a Kentuckian and a Georgian to the Supreme Court. The deed was done. Negroes did not surrender the ballot easily or immediately. . . . But it was a losing battle, with public opinion, industry, wealth, and religion against them. Their own leaders decried "politics" and preached submission. All their efforts towards manly self-assertion were distracted by defeatism and counsels of despair, backed by the powerful propaganda of a religion which taught meekness, sacrifice and humility. But the decisive influence was the systematic and overwhelming economic pressure. Negroes who wanted work must not dabble in politics. Negroes who wanted to increase their income must not agitate the Negro problem. Positions of influence were only open to those Negroes who were certified as being "safe and sane," and their careers were closely scrutinized and passed upon. From 1880 onward, in order to earn a living, the American Negro was compelled to give up his political power.

The attempt on the part of white racism to justify the reimposition of a servile condition upon the blacks took numerous forms. The performance of the blacks as legislators became the inexhaustible topic of poisonous caricatures. Their financial honesty was widely impugned. To be sure, not all blacks were honest; some undoubtedly were corrupt. Yet one would have supposed, amid the spate of white allegations against the blacks, that no white man had ever taken a penny that was not his own lawful property. Black ineptitude, black dishonesty, black inferiority—these were the obsessive themes of the white racists bent on returning the blacks in practical and legal effect to their former unfree state.

James S. Pike, a Northern journalist, wrote as follows in a book entitled *The Prostrate State: South Carolina Under Negro Government,* published in 1874:

The Speaker is black, the Clerk is black, the doorkeepers are black, the little pages are black, the chairman of the Ways and Means is black, and the

112

chaplain is coal black. At some of the desks sit colored men whose types it would be hard to find outside of the Congo.

That was the trouble, precisely: blackness—and all it connoted. There was no length to which white racism would not go, no depth to which it would not stoop, no lie, however vile, it would not fabricate, in order to supply a spurious foundation for its hatred and fear of the blacks. Nor, as the quotation from Pike suggests, was the South singular in its attitude. Du Bois observes:

Of all that most Americans wanted, this freeing of slaves was the last. Everything was black and hideous. Everything Negroes did was wrong. If they fought for freedom, they were beasts; if they did not fight, they were born slaves. If they cowered on the plantations, they loved slavery; if they ran away, they were lazy loafers. If they sang, they were silly; if they scowled, they were impudent. The bites and blows of a nation fell on them. All hatred that the whites after the Civil War had for each other gradually concentrated itself on them. They caused the war—they, its victims. They were guilty of all the thefts of those who stole. They were the cause of wasted property and small crops. They had impoverished the South, and plunged the North into endless debt. And they were funny, funny—ridiculous baboons, aping man.

The blacks had been promised land in the wake of their emancipation. But now they were cheated of the promise. The land was withheld from them. A Freedmen's Bureau was set up in 1865 to oversee the affairs of the former slaves. It was disbanded after seven years of fitful, frustrated existence. Its efforts had not been entirely fruitless. Among other achievements, it had succeeded in reducing the mortality rate of the freed slaves by 35 per cent over a span of four years. It had also provided various forms of relief and assistance for millions of destitute blacks. But in its main objective, the distribution of land to the landless blacks and their conversion into a self-subsisting peasantry, it fell far short of accomplishment. Its failure was the result of outright betrayal. The work of the Bureau was hampered everywhere by a myriad devices of racist reaction. Perhaps its principal achievement was the schools it established. For in the end, the trained leadership thus produced, extended and reinforced in other schools— founded, respectively, by Northern sympathizers and by some of the Southern legislatures that were dominated by representatives of the liberated blacks—played a role of crucial historic import.

Nothing was so decisive as this leadership in preventing the reinstitution of slavery by a Southern oligarchy resolved upon it and, after

1876, by Northern capitalism acquiescent for the sake of its economic self-interest. There was, in practical effect, a coalition between these two groups, to which the Republican administration of Rutherford Hayes had given its political sanction. The blacks were abandoned and delivered up to their white racist enemies. Their plight was desperate, their prospects dismal. It seemed that the Civil War and their expedient release from slavery had been no more than a fleeting interlude, a decade long, between two and one-half centuries of enslavement, and what, for all practical purposes, was the imminence of their re-enslavement. Wherever they turned, this desolating threat confronted them like a remorseless doom. The lineaments of the conspiracy were etched on the faces of the white racists, those stony, cement-gray faces inhospitable to mercy, inaccessible to compassion, intent upon their brutal hatred of the defenseless blacks. Between these blacks and the whites who stalked them as beasts in pursuit of their prey, there stood—uncertain, unpolicied, unprepared—the fledgling leadership of a people bewildered by freedom but resolved, now that they had attained it, to choose extermination rather than be returned to slavery. For their part, the white racists envisioned in exactly these alternatives the destiny of the outnumbered blacks. From this grisly situation the latter were rescued, though at frightful cost, by their leaders. It was a leadership without any clear grasp of the economic forces, North and South, competing for the labor of the blacks and poor whites. It was a leadership with little except an instinctive, rudimentary grasp of the political entities and of the social aspirations of the dissident collectivity known as the United States of America. But one thing it knew. It might grope, stumble, and blunder, yet it knew, and never relinquished the knowledge, that black men, black women, and black children would never, never again, be slaves in this land. Never again. At worst these leaders were in some instances illiterate, in a few other instances corrupt. At best they were over-disposed, like their white counterparts, to grandiose flights of rhetoric and perfervid appeals to abstract principles of eternal truth and justice. Yet there were able men among them, men of the amplest capacities by any test. Robert Brown Elliott, of South Carolina, F. L. Cardozo, also of South Carolina, Lieutenant Governor Oscar Dunn, of Louisiana—to name only a few—were the superiors of most of their white contemporaries. They were men of towering moral, as well as intellectual, stature. To them and their like, the emancipated blacks

114

were indebted for the calm judgment and clear foresight that deflected them from precipitate collision with white racism, which would otherwise have encompassed either their re-enslavement or their extermination. The white racists, balked of their prey, resorted to the Black Codes.

Every aspect of the lives of the blacks was policed and constrained by this repressive system. It was not necessary to re-enact the Fugitive Slave Law; there were other devices, legislative and extralegal. Dispossessed forcibly or fraudently of what small landholdings they had managed to secure for themselves, they were reduced, virtually, to serfdom by the necessity imposed upon them to subsist by "contract labor." They could not work unless, in this way, they were permitted to work, and if they did not work, they were subject to severe penalities for vagrancy and other incidents of the minute and comprehensive scheme of prohibitions and restraints by which the vengeful white racists pursued their unrelenting aim of herding them back into slavery. They were not, as were the Jews under Hitler, obliged to wear an identifying symbol. Their blackness sufficiently proclaimed their identity. But, as in the case of the blacks of South Africa at the present time, they were regulated by curfew and, except where their employment warranted their presence outside it, restricted to an area specifically demarcated for them.

The plantation, with its brutal regime and callous subjection, had been, in total effect, a concentration camp presided over by a paternalistic commandant in the form of a slave owner. Now even that element of paternalism, however perverse it was in any civilized terms, was gone. As if in fury at the sight of blacks no longer slaves, the white racists of the South were indefatigable in heaping outrages of mistreatment upon them, and in seeking and finding additional modes of imposing upon their victims the gruesome burden of their own white-racist barbarism. Lynching, torture, maiming, raping, castrating, humiliating, and inculcating fear: these were only some of the contrivances spawned by their diseased imaginations to execute the designs of their bestial cruelty.

It has been the professional custom of the historians of American culture, with certain exceptions, to speak of the enslavement of the blacks as though it were no more than an untoward incident in the radiant story of a remarkable group of white people; to assess the fact as if, however deplorable it might have been, the victims were after all black, and so this circumstance rendered the matter somehow less culpable; to see the whole issue against a national background of soaring utterances of civilized attachment and of resplendent personalities, such as the Founding Fathers, whose ownership of slaves was evidence not of moral backwardness but only of an ethical dilemma for which the ruling conventions of the age, rather than their racist hypocrisy, were responsible. George Washington's tenacious refusal to free his slaves during his lifetime, his brazen buying and selling of them, the resourcefulness and determination with which he made certain that never, so long as he lived, would his slaves be set free— this, in the view of most American historians, is merely testimony to the compactness and integrity of his character when judged by the standards of the age in which he lived. So with Thomas Jefferson. For all his moral writhings, in all their elaborate and calculated record (so, perhaps, to disarm posterity of censure), he nevertheless found it expedient to retain his ownership of slaves during his entire lifetime. Nor, apparently, was his treatment of his mulatto daughter above humane reproach; William Wells Brown's *Clotel, or the President's Daughter* contains the essential account of this affair. The South was not alone morally reprobate in its treatment of the blacks, although it would be indiscriminate to assign to otherwise enlightened men, like Washington and Jefferson, the same degree of moral squalor on the issue of slavery justly attributable to John C. Calhoun or Jefferson Davis. Strict impartiality, however, requires the observation that Washington's attitude toward freedom for his slaves in his lifetime was remarkable for the obduracy with which (allowing for the sole exception of his "mulatto man, William") he refused to entertain the notion. He evidently spoke of it, he certainly wrote about it, but as a practical matter he did nothing. His conduct in this regard was anything but admirable. The record is clear. He was throughout his lifetime a determined slave owner. The true measurement of any man pretending to greatness lies along a line drawn with Plutarchian evenhandedness precisely midway between his virtues and his vices. The reciters of the American story must bear this firmly in mind if their tale is to be anything more than the flattering distortions of portraitists too eager to please, too self-interested to be truthful.

Let the whole episode be laid bare in all its nightmarish horror. Place the mass slaughter of millions of Africans in the Congo by Leopold II of Belgium side by side in the historical record with the

116

mass slaughter of millions of European Jews by Hitler. Then bid the world to remember always, never forgetting, the one as well as the other. And let statesmen and their peoples do homage to the memory of slaughtered Africans and slaughtered Jews alike. Let Willy Brandt kneel in Poland at a memorial for murdered Jews. But let him kneel, too, at a memorial for murdered Africans. For if he remembers Hitler, as he should, he ought also to remember the fate of the Herreros and the bloodstained career in German Southwest Africa of the infamous Karl Peters. It must no longer seem, as for too long it has, that the value of human life is to be measured by ethnic categories. Thousands of American Indians in Brazil and Colombia are being exterminated at the present time in order to gain possession of their lands. There is scarcely a ripple of protest anywhere in the world. The Australian aborigines were brought close to extermination by the white Australian settlers with a like absence of widespread concern. The European Jews were abandoned to Hitler by the passive connivance of the nation-states of the world. Nor was the Vatican itself more compassionate. The fate of the Indians of North America foreshadowed these manifestations of racism, exactly as these were themselves prefigured by the Spanish massacres of untold millions of the Indians of South and Central America and the Caribbean.

4

THE FATE of the Indians of North America is a prime index to the historic forces that have shaped the American character. It is also one of the supreme determinants, political, economic, and social, of the evolution of the American society. The mass slaughter of the Indians of North America has steeped in blood, indelible as time, the extension of the national frontier. As historic actuality as well as tradition, the conquest of the frontier must be recognized as having left a profound impress and at the same time conferred a distinctive impulse upon the American society: the impulse to violence.

To the extent that it is scientifically warrantable to speak of an "American character," the evidence for it is to be validated mainly by a quintet of collective experiences, namely, African slavery, the Revolutionary War, the Civil War, the conquest of the frontier, and the vast tide of human migration that deposited nearly 45 million people from other lands on the shores of the North American continent. Of all these circumstances, none has so deeply permeated the national consciousness as slavery, but none has so definitively imparted its own inseparable traits to that consciousness as the conquest of the frontier. At any given moment, whatever the country may have been engaged upon, whether at home or abroad, the expansion of the frontier was pushed forward, a remorseless human wave crushing or eroding every animate and inanimate thing that stood in its path. It never

118

slackened, never faltered, never desisted, until at last the Bering Strait intervened against its violent, unremitting, and implacable encroachment.

Yet while this domestic epic was distilling its fateful strain into the formation of the national character, other sociological influences were also at work. Some historians, notably Daniel J. Boorstin and Louis Hartz, have propounded theories of the matrix from which the American character emerged, in which European cultural influences have been heavily discounted. That theirs is an erroneous thesis seems virtually self-evident. Leaving aside their unscientific mystification, which can command no excessive attention, it is sufficient simply to point to the genetic aspect of the matter. By any test of scientific common sense, there can be not the slightest doubt that the Europeans who colonized the North American continent carried their European heritage with them wherever they settled or penetrated. This heritage did not only consist of a body of cultural accretions—acquired learning, inculcated modes of thought, a distinctive complex of social attitudes and relations, a collective consciousness of specific group identity. It also consisted of a genetic structure. And it was generalized as well throughout the group, calculated to act upon an environment and to respond to ecological stimuli in a manner that was an index to the group's social uniqueness. In short, these transplanted Europeans, like all other human groups, were compounds of physiochemistry and social culture from which the former element could be excluded only at the certain risk of misreading their total significance as an animal species.

Liberal romanticists, such as Boorstin and Hartz, expend ponderous learning in a maze of disputation about the persistence or transiency of cultural influences. They exhibit little or no concern for what C. G. Jung summed up with such apt felicity as "the memory of the race." No one needs to be reminded that this insight of Jung's has a physiological base in the heritable apparatus of the genetic structure. "We are all the product of heredity and environment. The genes provided the blueprints and the carpenters, the environment the lumber" (Carleton S. Coon and others, Races). It can only be egregious error to view the European colonists of North America solely as the bearers of a culture whose burden they could discard in more or less short order upon contact with their new environment. This is to accord to the environment a sanction that does not so much depict as distort its influence.

119

It is a point of view characteristic of certain Europeans who, for whatever reasons, are anxious to disburden themselves of their European past. People such as these find it more congenial to set the temper of their minds in an intellectual outlook from which the residue of their European experience has been effectively banished. For them, and such as they, life began in the United States of America. They are therefore not so much commentators on the actuality or otherwise of European influence upon the cultural development of North America and the formation of the American character; they are, rather, confessors of their resentment of a Europe that begrudged them and their forebears an existence from which the generous promise and fulfillment of American life was wholly absent. These men can neither forgive nor forget the multitudinous slights and frustrations that marred their ancestral connection with Europe. No one can blame them for that. But they must be censured for importing into the context of social science prejudices which can have no valid place there and which belong, more properly, to those occasions of private discourse where emotion may be indulged at the expense of critical self-discipline. The central fact of the formation of the American character is the interaction of Europeans, first as colonial subjects and then as citizens of an independent nation, with an environment that, in its essential terms, was only partly physical. That is to say, the ecological circumstances were not composed simply of space stippled with land and water, plant and animal life. They were also comprised of a mass of non-Europeans, who were, specifically, Indians and Africans.

The colonists themselves were numerous, millennia-wrought, individual bundles of neurophysiology, conditioned by a vast range of evolutionary factors. This process of evolution had selected them in their former cultural and physical environment as Europeans. When they emigrated to North America, the ages-long influence of their evolutionary antecedents did not abruptly cease. It persisted, although diminishing gradually, until by interaction with the new environment it was no longer decisive in determining the character of the immigrants and their descendants. Something else, too, had occurred. There had been intermixture with other human, non-European groups. Hybridization had taken place. An adventitious train of genetic combination and recombination was set in motion. The biological result was a mutant species. Cultural circumstances reinforced the mutation.

The dialectic of challenge and response proceeded from the premise of the environment to a new human synthesis. Yet the process as a whole remained an evolutionary matter. The mutation from *Homo europeus* to *Homo americanus* took place at a cultural rate. There was no sudden leap. But, contrary to Boorstin and Hartz, it was not merely a question of vanished or persistent European cultural influences. It was, in fact, nothing less than the emergence of a new and distinctive human type from an intricate complex of evolutionary factors. Among these factors, European cultural influences (intellectual and otherwise) played an important but by no means a solitary role. It would be wrong to depreciate these influences after the fashion of Boorstin and Hartz. Yet it would be equally mistaken to exclude from consideration, as they do, the part played by human biology.

The fatal weakness of the exceptionalist position espoused by Boorstin and Hartz derives precisely from this failure. They have been so obsessed with the problems of cultural influences that they have lost sight of genetic elements that were no less determinant. Even so, their main preoccupation has been with providing warrant for the thesis that in the development of a distinctive American character, European intellectual influences were of relatively minor account. Historians who adhere to traditional middle-class values are prone to display undue preoccupation with "intellectual" influences. This tendency entraps them in the habit of formulating abstract and imprecise generalizations: abstract because they have no basis in scientific actuality; imprecise because they issue from too limited a compass of enquiry. There was an acculturating process by which at length former Europeans acquired the distinctive character of Americans. But there were also biological elements of the highest importance in the process. It was not only, and in no sense pre-eminently, a matter of intellectual influences disappearing or persisting or of the new environment acting upon its European influx as though the latter were a *tabula rasa*. The genetic factor, in interaction with the environment, was of pivotal consequence. Intellectual influences were potent though ancillary. But they might misleadingly be elevated to decisive importance by narrowing the study of their effect to the comparatively small segment of middle-class European settlers who inhabited the country during the first two centuries of its existence as a cisatlantic colony, or to those from the same stratum of society who came later.

With the second quarter of the nineteenth century, mass migration to North America began. The Irish came after 1846, the Germans after 1848, the Russian Jews after 1881, the White Russians after 1917. Between 1820 and 1969, the number of immigrants to the United States of America totaled 44,789,312. This was nearly five times the entire population of the United States in the year 1820. They came from all over the world. Hybridization occurred on a massive scale. So did genetic combination and recombination. This titanic wave of migration carried its own crest of intellectual influences wholly distinct from British liberal utilitarianism, the encyclopedism of the French Enlightenment, the romanticism of the German *Aufklärung*. Eighty per cent of the immigrants came from Europe: in absolute numbers, 35,593,649. Of the rest, more than 7 million came from within the Western Hemisphere itself; less than 1.5 million from Asia; 69,374 from Africa; roughly, 100,000 from Australia and New Zealand. In vast predominance it was a migration of white peoples. That was their common ethnic center. They also had something else in common: their membership in the militaristic caste of the all-conquering Christian communion, which had established its thralldom over the world. It was above all, then, a white Christian migration. These were the people in restless surge against the American frontier, in mine and forest, field and factory, on land, lake, river, and mountain, in action, thought, and dream, defining America as they themselves evolved, chrysalislike, to become one with the land, receiving its distinctive life in return for their own, and becoming, slowly becoming, created anew in the image of the land, and creating anew the image of the land, until at length they merged with it—Europeans, Asians, Africans, and Australians, New Zealanders, South and Central Americans, West Indians, and Pacific Ocean Islanders—to emerge at last, Americans.

The process was genetic, cultural, environmental, involving millions of human migrants. In preceding millennia they had trekked across the Asian steppes and traversed the Bering Strait into Alaska and thence onward. They had drifted and sailed on Atlantic and Pacific Ocean currents until they made landfall in the Western Hemisphere. They were Asians then, or Pacific Islanders, or others. But now they traveled by steamship across the Atlantic and were in the main white, European, and Christian. They constituted the raw human material, the primary genetic ingredients, from which a new and distinctive type of mankind would evolve.

It is important to bear in mind that the great leavening of this giant mass of people moving from east to west across the Atlantic was composed of social malcontents. They were in flight from want and famine, violence and terror; they were releasing themselves from religious constraint, economic exploitation, political subjection. Theirs was a dream of unprecedented freedom for self-fulfillment. The dream came true. This was the meaning of America for them.

Taken together as a many-millionfold collectivity, these immigrants were people characterized by a social tradition whose resolution of group problems, whether of an internal or external nature, was typically by resort to violence. Europe alone, from which the large majority of them came, had scarcely known a generation of unbroken peace in 1,000 years. War was its chronic and recurrent feature, as civil strife was the constant condition of its domestic society. The Christian civilization of Europe erected magnificent cathedrals to the greater glory of God and for the entombment of its celebrated warriors. The predominating group impulse of European civilization was violence in the form of war. That was the principal element of the social matrix from which these migrants to the Western Hemisphere had derived their definitive character as Europeans. They were in the main not the beneficiaries of violence. More largely than not, they were its victims. Yet they were all, to a nearly undifferentiated degree, the products of violence. With them they brought to the New World a social habit of violence, whether as sufferers or as perpetrators. This was equally true of their predecessors who had quit Europe for North America. Of them all it might be said with simple truth, from the first to the last European migrant, that they and their forebears for 1,000 years had either been active or passive continuators of a tradition of group violence deeply entrenched in their social customs and biologically encoded in their genetic structure. The European heritage that devolved upon America by way of the heirship of these migrants had other properties, of course; but the conditioned reflex of collective violence was its main bequest. Beside this tragic and overshadowing fact, this *damnosa hereditas,* overemphasis on "intellectual influences" is less than adequate.

When these migrants began their mass descent upon North America during the first half of the nineteenth century, their European forerunners had long since been busy with the extermination of the indigenous Indians and the extension of the national boundaries. They were settling the country, impelled by a relentless need for living space. Land was the inflexible imperative. To hold, enlarge, and maintain the possession of land demanded nothing less than a remorseless will to endure any sacrifice or, as it might chance, to commit any crime. If a single theme is to be abstracted from the many-faceted record of the conquest and settlement of North America, it must be the vast engrossment of migrant energies with the acquisition of land. This was only to be expected of people who had been, for the most part, landless in their European habitat. They gave themselves up to an orgy of overcompensation. Land hunger and its struggle for appeasement are the essential constituents of the settlement of North America by Europeans. They cleared the plains of bison and buffalo, drove the Indians from the land, and presently refused to allot any but the meanest parcels (and hardly those) to the former black slaves. They coveted the land; and the land was theirs. No means was too dishonorable, no path too crooked, no act too sordid, no crime too violent; they stopped at nothing in order to gain possession of the land. To extrude Mexico from the West and Southwest, they fought a war that was as unjust as the current twentieth-century Vietnamese adventure. And when they had established their suzerainty from the Atlantic to the Pacific, they asserted the Monroe Doctrine.

Meanwhile the country continued to be developed with propulsive energy. Railways and the telegraph linked it, as did steamboats on lakes and rivers; and electricity illuminated it. The great masses of nineteenth-century immigrants were the inheritors of a technology that transformed the terms of their existence. It was as if a magic wand had been waved over their lives. In literal truth, beggars became princes or—the American equivalent—tycoons. Such a revolution of possibilities would have been inconceivable in Europe; here, in North America, it was a mere commonplace. That the United States of America should seem to these migrants like the Promised Land flowing with milk and honey was not unwarranted. For they achieved here a level of personal fulfillment beyond their wildest imagining. Their dreams, however, did not realize themselves without effort, or with only a minimum, on the part of the dreamers. They toiled, transcending fatigue, undiscouraged by failure, because there was always a prospect of ultimate success. The rich, illimitable treasure they found in America was hope. Difficulties were often formidable; obstacles abounded. It never was simply a matter of a munificent inheritance into which they entered without let or hindrance as fortuitous heirs. America demanded everything they had but gave it back to them multiplied manifold.

The country extended them no empty promises. It redeemed every one without stint. A man might rise from pedlar to international banker, from factory hand to industrial magnate, from farm laborer to United States Senator. Aside from the will and capacity for hard work and imaginative enterprise, there was only one qualification: a white skin. Granted that, the rest was not easy, but it was rewarding. Despite its millions of black inhabitants, constituting the largest ethnic minority, the United States was a white man's country. The basic law of the land declared that all men were created equal. Yet "all men" did not include blacks. Interpreted in the sociological context in which the basic law was formulated, it was intended to mean only that all *white* men were created equal. Not blacks. They were slaves: subhuman. So the unparalleled promise and transforming fulfillment of American life was not designed to embrace blacks.

This was the state of affairs that the immense concourse of immigrants discovered on reaching America. The possibilities of enhancing the terms of existence proliferated in all directions. A new civilization, the American, was evolving out of an old culture that was European. As far as it went, this impression was true enough. But they would also discover on deepened acquaintance with the new land the existence of other formative influences. They would come to realize that the original Indian inhabitants of the land and the millions of black slaves transported from Africa had also suffused the fabric of the incipient American civilization with vital elements of their own indigenous cultures. Accordingly, the American civilization was a hybrid organism, as is the case with all such social agglomerations. The American civilization was not a cisatlantic transplant of European culture. Its genetic basis was predominantly European. So was its cultural basis. Again, in biological terms, its most numerous human constituents were European. But there were Asians, too, and Africans. There were also the primary migrants, the Indians. And the supereminent fact was that all these diverse peoples in their planet-wide variety were contributing, in the sum of their differences, that unifying character by which a collection of cultures coalesces into a civilization. Flinders Petrie has an interesting observation to make on this point:

The rise of the new civilization is conditioned by an immigration of a different people . . . it arises from a mixture of two different stocks. That effect of mixture cannot take place all at once. There are barriers of antipathy, barriers of creed, barriers of social standing, but every barrier to race fusion gives way in time. [Cited by C. D. Darlington in *The Evolution of Man and Society.*]

Nevertheless, it is of the first importance to recall the fact that whatever the hybrid character of American civilization, its cultural—and more narrowly—intellectual influences were dominantly European. Howard Mumford Jones's *O Strange New World: American Culture: The Formative Years* is a persuasive text on this theme. So is Carl Becker's *The Declaration of Independence: A Study in the History of Political Ideas.*

The social effect of this stupendous migration on North America was revolutionary. One of its main consequences was the widening of the customary divergence of outlook between the South and the other regions of the country. As a whole, the former rejected the newcomers; the latter welcomed them. Daniel J. Boorstin, in *The Americans: The National Experience* (Vol. 2), puts this matter as follows:

In the Southern states, however, slavery—the South's "Peculiar Institution"—fostered quite another attitude toward newcomers. While Boosters worried over how to attract and assimilate, in the half-century before the Civil War, Southerners were more and more concerned with how to extrude and separate.

Nor did the South regard the blacks as immigrants. This circumstance causes Boorstin some uneasiness. He eventually finds an explanation for it. "Southerners," he says, "did not count the Negro an immigrant primarily because they did not consider him a candidate for assimilation into their community." He adduces no evidence, however, for his thesis that the Southern test of whether or not anyone was an immigrant was that person's eligibility "for assimilation into their community." The true statement of the matter is that the South was a xenophobic community. In any case, the Southerners did not regard the blacks as persons. So there could be no question of any presumed "candidacy." But quite apart from their attitude toward the blacks, Southerners were disposed to regard themselves as separated from the rest of the country by their folk character, their preindustrial way of life, their distinctive customs and institutions. Most salient among the last-named was black slavery.

Boorstin speaks of the black slaves as "involuntary immigrants." But this is perhaps a contradiction in terms. It may be debatable whether

126

volition is a necessary element in the status of immigrant. It may be arguable that there is such a thing as enforced immigration. Refugees, for example, in search of sanctuary from terror may be considered, if you will, "involuntary immigrants." The case of the black slaves, however, was conspicuously different. They fled no terror in their native land; they sought no asylum elsewhere. The essence of their situation was that they were captives. Precisely, say, as the Jews were captives in the period of their Babylonian sojourn. No one, no historian, has ever referred to those Jews as immigrants. Exiles, yes. But immigrants, never. This is exactly the position of the black slaves and their descendants in America. They are properly to be regarded as captives and exiles. For what immigrants were ever sold into slavery against their will and transported to a foreign country against their will and, for two and one-half centuries thereafter, held as slaves against their will in that foreign country?

Boorstin writes:

Southerners who attacked immigration in the North somehow chose not to see Negroes as "immigrants." . . . From a 20th-century perspective, this way of thinking seems odd, for although Negroes, with negligible exceptions, had not come here willingly, they had other indices of immigrants in extreme form: they came from a great distance and from an alien culture. . . . American historians, adopting this Southern point of view, have never quite become accustomed to think of the Negro as an immigrant.

The sheer naïveté of this citation of indices of immigrant status is startling. "They [the blacks] came from a great distance and from an alien culture." So did the early Britons, enslaved by the Romans and transported to Rome. Yet has any historian ever referred to these Britons as immigrants? Such transfers of population on varying scales have been a frequent incident of human history. But this must be the first time that a scholar has sought to place enslaved people subjected to involuntary displacement and removal to a foreign country, by no means of their choice, in the category of immigrants. One is tempted to read into this attempt an aversion on Boorstin's part to the classification of immigrant; as a result of which, one might further suspect him of pique and an unscholarly peevishness at the thought that the lowly blacks have been excluded from this classification by a perverse exceptionalism on the part of Southerners and American historians.

There are other aspects of the black experience of abduction and enslavement across the seas to which the attention of historians has been insufficiently directed. On all the available evidence, it is clear that the European incursion into Africa was an instance, similar to that of the Roman conquest of Greece or the Spanish conquest of the Aztec Empire, of an inferior civilization successfully assaulting a superior. The extrusion of the Moors from Spain—the *Reconquista*—is another instance of a successful barbarian onslaught against a more advanced culture.

To argue that the black slaves and their descendants are to be considered immigrants because some of those incidents that are attached to them are characteristic of this category is a dubious proposition indeed. It is rather as if someone were to assert that a Hollywood motion-picture star should be regarded as a prince because he lived in royal style, or that an airplane should be classified as a bird because it flies. No, that simply will not do. The black slaves and their decendants are not immigrants. They were captives in enforced exile up to the moment of their emancipation after two and one-half centuries. At that point their status changed. They became not immigrants but liberated settlers. The blacks in America are the descendants of captive colonists once reduced to slavery. A simple illustration will make this clear. The white convicts and felons who were transported from England to New England and the Carolinas, and elsewhere in North America, have never been regarded as immigrants, although they also "came from a great distance and from an alien culture"; at least, not as immigrants in the sense in which the massive influx of Europeans beginning with the fourth decade of the nineteenth century may be viewed. Precisely as in the case of the African slaves, the British convicts were brought here in an unfree state. Like the African slaves, they had been deprived of choice in the matter. They came whether they wished to or not. When the terms of their imprisonment expired, they became free men and settlers. The African slaves and their descendants were, however, to be deprived of their liberty the whole of their lives. Yet they were, in fact, set at liberty after two and one-half centuries. When that happened, they also became free men—and settlers. So the black slaves of America and their descendants never were and are not now immigrants.

Between an indigenous—or, if not an indigenous, then a settled—population and immigrants, there exists as a rule a barrier of strangeness. Throughout the country, but especially in the South, any such barrier between the black slaves and their white owners had long been dispelled by generations of intimate contact. Strangeness there had been at the beginning, of course. What could have been more natural? On August 20, 1619, how could there possibly not have been strangeness between the "20 negars" sold off the "Dutch man-of-warre" and the Jamestown colony?

By the beginning of the eighteenth century, there were around 30,000 slaves in the North American colonies, of whom more than 20,000 were in the South. Peter M. Bergman's and Mort N. Bergman's *The Chronological History of the Negro in America* is authority for the following statistics: of a population of 173,150 in four Southern states —Maryland, Virginia, North Carolina, and South Carolina—in the year 1715, there were 46,700 blacks. Sixty per cent of the population of South Carolina was black, and so was more than 33 per cent of that of North Carolina. Of the 95,000 people of Virginia, 23,000, or 24.2 per cent, were black, and of Maryland's 50,000, 18.6 per cent, or 9,500, were black. As early, then, as the first decade of the eighteenth century, and long before that time, there cannot have been much room for strangeness between the black and white segments of the Southern population. Nor is the prospect or even the possibility of assimilation a valid criterion, as Boorstin suggests, of immigrant status. There are ethnic minorities everywhere in the world who have been regarded as unassimilable because they have either resisted assimilation or been deemed by the host country as unsuitable or even undesirable for assimilation. The Armenians in Turkey, the Sudeten Germans in Czechoslovakia, the Alsatians on the shifting border between France and Germany are a few of the numerous examples of peoples who, though unclassified as immigrants, have also been unassimilable for one reason or another.

Despite the protracted, blood-drenched tragedy of relations between whites and blacks in the South, the late Senator Richard B. Russell of Georgia is much closer to the truth of the matter than Professor Boorstin. Russell was reported by the New York *Times* to have said in the course of a civil-rights debate in the Senate: "I was brought up with them [meaning the blacks]. I love them." Probably true enough. The only flaw in the Senator's love was its restricted situation. He loved the blacks—in their places; which meant, of course, he loved them as long as they remained stratified in the social layers of the South right down at the bottom, where, loving them as he did, he could not doubt they properly belonged. That is the trouble. If the Senator's love (and that of many other white Southerners) for his black fellow Southerners were only capable of transcending the historical circumstances, the whole South would all the sooner and all the more surely accede to the moral leadership of a country that once it would have sundered. The urges that actuated it to this course were consistent with its racism and its backward economic ideology. Yet they were contradictory of the larger destiny proffered by the black presence in its midst. In a world that is predominantly nonwhite, the United States possesses in its black population the most valuable of all resources for conciliating, if it should choose to do so, the racial conflict that more deeply than anything else frustrates a just balance of the interrelations of mankind.

The Southern region of the United States, where the greater portion of the black inhabitants of the country has always been concentrated, has acquired an intimate contact with the social realities inherent in racial differences much surpassing that of any other region of the republic. The South so far has failed itself, failed the country, and failed the world in the moral quality of its response to the challenge of racial divergences. But precisely because the South still confronts the problem—often, as throughout its history, in desperation, though, curiously, never in despair—hope survives there. A new leadership is emerging, represented by men like Governor Jimmy Carter of Georgia and Governor John C. West of South Carolina, whose decency of inspiration in their approach to this tormented question augurs widespread moral uplift for the South, the country, and the world. On this matter of race, the Southern region of the United States may yet provide the enlightened leadership and illuminating example of which humanity so urgently stands in need. Indeed, the South may be the last best hope of America. Should this prove to be the case, little credit for it will be due to anyone like the late Senator Russell, who, despite his professed love for the blacks, was in fact an implacable foe of any measure calculated to improve their lot. The honest enmity of the Senator would have been more useful to the blacks than his pathological affection. It is not necessary to doubt or deny his declaration of love. One need only examine the quality of his passion. Of a piece with the feudal tradition that facilitates admixtures of love and contempt for one's presumed in-

130

feriors, it enabled the Senator and such as he to dissemble their
inveterate racism while feigning a sentimental regard for their serfs.
That the Senator should love the blacks and assert his intimate connection with them was in no sense unexpected, for those blacks, whom
he knew so well, were by any test the finest human beings he had
ever been associated with in all his life. The Senator's love for them
was perfectly natural. Unnaturalness arose from his racist misuse of
the sentimental attachment he so proudly confessed and, by his political actions, so grossly disfigured.

No student of racial conflict in the South however profound, no
observer however penetrating, no artist however illuminated—not even
William Faulkner—has so far succeeded in achieving and expressing
the full range and content of the involuted relationship between
blacks and whites in the South. At the very peak of his comprehension
of the multiprismed nature of this relationship, Faulkner's parochialism
curtails his vision, which, otherwise, might have been Dantesque. His
parochialism was the product of his white-racist reflexes conditioned
by the cultural environment of Oxford, Mississippi. Never was he able
to attain in his work the artistic transcendence of this limiting circumstance that would have invested him with universality. As a
regional writer, he ranks among the greatest. But purely as a writer,
without regard to place, unfettered in his comprehension by the
transient things of the human condition, a writer whose vision was
untrammeled by man's yesterdays, though irradiated by their passage,
detached from the present so as the more magisterially to preside
over it, and conceiving fearlessly of the future as flux and change and
grandly as a vista coextensive with the infinite—as such a writer,
Faulkner recedes from greatness. The sum of his insight, cast in a wist-
ful reflection that it is better to endure than to prevail, elucidates his
view of the destiny of the Southern blacks in their relationship with
the whites of the region. What he clearly has in mind, although it
can be deduced only from the muted undertones of his despairing
perception, is that from his standpoint it is better for the blacks to
endure and for the whites to prevail. So he envisions for the blacks a
homeostasis of perpetual suffering. This, and nothing else, is what he
means by enduring. He intends that the blacks shall persist throughout time as the prostrate figures upon whose neck a white foot is
planted forever in token of uncontested racial superiority.

For Faulkner, Dilsey, in *The Sound and the Fury*—who endured—

was, in the fictional terms of his artistic vision, the ideal black exemplar. She simply endured without a thought of prevailing. Her role, as delineated by her creator, was that of a black foster matriarch, generating as well as sustaining the values of survival amidst the decadence of a Southern white family to whom she was bound as a retainer. That she emerges in the end, despite Faulkner, as an elemental Magna Mater instead of a black wet nurse at whose patient and inexhaustible breasts generations of white Compsons suckle, unweaning and insatiable—that she thus emerges is a teeming paradox of Faulkner's racist contrivance. "That's the trouble with nigger servants, when they've been with you for a long time they get so full of self importance that they're not worth a damn. Think they run the whole family." Dilsey was indeed a "nigger servant." Yet she did rather more than "run the whole [Compson] family." She shielded their flickering animation with a strong, protective hand against the gusts of genetic decay that threatened to extinguish them. She presided over them as a household goddess, a deity vouchsafed to them for their preservation against their own compulsive decomposition. She cared for them with that ironic solicitude and invincible compassion that Southern blacks have so inversely lavished upon their white oppressors. "He touched my arm, lightly, his hand that worn, gentle quality of niggers' hands. 'Listen. This ain't for outside talking. I don't mind telling you because you and me's the same folks, come long and short.'" The same folks; which, in Faulkner's allegorical perception, transmutes the killing of Southern blacks by Southern whites from murder into symbolic group suicide.

Martin Luther King exhorted his followers not to shed the blood of whites. "If blood must be shed, let it be our blood." This love of Southern blacks for Southern whites is nothing short of a paradigm of the latent ability of the human species to transcend evil by redressing it with good. Out of it wells the protectiveness with which Dilsey shields Quentin from Jason's anger. "Hit me, den," Dilsey says, "ef nothin else but hittin somebody wont do you. Hit me." The incident closes, however, with Quentin calling her a "damn old nigger." Long before Faulkner's Dilsey, Dr. Samuel Johnson's "shepherd in Virgil" discovered "love to be a native of the rocks." Toward the end, Dilsey "led Ben to the bed and drew him down beside her and she held him, rocking back and forth, wiping his drooling mouth upon the hem of her skirt."

132

As a literary image of the congenital idiocy of white racism and the compassionate endurance with which blacks have suffered it, this metaphor of Faulkner's is unsurpassable. By the time he came, in 1950, to accept a Nobel Prize, however, Faulkner had moved beyond a mystique of enduring to a metaphysic of prevailing. "Man will not merely endure: he will prevail . . . because he has a soul, a spirit capable of compassion and sacrifice and endurance . . . the writer's duty is to write about these things."

But which genus of man did Faulkner have in mind: black man or white man? It is precisely this dualistic perception of man that fatally impairs Faulkner's title to artistic transcendence. Nevertheless, the passage of Faulkner's vision from enduring to prevailing reveals, despite his obdurate racism, an enlargement of his artistic comprehension. In its own terms, it is hardly less than revolutionary.

The coexistence of revolution and racism has always been a dominant feature of the evolution of the American society. Faulkner is simply, so to speak, an individual instance in point. The country as a whole has been in a state of unceasing revolution (using this word in its broadest significance) from its inception. To be an American is, virtually in terms, to be a revolutionary. The country is not hostile to revolution as such, it is merely intolerant of black revolution. Any black uprising, violent or nonviolent, is a disturbance of the racial *status quo* that goes to the very foundations of the society. For the country was founded on the social premise that blacks are not equal to whites, not even in group nomenclature; which explains to some extent the stubbornness of the opposition on the part of the whites to the equal though contrary term "black" as a collective description of the people they prefer to call Negroes. This word, "Negroes," is to them a comforting reassurance of their own caste superiority. The whole historic range of the connotation of the word "Negro" imports inferiority of one sort and another. Every human group, with the exception of the people designated Negroes, has chosen its own identifying description. Either they ascribe themselves to a given area of the earth, whence they become Englishmen, Frenchmen, Germans, or, on a larger generic scale, to an enveloping ethnic collectivity, such as white peoples. But the people styled Negroes by white Western society are denied the description, for example, of African blacks and, instead, are referred to as African Negroes. They are deemed not to be a member group of the nonwhite peoples of the world (like the Chinese and Japanese), but to be "Negroes." There is a stark linguistic equivalency between the terms "black" and "white," which the white racism of the Western world finds intolerable. Thus it saddles upon the black peoples everywhere a caste descriptive, "Negroes," the more securely to maintain them conceptually and empirically in the inferior status imposed upon them. Negro accommodationists are always easy to find. They abound everywhere, reaching out eagerly for the scraps and bones of "recognition" that the whites throw them to reward their abysmal lack of racial pride, which, of course, is not the same thing as racism. The latter is the former grown diseased. A healthy racial pride is a symptom of self-respect.

W. E. B. Du Bois once replied to a letter from a black youth who had asked him about the appropriateness of the group descriptive "Negro." Du Bois's position was that it mattered much less what you were called than what you did. But he went astray in this matter in two directions after making pedantic play with the possibilities of a Greek equivalent. First, he failed to give adequate consideration to the immense psychological burden of the word "Negro." Second, his scholarship would have been more usefully employed in a serious examination of the validity of the word in its application to the black peoples of the world. For it is as if these human groups came into being only with their discovery by the Portuguese, who called them Negro. Almost at once the term became a synonym for "slave," since the Portuguese lost no time in depriving these Africans of their liberty and carrying them to enforced servitude in Portugal. The word remains tainted by this historical circumstance and its social consequence of caste inferiority. It is a word of contempt. The Arabs, who are among the most energetic and persistent enslavers of black Africans, apply in their own language to these black slaves a term which is the historical equivalent of "Negro" and which, similarly, is fraught with disparagement and caste degradation. The word is "Zanj." There would be no reason to debate the question of the validity of the word "Negro" as a collective description of the black peoples of the world were it not for a white racism that is as virulent as it is pertinacious.

Although by no stretch of anyone's imagination an accommodationist, Du Bois erred nonetheless in this matter. Instead of treating it with condescending humor and dismissing it with a pompous, philosophical assertion of the superior importance of the substance of a thing to its name; instead of engaging in what amounted in effect to

134

a piece of intellectual persiflage, he should have contemplated and discussed in his reply to the black youth the anthropological inaccuracy of the term "Negro," and the resultant distortion of the history of the blacks that it has facilitated at the hands of white racism. Du Bois was wrong. His humor was misplaced; his historical sense, impeccable as a rule, gravely wanting in this instance. How would the whites react, he might have profitably considered, were the blacks to insist on calling them Blancos? Whatever the shortcomings of the whites, they at least are not lacking in racial pride. Tocqueville's observations, in *Democracy in America,* concerning Negroes are worth noting at this point.

The Negro makes a thousand fruitless efforts to insinuate himself into a society that repulses him; he adapts himself to his oppressors' tastes, adopting their opinions and hoping by imitation to join their community. From birth he has been told that his race is naturally inferior to the white man and almost believing that, he holds himself in contempt. He sees a trace of slavery in his every feature, and if he could he would gladly repudiate himself entirely. In contrast, the pretended nobility of his origin fills the whole imagination of the Indian. He lives and dies amid these proud dreams. Far from wishing to adapt his mores to ours, he regards barbarism as the distinctive emblem of his race, and in repulsing civilization he is perhaps less moved by hatred against it than by fear of resembling the Europeans. . . . The Negro would like to mingle with the European and cannot. The Indian might to some extent succeed in that, but he scorns to attempt it. The servility of the former delivers him over into slavery; the pride of the latter leads him to death.

Tocqueville has other opinions about Negroes.

The United States Negro has lost even the memory of his homeland; he no longer understands the language his fathers spoke; he has abjured their religion and forgotten their mores. Ceasing to belong to Africa, he has acquired no right to the blessings of Europe; he is left in suspense between two societies and isolated between two peoples, sold by one and repudiated by the other; in the whole world there is nothing but his master's hearth to provide him with some semblance of a homeland. The Negro has no family; for him a woman is no more than the passing companion of his pleasures, and from their birth his sons are his equals. Should I call it a blessing of God, or a last malediction of his anger, this disposition of the soul that makes men insensible to extreme misery and often even gives them a sort of depraved taste for the cause of their afflictions? Plunged in the abyss of wretchedness, the Negro hardly notices his ill fortune; he was reduced to slavery by violence, and the habit of servitude has given him the thoughts and ambitions of a slave; he admires his tyrants even more than he hates them and finds his joy and pride in a servile imitation of his oppressors. His intelligence is degraded to the level of his soul. The Negro is a slave from birth. What am I saying? He is often sold in his mother's belly and begins, so to say, to be a slave before he is born.

A brief look at Tocqueville's background may be illuminating. He was born early in the nineteenth century, and by the time he was about twenty-six he had visited the United States, made a study of its prison system, and published (in 1832) *Du système pénitentiaire aux États-Unis et de son application en France.* The visit to the United States and his investigations supplied him with the material for his celebrated study of American life and institutions, *De la démocratie en Amérique.* He was a gifted observer endowed with uncommon political insight. He took some part in public life and for a time in 1849 was Minister for Foreign Affairs. During his brief occupancy of this post, his *chef de cabinet* was the Comte de Gobineau, author of the *Essai sur l'inégalité des races humaines,* a pseudo-scientific treatise on ethnology, which has long been a prime source of mischief on this highly complex matter. Gobineau has been a high priest of modern racism, and there is some basis for the belief that the association between him and Tocqueville was not without influence on Tocqueville's own racial outlook. No one can have forgotten Gobineau's thesis that the white man alone is able to create culture. Nor will anyone need to be reminded that it was Gobineau who implied in his work an essential contradiction between liberty and equality.

At the heart of Tocqueville's social philosophy is this fundamental notion of the incompatibility of equality and liberty. Tocqueville celebrated privilege, and his characteristic pessimism drew much of its sustenance from his belief that privilege was doomed to extinction by social equality. Property seemed to him to be the last redoubt of privilege, so he espoused this economic institution with passionate ardor and ideological attachment. Like Gobineau, he was a racial chauvinist. His view of mankind was narrowly ethnocentric. The standards by which he assessed the capabilities of other human groups were European. Yet it never seemed to occur to him to reverse the process and evaluate Europeans by the standards of other human groups. Had he done so, his political insight might have been no less acute, but his comprehension of human cultures would have been

136

profounder. As the matter stands, he emerges as a political observer and an analyst of extraordinary penetration, but as a social theorist whose views on ethnology proclaim him a European racist similar to Gobineau and differing from the latter not so much in virulent prejudice as in the semblance of respectability. His self-regarding elevation of the "white man, the European" is no less intoxicated than Gobineau's. "Man par excellence" is Tocqueville's description of the "white man, the European," who also is "the first in enlightenment, power, and happiness."

Tocqueville's observations on the "United States Negro" must therefore be interpreted in the light of his white European racism. He can then be understood much better. He says of the "Negro":

Devoid both of wants and of pleasures, useless to himself, his first notions of existence teach him that he is the property of another who has an interest in preserving his life; he sees that care for his own fate has not devolved on him; the very use of thought seems to him an unprofitable gift of Providence, and he peacefully enjoys all the privileges of his humiliation. If he becomes free, he often feels independence as a heavier burden than slavery itself, for his life has taught him to submit to everything, except to the dictates of reason; and when reason becomes his only guide, he cannot hear its voice. A thousand new wants assail him, and he lacks the knowledge and the energy needed to resist them. Desires are masters against whom one must fight, and he has learned nothing but to submit and obey. So he has reached this climax of affliction in which slavery brutalizes him and freedom leads him to destruction.

Tocqueville reflects:

Seeing what happens in the world, might one not say that the European is to men of other races what man is to the animals? He makes them serve his convenience, and when he cannot bend them to his will he destroys them. [*Democracy in America*.]

The last sentence at least is incontestable.

A good deal of the relative complacency exhibited by the people called Negroes on the question of their correct group designation is a result of the want of social energy necessary to contest this additional indignity. Most, if not all, of their available energy has been absorbed by the struggle for survival. With them, it is always a stern business of the ordering of priorities. First things first, and first among them is survival. Only when the chances of survival have appeared to increase have some of them been able to give their attention to this question of their just ethnic designation. When Du Bois wrote his well-known letter to his young black correspondent, this matter of priorities doubtless was uppermost in his mind. When a man is on a gallows with his neck already encircled by the noose, he is unlikely to spend much time considering whether his name is correctly inscribed on his birth certificate. He is more likely to be scanning the mob of lynchers for a friendly face whose intervention on his behalf might stay the mob from its purpose. For a long time in America the primary business of the black people has been to distinguish here and there a friendly face amidst the howling concourse of savage white lynchers intent on a sacrificial rite of appeasement of their tribal god, racism.

The white Christian world of the West has worshiped two gods above all: the creature of their eschatology, the expropriated folk deity, Jehovah, of their age-old victims, the Jewish people; and their own indigenous god of race. They make collective war in the name of the former; in the name of the latter they make caste law. The social consequences of both of these theocratic institutions are indistinguishable from those of earlier cultures as a form of human sacrifice. A white lynch mob anywhere in America is as much engaged in a sacrificial rite as any group of Aztecs honoring their god or Cretans appeasing their Minotaur. The custom of human sacrifice persists throughout the whole record of human culture. Religious ritualism is merely one of its institutional forms; there are secular forms as well. A lynch mob is an instance.

On the level of deliberate social organization, however, war is its most massive expression. The technology of the white Western world, together with its fanatical devotion to the mystique of racial caste, has enabled it to practice the rite of human sacrifice on a scale unparalleled in the history of the animal species. Of all the divisions of mankind, the white groups are the most ardent devotees of this ancient custom. Not only do they sacrifice countless millions of their own groups by the institutional device of mass warfare; but by the social contrivance of caste distinctions on a basis of racial identity, they also make untold numbers of nonwhite sacrifices. Never has any sector of mankind exhibited such fidelity to its chosen god. For several centuries past, its principal victims outside its own group have, of course, been the nonwhite peoples, principally blacks, although it is only fair to say that the whites have probably slaughtered more of their own people than they have of any other group. In the first half of the twentieth century alone, they sacrificed upward of 100 million of themselves by institutional warfare, which is their favorite form of human sacrifice. Continuing the classical tradition of their European forebears, paralleled by Central American and other cultures elsewhere in the world, they have concentrated in particular, since the beginning of the twentieth century, on the ritual sacrifice of young people on a rapidly expanding scale.

In the First World War, the nations of Europe sent their finest youth in unrestrained numbers to die as human sacrifices on the institutional altars of intergroup warfare. So, too, twenty-five years later, in the Second World War. The United States was, for briefer periods, similarly engaged, during these two ritualistic episodes, in Europe, North Africa, and the Pacific; later on in Korea, as well, and then in Vietnam, where for more than a decade now it has been fanatically absorbed in mass human sacrifice, especially of the young. A characteristic feature of the practice of human sacrifice has always been its confinement to young people. It is always the old who condemn the young to die, who consign them to their fate as human sacrifices. The young are sacrificed to the gods of the tribe on the altars of battle. The old die in their beds. They are clever and resourceful at finding reasons for the young to die. But they never fight wars themselves. They are too decrepit for such a purpose; too cowardly to take the inherent risks. After all, they may lose their precious lives, be maimed, or otherwise hurt; and in their old age, too. So, instead, they instigate wars in order that they may carry on the immemorial custom of human sacrifice of the young. Yet, as soon as the young people of the world realize this—as they are gradually coming to do—and organize themselves powerfully enough to force the old men who make wars to go out and fight them, there will be no more war. This form of human sacrifice will have come to an end. Perhaps, however, another will take its place.

In the evolution of American society, the institution of human sacrifice expressed itself, typically, in the near extermination of Indians and the large-scale lynching of blacks. The latter was a regional, the former a country-wide, phenomenon. Both were the consequences of white racism. The massacre of the Indians was incidental to the expansion of the American frontier, which, itself, was a revolutionary process of the deepest import. Human sacrifice was practiced in the course of this development as a racial principle, much as the Nazis chose a religious basis for their maintenance of the custom in the case of the Jewish people; or, previously, like Leopold II of Belgium, whose racist rationale, justifying commercial greed, dictated the slaughter and maiming of millions of Africans in the Congo; or as in the instance of the French in Madagascar after the Second World War, whose massive atrocities were inseparable from their racist inspiration. The modern practice of human sacrifice is no longer restricted to the selective murder of the young by draft laws and other components of the ritual machinery of mass warfare. It is now carried out, as well, on the principle of racial caste.

Other urges, less atavistic and more immediate in their origin, were also operative in the extension of the American frontier. The pushing back of the frontier was, in a manner of speaking, the continuous obbligato against which the raucous melody of the evolution of the American society was counterpointed. It began at the very beginning of the country's existence and continued throughout all its embroilments, domestic as well as foreign. Nothing interrupted the process. Neither the War of Independence, the War of 1812, the Civil War, the Mexican and Indian wars (which, indeed, were an integral part of the process), or the Spanish-American War late in the nineteenth century. In essence it was a revolution, with no lesser objective than to transform the life of a continent and subdue it to the needs of new ownership. A multitudinous tide of European migrants rolled across the country, impelled by the desire for freedom, the spur of the prospect of self-fulfillment, lust for gold, greed for land, and the Christian imperative of white racism. As the pioneers spread out and penetrated, acquired and prospered, slaughtered and subjected, the blacks toiled, were shackled, and endured. The Indians fought, resisted, and were massacred.

Gunpowder overcame the Indians as it had the Africans and, earlier, the Indians of Central America, the Caribbean, and Mexico. It is an interesting reflection that the Chinese, on discovering gunpowder, diverted it into the relatively harmless production of firecrackers. The Europeans adapted it to the manufacture of guns. With this new weapon they conquered the world. The white groups of mankind are the people of the gun. This instrument of death is the deity they worship and upon whose altar they offer up numberless millions of human sacrifices.

140

5

THE GUN has been the principal architect of the American society. Without their possession of the gun, the European migrants would have been repulsed and contained by the North American Indians. Without their possession of the gun, the fauna of the great plains would have had a better chance of survival against their penchant for indiscriminate slaughter. Without their possession of the gun, the frontier would have resisted conquest, delaying and protracting it until, perhaps, the moral evolution of the migrants had progressed to the point of an understanding respect for the life of the land. But the gun eliminated the need for moral progress while it facilitated the advance of the covered wagon. In the ensuing event, Indians were decimated and certain forms of wild life all but exterminated. Nor did the destruction of life stop there. It extended to stream and lake and river, mountain, valley, and forest, ocean and air. The covered wagon conveyed white Christian culture throughout the land; and, in an ecological sense, it conveyed pollution. The destruction of the environment that began on this continent with the early European settlements in North America has traditionally been concealed or ignored by historians eager to celebrate the technological triumphs of white culture. The American frontier was extended at such an excessive cost of human values that, as in the present instance of the Vietnam war, the whole American society is branded with an indelible impress of wanton deceit and murderous cruelty. The European incursion into North America developed into an ethnic revolution that overthrew the cultural values of the indigenous Indian civilization and replaced them by an ethnocentric monotheism whose religious precept was peace but whose secular practice was war. The crucifix was its heavenly symbol, the gun its earthly sovereign.

Upon these twin foundations, the cross and the gun, the transplanted European culture established itself in the North American environment. It moved from a scattered nucleus of agricultural and trading-post communities to a sparsely populated preindustrial society, thence through industrialism to advanced technology. These developments manifested themselves as a general principle of social and economic co-operation that made possible the large-scale organization of steamboat transport, the country-wide extension of the railroads, the telegraph and electricity, as well as the factory system. It also made possible the successful penetration of the covered wagon into the undiscovered continent and the survival of the pioneer settlements, as it had made possible the survival of the earlier settlements of New England colonists.

Co-operation ensured the triumph of the new culture, yet the very magnitude of the task confronting these vigorous and intrepid people left them perhaps too little time for contemplating the moral issues involved in their headlong and remorseless advance across the land. The material prosperity they quickly achieved also provided them with too little incentive for such exercises in moral self-examination. They were people in a hurry. Problems had to be solved at once; rivers to be bridged, mountains to be climbed, cold and heat to be endured, dangers to be faced, Indians and rattlesnakes, buffalo and bison to be killed; food to be procured, hunger and thirst to be assuaged; land to be taken and held, gold to be prospected and mined; individual self-assertion to be attained at any price—and all in a hurry. No time for spacious reflection, for leisurely refinements of distinctions between good and evil. No time for anything but getting ahead. No space for a grand design of overarching social import. No inspiration save the instinctual tropism of material success against the environment. They covered the land like a stupendous army of warrior ants on the march, destroying everything in their path and erecting termitaries along the way as monuments to their victorious passage. And since they were in such imperious haste, with problems of such remorseless urgency to be solved, they resorted to short-run devices that favored what was immediate and expeditious over what might be more broadly effective as a long-term solution. They were under unrelenting necessity to get going and to keep going, to get there and then to get moving again, and over and over again, until their appetite for land and their craving for gold could propel them no longer.

Indispensable to the whole enterprise, given their haste and greed, and given, too, their racist conviction of caste superiority, was the gun. To them its primary virtue was that it facilitated quick and decisive solutions of what might have otherwise been delaying or intractable problems. The gun disposed, decided, cleared the way, overcame the enemy. The gun was guardian, protector, defender, avenger. The gun was champion, the gun was magic, the gun was god: the white man's god. And so, the gun created the American society in its own image. Reciprocally, in its worship, a national shrine was erected to violence. And there, the whole culture—except the blacks —did reverence. The blacks were not permitted in those sacred precincts. They were discouraged from the use of guns. The gun was a caste weapon, the white man's weapon. It might be used against blacks but, so far as this could be arranged, never by them. Later on the white groups of North America and Europe, after the Second World War, would propose a convention by which arms should be withheld from Africa. The same principle was here at work. Black Africans, like black Americans, should not be allowed to use guns. Perhaps it was thought that they had too much to avenge. In any case, precisely as the sword was once a caste weapon and not permitted to be used by serfs or other inferior members of the social hierarchy, so the gun, also a caste weapon, must not be permitted to be used by blacks, who are, of course, caste inferiors in the white-racist stratification of mankind.

The national shrine erected to violence in the American society did not take the form of a hallowed artifact confided to a consecrated structure. It evolved instead as a group ethos, a conditioned and collective reflex, a national characteristic. "Violence," said H. Rap Brown, "is as American as cherry pie." He was right. The only trouble with the statement was that so incontrovertible a truth should have issued from the lips of a black man.

Yet while violence and the gun were sovereign in the settlement of the country, it would be a misstatement to assert that they alone conferred upon the new community a distinctive common form and national content. These migrants making their way across the country were the outriders of a social revolution, a turbulent cortège that had set out across the Atlantic from Europe two centuries earlier. Their curiosity and vigor, their conviction of the possibilities of social transformation on a scale matching the vast reaches of the newly discovered land, their resolution and hardihood, their intrepidity and imagination, their will, their courage, their enterprise—these all entered into the conquest of the American frontier, and each in turn and in sum contributed its own quantum of energy, its own inspiration of contour and definitive character, to the evolution of the American society. But this point must be grasped above all: it was in truest essence a revolution, a class revolution, whose initial impulse was religious but also economic, and which developed in due course, when it had been reinforced by subsequent influxes of the disaffected and outcast from Europe, into a massive effort to create across the Atlantic a new world liberated from the feudal shackles and obsolete ideology of the old. In their attempt to do so, these migrants shackled other human beings, notably millions of blacks. That was a monstrous tragedy. Yet a single fact remains untainted by any evil or short-coming: they dared to dream anew.

In the dreaming and the doing, they expressed the whole complex of circumstances, biological as well as cultural, by which they were molded. Originally European—and this implies both a genetic and sociological conformation—they gradually evolved in the transatlantic environment through the normal biological process of selection into a new and definitive human type, the American. An old, multitudinous variety of antecedents and the widely diversified environment they encountered across the Atlantic determined the selection. They had to deal with the environment to respond effectively to its challenge. Organization was their prime tool for this purpose. The value of co-operation thus became self-evident. Community in turn became the political expression of the need to organize and co-operate for the conquest of the environment. On these facts alone there would be nothing in the process of becoming American to set it apart from the experience of other human groups throughout recorded history in their struggle for survival. But there are other facts to be taken into account. For one, intellectual influences played a role of the most distinct consequence.

If the Protestant ethic, especially in its Calvinist inspiration, was the main religious spur to the settlement at Jamestown in 1607; if,

144

indeed, as Max Weber, in *The Protestant Ethic and the Spirit of Capitalism*, and R. H. Tawney, in *Religion and the Rise of Capitalism*, would have it, this imperative not only sanctified but also set in motion the social energies that created the modern capitalist system, then, equally, the world-transforming impetus conducted into the organization of transatlantic society by Social Darwinism must be recognized. The roots of this secular development had long since been implanted deeply and luxuriantly in the capitalist organization of society by the Protestant insistence upon the supreme value of the individual responsible only to God. The notion of individual responsibility, whose sole arbiter on earth was private conscience, could locate its philosophical ancestry in the Reformation. The notion of the social contract, which so deeply permeated the political consciousness of the settlers and their pioneering attempts at communal organization, was part and parcel of liberal thought in England in the seventeenth century. The religious dissidents carried it with them across the Atlantic. So also did they carry the English common law, by which they regulated their communal relations and which in time became in most of the jurisdictions of the new country a basic portion of the governing law.

The corpus of political exposition contained in *The Federalist* bears patent evidence of European intellectual influences. These luminous essays on civil polity are no less original for that, but it can only distort the truth to deny their profound indebtedness to European sources or to dismiss these latter as though American enlightenment had simply occurred, full-grown and mature, by some process of collective ingeneration. The fact is that only gradually did the European colonists and subsequent immigrants slough off their Old World origin and its concomitant traits of ethnic character. Only gradually did they become sufficiently removed from their ancestral past and its genetic and cultural consequences to be differentiated as *Homo americanus*. It did not take a single generation, or two or even three generations. For necessarily involved, in addition to survival by selection in the new environment, was the pure biological process of genetic combination and recombination. When this had occurred—and the process might be longer or shorter in individual instances—an American emerged. By then he had both adapted and transcended his pristine European influences, intellectual and otherwise. But they were his influences, and it is simply pointless to deny it.

The counterargument that new immigrants may become Americans in short order merely by a period of residence here and a rejection of European influences is the emotional resort of immigrants over-anxious to regard themselves as Americans. (These are the people who also become, in equally short order, superpatriots.) But this point of view does much less than justice to the genetic and cultural truth of the matter. No one, surely, needs to be reminded that as late as the last years of the nineteeenth century and the early years of the twentieth, one of the greatest of American writers, Henry James, was still preoccupied with the then contemporary influence of European culture on American thought and matters (see *The Ambassadors*). Nor was he alone in his preoccupation. The servility of American social ideas and practices to European norms was scandalous outrage to the sensibilities of many American commentators. Europeans indulged their ethnocentrism to the utmost at the expense of Americans who had, with little or no resistance, accepted the notion that in the realm of "civilized" forms and behavior what was European was by that fact superior to what was American. It was long after the Civil War and well toward the end of the century before American writers, for example, acquired enough self-confidence to cease imitating British letters and assert their native inspiration as indubitably equal.

A social history of the United States up to the First World War, if it were accurate and not mistakenly chauvinistic, would be to a considerable extent a record of the persistence of European influences on the evolution of the American society and on the habits of thought of the transatlantic immigrants, who make up by far the largest segment of the population.

Yet more important than the precise degree of European influences is the larger question of their meaning. No one can fail to recognize the revolutionary impulse that drove these numerous millions, often in peril and still oftener in discomfort, across the ocean waste to a strange land. They were almost always people in revolt, either actual and explicit or inarticulated and latent, against the tradition-bound limitations of their European existence. Whether fomenters of revolution or its victims, they all had one thing in common: a conception of a personal existence replete with fulfillment of which, for centuries, Europe had starved them and their forebears. In an active and immediate sense, they aimed at a transformation of their customary lives, an inversion of the Old World order of society. They

146

wanted to ascend from lower to upper stations in free and open competition, the issue being determined by ability regardless of birth. Their aspiration was social freedom, and this was attained by every white immigrant immediately upon arrival in America. It was in effect a personal revolution successfully consummated by the sole act of crossing the Atlantic, always provided one were white.

One then set about becoming an American. Whiteness was the open sesame to the caste structure. With this ethnic classification, you were on your way. Your integration into American society would occur, as a matter of course, on a level that was in any event higher than that on which the integration of blacks had occurred. The blacks had been integrated into the society as untouchables. They were pariahs, as the untouchables of India were pariahs. But just as the untouchables of India were nonetheless Indians, so were the black untouchables of America nonetheless Americans. The untouchables of India were Indians with a completeness and authenticity sealed by history and sociology. No newcomers to India could be, after two or three generations, or, still less, claim to be, Indian with the profound ethnic validity that the untouchables could. In the same way, no new-comers to North America could be, after two or three generations, or, still less, claim to be, American with the profound ethnic validity that the black untouchables could. One of the salient defects of the leadership of the black untouchables in the United States is its mis-conception of the caste position of the black untouchables. With few exceptions—and Booker T. Washington is foremost among these—the leadership of the black untouchables in America has formulated its demand for release from the caste restrictions of untouchability in the language of "integration." This leadership has, in fact, been clamoring for what the black untouchables already possess. For the black untouchables have, for some fourteen generations or more, been integrated into the caste structure of American society exactly as the untouchables of India have been integrated into the caste structure of Indian society for millennia. The leadership of the black untouchables in America has therefore been attempting to solve a problem that in actuality does not exist. It has been making vociferous demands for "integration" when the real problem is social mobility; that is, social freedom. It is the immediate conferment of this attribute upon any white immigrant to America that essentially distinguishes him or her from the black American untouchables. This tendency of black leadership in America to set up straw problems rather than confront concrete issues that should compel attention is the typical behavior of people whose past experience has caused them to doubt their capacity for dealing successfully with surrounding actualities.

The white immigrant, once arrived in America and having automatically, as a reward for whiteness, been accorded social freedom, discovered that there was almost unlimited work to be done building, consolidating, and expanding the country. And the conditions of labor, in the tremendous scope of their promise, were revolutionary in the magnitude of reward they held out for performance. Labor in America —and here indeed was revolution—was engaged in organizing itself to challenge the vested right of a master to dictate the terms and remuneration of a laborer's service, and to establish its own right to negotiate an equitable return as its share of the capitalist enterprise. It was a frontal attack on the concept of surplus value, which Karl Marx had detected as the instrument by which capital in an industrial society reduces labor to wage slavery. Short of equal ownership of the means of production, the organization of labor as a countervailing monopoly offered the surest prospect of economic equality and its corollary, social equality, for the immigrant. But the real contest was for power: the power to dispose, rather than be disposed of; the power to own, to enjoy, to decide; the power to choose or, simply, abstain from choice. And the locus of this power was property, expressed either as the substance of ownership itself or as the right to ownership and the exploitation of ownership. The struggle between capital and labor was, in ultimate terms, a struggle for the ownership and control of the state power. In its nineteenth-century outcome, the victory went to capital. That was the meaning of the defeat of the Knights of Labor in its fatal conflict with the American Federation of Labor over the eight-hour day, a conflict that capital was not slow to aggravate in order to divide labor and so secure its own conquest of the state power. The same meaning is also to be read into the failure of the efforts of Samuel Gompers in 1886 to achieve the objective of the eight-hour day. The violence in Haymarket Square was a pretext, avidly seized upon by capital, to rally public sentiment against unionism in the name of law and order. When the workers struck the Pennsylvania and the Baltimore and Ohio railroads in 1877, violence was again a tragic accompaniment, which in its cumulative effect provided occasion for federal intervention. United States troops were sent to the scene and broke the strike. But perhaps the most graphic impression of the nineteenth-century power commanded by capital vis-à-vis labor might be seen in the ruthless self-assurance and sanguinary violence with which the Carnegie Steel Company smashed a strike organized by the Amalgamated Association of Iron, Steel and Tin Workers, at Homestead, Pennsylvania, in 1892. The American Railway Union went on strike two years later, also to resist a wage reduction. Here, too, violence erupted. Federal intervention took place by way of the dispatch of military units to Chicago and by the use of the Sherman Antitrust Law against the union. This combination of military (or paramilitary) force and legal sanctions was marshaled by capital against labor in one clash after another until 1932 and the passage of the Norris–LaGuardia Anti-Injunction Act. Under the New Deal of Franklin D. Roosevelt's administration, the legal position of the labor unions was vastly enhanced. For the first time, the grip of capital on the ownership and control of the state power was visibly loosened. The Norris–LaGuardia Act was supplemented by the Railway Labor Act of 1934 and the National Labor Relations Act of 1935. But the conflict between these two major economic forces was by no means at an end. Labor had grown stronger, yet power in the society—the collective state power—continued to gravitate toward whichever side exerted, at any given moment or in any complex of circumstances, the greater influence upon its field of interest.

The role of black labor in the struggle was confined, for the most part, to its remote perimeter; although, as early as 1850, an attempt had been made in New York City to organize black workers into a trade union. The workers' movement in the United States was racist from its earliest beginnings. It refused to admit blacks to its ranks and restricted them to segregated unions. By 1890, the year after A. Philip Randolph was born, there were more than 30,000 blacks organized in segregated unions on a craft basis. While the American Federation of Labor asserted the principle of unity among all workers irrespective of race, it did not hesitate at the same time to admit craft unions openly racist in their exclusion of black workers. Its sole concession to its declared ideal of unsegregated labor was in its conniving at an arrangement by which racial exclusion clauses were omitted from union constitutions, but white workers gave a secret undertaking not to propose blacks for membership. An exception was the United Mine Workers, to which black workers as a rule were freely admitted. The Bergmans calculate that in the year 1900, of "91,019 dues-paying members in the United Mine Workers . . . 20,000 were Negroes." But progress was gradual, and when in frustration black workers tried to organize an independent movement (the National Brotherhood Workers of America), white opposition, crystallizing in the American Federation of Labor, rendered it abortive. Yet an important advance was made in the year 1919. The American Federation of Labor passed a resolution against racial discrimination in union membership. It would be a long time before its translation into actual practice would occur, but it nonetheless represented something of a revolution in the philosophy of the white labor movement. In the same year, porters at Pennsylvania Station in New York founded the Brotherhood of Railway Station Attendants. The following year, the Brotherhood of Dining Car Employees was established. By 1925, A. Philip Randolph had organized the Brotherhood of Sleeping Car Porters. The subsequent development of this trade union is an important part of the economic history of the blacks in America.

Efforts at formal organization of black workers into trade unions or to secure their admission to such bodies were made against a background of continuous and wide-ranging participation by these workers in the building of the country as a whole.

Courts and legislatures alike participated in the labor struggle, and only gradually, with the advent of the twentieth century and the growing expansion of social consciousness, was labor able to win a footing of economic equality with capital. To do so, it was obliged to become as monopolistic as its corporate antagonist. The conflict had begun before the Civil War and continued after the termination of that struggle. It proceeded apace with the expansion of the frontier and the always increasing subordination of agrarianism to the industrial development of the country.

As a contribution to perspective, it is useful to bear in mind that the Battle of the Little Big Horn was fought and, subsequently, Chiefs Crazy Horse and Sitting Bull defeated as the counterrevolution of the white South was dismantling the fragile structure of Reconstruction. In the same way, some sense of historical proportion may be retained through selective awareness of critical episodes occurring, in some instances simultaneously and in others successively, against the background of the evolution of the national society. Two themes were mainly dominant. One was, of course, the expansion of the frontier, the aggrandizement of the country under the intoxicating stimulus of its Manifest Destiny. Here, a colossal and relentless energy was at work. Louisiana and Alaska were purchased and Texas annexed. The Oregon country and California were acquired. Along the Santa Fe, California, and Oregon trails trekked the pioneers. A century before the Gold Rush of 1848, the enticement of land and the prospect of amassing wealth had begun to lure them westward. Not even the enormous wastes of the Pacific Ocean could interpose an effective barrier against this stupendous tide of acquisitiveness. Thousands of miles distant from the coast of California, Hawaii and the Philippines were made client territories; the one to become, eventually, a state of the Union, the other to continue for almost fifty years its colonial exist-ence as an American satellite.

The other theme was slavery until the emancipation, after which it modulated into the struggle to organize labor in self-defense against corporate capitalism. Yet the racial question implicit in the presence of a large number of nonwhite people in the American population continued to dominate national developments in one form and another. Off stage at all times in the absorbing drama of the evolving country was the suppressed figure of a black man, waiting, waiting. The greatest social revolution in the history of the human species was un-folding, and among its chief protagonists were the blacks, at present free though formerly slave, yet even now scarcely better off than slaves. The organization of the factory system, the extension of the railroads, the construction of turnpikes and canals, a huge and intri-cate network of transport and communication, the transformation of rural communities into urban centers, the making of Americans—to all these things the blacks were virtually indispensable. But they were either derided in social theory or disregarded in political practice; or, what was worse, they were treated with a psychopathic malignity of which murderous cruelty was the prime ingredient.

The curious fact about the post-Reconstruction era and the suc-ceeding decades up to the emergence of Marcus Garvey after the First World War is the absence of any single commanding black voice raised in protest against the atrocities that were being perpetrated against the blacks of the United States during those years. Samuel Eliot Morison writes:

Altogether, the thirty years from 1890 to 1920 were the darkest for the dark people of America. And, sad to relate, a perverted form of democracy was responsible. . . . In general the Southern Negro submitted to his own

151

abasement and accepted the degraded status that his former masters forced upon him. His fellows in the North did nothing to help. No leaders then arose to fire his sullen heart with courage and determination to resist. For that he had to wait a century after Gettysburg.

The salient black figure of the period when the Black Codes were reintroduced in the South, and every vestige of the era of Reconstruction obliterated, was Frederick Douglass. But he was by now an embering fire. The flame that earlier had seared the slave owners and their supporters, and enkindled so much of the ardor of the abolition movement, was still alight but burned with diminished intensity. Douglass had become an office seeker. His first appointment was in the ironic vein of the anticlimactic nature of his later career. He was appointed United States Marshal of the District of Columbia by President Hayes, whose treacherous betrayal of the blacks had ended the Reconstruction era and delivered the black freedmen once more into the power of the white racist South.

Hayes was an enemy of the blacks, but he was not for that reason without cunning. To consummate the bargain by which federal troops were withdrawn from the South, Hayes, on succeeding to the Presidency, deprived the victims of his treachery of the one voice that, had it been raised on their behalf, would have drawn to their plight the attention of the world. He bought Douglass for the price of one of the minor offices in the gift of the American President. Some measure of insight into the underlying circumstances, from Douglass's standpoint, may be gained by reading his own estimate of the deplorable affair (in *The Life and Times of Frederick Douglass*).

On the 4th of March in that year [1881], I happened to be United States Marshal of the District of Columbia, having been appointed to that office four years previous to that date by President Rutherford B. Hayes. This official position placed me in touch with both the outgoing President and the President-elect. By the unwritten law of long-established usage, the United States Marshal of the District of Columbia is accorded a conspicuous position on the occasion of the inauguration of a new President of the United States. He has the honor of escorting both the outgoing and the incoming Presidents, from the imposing ceremonies in the U.S. Senate Chamber to the east front of the Capitol, where, on a capacious platform erected for the purpose, before uncounted thousands and in the presence of grave Senators, Members of Congress, and representatives of all the civilized nations of the world, the presidential oath is solemnly administered to the

President-elect, who proceeds to deliver his inaugural address, a copy of which has already been given to the press. In the procession from the Senate I had the honor, in the presence of all the many thousands of the dignitaries there assembled, of holding the right and marching close by the side of both Presidents. . . . I felt myself standing on new ground, on a height never before trodden by any of my people, one heretofore occupied only by members of the Caucasian race. . . . Personally it was a striking contrast to my early condition. Yonder I was an unlettered slave toiling under the lash of Covey, the Negro-breaker; here I was the United States Marshal of the capital of the nation, having under my care and guidance the sacred persons of an ex-President and of the President-elect of a nation of sixty millions, and was armed with a nation's power to arrest any arm raised against them. . . . I rejoiced in the fact that a colored man could occupy this height.

That was the public aspect of the matter. But what private impulse had led him to this height, as he esteems it? Once more in his own words:

When the War for the Union was substantially ended, and peace had dawned upon the land, as was the case almost immediately after the tragic death of President Lincoln, when the gigantic system of American slavery which had defied the march of time and resisted all the appeals and arguments of the abolitionists and the humane testimonies of good men of every generation during two hundred and fifty years, was finally abolished and forever prohibited by the organic law of the land, a strange and, perhaps, perverse feeling came over me. My great and exceeding joy over these stupendous achievements, especially over the abolition of slavery (which had been the deepest desire and the great labor of my life), was slightly tinged with a feeling of sadness. I felt that I had reached the end of the noblest and best part of my life. . . . Then, too, some thought of my personal future came in. . . . I was still in the midst of my years, and had something of life before me, and as the minister (urged by my old friend George Bradburn to preach antislavery, when to do so was unpopular) said, "It is necessary for ministers to live.". . . I could not now take hold of life as I did when I first landed in New Bedford, twenty-five years before; I could not go to the wharf of either Gideon or George Howland, to Richmond's brass foundry, or Ricketson's candle and oil works, load and unload vessels, or even ask Governor Clifford for a place as a servant. Rolling oil-casks and shoveling coal were all well enough when I was younger, immediately after getting out of slavery. Doing this was a step up, rather than a step down, but all these avocations had had their day for me, and I had had my day for them. . . . A man in the situation in which I found myself has not only to divest himself of the old, which is never easily done, but to adjust himself to the new, which is still more difficult. . . . But what should I do, was the question.

Hayes supplied the answer. The effect of Douglass's seduction by public office was catastrophic for the black freedmen of the white racist South. Not one black voice of compelling stature then remained to be lifted on their behalf. Few white voices of any significant authority were raised, yet this was only to be expected. Those that were so raised—like those of the novelist George Cable and Walter Hines Page of *The Atlantic Monthly*—were driven out of the South. Never, even in the dire extremity of their actual enslavement, had the blacks been so utterly abandoned. The general white attitude toward them amounted to no more than this: "After all, they are free now. What more are we supposed to do for them?" And the Northern blacks, bereft now of liberal white concern to stir their sluggish interest in their fellow blacks to active protest, enwrapped themselves in apathy and silence. "Murder, killing and maiming Negroes," writes W. E. B. Du Bois in his *Autobiography*,

raping Negro women—in the 80's and in the southern South, this was not even news; it got no publicity; it caused no arrests; and punishment for such transgression was so unusual that the fact was telegraphed North. Lynching was a continuing and recurrent horror during my college days: from 1885 through 1894, 1,700 Negroes were lynched in America.

But Frederick Douglass, while not silent, took up the meliorist position of comparing their improved circumstances at that time, as he viewed them, with the conditions of their past enslavement.

Bad as is the condition of the Negro today at the South, there was a time when it was flagrantly and incomparably worse. A few years ago he had nothing—he had not even himself. He belonged to somebody else, who could dispose of his person and his labor as he pleased. Now he has himself, his labor, and his right to dispose of one and the other as shall best suit his own happiness. He has more. He has a standing in the supreme law of the land—in the Constitution of the United States—not to be changed or affected by any conjunction of circumstances likely to occur in the immediate or remote future. The Fourteenth Amendment makes him a citizen, and the Fifteenth makes him a voter. With power behind him, at work for him, and which cannot be taken from him, the Negro of the South may wisely bide his time. The situation at the moment is exceptional and transient. The permanent powers of the government are all on his side. What

154

though for the moment the hand of violence strikes down the Negro's rights in the South, those rights will revive, survive, and flourish again. They are not the only people who have been, in a moment of popular passion, maltreated and driven from the polls. The Irish and Dutch have frequently been so treated. [*Life and Times.*]

It is not to justify so much as to understand Douglass's argument that we recall how, only a little while before, Senator Charles Sumner's appeal in the Senate for the right of the vote for the freedmen was dismissed with the retort that such legislation was unnecessary, for "the Negro was rapidly dying out, and must inevitably and speedily disappear and become extinct." Douglass commented that "inhuman and shocking as was this consignment of millions of human beings to extinction, the extremity of the Negro at that date did not contradict, but favored, the prophecy. The policy of the old master-class, dictated by passion, pride, and revenge, was to make the freedom of the Negro a greater calamity to him, if possible, than had been his slavery." Douglass was remarking on the subject of a proposal to instigate the exodus of the black freedmen from the South, a proposal favored by those he referred to as "leading colored men of the country."

Yet, taken altogether, this was a new Douglass or, at any rate, not the Douglass of old, who had channeled his tidal eloquence in uncompromising spate against the institution of slavery. This was a Douglass grown not less moral but more mellow, reasonable rather than evangelistic, a crusader still but a cross-bearer no longer. Douglass had tasted public office, and he had acquired a sense of the balancing restraints, a notion of the reflective equipoises, that accompany the possession of power. His counsel was sought by Presidents of the United States, his friendship by the eminent in all walks of life. On the death of his first wife he had married a white woman. The successive offices he held—United States Marshal of the District of Columbia, Recorder of Deeds of the District of Columbia, and Minister and Consul General to the Republic of Haiti—all had the effect of detaching him from partisanship, though not diminishing his attachment to the cause of the black freedmen. Yet, as an active force from day to day in developments affecting the blacks of the United States, his role was necessarily limited and conditioned by his acceptance and enjoyment of public office. He now had the time as well as the inclination to discuss the niceties of protocol surrounding the office of United States Marshal of the District of Columbia, and to justify his exclusion by President Hayes from carrying out certain of the traditional duties of the office. His revolutionary fervor had abated, and, in a historical metaphor for which he displayed some fondness, his passion for Rome was tempered by his growing reverence for Caesar. Nothing else so dramatizes the decline of the great revolutionary as his temporizing assessment of the plight of the black freedmen in the South. To repeat the relevant passage: "With power behind him, at work for him, and which cannot be taken from him, the Negro of the South may wisely bide his time. The situation at the moment is exceptional and transient." This is the language of a social democrat in metamorphosis from the revolutionary figure he had once been. Accession to public office frequently has this effect, but it was a tragedy for the Southern blacks that their natural leader, whose greatness had been so magnificently attested by his devotion to their cause, was now grown moderate and his counsels to them more designed to reassure his federal patrons than to reawaken the resistance of his fellow blacks to the enormities being revived and practiced against them. Frederick Douglass in full revolutionary battle against the intolerable evil that was slavery moved in close and natural intimacy with the revolutionary rhythm of America itself, and was for that reason a towering national figure. Frederick Douglass in tepid retrenchment of his once impassioned zeal for the rights of his fellow blacks went counter to that rhythm and, while he remained of large historical significance, became an officeholder, a beneficiary of federal patronage. Hayes had done to Douglass in this symbolical fashion what white mobs have so often inflicted in actuality upon black men: he had castrated him. It was not that Douglass ceased to speak out for his people, but his tone now was one of eunuchoid accommodation. It was not that he ceased to exhibit lofty indignation. He seemed no longer capable of flaming anger. He was not so much tamed as tethered—a lion on a chain. So there he was, Frederick Douglass, with his federal job and his white wife at the end of it all.

There had been portents in the sky. Douglass tells about a return visit to his former owner, when the latter addressed him as "Marshal Douglass," in deference to his position as United States Marshal of the District of Columbia: "Hearing myself called by him 'Marshal Douglass', I instantly broke up the formal nature of the meeting by saying, 'not *Marshal*, but Frederick to you as formerly.'" Whatever might be inferred from this incident as to Douglass's modesty, an equal inference must be drawn as to his accommodationism. His relationship to his former master had undergone a revolutionary change in the more than forty years that had elapsed. The eagerness he displayed to return his erstwhile owner to the more comfortable mode of the master-slave form of address might be thought to have betrayed on Douglass's part a sentimental regard incompatible with the self-respect to be expected of a man of his fiber who had personally experienced the horrors of slavery. Nor did the old slave owner perform out of character on his deathbed, as then he was. "Frederick, I always knew you were too smart to be a slave, and had I been in your place, I should have done as you did." To which Douglass replied: "Capt. Auld, I am glad to hear you say this. I did not run away from *you*, but from *slavery*; it was not that I loved Caesar less, but Rome more."

There is about this episode almost the flavor of a nostalgic regret that the quondam slave had been obliged to desert his master. No reflection on the latter had been intended; it was simply a protest against the institution of slavery.

The ability of some slaves to distinguish between slavery and slave owners is a unique feat of moral casuistry. In Douglass's case, it accedes to a special interest because of his gradual descent from the abolitionist heights of social revolution to a postemancipation plateau of social accommodation.

In 1876, a century after the War of Independence, the infamous compromise was negotiated between big business and the South by which Reconstruction was terminated and the black freedmen all but relegated to their pre-Civil War condition of servitude. In that very year, on April 14, Douglass spoke at the unveiling of the Freedmen's Monument, in memory of Abraham Lincoln, in Lincoln Park, Washington, D.C., He said, in part:

We fully comprehend the relation of Abraham Lincoln both to ourselves and to the white people of the United States. . . . Lincoln was not, in the fullest sense of the word, either our man or our model. In his interest, in his associations, in his habits of thought and in his prejudices, he was a white man. He was pre-eminently the white man's President, entirely devoted to the welfare of white men. He was ready and willing at any time during the first years of his administration to deny, postpone, and sacrifice the rights of humanity in the colored people in order to promote the welfare of the white people of this country. . . . He came into the Presidential chair upon one principle alone, namely, opposition to the extension of slavery. His arguments in furtherance of this policy had their motive and mainspring in his patriotic devotion to the interests of his own race. To protect, defend, and perpetuate slavery in the states where it existed Abraham Lincoln was not less ready than any other President to draw the sword of the nation. He was ready to execute all the supposed constitutional guarantees of the United States Constitution in favor of the slave system anywhere inside the slave states. He was willing to pursue, recapture, and send back the fugitive slave to his master, and to suppress a slave rising for liberty, though the guilty master were already in arms against the Government. The race to which we belong were not the special objects of his consideration. Knowing this, I concede to you, my white fellow-citizens, a pre-eminence in this worship at once full and supreme. First, midst, and last, you and yours were the objects of his deepest affection and his most earnest solicitude. You are the children of Abraham Lincoln. We are at best only his step-children, children by adoption, children by force of circumstances and necessity. . . . But . . . we entreat you to despise not the humble offering we this day unveil to view, for while Abraham Lincoln saved for you a country, he delivered us from a bondage, one hour of which, according to Jefferson, was worse than ages of the oppression your fathers rose in rebellion to oppose. . . . Our faith in him was often taxed and strained to the uttermost, but it never failed. . . . When he strangely told us that we were the cause of the war—when he still more strangely told us to leave the land in which we were born—when he refused to employ our arms in defence of the Union—when, after accepting our services as colored soldiers, he refused to retaliate our murder and torture as colored prisoners—when he told us he would save the Union if he could with slavery—when he revoked the Proclamation of Emancipation of General Frémont—when he refused, in the days of the inaction and defeat of the Army of the Potomac, to remove its popular commander who was more zealous in his efforts to protect slavery than to suppress rebellion—when we saw all this, and more, we were at times grieved, stunned, and greatly bewildered; but our hearts believed while they ached and bled. Nor was this, even at that time, a blind and unreasoning superstition. . . . We saw him, measured him, and estimated him. . . . We came to the conclusion that the hour and the man of our redemption had somehow met in the person of Abraham Lincoln.

No one knew better than Douglass that Abraham Lincoln did only what he was constrained to do, and no more. But no one could have dissembled this knowledge in more magnificent rhetoric. The question is: Why did he conclude that it was better to be charitable than to be just? For whose advantage? It cannot, surely, have been for the benefit of his fellow blacks in the South then about to be returned, shackled hand and foot by the secret terms of a nefarious arrangement between Republicans and Democrats, to further decades of brutal suppression. It cannot have been for the benefit of his fellow blacks elsewhere in the country, who had no need of his panegyric adornment of Abraham Lincoln. To whose attention, then, were these lapidary utterances really directed? Departing from charity only in order to be just, one cannot help detecting a particle of self-interest in Douglass's soaring benediction. This was Douglass the officeholder. In him passion now was not spent; it had simply been redirected to the pursuit of his own self-interest. He had not grown cold to the cause of his people, or even lukewarm, but he had rearranged his priorities. He had done his work—as unquestionably he had—and now he was taking his wages. The succession of federal appointments, the white wife, the temperate, calculated utterances, the confidence of Presidents, the friendship of the eminent—a man's mountaintop, when gained, either afflicts him with vertigo or induces in him a self-enraptured quietism, a narcosis of the heights. The latter was the case with Frederick Douglass.

It is not to detract from his indubitable greatness to say that he never was deficient in vanity. The misfortune from the standpoint of the black freedmen was that this profoundly human weakness was too clearly evident to his enemies and theirs—the racist whites. These latter were not slow to turn it, with every aspect of well-meaning, against him. The result was that they thereby succeeded in decapitating the black freedmen of their most distinguished and respected leadership. So that the question arises to tantalize historical speculation: had Frederick Douglass accepted John Brown's invitation to accompany him to Harpers Ferry and died in battle there or afterward shared John Brown's fate, would he perhaps have deserved in the end to rank with no lesser figure in the pantheon of American greatness than General Robert E. Lee? As it turned out, the last twenty years of his life owe their luster more to the afterglow of sunset than to the luminous rays of the afternoon sun. For Douglass, the postlude of the Civil War and the emancipation was anticlimactic. Here, painted with his own unconscious brush, is a portrait of the lion in captivity.

Although I was not a delegate to this National Republican Convention [1888], but was, as in previous ones, a spectator, I was early honored by a spontaneous call to the platform to address the convention. It was a call not to be disregarded. It came from ten thousand leading Republicans of the land. It offered me an opportunity to give what I thought ought to be the accepted keynote to the opening campaign. How faithfully I responded will be seen by the brief speech I made in response to this call. It was not a speech to tickle men's ears or to flatter party pride, but to stir men up to the discharge of an imperative duty. It would have been easy on such an occasion to make a speech composed of glittering generalities, but the cause of my outraged people was on my heart, and I spoke out of its fulness, and the response that came back to me showed that the great audience to which I spoke was in sympathy with my sentiments. [*Life and Times.*]

While Douglass was proclaiming at that convention, and later from the hustings, his undying loyalty to the Republican party, the Southern blacks were experiencing the severities of a period of repression that had been ushered in by the connivance of that party with its opposite number. "This was an era of lynchings," writes Morison "which reached their apex in 1892 with 226 extra-judicial mob-murders, 155 of them Negroes." Douglass had been recalled in 1891 from Haiti, where he had spent the two previous years as Minister and Consul General, the last of his federal jobs. He implies that his immurement in federal offices of profit during two critical decades of the post-reconstruction period is to be attributed to financial necessity, on the one hand, and, on the other, to his unfitness for any specific job now that

the antislavery platform had performed its work, and my voice was no longer needed. . . . I felt it was necessary for me to live, and to live honestly. But where should I go, and what should I do? . . . My public life and labors had unfitted me for the pursuits of my earlier years, and yet had not prepared me for more congenial and higher employment. . . . But what should I do, was the question. [*Life and Times.*]

He lectured, and he engaged in journalism and in banking. The first activity was remunerative, the other two disastrous. Lecturing meant, as it usually does, an itinerant existence, which, however profitable it may be, is also unsettling. Then, too, with the emancipation of the slaves, public interest in the question had waned. No career now lay open, as hitherto, to an ex-slave able to narrate his experiences, as well as denounce slavery, in eloquent and moving language. Othello's occupation was gone. In his profound gratitude and relief at being given the post of United States Marshal, he failed to discern President Hayes's cunning misuse of him and was insensible to the task that still awaited his superlative gifts in the vacant leadership of the black

160

freedmen oppressed by vengeful white racism with the sanction, tacit or expressed, of both major political parties.

For a time he thought of founding an Industrial College for Negroes. In a letter to Harriet Beecher Stowe, he wrote:

Prejudice against the free colored people in the United States has shown itself nowhere so invincible as among mechanics. The farmer and the professional man cherish no feeling so bitter as that cherished by these. The latter would starve us out of the country entirely. At this moment I can more easily get my son into a lawyer's office to study law than I can into a blacksmith's shop to blow the bellows and to wield the sledgehammer. . . . We must become mechanics; we must build as well as use furniture; we must construct bridges as well as pass over them, before we can properly live or be respected by our fellow men. We need mechanics as well as ministers. We need workers in iron, clay, and leather. We have orators, authors, and other professional men, but these reach only a certain class, and get respect for our race in certain select circles. . . . We must not only be able to black boots, but to *make* them. [*Life and Times.*]

Douglass here foreshadows Booker T. Washington's subsequent view of the economic destiny of the emancipated blacks in America. It is probable, in fact, that Washington's position in this matter was directly influenced by Douglass.

But if Douglass was, as we have seen, not acquiescent in the resurgence of white racist power in the South (though his absorption in federal jobs certainly made him more or less quiescent), what, then, of Booker T. Washington? We may cite the latter's contemporary and his philosophical opponent W. E. B. Du Bois, from *Dusk of Dawn:*

At a time when Negro civil rights called for organized and aggressive defense, he broke down that defense by advising acquiescence or at least no open agitation. During the period when laws disfranchising the Negro were being passed in all the Southern states, between 1890 and 1909, and when these were being supplemented by "jim-crow" travel laws and other enactments making color caste legal, his public speeches, while they did not entirely ignore this development, tended continually to excuse it, to emphasize the shortcomings of the Negro, and were interpreted widely as putting the chief onus for his condition upon the Negro himself.

There was little temperamental affinity between Washington and Du Bois. Indeed, it might be concluded from reading accounts of such personal contact as there was between them that they disliked each other. Certainly their respective approaches to the common problem of the condition of their fellow blacks were deeply divergent from the standpoint of method as well as objective. Washington was born into slavery in Virginia; the year 1856 seems to be preferred by scholars. He was given the name Booker Taliaferro by his mother. The surname she bestowed upon him might have been indicative of his paternity. But much of all this concerning Washington (the name he chose for himself) remains obscure or obliterated by the customs of slavery. In a sense so primal and absolute as almost to suggest that he was, virtually, his own creator, Washington was the architect of his life. He asked his mother for a book by which he might teach himself to read. By some means or other—and the effort involved in the prevailing circumstances was not less than superhuman—she managed to obtain for him "an old copy of Webster's 'blue-black' spelling book, which contained the alphabet, followed by such meaningless words as 'a', 'b', 'ca', 'da'. I began at once to devour this book, and I think that it was the first one I ever had in my hands."

Du Bois's childhood introduction to letters was a world apart in its profound and formative difference. His introduction to the world itself was, qualitatively, a planet's distance away from the scene and circumstances of Washington's birth. Washington was born at such an extremity of creature squalor and social degradation that, by comparison, Du Bois was ushered into existence with all the appurtenances of a royal event. Washington wrote in his autobiography, *Up from Slavery:*

I was born a slave in Franklin County, Virginia. I am not quite sure of the exact place or exact date of my birth, but at any rate I suspect I must have been born somewhere and at some time. As nearly as I have been able to learn, I was born near a crossroads post-office called Hale's Ford, and the year was 1858 or 1859. I do not know the month or the day. The earliest impressions I can now recall are of the plantation and the slave quarters— the latter being the part of the plantation where the slaves had their cabins. My life had its beginning in the midst of the most miserable, desolate, and discouraging surroundings.

By contrast, Du Bois's account of his own beginnings reads with an unintended smugness. He says in his *Autobiography:*

I was born by a golden river and in the shadow of two great hills. . . . The house of my birth was quaint, with clapboards running up and down, neatly trimmed; there were five rooms, a tiny porch, a rosy front yard, and unbelievably delicious strawberries in the rear.

I was born [says Washington] in a typical log cabin, about fourteen by sixteen feet square. In this cabin I lived with my mother and a brother and sister till after the Civil War, when we were all declared free. . . . There was no wooden floor in our cabin, the naked earth being used as a floor. . . . Three children—John, my older brother, Amanda, my sister, and myself—had a pallet on the dirt floor, or, to be more correct, we slept in and on a bundle of filthy rags laid upon the dirt floor.

Du Bois traces his ancestry on his father's side back to

the black Burghardts [who] were a group of African Negroes descended from Tom, who was born in West Africa about 1730. He was stolen by Dutch slave traders and brought to the valley of the Hudson as a small child. [My mother was a descendant of] two French Huguenots, sons of Crétien Du Bois, [who in the early seventeenth century] migrated from Flanders to America. . . . They were in all probability artisans descended from peasants; but the white American family declares they were aristocrats, and has found a coat of arms which they say belongs to them.

Washington declares:

Of my ancestry I know almost nothing. . . . In the days of slavery not very much attention was given to family history and family records—that is, black family records. My mother, I suppose, attracted the attention of a purchaser who was afterwards my owner and hers. Her addition to the slave family attracted about as much attention as the purchase of a new horse or cow. Of my father I know even less than of my mother. I do not even know his name. I have heard reports to the effect that he was a white man who lived on one of the near-by plantations. Whoever he was, I never heard of his taking the least interest in me or providing in any way for my rearing.

As for early schooling, Du Bois says:

In the public schools of this town [Great Barrington, Massachusetts], I was trained from the age of six to sixteen, and in the town schools, churches, and general social life, I learned my patterns of living. I had, as a child, almost no experience of segregation or color discrimination. My schoolmates were invariably white; I joined quite naturally all games, excursions, church festivals; recreations like coasting, swimming, hiking and games. I was in and out of the homes of nearly all my mates, and ate and played with them. I was as a boy long unconscious of color discrimination in any obvious and specific way.

But here is Washington:

I had no schooling whatever while I was a slave, though I remember on several occasions I went as far as the schoolhouse door with one of my young mistresses to carry her books. The picture of several dozen boys and girls in a school room engaged in study made a deep impression upon me, and I had the feeling that to get into a schoolhouse and study in this way would be about the same as getting into paradise. . . .

I was asked not long ago to tell something about the sports and pastimes that I engaged in during my youth. Until that question was asked it had never occurred to me that there was no period of my life that was devoted to play. From the time that I can remember anything, almost every day of my life has been occupied in some kind of labour.

The contrasts between these two lives can be extended indefinitely. They represent almost, as it were, the light and the dark of the black experience in America. There could be little ground of belief or expectation common to two such vastly divergent beginnings. In actual fact, there would be more to bind Washington and the former slave owners together and render them congenial to each other than there would be between the bourgeois Negro scholar from New England and the Negro college administrator who had propelled himself with inconceivable pain and massive power of will from the abysmal depths of slavery. As for Washington and Frederick Douglass, though their origins were similar, their temperaments differed incisively. There was no point of his development at which, it may be deduced, Washington would have denounced the institution of slavery with the incandescent passion that enkindled Douglass and illuminated his audiences. The evidence suggests that Washington, while not less opposed to slavery, would have expressed his hostility in language that more nearly reflected his characteristic restraint. As he was to say in later years:

I pity from the bottom of my heart any nation or body of people that is so unfortunate as to get entangled in the net of slavery. I have long since ceased to cherish any spirit of bitterness against the Southern white people on account of the enslavement of my race.

Yet Washington, despite the fact that he was of a less combustible temperament than Douglass, was nonetheless more directly descended from the latter than was Du Bois in his attitude toward relations between blacks and whites outside the compass of slavery. Du Bois was fundamentally hostile to white people in general; Washington and Douglass were basically friendly to them. Both the latter, in their successive phases, advocated industrial training for blacks as the best way out of the economic blind alley and as a sure path to social upliftment for their ethnic group. Washington eventually carried this plan into effect by his development of such a school at Tuskegee, Alabama. The year of the founding of this institution was 1881, and the day, July 4. At this time the counterrevolution of white racism against Reconstruction was in full swing. The Black Codes had been reinstituted, the black freedmen effectively disfranchised. During these years an average of fifty blacks were being lynched annually, and the inertia of powerlessness had deepened their apathy and deprived the black population of the South of the slightest particle of collective will to resist. Douglass's response to this state of affairs has already been noted; a response conditioned significantly by his having been taken, so to speak, into the enemy camp. There he was, the great Frederick Douglass, tranquilized by the treacherous President Hayes with a succession of federal appointments, and subdued by his marriage to a white woman. There—without so much as a visible urge to shake the pillars of the temple, let alone pull down the structure that was, in practical effect, an inhuman prison for his people. At best, he could only compare the present to the past and take comfort in the fact that he and his fellow blacks were no longer slaves. What was Washington's reaction to the white racist counter-revolution? That he was conscious of the need to define his attitude is plain in his autobiography. There is indeed an aura of apology about his attempt at self-justification.

Though I was but little more than a youth during the period of Recon-struction [he suggests that this period encompasses the years from 1867 to 1878], I had the feeling that mistakes were being made, and that things could not remain in the condition that they were in then very long. I felt that the Reconstruction policy, so far as it related to my race, was in a large measure on a false foundation, was artificial and forced. In many cases it seemed to me that the ignorance of my race was being used as a tool with which to help white men into office, and that there was an ele-ment in the North which wanted to punish the Southern white men by forcing the Negro into positions over the heads of the Southern whites. I felt that the Negro would be the one to suffer for this in the end. Besides, the general political agitation drew the attention of our people away from the more fundamental matters of perfecting themselves in the industries at their doors and in securing property.

This remained his philosophical position and informed his strategy in dealing with the racial question throughout his public life. No

165

politics for black people, or, at any rate, as little as was practicable. Instead, large-scale concentration on industrial training for vocational purposes. Learn to make bricks, build wagons, sew and launder, but stay away from politics. "Of course," he says, speaking of the post-Reconstruction era, "the colored people, so largely without education, and wholly without experience in government, made tremendous mistakes, just as many people similarly situated would have done." He nevertheless believes that "not all the colored people who were in office during Reconstruction were unworthy of their positions." Yet, summarizing his highest wisdom in the whole matter, he wishes that

by some power of magic I might remove the great bulk of these people [those blacks with ambition for employment in the federal civil service] into the country districts and plant them upon the soil, upon the solid and never deceptive foundations of Mother Nature, where all nations and races that have ever succeeded have gotten their start—a start that at first may be slow and toilsome, but one that nevertheless is real.

The amelioration of the general problem then confronting the freed blacks seemed to Washington to consist of the development of a self-sufficient peasantry reinforced by industrial artisans; for the rest, abstention from politics, supplemented by a policy of making friends among well-intentioned whites. He does note, although with something like reluctance, the terroristic vigilantism of the Ku Klux Klan. This puts him in mind of the "patrollers" during slavery.

It was while my home was at Malden that what was known as the "Ku Klux Klan" was in the height of its activity [1877]. The "Ku Klux" were bands of men who had joined themselves for the purpose of regulating the conduct of the coloured people, especially with the object of preventing the members of the race from exercising any influence in politics. They corresponded somewhat to the patrollers of whom I used to hear a great deal during the days of slavery, when I was a small boy. The "patrollers" were bands of white men—usually young men—who were organized largely for the purpose of regulating the conduct of the slaves at night in such matters as preventing the slaves from going from one plantation to another without passes, and for preventing them from holding any kind of meetings without permission and without the presence at these meetings of at least one white man.

Like the "patrollers" the "Ku Klux" operated almost wholly at night. They were, however, more cruel than the "patrollers". Their objects, in the main, were to crush out the political aspirations of the Negroes, but they

166

did not confine themselves to this, because schoolhouses as well as churches were burned by them, and many innocent persons were made to suffer. During this period not a few coloured people lost their lives.

As a young man, the acts of these lawless bands made a great impression upon me. I saw one open battle take place at Malden between some of the coloured and white people. There must have been not far from a hundred persons engaged on each side; many on both sides were seriously injured, among them being General Lewis Ruffner, the husband of my friend Mrs. Viola Ruffner. General Ruffner tried to defend the coloured people, and for this he was knocked down and so seriously wounded that he never completely recovered. It seemed to me as I watched this struggle between members of the two races, that there was no hope for our people in this country. The "Ku Klux" period was, I think, the darkest part of the Reconstruction days.

I have referred to this unpleasant part of the history of the South simply for the purpose of calling attention to the great change that has taken place since the days of the "Ku Klux". To-day there are no such organizations in the South, and the fact that such ever existed is almost forgotten by both races. There are few places in the South now where public sentiment would permit such organizations to exist.

Washington published his autobiography in the year 1901, at a time when the Ku Klux Klan was certainly no less active than it had been in the preceding two decades. There is a moral astigmatism about Washington on the subject of black-white relations in the South that cannot be explained simply by adverting to his fanatical love of this region of the United States. Great men—and Booker T. Washington without the slightest question was a great man; as were Frederick Douglass and W. E. B. Du Bois—have loved their native places before this and yet have been able to avoid the uncritical ranting indistinguishable from outright misrepresentation of which Washington was guilty concerning Southern white racism toward the blacks. Was it hypocrisy? Was he merely dissembling his actual feelings in the matter? Or was he simply intent on the traditional Negro game of telling the white man only what the latter wished to hear? Or was he wishfully making unfounded statements in the hope that they might by some miracle turn out to have been self-fulfilling prophecies? Whatever his motive, his assessment of white racism in the South at most times represents, on any view, the subordination of objective reality to the egoistic necessities of a personal vision. He saw what he wished to see. More accurately, he *said* he saw it. Alteration of the

167

focus of vision is a well-known technique of survival. Negroes—and Washington pre-eminently among them—have long been masters of it. Martin Luther King was in his turn to exhibit this characteristic in a degree barely surpassed by Washington himself. Douglass substituted rationalization for it, as in his attitude toward the post-Reconstruction South. Du Bois did not necessarily see things as they were more clearly than either Douglass or Washington, but he did insist on rendering the content of his vision with uncompromising clarity. During these years of brutal reaction when Southern white racism stopped at nothing to reinvest the blacks with the bonds of servitude, which after two and one-half centuries they had only just cast off, Washington saw no evil, heard no evil, spoke no evil, thought no evil, did no evil. He was busy building Tuskegee. A laudable preoccupation. But was it enough? Was it a just price for his silence in the teeth of his certain knowledge of the torment and oppression of his fellow blacks? And if it was not, if indeed it was a betrayal, as on the part of Frederick Douglass it was, then might it yet be warranted by any pragmatic test, even the most cynical, of its actual outcome? Washington says in *Up from Slavery:*

When it is considered that the laying of this cornerstone took place in the heart of the South, in the "Black Belt", in the centre of that part of our country that was most devoted to slavery; that at that time slavery had been abolished only about sixteen years; that only sixteen years before that no Negro could be taught from books without the teacher receiving the condemnation of the law or of public sentiment—when all this is considered, the scene that was witnessed on that spring day at Tuskegee was a remarkable one. I believe there are few places in the world where it could have taken place.

Perhaps. Yet should not some doubt have gnawed at his conscience more insistently than it seems to have done, that even the building of Tuskegee could not justify what can only be described as his moral purblindness? It was one thing—and a magnificent thing—to erect and develop the great institution of Tuskegee; it was quite another thing—and a deplorable thing—to sublimate his consciousness of the sufferings of his people in a program that condemned them to further mutilation of their spirit while it brought comfort and a soothing release to the savagery of their white racist oppressors.

On Washington's death in 1915, W. E. B. Du Bois wrote of him as follows (in his *Autobiography*):

168

The death of Mr. Washington marks an epoch in the history of America. He was the greatest Negro leader since Frederick Douglass, and the most distinguished man, white or black, who has come out of the South since the Civil War. His fame was international and his influence far-reaching. Of the good that he accomplished there can be no doubt: he directed the attention of the Negro race in America to the pressing necessity of economic development; he emphasized technical education, and he did much to pave the way for an understanding between the white and the darker races.

On the other hand, there can be no doubt of Mr. Washington's mistakes and shortcomings: he never adequately grasped the growing bond of politics and industry; he did not understand the deeper foundations of human training, and his basis of better understanding between white and black was founded on caste.

We may generously and with deep earnestness lay on the grave of Booker T. Washington, testimony of our thankfulness for his undoubted help in the accumulation of Negro land and property, his establishment of Tuskegee and spreading of industrial education, and his compelling of the white man to think at least of the Negro as a possible man. On the other hand, in stern justice, we must lay on the soul of this man a heavy responsibility for the consummation of Negro disfranchisement, the decline of the Negro college and public school, and the firmer establishment of color caste in this land.

It might be argued that Du Bois's principal grievance against whites was that he was not himself white. There is reason to believe that this might not be an inaccurate location of the wellspring of his profound disesteem for the whites, who, after all, refused to treat him as a white man. It may be an unfair speculation, but it is irresistible to conjecture what he might have been like in his attitude toward the black-white problem had he been a white man. Granted his innate sense of justice, but granted also his temperamental aloofness and intellectual arrogance, his New England Brahmanism, what role would he have played, as a white man, in the racial conflict of his time? The suggestion may not be wide of the mark that he would have plunged into the struggle on the side of the oppressed, as others of his cultural type and attainments had done, notably, Wendell Phillips, William Ellery Channing, and Theodore Parker. But this perhaps would have been governed in Du Bois's case by the historical milieu. There can be little doubt that he would have been an abolitionist in the pre-Civil War era. Equally probable is it, however, that, assuming he were white, he would have been quite as removed from the arena as was, say, William James, during the post-Reconstruction period. Nor can the suspicion be dismissed altogether out of hand that, granted only he were white, he would have been capable of the attitude expressed in Emerson's advice to the abolitionists that they should "love their neighbors more and their colored brethren less." Yet the fact is that he was a black man in the sociological context of the United States of America. Speculation as to what he might have done had that not been the case may light up the dark side of the possible, but it also tends to obscure the tremendous actuality that was W. E. B. Du Bois. With Frederick Douglass and Booker T. Washington, he ranks as an equal member of a great revolutionary triad, precisely as later on Marcus Garvey, Malcolm X, and Martin Luther King might be seen to constitute another trinity of black revolutionaries.

All of these men were revolutionaries, each in his own fashion, against white racism. But while the descent from Douglass to Washington is lineal, it is collateral from Douglass and Washington, on the one hand, to Du Bois, on the other. Washington and Douglass were pragmatists, while Du Bois tended to be an ideologue. Neither of Du Bois's predecessors (they were also his contemporaries in the racial struggle) was in any decisive degree motivated by ideological considerations, except in so far as they might, and did, appeal to humanitarian traditions. On the other hand, Du Bois was a theorist of the human condition, a historian deeply acquainted with the blunders, the aberrancies, the triumphs and tragedies of trial and error bestrewing the path of the human species. He was also a sociologist acutely sensitive to the frailty of the ramshackle structure that is human society. Yet, as a scholar, he was inclined to deal in abstractions, which, whatever their foundation in brute fact, tended to divest issues of their flesh and blood, and to represent them as components of an impersonal process. All of these elements, present in Du Bois so that he never was compactly of one piece, converted him into an extraordinarily intelligent amalgam of the seething contradictions at the heart of American life. Powerful opposing tensions and scrupulous and intricate balances made him a hybrid to a degree unapproached by either Douglass or Washington: a New England Puritan who boasted of his enjoyment of "wine, women, and song"; a fastidious Brahman who did not shrink from contact with the creature squalor of the rural South; a scholar who was also the active organizer of the

170

political movement of Pan-Africanism; a disciple of William James, Josiah Royce, and George Santayana, who later became an apostle of Lenin. At the center of this vortex of contradictions was a brilliant mind indefatigably curious in its pursuit of knowledge, uncompromisingly critical in its evaluation of world society, inveterately hostile to white racism.

A shaft of irony glances off this reflection. For it is evident that there really was less in common (setting aside their blackness, as well as their converging commitment to racial justice) between, on the one hand, Du Bois and, on the other, Douglass and Washington than there was between Du Bois and any of the brilliant constellations of intellects, North and South, whose consuming motivation was dispassionate inquiry into the causes of things. But the peculiar circumstances of American life dissevered Du Bois from his natural compeers and associated him with those between whom and himself there was an ethnic connection: a connection whose inexorable demand was that he forgo all else and give his superlative mind to the cause of racial redemption. As he was fond of quoting from Goethe: "Thou shalt forego; shalt sacrifice."

All of his long life he made himself an unwearying protagonist in the remorseless struggle. He was subjected to every ignominy that a racist culture could devise, and he endured every humiliation it could impose. To a man of his magnificent gifts and attainments, life in America can only have been measureless spiritual agony. He sustained it, however, for more than ninety years, until he chose exile in Africa for the final three years of his life. What resemblance there was between Frederick Douglass and himself was confined to that period in Douglass's life before the Civil War—and indeed during the Civil War—when in clarion speech and writing he bared the horrors of slavery before the uneasy conscience of America. The postwar Douglass, the courtier-statesman, had little in common with Du Bois.

Washington, a dozen years older than Du Bois, was in his approach to the racial problem related to Douglass as accommodation is to moderation. He differed from Douglass to the extent that his was an extension in degree of the latter's fundamental attitude. Douglass and Washington counseled industrial training for blacks; Douglass and Washington centered the academic aspirations of blacks around a vocational college; Douglass and Washington offered blacks the consolation, and whites the justification, that whatever the present sufferings of the blacks under the iron repression of the post-Reconstruction era, their lot was infinitely better than it had been during slavery. Their point of view is explicable only when it is recalled that they were both slaves during the early years of their lives (Douglass, indeed, until he was a young man). Remembering how it had been with them and with others like them, they were inclined to view any condition short of slavery as tolerable, at least. This may have been understandable, yet it contributed little to bettering the lot of the Southern blacks groaning once more under a revived and virulent despotism. Their reaction to the post-Reconstruction era was not altogether dissimilar from the outlook expressed by a prayer of which Martin Luther King was fond: "Lord, we ain't what we goin' to be; we ain't what we want to be; but thanks, Lord, we ain't what we was." "Amen" would have been the joint and several response of Washington and Douglass.

Not so, however, of Du Bois. He was quite young, not yet out of his teens, when the post-Reconstruction period began, and at the time of Frederick Douglass's death in 1895, he was just beginning his public career. But Washington, then in his early forties, was approaching the height of his national fame as a sober conciliator of the deadly racial struggle that was tearing at the vitals of America. In 1895 Washington made his celebrated speech at the Atlanta Exposition. But well before that time he had formulated to his own satisfaction a basic philosophy for his personal guidance:

My own belief is, although I have never before said so in so many words, that the time will come when the Negro in the South will be accorded all the political rights which his ability, character, and material possessions entitle him to. I think, though, that the opportunity to freely exercise such political rights will not come in any large degree through outside or artificial forcing, but will be accorded to the Negro by the Southern white people themselves, and that they will protect him in the exercise of those rights. Just as soon as the South gets over the old feeling that it is being forced by "foreigners", or "aliens", to do something which it does not want to do, I believe that the change in the direction that I have indicated is going to begin. In fact, there are indications that it is already beginning in a slight degree. [*Up from Slavery.*]

The divergence between Washington and Du Bois at this point is so wide as to be unbridgeable. The former's concession of caste superiority to the racist whites, implicit in his fostering of the prospect

172

that contingent upon the Negro's "ability, character, and material possessions" the Southern whites in their *Herrenvolk* benevolence would confer his political rights upon him, was gall and wormwood to Du Bois. He would have none of that, in principle, and he saw no chance of it in actuality. He wrote in his *Black Reconstruction in America, 1860–1880:*

The effect of caste on the moral integrity of the Negro race in America has thus been widely disastrous; servility and fawning, gross flattery of white folk and lying to appease and cajole them; failure to achieve dignity and self-respect and moral self-assertion, personal cowardliness and submission to insult and aggression; exaggerated and despicable humility; lack of faith of Negroes in themselves and in other Negroes and in all colored folk; inordinate admiration for the stigmata of success among white folk: wealth and arrogance, cunning, dishonesty and assumptions of superiority; the exaltation of laziness and indifference as just as successful as the industry and striving which invites taxation and oppression; dull apathy and cynicism; faith in no future and the habit of moving and wandering in search of justice; a religion of prayer and submission to replace determination and effort.

And, he might also have added, a fatal weakness for resorting to words in preference to action. *Quand dire, c'est faire* is their collective motto, these black idolators of *la parole performative.*

Washington's acceptance of white caste superiority is further exemplified by his attitude toward the invitation to him to speak at the Atlanta Exposition. "The Atlanta officials," he declared in his autobiography, "went as far as they did because they felt it to be a pleasure, as well as a duty, to reward what they considered merit in the Negro race." This was the tragic fallacy at the heart of Washington's position: he had yielded to the white racists the capacity to "reward what they considered merit in the Negro race." That was a wretched capitulation, which can only be understood in the light of his previous enslavement. Accuracy requires it to be said, moreover, that this remains at the present day the attitude of many blacks who, unlike Booker T. Washington, have never been slaves. For them there is no excuse. But Washington at this time, 1895, was about to deliver his epoch-making address at the Atlanta Exposition. He began by reminding his hearers that "one-third of the population of the South is of the Negro race." He proceeded to speak of Negroes as "ignorant and inexperienced," and he remarked ironically,

173

it is not strange [and here he speaks of the Reconstruction era] that in the first years of our new life we began at the top instead of at the bottom; that a seat in Congress or the state legislature was more sought than real estate or industrial skill; that the political convention of stump speaking had more attractions than starting a dairy farm or truck garden.

In other words, he disapproved of the political gains made by Negroes during Reconstruction. They would have been better off, he suggests, in landholding, in acquiring industrial skills, or in farming or peasantry. He then went off at something of a tangent and admonished his fellow Negroes to "cast down your bucket where you are." He meant, he says, "Cast it down in making friends in every manly way of the people of all races by whom we are surrounded. Cast it down in agriculture, mechanics, in commerce, in domestic service, and in the professions." And here he asserts the fundamental canon of his philosophy:

Our greatest danger is that in the great leap from slavery to freedom we may overlook the fact that the masses of us are to live by the productions of our hands, and fail to keep in mind that we shall prosper in proportion as we learn to dignify and glorify common labour and put brains and skill into the common occupations of life. . . . No race can prosper till it learns that there is as much dignity in tilling a field as in writing a poem. It is at the bottom of life we must begin, and not at the top. Nor should we permit our grievances to overshadow our opportunities.

The sum and substance of this passage is the ratification of the institution of caste and the position of Negroes as the lowest stratum in the American society. This is the meaning behind all the high-souled rhetoric. But he goes on to define his conception of being, nevertheless, an American, despite the inferior caste position he humbly accepts.

To those of the white race who look to the incoming of those of foreign birth and strange tongue and habits for the prosperity of the South, were I permitted I would repeat what I say to my own race, "Cast down your bucket where you are". Cast it down among the eight millions of Negroes whose habits you know, whose fidelity and love you have tested in days when to have proved treacherous meant the ruin of your firesides. Cast down your bucket among these people who have, without strikes and labour wars, tilled your fields, cleared your forests, builded your railroads and cities, and brought forth treasures from the bowels of the earth, and helped make possible this magnificent representation of the progress of the South. Casting down your bucket among my people, helping and encouraging them as you are doing on these grounds, and to education of head, hand, and heart, you will find that they will buy your surplus land, make blossom the waste places in your fields, and run your factories. While doing this, you can be sure in the future, as in the past, that you and your families will be surrounded by the most patient, faithful, law-abiding, and unresentful people that the world has seen. As we have proved our loyalty to you in the past, in nursing your children, watching by the sickbed of your mothers and fathers, and often following them with tear-dimmed eyes to their graves, so in the future, in our humble way, we shall stand by you with a devotion that no foreigner can approach, ready to lay down our lives, if need be, in defence of yours, interlacing our industrial, commercial, civil, and religious life with yours in a way that shall make the interests of both races one.

This is what commentators like Daniel Boorstin and Oscar Handlin do not understand, this attitude on the part of a man like Booker T. Washington, a former slave. Washington does not see himself as a "foreigner," but as native to the South, and he reserves the appellation "foreigner" for "those of foreign birth and strange tongue and habits," that is, for the millions of European immigrants who were at that time debouching in a massive tidal wave upon the shores of America, and whom Henry George described as "human garbage." Washington knew that, by contradistinction, he and his fellow blacks of the South and elsewhere in the land were not "of foreign birth and strange tongue and habits." He knew that they were Americans, even though of an inferior caste in a racist society. They were Americans. He knew that. But up to this day people like Boorstin and Handlin do not. Washington understood, as they do not, what Wilbur J. Cash means when he writes, in *The Mind of the South*, of the relationship between Southern whites and Southern blacks as being

nothing less than organic. Negro entered into white man as profoundly as white man entered into Negro—subtly influencing every gesture, every word, every emotion and idea, every attitude.

Washington comes now to the climax of his address:

In all things that are purely social we can be as separate as the fingers, yet one as the hand in all things essential to mutual progress.

He drives the point home:

There is no defence or security for any of us except in the highest intelligence and development of all. If anywhere there are efforts tending to

175

curtail the fullest growth of the Negro, let these efforts be turned into stimulating, encouraging, and making him the most useful and intelligent citizen. Effort or means so invested will pay a thousand per cent. interest. These efforts will be twice blessed—"blessing him that gives and him that takes."

There is no escape through law of man or God from the inevitable:—

"The laws of changeless justice bind
Oppressor with oppressed;
And close as sin and suffering joined
We march to fate abreast."

The wisest among my race understand that the agitation of questions of social equality is the extremest folly, and that progress in the enjoyment of all the privileges that will come to us must be the result of severe and constant struggle rather than of artificial forcing. No race that has anything to contribute to the markets of the world is long in any degree ostracized. It is important and right that all privileges of the law be ours, but it is vastly more important that we be prepared for the exercise of these privileges. The opportunity to earn a dollar in a factory just now is worth infinitely more than the opportunity to spend a dollar in an opera-house.

. . . [there will be a] higher good that, let us pray God, will come, in a blotting out of sectional differences and racial animosities and suspicions, in a determination to administer absolute justice, in a willing obedience among all classes to the mandates of law. This, then, coupled with our material prosperity, will bring into our beloved South a new heaven and a new earth.

The main elements of his address were: the great labor potential of the black population of the South; the need for the blacks to realize that their best hope of progress lay in the South; the fact that this progress would be realized through training in industrial skills; the need for the white South to help train, and avail itself of, this large reservoir of black labor; economic co-operation but, at the same time, social separation; the mutual interdependence of the white and the black South; the folly of "agitating" questions of social equality; preparation by the blacks for the rights to which they are entitled; the priority of economic goals over cultural aspirations; and an appeal for an end, in time, to racial animosities, for impartial justice, and for submission by both blacks and whites to the law.

His paramount concern was with economic advancement for his fellow blacks. To him, this was, immediately at any rate, more important than anything else. It was, in fact, from his standpoint, the key to the solution of the entire problem. He deprecated participation in politics and frowned upon the "agitation" of questions of social equality. Reduced to their simplest essentials, his proposals to the South were for economic co-operation and social separation. He emphatically did not envisage the latter-day development known as integration, nor would he have favored it.

More than once in the course of his speech at the Atlanta Exposition, he referred to "foreigners," by which, quite clearly, he meant the European immigrants then pouring into the country. They were people of "foreign birth and strange tongue and habits." They were not Americans. He and his fellow blacks were Americans, he was implying, although admittedly of an inferior caste. Moreover, he assured the white South, "we shall stand by you with a devotion that no foreigner can approach, ready to lay down our lives, if need be, in defence of yours."

The attitude exhibited toward foreigners by the great black leader had its roots in the early American tradition of nativism. This cultural incident might occur (as it did in the colony of Massachusetts within three or four decades of the landing at Plymouth) in the form of anti-Catholicism. Or it might occur in the guise of regulations conferring upon the native-born prior right to the possession of land. It might also be expressed as hostility to free immigration. Toward the end of the nineteenth century and during the early years of the twentieth, the Restrictionists made their historical appearance. But they had been preceded in the eighteenth century by some of the most notable among the Founding Fathers. Benjamin Franklin opposed free immigration; so did Alexander Hamilton and Thomas Jefferson.

It was therefore as a black Restrictionist that Booker T. Washington made his slighting references to "foreigners."

Washington's address is, from a purely emotional point of view, the most accurate expression of the feelings of Southern blacks toward Southern whites ever uttered by any public figure of comparable distinction in the United States. The closest any other has come to it was when Martin Luther King counseled his followers that if blood must be shed in the South, then "let it be our blood, and not theirs." This is the love that passes Northern understanding, this transcendent love of Southern blacks for Southern whites, despite everything. Neither is it to be explained by the usual glib catalogue of Freudian hypotheses. It is probably much more the result of profound cultural hybridization intimately related, as well, to a long and persistent process of genetic combination and recombination. But there have also been psychological imponderables at work between these two groups, fusing them, beneath an exterior surface of violence and oppression, into a singular social entity.

Doctrinally, the present-day Black Muslims attempt to carry out in secular practice (no reference here to their theology) Washington's precept of social separatism. So also in general do the black nationalists. These two factions differ from Washington, however, in the prescribed degree of separatism. The latter recommended economic cooperation; but the former two groups advocate, on the whole, complete separation from whites to the extent of an autonomous state of their own within the country. Washington, of course, would have regarded this as undesirable and impractical. Yet there is a distinct resemblance between the solutions they all put forward. The difference arises from the more exclusive, as well as comprehensive, character of the proposals of the Black Muslims and black nationalists.

Nevertheless there is a clear ideological line of descent from Frederick Douglass through Booker T. Washington to Martin Luther King in so far as a supreme attachment to the South goes. With these men it amounted to hardly less than a fundamental religious belief. They worshiped the South, however much they might—and did—disapprove of certain Southern customs and institutions. And they were at one in wishing to preserve unimpaired all they conceived to be of human value in the South. They were, each in his own generation, hopeful of the South and attached to the view that whatever the present condition of the blacks there, it had been immeasurably worse in the past and was measurably better now.

It cannot, however, be forgotten that Washington delivered his address on the eve of *Plessy* v. *Ferguson*, which was decided by the United States Supreme Court in 1896. It remains an interesting speculation how far the majority of the Court may have been influenced in their judgment by Washington's advocacy a year earlier of social separation between the races. The "separate but equal" thesis, which the Court propounded, went somewhat beyond Washington's essentially more conservative position. Backward as the thinking of the prevailing majority on the Court was in this instance, Washington's was still more reactionary. Yet it must be borne in mind that in 1883 the Supreme Court had ruled unconstitutional the Civil Rights Act of

Bibliography

Nolen, Claude H.

The negro's image in the
South

Lexington, University of Kentucky
Press

1967

325.75
N 792

1875 (which guaranteed the blacks equal rights to public accommodation), so that Washington was, in effect, dealing with things as they were when he spoke at the Atlanta Exposition. In his behalf it may be argued that whatever he might have preferred, he was obliged to confront the actualities. And so he did. He was, after all, a single individual severely limited in such influence as he might exert upon the existing situation, and powerless to modify it by a frontal assault developed out of his deepest convictions. His address is not least interesting as an exercise in the tactics and strategy of powerlessness. Very different was the position of the Supreme Court. There, in that august body, resided the power to chasten and constrain society into just courses. There, too, was an incumbent duty to do so. There, and not with Booker T. Washington, lay the responsibility for the tragic betrayal of civil rights that it would take half a century to expiate and repair.

Frederick Douglass, "the noblest slave that ever God set free," died in that year, 1895. One year later W. E. B. Du Bois published *The Suppression of the African Slave-Trade to the United States of America, 1638–1870,* the first in a monumental series of investigations into the historical facts, as distinguished from historical prejudices, of the coming of the blacks to North America, the subsequent course of events, and the sociological circumstances in the land of their involuntary exile, which later became the country of their voluntary adoption. This first publication by Du Bois was his doctoral thesis, the degree being awarded him by Harvard University in 1896, the year Booker T. Washington delivered a commencement address there and was the recipient of an honorary degree.

Unlike Douglass and Washington, Du Bois was not a Southerner. Perhaps for this reason he was able to take a more detached view of the region as a whole. In any case, Du Bois was a deviant instance among the outstanding blacks produced by the racial conflict in the United States. He fitted no previously established pattern. And while he was a significant influence, he seems to have been uninfluenced except by an overwhelming intellectual passion for justice generated by his own convictions.

Aside from the brilliance of their intellects, their extraordinary lucidity, the uncompromising clarity with which they were capable of delineating their points of view, there was little in common between Du Bois and either Douglass or Washington. Until the emancipation, there were in Douglass modes of address and intensities of passion comparable to those that typified Du Bois when he embarked upon his phase of the struggle against white racism. But after emancipation Douglass declined, as if from psychic exhaustion, into a kind of moderation that divided his public career into two sections, of which the first was clearly more admirable than the second. With the Douglass of the latter epiphany Du Bois had nothing in common except mutual partisanship in a continuing struggle in which Douglass had untimely sheathed his sword.

But at no time whatever can there be said to have existed between Washington and Du Bois even this nominal bond of partisanship. It is true that there was a point at which Du Bois wrote, in his *Autobiography:*

In 1905 I was still a teacher at Atlanta University and was in my imagination a scientist, and neither a leader nor an agitator; I had much admiration for Mr. Washington and Tuskegee, and I had in 1894 applied at both Tuskegee and Hampton for work. If Mr. Washington's telegram had reached me before the Wilberforce bid, I should have doubtless gone to Tuskegee. Certainly I knew no less about mathematics than I did about Latin and Greek.

Since the controversy between me and Washington has become historic, it deserves more careful attention than it has had hitherto, both as to the matters and the motives involved. There was first of all the ideological controversy. I believed in the higher education of a Talented Tenth who through their knowledge of modern culture could guide the American Negro into a higher civilization. I knew that without this the Negro would have to accept white leadership, and that such leadership could not always be trusted to guide this group into self-realization and to its highest cultural possibilities. Mr. Washington, on the other hand, believed that the Negro as an efficient worker could gain wealth and that eventually through his ownership of capital he would be able to achieve a recognized place in American culture and could then educate his children as he might wish and develop their possibilities. For this reason he proposed to put the emphasis at present upon training in the skilled trades and encouragement in industry and common labor.

These two theories of Negro progress were not absolutely contradictory. Neither I nor Booker Washington understood the nature of capitalistic exploitation of labor, and the necessity of a direct attack on the principle of exploitation as the beginning of labor uplift. I recognized the importance of the Negro gaining a foothold in trades and his encouragement in industry and common labor. Mr. Washington was not absolutely opposed to college training and sent his own children to college. But he did minimize its importance, and discouraged the philanthropic support of higher education. He thought employers "gave" laborers work, thus opening the door to acquiring wealth. I openly and repeatedly criticized what seemed to me the poor work and small accomplishment of the Negro industrial school, but did not attack the fundamental wrong of giving the laborer less than he earned. It was characteristic of the Washington statesmanship that whatever he or anybody believed or wanted must be subordinated to dominant public opinion and that opinion deferred to and cajoled until it allowed a deviation toward better ways. It was my theory to guide and force public opinion by leadership. While my leadership was a matter of writing and teaching, the Washington leadership became a matter of organization and money. It was what I may call the Tuskegee Machine.

Thus Du Bois summarizes a lifetime of sustained criticism of Booker Washington and inflexible disagreement with him. It is not too much to say that Du Bois held Washington contributory to the abysmal decline in the status of the Southern blacks in the post-Reconstruction period. He reviews the consequences of his opponent's policy as follows:

This brings us to the situation when Booker T. Washington became the leader of the Negro race and advised them to depend upon industrial education and work rather than politics. The better class of Southern Negroes stopped voting for a generation. Then with the shift of population toward the North, there comes the present situation when out of 12,000,000 Negroes, 3,000,000 are in the North and 9,000,000 in the South. Those in the North and in Border States vote. Those in the South are seriously restricted in their voting, and this restriction means that their political power is exercised by the white South, which gives the white South an extraordinary political influence as compared with the voters of the North and East.

The disfranchisement of Negroes in the South became nearly complete. In no other civilized and modern land has so great a group of people, most of whom were able to read and write, been allowed so small a voice in their own government. Every promise of eventual recognition of the intelligent Negro voter has been broken. In the former slave states, from Virginia to Texas, excepting Missouri, there are no Negro state officials; no Negro members of legislatures; no judges on the bench; and usually no jurors. There are no colored county officials of any sort. In the towns and cities, there are no colored administrative officers, no members of the city councils, no magistrates, no constables, and very seldom even a policeman.

181

In this way, at least eight million Negroes are left without effective voice in government, naked to the worst elements of the community.

Beyond this, caste has been revived in a modern civilized land. It was supposed to be a relic of barbarism and existent only in Asia. But it has grown up and has been carefully nurtured and put on a legal basis with religious and moral sanctions in the South. First, it was presented and defended as "race" separation, but it was never mere race separation. It was always domination of blacks by white officials, white police and laws and ordinances made by white men. The schools were separate but the colored schools were controlled by white officials who decided how much or rather how little should be spent upon them; who decided what could be taught and what textbooks used and the sort of subservient teachers they wanted. In travel, separation compelled colored passengers to pay first-class for second- or third-class accommodations, and to endure on street cars and trains discrimination of all sorts. Ghettos were built up in nearly all Southern cities, not always sharply defined but pretty definite, and in these, Negroes must live, and in them white vice and crime might find shelter and Negro delinquency go unpoliced. Little attention was paid to lighting, sewerage, and paving in these quarters.

Besides this, a determined psychology of caste was built up. In every possible way it was impressed and advertised that the white was superior and the Negro an inferior race. This inferiority must be publicly acknowledged and submitted to. Titles of courtesy were denied colored men and women. Certain signs of servility and usages amounting to public and personal insult were insisted upon. The most educated and deserving black man was compelled in many public places to occupy a place beneath the lowest and least deserving of the whites. Public institutions, like parks and libraries, either denied all accommodations to the blacks or gave them inferior facilities.

It is difficult to see what Booker T. Washington could have done about all this, and difficult to see how Du Bois could reasonably have expected of him anything like effective counteraction in the circumstances. Du Bois himself, in *Black Reconstruction in America,* quotes someone whom he describes as "a distinguished white Southerner" in 1885:

Is the freedman a free man? No. We have considered his position in a land whence nothing can, and no man has a shadow of a right to drive him, and where he is being multiplied as only oppression can multiply a people. We have carefully analyzed his relations to the finer and prouder race, with which he shares the ownership and citizenship of a region large enough for ten times the number of people. Without accepting one word of his testimony, we have shown that the laws made for his protection against the habits of suspicion and oppression in his late master are being constantly set aside, not for their defects, but for such merit as they possess. We have shown that the very natural source of these oppressions is the surviving sentiments of an extinct and now universally execrated institution; sentiments which no intelligent or moral people should harbor a moment after the admission that slavery was a moral mistake. We have shown the outrageousness of these tyrannies in some of their workings, and how distinctly they antagonize every State and national interest involved in the elevation of the colored race. Is it not well to have done so? For, I say again, the question has reached a moment of special importance. The South stands on her honor before the clean equities of the issue. It is no longer whether constitutional amendments, but whether the eternal principles of justice, are violated.

In the light of his own citation, Du Bois appears fanatical rather than fair-minded in his criticism of Washington. Exactly how was Washington to go about the task that Du Bois would evidently have wished him to undertake, namely, the defiance and dismantling of the Black Codes? Du Bois never quite says how, except that, in his judgment, Washington should have assumed a position of militancy instead of accommodation. But militancy to what practical effect? Precisely how would such a stance have altered or checked in the slightest degree the fiendish resolve of white racism to subject the black freedmen to all the incidents of their former status? How was Washington to accomplish this braking of white power in the South when the capitalists of the North and South had already struck their bargain, with the connivance of the federal administration, by which in Du Bois's own words,

Southern landholders and capitalists would be put in complete control of disfranchised black labor. The Democrats promised to "guarantee peace, good order, protection of the law to whites and blacks", or, in other words, exploitation should be so quiet, orderly and legal, as to assure regular profit to Southern owners and Northern investors.

Du Bois does not say, unless by implication, what he would have done had he been in Washington's shoes as leader of the blacks in America at that historic moment. It can be assumed that he would have inveighed against iniquities and advertised as widely as he might the monstrous complicity of a country professing to be civilized in the barbaric oppression of millions of its inhabitants. He would scarcely have failed to do less than this. Yet the question remains: to what purpose? He would thereby have shown himself finely tempered in his attachment to the cause of his despised and subjugated fellow blacks, and of impeccable ardor in his devotion to the moral conventions that should regulate the interrelations of human beings. But what concrete impact should he have made upon the objective conditions? It is a question with which Du Bois does not trouble himself, but one he neglects in order to assail Washington on the score of the latter's surrender to white racism.

Here Du Bois is unjust to Washington. What he really wanted Washington to engage in, although he himself showed no particular stomach for it, was armed revolutionary struggle. This is not to suggest that Du Bois was a physical coward or anything of the sort. But it is quite explicitly to say that he must have been well aware that nothing short of an organized uprising of the blacks in the South to change by force the laws, customs, and institutions that oppressed them could have made any impression on the existing state of affairs. And he must have been equally aware that such an attempt was inescapably foredoomed to failure, with consequences far worse for the blacks than even the hideous nightmare they were already enduring. Washington's view of the circumstances in which his fellow blacks were entrapped was acute and commodious. His judgment was cool; his objective, survival for the blacks. To survive, they must endure, as they had done throughout two and one-half centuries of slavery. Coldly, carefully, he adapted his tactics to his objective.

Du Bois's objective was "manly self-assertion," which, in the prevailing circumstances, meant the decimation of the blacks by the white racists.

It was at bottom—this divergence between the two men—a difference of fundamental outlook. For Du Bois, the gesture was of immense importance for the sake of its sheer symbolism. For Washington, the result of an act or process was its supreme justification; the engineering thought and ancillary deed being pliable instruments to secure the desired outcome. Du Bois was Trotsky to Washington's Stalin—a moral Stalin, if this is conceivable; or, again, Milovan Djilas to Marshal Tito.

Yet, if the opinion is tenable that Du Bois's greatest weakness was, as is the case with many scholars of the first rank, a tendency "to mistake fastidiousness for holiness," it can equally be charged against Washington that he was too deeply rooted in the belief that the normative values of the white segment of the national society were unquestionably the standard for blacks to emulate. Sometimes he carried this attitude to ludicrous extremes. "For example, you never see a Negro braiding his hair in the same way as a Chinaman braids his, but he cuts his like the white man. The Negro is seeking out the highest and best as to quality" (*The Negro in the South*). There can be little doubt that his aesthetic values in this regard profoundly influenced his own and succeeding generations of blacks in their slavish imitation of white modes and the superior consequence they uncritically attributed to whatever was white. Nor was this outlook confined to the black middle class. Although they were conspicuously directed by it, the rest of the black group as a whole also set its social values in complete subservience to the white norms that commanded Booker Washington's adulation. This was a disservice to his fellow blacks, which, from a psychological point of view, had the effect of riveting more securely upon them the enshackling consciousness of racial inferiority. Washington was a complex and fascinating man, and it is not easy to determine with certainty where genuine conviction ended with him and revolutionary strategy and tactics began. For he was a revolutionary, perhaps the greatest of all American revolutionaries, black and white. Setting aside the absurdities of his aesthetic opinions, at any rate on their surfaces, it is pertinent to ask how far Washington was motivated in such pronouncements by the well-known Negro habit in dealing with whites of "yessing them to death."

A principal technique of Negro survival in the United States has been the art of flattery. It is not quite the same thing as "Uncle Tomming," which embodies, characteristically, an element of clowning, with the necessary overtones—so reassuring to whites—of self-disparagement. Washington's was, rather, the practice of the courtier's art. The emperor was arrayed in royal purple and gold even when the emperor was stark naked. At the same time, Washington was probably a racial hybrid, and it must remain uncertain to what extent he was, whether consciously or unconsciously, expressing in certain of his aesthetic views a predetermined genetic preference. It is possible to regard as a revolutionary tactic Washington's declared attachment to white values as being inherently superior. He expressly encouraged imitation by his fellow blacks for the sake of the latter's redemption

185

from the curse of inferiority. This tactic is as fascinating to contemplate as the man himself, and discloses a panorama of revolutionary design hitherto obscured by outrage at his depreciation of the physical traits of blacks.

Clearly, where Washington was concerned, black was not beautiful in the light of the cosmetic values to which he gave preference. Black was beautiful for other reasons: because it was heroically enduring and clairvoyant in its farsightedness; because it knew how to wait; because it was self-disciplined with the tough, indurated temper of cold steel; because it could appraise its own strengths and weaknesses and those of its enemies with a dispassionate accuracy that was the product of a coolheaded realism; because it knew that the time to assert a right was not, as Daniel Webster declared, when it was called into question, but when you are strong enough to do so. In Washington's hour of leadership of the black people of America, their collective strength was at an especially low ebb. More perhaps than anyone else, he knew this to be so. Not even Frederick Douglass at this particular point possessed quite the same degree of intimate awareness of this fact. Certainly Du Bois, with the romantic passion of the bourgeois intellectual for revolutionary solutions, did not. Washington knew the weakness of his people and, by sobering contrast, the overwhelming might of their enemies. He was the captain of his people and, certainly from 1895, their undisputed leader. What was the correct revolutionary strategy to be adopted in the situation he faced? Even if one granted the converse assumption that Washington was not a revolutionary, one would nevertheless be obliged to recognize that he acted as a true revolutionary, and not simply as a spouter of revolutionary verbiage, would have done.

Having coldly assessed his position vis-à-vis the enemy and concluded that a frontal attack on him, his customs, and his institutions would be suicidal for his own people, he adopted the strategy of delay and avoided at all costs a pitched battle. He bided his time and counseled his people to be patient. Their hour was not now, not yet. Their strategy must be one of survival and their tactics adjusted accordingly. Survival was all, at that stage. If survival could only be procured and maintained, the succeeding generations, as inheritors of demographic advantages (for example, weight of numbers accruing from exponential increases of the black population), would then be in a far stronger position to confront the enemy on his own terrain.

186

For the moment, therefore, an iron self-discipline in the face of unspeakable oppression and a calm acceptance (though not resignation) of the forbidding realities were the revolutionary tactics to be put into effect. A leader more covetous of glory for himself and less scrupulous of the immediate survival and long-term welfare of his people would have uttered vaunting noises and hollow challenges, the inevitable response to which would have been the massacre and perhaps near-extermination of the black people.

To no one as to Booker T. Washington do the black people of the United States owe so deeply the sheer fact of their survival. There would have been no help for them from any quarter in the world. Africa was powerless, prostrate, and wholly occupied as an exploited enclave of the European imperialists. Asia was hardly in better case and, in any event, had no relationship to the blacks of America such as, the fortuitous incident of skin color aside, might have stirred them to protest. And, for the rest, the Asians themselves (not even the Japanese excepted) were too weak to be of any influence in the matter. There would be no assistance forthcoming from any quarter. Scarcely a voice would be raised to any practical effect. It is well to remember that at this time black people were being massacred almost at will by the white colonial powers in numbers of instances. Here and there an individual outcry might be raised among the whites, but only to be stifled or ignored. In these ill-omened circumstances, Washington preserved his people from catastrophe. He obtained a breathing space for them. This was their most crucial need. Without the period of time he procured for them, their plight, already desperate, would have been utterly hopeless. With the years he won for them, they obtained not safety, but a fighting chance. Thus did Washington fulfill his revolutionary mission. Despite his detractors, he is in deepest truth the savior of his people, in profoundest essence a black American revolutionary.

If to be a revolutionary is to be something more than an igniter of causes from whose conflagration the worst sufferers and most numerous victims are those on whose behalf the fire was started, then Washington was such a revolutionary. If to be a revolutionary is to be tough and disciplined, monumentally patient, transcendently enduring, flexible in tactics and farsighted in strategy, calculating available means with clearheaded accuracy and adjusting them to the desired end with cold precision, then Washington was such a revolutionary. If to be a revolutionary is to know your enemy's weaknesses and exploit them, and to know your own and strengthen them, to bide your time while confiding your cause to your calmest judgment, clearest vision, and deepest wisdom, and to see the grand design of revolution as an exercise of unyielding will reinforced by unwavering intelligence, then Washington was such a revolutionary. If to be a revolutionary is to realize that revolution is not a rigid obsession with a single means of attaining a desired goal, but a pragmatism of approach that embraces all means, and that weapons to be employed in the struggle are limitless in their variety (their choice depending on improvisation as well as deliberation), if to be aware of these things— and resolutely to carry them out in practice—is to be a revolutionary, then Washington was such a revolutionary. If to make measured statements based on unquestionable facts, and not merely release impassioned utterances that do not so much articulate the highest wisdom as testify to unbalancing emotions—if to do so is to be a revolutionary, then Washington was such a revolutionary.

Admiration for Du Bois should not blind anyone to the fact that, as a revolutionary—and Du Bois was a revolutionary—his temper was less formidable than Washington's. His intellect was sharper, his academic training had been carried out on a far higher level, he possessed a knowledge of world history and of the interior workings of human societies vastly superior to anything that Washington could boast. He was a scholar of the utmost distinction, a writer of eminent gifts, a speaker of forceful conviction. But he was unmistakably inferior to Washington as an administrator. He had no comparable talent for successfully combining people and extracting from them their highest energies in pursuit of a common goal. He did not suffer fools gladly, for which no one can blame him. But he also did not suffer them at all, and since much of the business of life is carried out by people who, accurately if uncharitably, may be deemed fools, Du Bois found ordinary human intercourse somewhat wearing. His work with the Pan-African Congress, which he initiated, demanded abilities of organization that depended more on his personal prestige than upon his powers of persuasion and compromise. He was indubitably successful in this enterprise, and while perhaps no specific accomplishment of a concrete political nature can be demonstrated as an outcome of his efforts, it is nevertheless the fact that much of the present-day consciousness among black people the world over of the intimate relationship of Africa to their history derives from Du Bois's dream of a united Africa providing leadership and inspiring redemption for downtrodden blacks everywhere. In all these things and in all these ways Du Bois outshone Washington as the evening star at night outshines the daystar at noon.

But in one respect—to select only one—the brilliance of Washington far exceeded Du Bois's refulgence, and this was in Washington's instinctual grasp of the possibilities of effective action within the governing realities of the American society. Washington was so profoundly attuned to the imperatives of the country and, in particular, of the South that he sensed the least tremor of national disquiet on its remotest perimeter. So, precisely as Frederick Douglass had once refused, though with ardent sympathy as well as attachment to the design, to accompany John Brown to Harpers Ferry, deeming the enterprise valiant but foolhardy, Booker T. Washington in his turn restrained himself from fomenting among his fellow blacks in the South a resistance that he well knew could only provoke a ferocious counterstroke. The result would thus have rendered the attempt worse than futile, and the cost to the black victims of his irresponsibility would have been beyond the power of generations to retrieve.

Du Bois was incapable of such restraint. Although he never counseled violence, he had no positive approach to the problems of the Southern blacks that counterpoised Washington's position in the matter with either judiciousness equal or foresight as perspicuous. His countervailing approach to Washington's cautious posture was the advocacy of an elitist program for the "Talented Tenth." Hardly anything else reflected so clearly the intellectual exclusiveness that typically obtruded itself into Du Bois's solutions to the racial problems of American society. Yet it would be gravely to underestimate his influence on the twentieth-century development of black nationalism in the United States if his intellectual romanticism were the sole yardstick applied to his activities. He grew more intransigent in his opposition to white racism as he grew older, more obdurate in his refusal to compromise with it in any of its aspects. He was perhaps all the more hostile to it because of the devastating insight into himself provided by his realization that, as he says in *Dusk of Dawn,*

had it not been for the race problem early thrust upon me and enveloping me, I should have probably been an unquestioning worshipper at the shrine

189

of the social order and economic development into which I was born. But just that part of that order which seemed to most of my fellows nearest perfection seemed to me most inequitable and wrong. . . . What the white world was doing, its goals and ideals, I had not doubted were quite right. What was wrong was that I and people like me and thousands of others who might have my ability and aspiration, were refused permission to be a part of this world.

Rejection creates revolutionaries; acceptance makes conservatives. This is a classic axiom of sociological development.

Du Bois was by his own confession no exception to the general rule. His bitterness was that of a *nouveau arrivé* refused admission to an exclusive club. Hell hath no fury like a parvenu scorned. For all of his life, he was relegated to looking from the outside through the lighted window into the elegant precincts of a room whose high-vaulted ceiling and tapestried walls enclosed his peers, shielding them from casual contact with the vulgar, protecting them against the coarse clamor of the world without; and materializing to satisfy their unspoken needs dignified old servitors with deferential voices more subdued than the quiet rustle of the New England newspaper slipping to the carpeted floor from the ivory-colored, blue-veined hands of the venerable aristocrat asleep in his deep leather chair in the bay of the far window. It is sad that people should harbor such ambitions and sadder still that they should go unsatisfied, especially when they are thereby driven to spend all their lives (and in Du Bois's case, an unusually long life) in a vain though ceaseless assertion of proof of their *arriviste* credentials, their eminent suitability for membership in a club partly composed of *arrivistes* like themselves, with only one difference—and this the tragic, irreparable difference—that they were white, and he was black.

With such a hair shirt on his back morning, noon, and night, it was no wonder that Du Bois was characteristically peevish and easily given to taking offense. The man was in torment. Yet this was only a single aspect of him. It may be remarked that had he been a colonial subject of Portugal, he would have been accorded the rank, style, and white man's privileges of an *asimilado;* had he been a French colonial subject, the honorific white man's status of *évolué*. Had he been a British colonial subject, the British would have seen to it that he was admitted to the club as a special exception, treated as an honorary white man, and made colonial secretary or governor. They would

190

have knighted him, and as Sir Burghardt Du Bois, he would have been intellectually estimable, politically reliable, and ideologically harmless. But the Americans, with their crude oversimplification of racial categories, could only make an enemy of him, and a dangerous and an embittered enemy he became and remained to the end of his days. No one—neither Frederick Douglass nor Booker T. Washington, Marcus Garvey nor Martin Luther King, Adam Clayton Powell nor Malcolm X—so profoundly influenced the thinking of the black intelligentsia for fifty years as did W. E. B. Du Bois.

Beyond his embitterment there was his magnificent intellect. Throughout the major portion of his ninety-five years, he applied this superb instrument to a scalpeling analysis of the racial issue in America in all its open manifestations and secret disguises. In a massive series of enlightening studies, he revealed with cold fury and pitiless accuracy the racial squalor of America behind its glittering façade of fine professions of human equality. His work is a towering monument to his gigantic industry, his lucent scholarship, his marmoreal integrity, and his capacity for remorseless hatred. Du Bois hated as few blacks before him or after him have done. Yet his hatred was never an unbalancing factor in his work, which testifies to the scrupulous equipoise of his intellect. Undoubtedly, it generated some, at least, of the colossal energy with which he devoted himself to exposing the stupendous fraud perpetrated as American history, especially in so far as it obscures or misrepresents the true record of the racial issue and the role of the blacks in the building of America. His singular achievement from the standpoint of his dominating emotion —hatred of the white man's lies—was a feat of his tremendous will, in that he succeeded in making hatred the servant and not the master of his sovereign powers of mind. He made it serve the demands of his fastidious intellect and never permitted it to dictate his premises or deform his conclusions. He possessed up to the end the remarkable faculty of remaining *au dessus le combat* while deeply engaged in conflict.

Paul Robeson and Kwame Nkrumah are only two of the international figures he influenced. It may be thought that both of these men are fallen idols. Where are they now? This question reveals its own limitations. For it is not what happens to a man, but the outcome of his dominant ideas that is, finally, of importance. The ruling ideas of these men, and others like them, all have a common center, which is the destruction once and for all, for the sake of mankind, of the monstrous myth of the supremacy of the white race. Du Bois was not the first black man to dedicate himself to this crusade, but few blacks have been so successful in galvanizing other blacks (and whites, as well) into awareness of the crass intellectual fraudulence of white racism. The contempt that so many blacks possess in increasing measure for this tawdry scheme of ethnic pretensions derives a good deal of its explicit rationale from the work of W. E. B. Du Bois. On the theory that his inspiration in this respect could have had a genetic origin, it may be illuminating to reproduce from his *Autobiography* a reference to his paternal grandfather. "I saw grandfather but once, when I was 15 and he 77. Always he held his head high, took no insults, made few friends. He was not a 'Negro'; he was a man!" It may be thought that this is how Du Bois should have responded in sum to the black youth who once wrote to him asking his view of the ethnic appropriateness of the term "Negro." Yet whatever the failure of his sense of occasion in that incident, it is a fact beyond all controversy that fixed and immovable in the very core of his being was this view of himself: "I am not a 'Negro'; I am a man!" Holding fast to this conviction for most of his life, he inspired others to attach themselves, as storm-tossed mariners to a mast, to the same standpoint.

Du Bois went well beyond this principle and showed by the example of his life and work the sacred necessity to oppose with all one's might and to its final eradication the cancerous moral evil of white racism. His point of departure may have been, as he himself has indicated, a private reaction to his personal standing in the white man's world. It could have been, perhaps, no more than pique to start with. Yet, however that may be, it soon transcended the scope of an individual grievance and attained the scale of a massive crusade to force his country to redeem the magniloquent and, thus far, fraudulent terms of its fundamental constitution.

Du Bois and Washington were not irreconcilably at variance with each other in their specific proposals. They both contemplated higher education for blacks. In Du Bois's case, the emphasis was academic; in Washington's vocational. Washington envisaged economic advancement as the key to the black predicament; Du Bois saw the probable solution in intellectual progress. These approaches were not basically dissimilar. They might indeed be thought to have been complementary. But there were divergences of degree between them, and where these became crucial and, in the actual event, sundering was in the political objectives they were designed to effectuate. Du Bois aimed at more vigorous political activity on the part of the blacks led by the elite corps of the group that he dubbed the Talented Tenth. This was the major synthesis that he strove to realize in action. He envisioned enlightened political leadership of blacks by blacks as the straight path to the Promised Land. On the other hand, Washington eschewed politics for blacks in his program and placed the greatest weight upon participation in the national economy by blacks trained in industrial skills. The one approach was political; the other, economic. It should not have been difficult to harmonize these approaches and blend them into a co-operative drive in single harness to the common goal of endowing the emancipation of the blacks with assurance of equal access to the resources of the American society. They were, after all, these twin approaches, two sides of the same coin.

Nothing should have been simpler, given, especially, the dire straits the blacks were in, than to accommodate politics and economics to each other for the sake of the overriding objective. This expectation foundered, however, on the shoals of the dramatic differences in personal temperament between the two protagonists, Washington and Du Bois. Had they been capable of working together, the blacks in America would have been led by as formidable a duumvirate as might be found anywhere, and their situation (above all in the South) improved incalculably. But that was altogether too much to hope for. It was unrealistic. Du Bois and Washington differed as sea from land. The former was all fluid intellect and tidal conviction; the latter earthbound and accommodating to every characteristic of the terrain. They could meet, and they did meet, but they could not merge with each other. From the point of view of black Americans, this was the greatest failure in the whole tragedy of their leadership. The opposition that deepened into mutual hostility between these two magnificently gifted men was exploited by whites, who realized the threat that such a coalition would pose to their design to rein in the pace of black progress to a crawl and its scope to no more than was represented by three-fifths of a man. So Du Bois recoiled from Booker Washington to the Niagara Movement and, subsequently, to the founding of the National Association for the Advancement of Colored People. Washington, immovable, remained at Tuskegee, whence, until his death in 1915, he presided over the destinies of blacks in America. Washington possessed a skillful guerrilla fighter's respect for the nature of the terrain. He would not expose himself or his followers to enemy fire while he was emplaced in a dangerous pass. Du Bois was more in the tradition of the romantic revolutionary to whom a lost cause is as much a matter of honor as one that is triumphant. While Washington played for time, Du Bois sought to bring the enemy to battle. Washington was cautious, realistic; Du Bois, venturesome and contemptuous; Washington, shrewd and farsighted; Du Bois, brilliant and visionary.

The differences between the two men went even deeper. Where Du Bois celebrated the African past of the black Americans, Washington denigrated it. To the former:

There can be no doubt but that the level of culture among the masses of Negroes in West Africa in the fifteenth century was higher than that of Northern Europe, by any standard of measurement—homes, clothes, artistic creation and appreciation, political organization and religious consistency. [*The World and Africa.*]

He also cites R. E. G. Armattoe:

Throughout the whole of the Middle Ages, West Africa had a more solid politico-social organization, attained a greater degree of internal cohesion and was more conscious of the social function of science than Europe.

Then Du Bois asks: "What stopped and degraded this development?" And he answers: "The slave trade; that modern change from regarding wealth as being for the benefit of human beings, to that of regarding human beings as wealth."

Note in contradistinction Washington's point of view concerning his African past:

In his native country, owing to climatic conditions, and also because of his few simple and crude wants, the Negro, before coming to America, had little necessity to labor. You have, perhaps, read the story, that it is said might be true in certain portions of Africa, of how the native simply lies down on his back under a banana-tree and falls asleep with his mouth open. The banana falls into his mouth while he is asleep and when he wakes up he finds that all he has to do is to chew it—he has his meal already served.

Washington speaks, too, of the nakedness of the Africans in their native habitat.

The economic element [in the New World] not only made it necessary that the Negro slave should be clothed for the sake of decency and in order to preserve his health, but the same considerations made it necessary that he

194

be housed and taught the comforts to be found in a home. Within a few months, then, after the arrival of the Negro in America, he was wearing clothes and living in a house—no inconsiderable step in the direction of morality and Christianity. True, the Negro slave had worn some kind of garment and occupied some kind of hut before he was brought to America, but he had made little progress in the improvement of his garments or in the kind of hut he inhabited. As we shall perhaps see later, his introduction into American slavery was the beginning of real growth in the two directions under consideration. [*Negro in the South.*]

He rationalizes the institution of slavery, finding ex post facto justification for it in numerous instances of what he describes as consequent "improvements" in the condition of the transported Africans. He declares:

To begin with let me repeat that at first, at least, the underlying object of slavery was an economic, and an industrial one. The climatic and other new conditions required that the slave should wear clothing, a thing, for the most part, new to him. It has perhaps already occurred to you that one of the conditions requisite for the Christian life is clothing. So far as I know, Christianity is the only religion that makes the wearing of clothes one of its conditions. A naked Christian is impossible—and I may add that I have little faith in a hungry Christian.

Washington was so profoundly materialist in his thinking that he regarded industrial training and economic enterprise as the twin pillars of the gate to the Christian Kingdom of Heaven. He says so in explicit terms:

I believe that enough facts can be given to show that economic and industrial development has wonderfully improved the moral and religious life of the Negro race in America, and that, just in proportion as any race progresses in this same direction, its moral and religious life will be strengthened and made more practical.

Despite his disclaimer in the course of an address, "The Economic Development of the Negro Race Since Its Emancipation," that "I would not have you understand that I emphasize material possessions as the chief thing in life or as an object within itself," evidence abounds and is persuasive that Washington considered the materialistic foundation of economics and industry to be the indispensable basis of "the moral and religious life" of a Christian, whether white or black. He saw the American white man as the foremost exemplar, from this point of view, of the human species. And he recommended that black Americans imitate the American white man. They were in any event "imitative" by their group ethos, he said, and they could not do better than apply their mimetic gifts to reproducing for their own advancement the characteristic traits of the American white man.

It would be easy and as foolishly glib to attribute this sort of attitude to "self-hatred." Deplorable as it is—and there is no conceivable ground on which it can be defended—it may nevertheless be understood if we allow that Washington was simply expressing an aesthetic preference to which he was of course entitled. His father was probably a white man. And only in the fallacious and distorting ethnology of the United States would Washington have been constrained, as he was, within the racial connotations of the descriptive term "Negro." In a civilized society he would have been a man free to assert his aesthetic preferences without incurring a pseudoscientific imputation of "self-hatred." But such an assertion, when made in the historical circumstances of Washington's day, and considering the preceding centuries of black enslavement, acquires an altogether different cutting edge. It then cleaves straight to the heart of black self-respect, suggesting, as it does, biological comparisons that imply ethnic criteria according to which "like the white man" is the sovereign test of acceptability. An aesthetic preference, as Washington's might have been, could not, however, be asserted without inevitable ethnological consequences. These in turn were bound to react upon the entire situation of the black Americans and, so doing, generate widespread conviction among the group that "black was ugly." On the adverse side of his formidable record as a black revolutionary must be placed this tragic failure to appreciate the intimate relationship of racial aesthetics and power politics. In sheer terms of group self-respect, this unfortunate predilection for white norms was seriously damaging to black self-conception. Its throttling stranglehold on the consciousness of the group as a whole would only be broken two generations later by the minting of the converse revolutionary slogan: Black is beautiful.

Meanwhile Washington hammered away at his theme of the superiority of the white man and his civilization. He contrasts the North American Indian with the black man.

The Indian refused to submit to bondage and to learn the white man's ways. The result is that the greater portion of the American Indians have

196

disappeared, the greater portion of those who remain are not civilized. The Negro, wiser and more enduring than the Indian, patiently endured slavery; and contact with the white man has given him a civilization vastly superior to that of the Indian.

The Indian and the Negro met on the American continent for the first time at Jamestown, in 1619. Both were in the darkest barbarism. There were twenty Negroes and thousands of Indians. At the present time there are between nine and ten million Negroes and two hundred and eighty-four thousand and seventy-nine Indians. . . . The Negro . . . has had the good sense to get something from the white man at every point where he has touched him—something that has made him a better and stronger race.

One of the salient features of Washington's thinking is its black racism, with its ever-present component of Christian allegiance. He defers to the white race as the superior in the scale of civilization, but he everywhere posits his argument in racial terms, the "Negro race," the "white race," and "other races" being the constant staple of his discourse. He foreshadows the position of the present-day *Ebony* magazine on the spectacular progress of the black Americans by comparison with other blacks elsewhere in the world:

Let me make this statement with which you may or may not agree: In my opinion, there cannot be found in the civilized or uncivilized world ten millions of Negroes whose economic, educational, moral and religious life is so advanced as that of the ten millions of Negroes within the United States. If this statement be true, let us find the cause thereof, especially as regards the Negro's moral and Christian growth. In doing so, let credit be given wherever it is due, whether to the Northern white man, the Southern white man, or the Negro himself. If, as stated, the ten millions of black people in the United States have excelled all the other groups of their race-type in moral and Christian growth, let us trace the cause, and in doing so, we may get some light and information that will be of value in dealing with the Negro race in America and elsewhere, and in elevating and Christianizing other races.

His fundamental attitude is indistinguishable from that of a white Christian conservative American deeply imbued with the spirit of Manifest Destiny and alight with the conviction of a world mission. It will be impossible to grasp the ethos of black Americans in the main (not that of the dissentient minority) if it is not understood that up to this day they are closer in their thinking to Booker T. Washington— and the governing rules of their group behavior are in more intimate consonance with the standards he prescribed—than they are to any other representative figure in American history. The blacks of America are conservative—like Booker Washington; Christian—like Booker Washington; profoundly conscious—like Booker Washington—of being, with their former white owners, archetypal Americans; firmly persuaded of the Manifest Destiny of their country as the missionary headquarters of the Christian world charged with the duty to carry the message to the four corners of the earth, to convert and elevate other races, and to make the world over in the American image.

In the deepest sense, the South is that region of the country which is most distinctively American. It is more so than New England, since the latter has retained in its temper and institutions ties with English traditions that have long since been abandoned in the folk mores of the South. A more conscious and sustained effort was made in the New England states to maintain the English heritage than was the case in the Southern region of the United States. This circumstance is itself testimony to the predominating influence of slavery. Its early abandonment in the New England states and its centuries-long persistence in the South defined a regional difference expressed in the former instance by the development of a transatlantic culture with well-tended English roots and, in the latter, by a largely self-generating culture within conditions of relative social isolation. As a direct consequence of slavery, a type of culture evolved in the South that, although not indigenous, was nevertheless a more faithful reflection of the characteristic circumstances of the New World and, specifically, of the United States than was the culture of the New England states. At the heart of the culture of the South was slavery, and at the heart of that institution were two human groups bound together either as white slave owners or, in any event, as white members of the higher caste who exerted rights of overlordship against the black slaves that constituted the lower caste. A process of organic fusion occurred between the two groups, the upper-caste whites and the lower-caste blacks, which, in its regional form and cultural essence, was the most distinctively American of all evolutionary developments of a social nature on the North American continent. The whites and blacks involved acquired a definitive American character. In a sense that excludes, of course, the North American Indians, these whites and blacks of the South emerge as prototypical Americans: the whites as upper-caste Americans; the blacks as lower-caste Americans; yet both groups

198

jointly as Americans, with an original, though not indigenous, title conspicuously beyond dispute.

It is out of a profound knowledge of this fact that Frederick Douglass, Booker T. Washington, and W. E. B. Du Bois—to cite only this great triumvirate—consistently distinguish themselves and other black Americans from "immigrants" and "foreigners," those, in Washington's language, "of foreign birth and strange tongue and habits." The blacks—especially the Southern blacks—have long known that they and the Southern whites, of all the universal variety of the inhabitants of this country, are Americans. Of particular concern is the difference in approach of these three giants—Douglass, Washington, and Du Bois—to the problem of enduing this fact with revolutionary significance: that is, each leader's approach to the problem of elevating from lower caste to equal caste the national status to which black Americans have traditionally been confined. The real argument is not now, nor has it ever been, except from the standpoint of "immigrants" and "foreigners," whether the blacks are in fact Americans, but whether or not they are to be expected to remain passive and content as lower-caste Americans; and if not, then how soon, how fast, and by what methods shall their status be made equal. No one in his right mind has ever thought of black Americans as immigrants. But there has always been (and there is no less today) ample reason to regard them as lower-caste Americans. Of this latter truth there can be no question whatever. And this is what the black upheaval is all about: a continuing effort by black Americans to move up from lower to equal caste in a racially stratified society.

We must see this upheaval, if we are to be accurate in our historical perception, as a continuous process extending throughout the well-nigh three and one-half centuries of the connection of blacks with this country. Only in this light will contemporary developments be deeply understood. It must be realized that Denmark Vesey and Nat Turner are the direct ancestors of Malcolm X and H. Rap Brown, that the voice of black protest has never been completely stilled in America, and that black insurrectionary activity has never long lain dormant. It must be appreciated, too, that the black condition at any given time in all its communal violence and social tragedy has always been an element in the pattern of force and upheaval characteristic of the evolution of American society. To be unaware of this fact is certainly to be unable to evaluate the present state of affairs.

Black insurrection has always occurred within American society on a volcanic principle of periods of quiescence alternating with eruption. But a volcano that is only sporadically active is nonetheless a volcano. As such, black insurrection has never been absent among the sociological features of the United States. In another metaphor, it may be described as a variable in the vast calculus of social evolution, in which national violence is a constant.

There has never been unanimity among the blacks as to how best their caste position might be improved. Indeed, between Washington and Du Bois there was a deep gulf fixed. Their differences took on even an international dimension. According to Du Bois in his *Autobiography:*

Mr. Washington was in Europe in 1910 and made some speeches in England on his usual conciliatory lines. John Milholland, who had been so dominant in the organization of the National Association [the National Association for the Advancement of Colored People], immediately wrote me and said that American Negroes must combat the idea that they were satisfied with conditions. I, therefore, wrote an appeal to England and Europe, under the signature of a group of colored friends so as not to involve the N.A.A.C.P. officially:

"If Mr. Booker T. Washington, or any other person, is giving the impression abroad that the Negro problem in America is in process of satisfactory solution, he is giving an impression which is not true."

The statement continues along those lines. Then, says Du Bois:

In further emphasis of this statement and in anticipation of the meeting of the proposed Races Congress, Mr. Milholland arranged that I should go early to London and make some addresses.

Elsewhere Du Bois describes Mr. John Milholland as an "earnest liberal" and refers to him as having been "so influential in the organization of the Association with paid employees and an office." Some white liberals were, and are, false friends. But Mr. John Milholland clearly was not among them.

The struggle between Booker T. Washington and W. E. B. Du Bois for the "souls of black folk" in America was a morality play without a protagonist of evil. Yet its intrinsic drama was not thereby diminished.

According to Du Bois, in *Dusk of Dawn,* Booker T. Washington

advised submission to segregation . . . in order that this bending to the will of a powerful majority might bring from that majority gradually such sympathy and sense of justice that in the long run the best interests of the Negro group would be served.

Du Bois opposed this on the ground that

unless the dominant group saw its best interests bound up with those of the black minority, the situation was hopeless; and in any case the danger was that if the minority ceased to agitate and resist oppression it would grow to accept it as normal and inevitable.

Eventually, however, Du Bois advocated "self-segregation on the part of colored people," and he saw, as Washington had, that the operative fulcrum by which blacks might lever themselves up was a matter of economics. Where Washington sought this fulcrum in the training of blacks as artisans to secure their entry into industry, Du Bois thought it might be found in their potential power as consumers.

They were not so far apart, after all. But the controversy between these two gifted and farsighted men divided the allegiance of the blacks at a crucial moment in their history and confused their planning for the future. Defying Washington and his great Negro monument, Tuskegee, Du Bois founded the Niagara Movement, from which emerged the National Association for the Advancement of Colored People.

The reconciliation between the two institutions has long been complete. It might not be wholly accurate to say that it was consummated by the break between Du Bois and the NAACP in 1934. But the NAACP could no longer contain Du Bois, except by surrendering to him the autonomy his towering stature demanded. This it would not do, and Du Bois strode off to Atlanta University, still thinking with the fresh and independent vitality that distinguishes so much of his work.

The NAACP took the path of compromise between Booker T. Washington's submission to segregation and W. E. B. Du Bois's self-segregation. It chose the goal of integration. As far back as 1916, when it succeeded in getting the Supreme Court to strike down the grandfather clauses, and 1917, when it delivered a great hammer blow to residential segregation, this goal had been its aim, whether explicitly formulated or not. The Niagara Movement itself was an instance of racial integration; so was the NAACP. It is, perhaps, a reflection not devoid of interest that the black community is divided at the present time on precisely this question: Segregation or integration; by which is meant segregation in Du Bois's sense as against integration in the planning and purpose of the NAACP. The conflict between Du Bois's philosophy and that of the organization he was instrumental in founding continues. Some irony may be seen in the historical circumstance that, contrasted with the NAACP, Booker T. Washington and W. E. B. Du Bois both envisaged a similar solution to the dilemma confronting blacks in racist America: self-segregation. They differed only in the spirit motivating the solution. In the one case, tactical submission, in the other, defiance.

It is Du Bois's solution that the black nationalist movement has adopted, with, of course, circumstantial variations.

The fact that the NAACP has espoused the cause of integration from its beginning is not unconnected with the racial composition of its founders, some of whom were white and others of whom were black. It must also be recognized that for much of its existence it has been a middle-class organization, with middle-class objectives. Integration, in the actual practice of the NAACP, has little to do with the lower-class blacks. I do not mean that it has not fought lynching, the poll tax, and the whole vast array of horror and inequity inflicted upon blacks by the dominant white majority in America. I do not mean that it has ignored the fearful actualities of black lower-class life in America or excluded this stratum of blacks from its aims and activities, its practical assistance and theoretical aspirations. But in reaching out for integration, it gave insufficient thought, certainly at first, to the brute economic facts of American life. The result was that it betrayed itself into seeking political solutions for economic problems, and, to the extent that it did envisage and emphasize economic solutions, these were more or less limited to ameliorating the condition of the black middle class.

This may have been the unintended consequence of a lack of the material resources necessary to mount a wider attack upon the whole black problem. But it might also be thought to bear some relation to the fact that the black middle class, composed as it traditionally was of lighter-skinned blacks, was able to use its higher social position with its concomitant educational advantages, to press more effectively for the immediate attention of the NAACP, and to secure it. Nor is it irrelevant that the NAACP itself was largely staffed by the representatives of the black middle class. Their class interest expressed itself in a certain insensitivity to the fundamental economic

202

problems of the black lower class, who were darker-skinned than they and, therefore, lower in the social scale, simply, although not exclusively, by virtue of that fact. To people such as they, their class position vis-à-vis the darker-skinned blacks blinded them to the fact that for people without jobs, without food, without shelter, without clothing, without self-respect, and without hope, integration could be nothing but a ghastly mockery. For the black middle class, it was a different story; they stood to benefit, with their better education and closer ethnic resemblance to the masters. But for the lower-class blacks, the NAACP, in this aspect of its program and pursuits, offered only wormwood and gall. The estrangement between the NAACP and the black lower class continues to this day. Hence the Black Muslims, Black Panthers, and other such groups.

The economic bridge that A. Philip Randolph sought to construct between a segment of the lower-class blacks and the middle-class blacks served by the NAACP was much less sturdy and its span considerably shorter than it might have been because of the hostility of the white unions. Blacks have encountered no foe so inveterate. The white labor movement, it is fair to say, has been a monumental barrier to the economic progress of blacks in America. In the midst of the Second World War, only extraordinary pressure exerted by Randolph upon the American President sufficed to extort an official directive against racial discrimination in industries vital to the war effort; and this was accomplished in the teeth of rabid opposition by the white unions.

It is not intemperate to say that white Americans have, as a whole, shown less regard for the national interest than for the preservation of racism. The career of A. Philip Randolph clearly makes this point. Economic activity is the mainspring of American life. A tremendous reservoir of black labor lay to hand virtually untapped. The country's productivity, gigantic though it was, nevertheless remained deficient to the extent of the exclusion of black labor from the industrial process. But not even self-interest could enlighten the white racists who dominated the labor unions. In the prevailing circumstances, Randolph's Brotherhood of Sleeping Car Porters is an American saga, and Randolph an authentic hero. He stands with the NAACP rather than with Du Bois and Booker T. Washington in his support of integration as against self-segregation; yet with this difference: he gave an emphasis to the path of economic advancement for blacks, which was muted, by comparison, in the program of the NAACP. At this point, he is closer to Du Bois and Washington. He may even be regarded as having attained in his work a fusion of the main drives represented by the NAACP, on the one hand, and Washington and Du Bois on the other; that is, he combined the former's goal of integration with the latter's aim of building, as a principal objective, economic strength for blacks.

This, in fact, characterizes all black radical reform and all black insurrectionary movements. They all have this one preoccupation in common: the amassing and marshaling of economic power. Where they differ from, say, the NAACP and the National Urban League, is at this point exactly. The National Urban League came into being in order to extend something in the nature of social service to the black migrants to the cities. It formulated no large-scale program to cope with the massive economic requirements of these urban settlers. In all realism, it was unable to do so. Where would the jobs have come from? Some jobs it did provide, but these were so few relatively to the mass of black unemployment as to be almost negligible. Nor, for some considerable time, was it actively engaged in the brutal struggle for political reform. Its policies touched the sphere of politics only marginally and, for the most part, were conceived and applied with the spirit and purpose of "social work." The NAACP, while it exhibited in general an inadequate concern with the organization and development of black economic resources, concentrated on the application of political techniques within the American system to the problem of black betterment. It maintained a legislative lobby at Washington and co-operated with friends in both parties to secure its objectives. Its central interest lay in the field of civil rights, but if it fought tenaciously, as it did, for the restoration of voting rights of which blacks were dispossessed after the Compromise of 1876, and if it fought unrelentingly, as it did, for the repeal of the poll tax and other forms of black disenfranchisement, it yet remains a fact that its paramount objectives were political in character rather than economic.

It is, of course, often difficult to disentangle these two strands in the whole skein of domestic interrelations. Where politics ends and economics begins is a constantly shifting line of demarcation. But a particular emphasis may nevertheless be discernible, and in the case of the NAACP, it was political. This is perfectly understandable. Politics, practiced in conformity with the governing code of the American system, is a tool of gradualism, a technique of indirection. The approach by way of a direct attack upon the economic problem is more immediate, with possibilities of dynamic urgency posing threat and menace to the *status quo*. Yet it must be admitted that this approach was blocked by the labor unions, who stood obdurately in the way and were reinforced by the vested interests of big business. Having to choose between a frontal challenge to this combination and its political circumvention, the NAACP chose the latter, which is the path of democratic reform. The more radical black movements, in all their multitudinous variety, as well as divergent degrees of impotence, have tended to choose the former. These have seen the "coming of the Lord" as an economic and not a political manifestation. Quite naturally; for, as a short-term measure for the relief of hunger, money will buy bread while elevation to political office, given the enfeebled minority representation on the part of blacks, would only proffer prestige.

None of these reflections can illuminate the plight of black Americans so starkly as the American concept of race, and none can elucidate it so persuasively as the American practice of this concept.

"We threat the Negro right," said Mr. Dooley. "He has plenty to do and nawthin' to bother him an' if he isn't satisfied he be hanged. . . . Th' black has many fine qualities. He is joyous, light-hearted, an' aisily lynched." One would look far to find a more apposite summary of the Southern attitude toward blacks in its historic expression. Nor was it confined to the South, as the draft riots of 1863 in New York City showed, to cite only a single other example of a nation-wide outlook and practice.

The Redeemers of the South—who subverted and destroyed the position reached by blacks in the Reconstruction era—had their counterparts everywhere in the country. The Ku Klux Klan are merely the best known among their agencies and, in an organizational sense, the most persistent. However they have differed in their animating philosophy or particular objectives, they have all employed the same instrument to effectuate their aims: violence. This tactic, as a means of procuring goals, has been pandemic in American society from the outset. The United States is a product of violence. Black Americans have been foremost among its victims, but they have not been the only victims.

Was it vanity, then, or masochism (it can scarcely have been ignorance) that impelled the late Martin Luther King to advocate nonviolence as a countertactic on the part of blacks? In making a considered response to this question, it must be borne in mind that he went so far as to counsel blacks to abdicate even the right of self-defense. Plainly, it is one thing to initiate violence; it is one thing to meet a degree of violence with disproportionate violence; it is one thing to espouse violence and incite others to it; but it is quite another to disseminate the principle of nonviolence and to indoctrinate disciples with it in a society whose dedication to violence is its most salient feature. This is the road to Belsen, Buchenwald, Treblinka, Dachau. Anyone who counsels the people whom he leads to take this road is not an exponent of love but a practitioner of sadism. Looking at the brute state of human evolution without the distorting lenses of liberal idealism, one conclusion, and one alone, is possible: Martin Luther King, in his role as an apostle of nonviolence by blacks, was as dangerous a threat to the continued existence of blacks in America as any self-styled revolutionary at the opposite pole. What King and the latter both exhibit in common is a profound naïveté in the face of the consuming impulse of the American society to mass destruction. The fate of the North American Indian should be sufficient warning.

Here was a man, Martin Luther King, who talked glibly of the "redemptive power of unmerited suffering" without, it seemed, overmuch thought for the possibility that the suffering he so nobly conceived might attain its ghastly culmination for blacks in American gas ovens and crematoria. What pathetic belief, despite all the evidence to the contrary, gave him to suppose that the Nazi visitation upon the Jews of Germany could not happen here as a "final solution"? Was he simply ingenuous or, well knowing what he risked not only for himself, did he nevertheless go in search of an acclaimed martyrdom in full awareness of the holocaust he courted for his people? As with saints, in general, was King's a case of monumental egotism masquerading as humility? A pathologic ambition for fame at whatever cost to the blacks upon whose cause he was so recklessly inscribing his career? For reckless it was, however cloaked by Christian piety. Reckless, and worse, because what he was doing was nothing more nor less than conditioning the blacks who followed him into going unresisting to the gas ovens. Had that man got his way, they would have gone by way of the concentration camps, which are not unknown in America, singing spirituals and clapping their hands right into the extermination chambers. And as they went, they would undoubtedly have invoked the blessing of Almighty God upon their executioners. How inspiring! How Christian! Had Brother Martin himself not told them time and again: "If blood must be shed, let it be your blood and not theirs"? Can it be wondered at that he was awarded the Nobel Peace Prize and the support and admiration of every white liberal in America who believes, in the unformulating depths of his unconscious, that the best thing that could happen to blacks in America would be their mass extermination followed by suitable expressions of civilized remorse? Hence the apotheosis of Martin Luther King. In any case, it is no longer worth troubling about. King is dead, and much of what he preached with him. Neither he nor his message will be resurrected for some considerable time to come in relations between blacks and whites in America.

Blacks were saved, at least for the time being, from the fate that King's simplistic Christianity was contriving for them by the intervention of Malcolm X. To this man, more than to any other, blacks owe their retention of the normal animal impulse to self-preservation, of which King had sought to strip them as the price of his lust for a pre-eminent niche in history. Malcolm X recalled blacks to their senses by reminding them of the nature of the beast by which they were confronted. This was necessary for the sake of their survival. Christianity is too sophisticated a creed for blacks, who tend, as a group, to be literal-minded; which explains their susceptibility to fundamentalist doctrines.

All white people do not partake of the generic nature of the beast that is white supremacy. Some are free of racial prejudice. But they are—alas!—in a tiny minority; multiply them, even if you will, by all the blacks who, each in turn, will offer their complement of positive exceptions to the sum total. Cumulatively, nonetheless, they remain a small, a very small, fraction of the preponderating mass of white racist Americans. Malcolm X did not make this point in the beginning; in fact, he would probably have denied its validity. In the end, however, he did make it. By then he had opened the eyes of large numbers of blacks to the sinister possibilities of Martin Luther King. It was not that King was a bad man, except in the sense that all men of overweening ambition are bad. It was simply that he was an inopportune man. At the conjuncture at which he occurred, his primary service to the black struggle in America was an attempt to substitute righteousness for effectiveness. Gandhi's tactic of passive resistance and nonviolence succeeded in India in special circumstances. It should have been clear to King, as it was to anyone who gave the matter half a moment's thought, that these conditions did not exist in the United States and were not reproducible here. But visionaries are notorious for their inability to make distinctions. All God's children are equally ready to enter His kingdom at any time. Moreover, in their hands—these visionaries—historical analogies become more dangerous than ever. They are, in any case, not to be trusted with history; for their innate tendency is toward dismantling the past so as to be unencumbered by experience in projecting the future.

The fate of any people unresolved and unready to fight, *by any means,* for their survival has been extermination. One glance, hardly more, at the human record will suffice to make this clear. King must have known this; or, if he did not, then why not? He seemed, on the whole, fairly intelligent; reasonably well educated, in the narrow, synthetic sense of this term; not unaware of the vast gulf between the actualities of human bigotry he knew so intimately and the aspirations he preached so eloquently. He was, when all is said and done, no fool. Then, was he a charlatan? Equally, no. More than anything else, he was a Christian mystic from the black Bible Belt who was seduced by political opportunism into a career as a populist demagogue. The love he preached lacked cleanliness and astringency. It was Dostoevskian, a fetid compost of suffering for putrescence' sake. In Dostoevsky, love does not redeem; it only rots. Suffering is the great human end, and human love a means to that end. What must be achieved at all costs is the transcendency of suffering by greater suffering—not love; suffering. It is an example of Slavic pathology, which has some counterpart in Hindu mysticism, with its notion of karma and expiation through suffering.

Gandhi's political astuteness, his precise sense of possibilities, enabled him to adapt with extraordinary success this element of Hindu religious ideology to the realities of Indian life. The synthesis he essayed and, to a remarkable extent, attained was in essence pragmatic. He was no ideologue. The aim was the extrusion of the British from India and the re-establishment of Indian independence. This, and not the indoctrination of the Indian masses with an ideology of love and suffering for its own sake, was his supreme objective. Nor is the difference between Gandhi and King the difference between Dostoevsky and Tolstoy. The latter's Christianity was closer in its inspiration to transplanted Western sources, while Dostoevsky's exhibited a nearer kinship to its Oriental provenance. The difference between Gandhi and King was in their respective conceptions of the pragmatic functions of a scheme of ethical values. Where Gandhi came to greatness, and King did not, was precisely here. Gandhi carried out his role, whatever his private shortcomings, as an instrument of the Indian masses; for King, on the other hand, his followers were the instrument. His acceptance of a Nobel Peace Prize sealed his captivity. More than ever before, he was the prisoner of an idea. He might, like Gandhi, have been its Praetorian Guard. But he lacked the necessary sophistication.

Here we touch upon a prime defect in the traditional leadership of blacks in America: this tendency to submit the cause of black freedom to the governance of ethical systems inflexible in their deference to the established order. This has been known as "operating within the system." It is a middle-class approach, which at length has been repudiated by the leadership of the insurgent lower classes. Yet I do not wish to imply here the abandonment of this approach by the old-line black organizations. They continue to adhere to it, whence the conflict between them and the younger groups. This is especially true of the National Association for the Advancement of Colored People. One of the main reasons underlying the moderate philosophy and practice of this group is the fact that its effective leadership has long been either actively exercised or profoundly influenced by liberal whites. Among these, Jews have been prominent. Until the establishment of the state of Israel, Jews tended as a group to be pacific and averse to violence. In the course of their long history, they have also acquired a collective sensitivity extraordinarily alert to the ways of power. They, above everyone, are aware that Acton's maxim "Power corrupts" is fatally incomplete unless it is recognized that, even more than corrupting, power destroys. Lacking power in the sense that white Anglo-Saxon Protestants have possessed it in the American society, Jews as a whole were inclined to confront it with caution while, nevertheless, insisting upon their timeless role as the guardians of justice for all men. In the balance thus struck, a moderating element obtruded into their counsels to the NAACP, which buttressed and reinforced the traditional conservatism of the black coleadership under the benevolent patronage of the white Christian liberals.

Walter White, who for many years held the executive secretaryship of the organization, was a black man who looked white. He would indeed have, in fact, been considered a white man in any country that, unlike the United States, is sane on the subject of race. He was at one time married to an olive-skinned black woman. A divorce occurred, and he then married a white woman. Although he was by all odds one of the most effective propagandists for black rights the NAACP had ever recruited to its staff, a serious question now arose as to whether or not his marriage to a white woman had impaired his usefulness to the organization. For he had shown that he was not one of those good Negroes who just didn't hold with race mixing on that level; not one of those good Negroes who knew their place, which was never to be found in any white woman's bed.

Blacks have survived in America by their success in reassuring whites that in no circumstances whatever are they likely to be much of a threat. When they have failed to do so, as in the instance of the Black Panthers, as a group, or Malcolm X, as an individual, they have been liquidated. Not only have blacks refined in an uncommon degree the art of accommodation for survival's sake, they have also developed a vocabulary of accommodation whose semantic nuances convey meanings with all the internal precision of diplomatic exchanges cloaked in exterior circumlocution. As among themselves, of course, a private language for purposes of folk interchange does exist. It is only to be expected that a primary motivation has been the desire to communicate with each other, even in the presence and hearing of whites, if need be, without the latter being privy to its substance. Whites show their awareness of this intention by picking up as fast as they can the ever-changing constituents of this esoteric language and transforming them into fashionable jargon.

But what whites, in general, do not succeed in accomplishing is penetration into those psychological hinterlands in which blacks have been driven and herded together as refugees from white terror. Here, truly, one must be black in order to gain entry, for only blacks have confronted day by day the peril of remaining alive, surrounded by a hostile white society that would not stop short of murder to keep them abject and servile. To exist in such conditions for well-nigh 400 years has required superhuman alertness, superhuman cunning, superhuman resourcefulness, superhuman endurance, superhuman strength, superhuman swiftness, superhuman intelligence. The black American has had to have them all. And, make no mistake, he has them. He is the toughest, shrewdest, wiliest human being in America. He got this way by avoiding, somehow, the reservations where the Indians have been sequestered by their exterminators. In the process, he developed the psychic resource of "soul." The closest equivalent, perhaps, to this concept in the folk lexicon of the Western world is the *duende* of the Spanish gypsies. There are Hebraic elements in the concept of *duende* that receive expression in the art of flamenco. A Jew has "soul"; so has a gypsy; so has a black. It is a private folk mystique in each case, and no transliteration is possible. Yet communication is. For these three peoples have in common an experience, unique and unifying, of the monster—man—whose only redeeming trait is that he aspires intermittently to humanity.

Norman Mailer, like so many other white liberals, may vent his anger and resentment at the repetitious claims of blacks nowadays to be "more beautiful . . . better endowed sexually . . . stronger . . ." and so on. Perhaps he has stopped to consider (although his present-day impeachments do not make this crystal clear) how far blacks have traveled—in America—in order to reach this point, and the road they have traveled by. Perhaps, too, he has thought of how long, how long. Maybe. He is, after all, white. From the standpoint of a black man, it really is unnecessary to say anything more.

The transition from Mailer to a consideration of black women has a certain self-consistent logic about it. For Mailer is, superlatively, the gifted son, often prodigal but always welcomed back from his errant wanderings with the warmth of rejoicing that heaven reserves for its favorite sinners. But if Mailer is *primus filius,* the black woman in America has a larger claim still, historic as well as contemporary, to the symbolic status of Magna Mater. This is true of the black woman everywhere in this country, but especially true of the black woman in the South. Not only has she been the fecund mother; not only has she been the devoted protectress; but she has, above all, been the indispensable condition of the survival of blacks in America. There is a lot of glib talk, conspicuously uninformed, by people like the sociologist Daniel Patrick Moynihan, about the female-headed "Negro" family. These white "experts" all have one thing in common: a profound ignorance of the psychological background of the black struggle to survive in America. They know something of the material aspects of the matter: how much unemployment, how much lynching, how much castration, how much welfare relief, and other data of this sort. But of the magic of black survival and proliferation into 25 million and more inhabitants in a land where they have constantly been threatened with extinction—of these things these white "experts" know nothing. The black mother has been like a she-wolf suckling, in legendary fashion, the black foundlings whose destiny it may be to become the true founders of democracy in America.

The education of the black woman (for example, in the South), as opposed to the relative neglect accorded the black male, as a matter of family policy, was a carefully wrought design calculated to protect the group, as a whole, in the hostile conditions imposed upon it. The Jewish people adopted a similar expedient amidst the disfavoring circumstances of ghetto life.

And now, the expanding education of the black group has had unforeseen consequences. The sit-ins in the South (in restaurants, department stores, supermarkets) and general militancy on the part of the first extensive crop of black college students set off an explosive chain of related movements, not only on white campuses in America but also among students throughout the world. Here is where it all began, with the black college students in the Deep South of the United States. They were the primary agents of the world-wide revolt against the older generation by the younger. This is not to suggest that they formulated this development as a conscious plan of action, but there can be no denying the consequences of the initial protests by the first large-scale harvest of black college students.

It is not without irony that a Woolworth cafeteria in an obscure Southern city may someday be regarded as the historic site of the founding movement for the final overthrow of the values of a Western society in an advanced stage of decomposition.

Federal Judge J. Waties Waring, a South Carolina aristocrat, who delivered the decisions in the Clarendon County cases in South Carolina that led to the antisegregation pronouncement of the United States Supreme Court in 1954, was forced by hostile racists to leave Charleston, where his family had resided for generations, 300 years and more. He went north and spent the last years of his life there. He once discussed with me the future of race relations in America at dinner at the home of Mrs. Edna Merson, who has devoted many years of her life to the struggle for civilized relations between blacks and whites. "Write off the older generation," was Judge Waring's recommendation. "It's hopeless to try to do anything with them. It's the young people who will change things."

Perhaps Judge Waring was right. He also said, in explanation of why black progress tended to be slow and sporadic: "Negroes are made to fight so hard for every little inch of gain in their struggle that every time they take a single step forward they are obliged to sit down and rest."

Simply as exegesis to Judge Waring's views, however, the Fabian tactics of the traditional Negro leadership in the centuries-old conflict with white supremacy can be remarked. As Fabius Cunctator's military plan was to avoid a pitched battle with Hannibal, so has black leadership retreated, as a rule, from direct engagement with white power. They are perhaps aware that Lake Trasimene and Cannae led in the end to Zama. Yet even if they are not, their tactics of delay and disengagement have secured, so far, the survival of the black group. At Zama Hannibal's elephants were stampeded by the strategy of Scipio Africanus. In their berserk fright these fighting animals inflicted confusion and disarray on Hannibal's forces. It is an interesting speculation whether the role of Hannibal's elephants is being re-enacted by some of the militant black groups in this struggle against the internal imperial might of the new Rome on the Potomac.

The best strategy capable of adoption by black Americans in this continuing struggle is a combination of flexibility and pragmatism. Incarceration in ideology, imprisonment in dogma, must be avoided at all costs.

The name of Marcus Garvey has already been mentioned. This black Jamaican stirred and implanted feelings of pride in their African heritage among black Americans to an extent never before equaled (let alone surpassed) by any other black leader. Garvey, singlehanded, transformed the racial consciousness of black people in America into a potent instrument of psychological uplift. He moved large numbers of blacks from a defensive to an aggressive position on the subject of race. The slogan "Black is beautiful" was not minted, except perhaps in the literal sense, by Stokely Carmichael. It was Garvey's distinctive coinage that, in Carmichael's rhetoric, received the contemporary verbal expression. But the message came straight from Garvey. No one since Frederick Douglass and before Malcolm X had so aroused and rallied the pride of Negroes in the sheer fact of being black. It is impossible to separate a man from his innate and distinctive gift. Garvey possessed remarkable powers of oratory, and, like Martin Luther King, he had a dream. In his case, it was the dream of returning to Africa. That it was a dream largely impracticable of realization never seemed to occur to him; or, if it did, he concealed it from his followers. He spoke as though the then colonial powers in Africa did not exist; but, assuming they existed, were either not in a position to oppose his ambition or in their beneficence would refrain from frustrating it. The practice of oratory is the administration of a powerful drug, soporific or kinetic as the case may be, to numbers of people; but one is obliged, as a condition of so doing, to administer it to oneself also. Oratory is incantation, and incantation is magic. The price of putting people under a spell is that one inevitably puts oneself under the same spell.

Even if the orator is a cynic and does not really believe what he is saying, he must for the moment of oratory, at any rate, embrace the belief he is professing or make a persuasive show of infatuation; unless, in the instance of orators possessed by overwhelming causes— Frederick Douglass inveighing against slavery; Winston Churchill exhorting Britain against Hitler—unless in such instances of palpable possession, the motives of the orator are appropriate objects of critical scrutiny. By this test, Garvey passes muster. He was a little, fat black man, in W. E. B. Du Bois's unflattering description, who had known in his own person, and witnessed in that of other blacks, the humiliation of colonialism in its protean guises. His sense of outrage found currency in the rhetoric of protest. He struck shrewdly at the very foundation stone of the theory and practice of colonialism: the belief on the part of the colonial power that its subjection of an exploited people is warranted by their self-evident state of ethnic inferiority. So, against this, he opposed and asserted the supreme heritage of Africa, the unequaled wealth of its great historic past, as the massive material basis for a deep, psychic restoration of black pride. That is where he began. His appeal was to the black unconscious primarily, and to effectuate it, he recruited a black historical past that was no more falsified than the national history of any white group. He knew that history was a harlot who would sleep with anyone for the right price. He said farfetched and absurd things about the African past, things he did not know to be true, perhaps did not even *feel* to be true; but so long as they were useful in the apocalyptic task he had set himself of liberating black men's thinking about themselves, and black men's ways of seeing themselves, from the centuries-long enslavement to white men's lies, they were justifiable. It wasn't playing

214

the game. The victims should always be more moral than the oppressors. Otherwise the springs of cleansing guilt will dry up—say the oppressors. Garvey lied about the African past just as any white nationalist lies about the European or North American past. No more, and no less. But he did not stop there. He organized the United Negro Improvement Association, a crude instrument of racial propaganda, which disclosed Garvey's shortcomings with naked clarity. In time he was sent to prison on the usual charges, but not before he had "ennobled" numbers of his followers and created a kingly court in which Dukes of Ashanti, Counts of Ghana, Princes of Nigeria, and Knights of the Order of Sierra Leone abounded. Negroes simply love these grandiose titles. Give them the least chance, and the first thing, or almost the first thing, they do is confer titles of nobility upon themselves; as at the Haitian court of Christophe, where Dukes of Lemonade and Marquises of Sugar Cane were as numerous as the noblemen of the chamber pot at the court of a French sovereign.

Garvey's ideological successors have mainly been West Indians like himself, who also emigrated to the United States. If they were born in the United States, as in the case of the late Malcolm X, they nevertheless have had some family connection with the West Indies. Senator Patrick McCarran of Nevada made West Indians the particular object of his excluding legislation when, in discussing the provisions of his Internal Security Act of 1950, he singled out those "broad-minded West Indians" as aliens to be kept out, rigorously.

After Garvey's imprisonment in an Atlanta jail by the United States government, on a charge of using the mails to defraud, and his subsequent release, he was deported to his native Jamaica. He had a brief fling at local politics, and, finding the stage too small and the audience too parochial for his talents and ambitions, he went to London. There, one winter afternoon, he stood on the pavement of the Gray's Inn Road, apparently sunk in thought, and leaning with a forlorn air on a cane he carried. He was short of stature, and he wore an astrakhan coat, dark and tightly buttoned against the damp cold. There he was, at the end of it all, a voluntary exile in the imperial bastion of the great colonial power against whom he had tilted, and, as it seemed at the time, so futilely. He stood alone— Samson among the Philistines. Yet in his eyes the old dream was still alive. Garvey gazed beyond the street, beyond London, beyond England, oblivious to the noise of the passing traffic, oblivious to the past, in the spell of his dream. Whatever men might say, Garvey had not failed. He had been humbled into seeking sanctuary in the land that had been a principal agent in the enslavement of Africa, whose past he had so powerfully invoked and to whose future he had so eloquently appealed. Although solitary and abandoned on the Gray's Inn Road in the twilight of a late winter afternoon, he still commanded the allegiance of Time as the prepotent British Empire could not. Garvey's dream would come to fruition and flourish long after that mighty empire had crumbled to dust.

Despite colonialism in the classic form in which it has existed in the British colonies in the West Indies, Africa, and elsewhere, it is nevertheless true that a West Indian, on coming to the United States of America, experiences, as a nearly invariable rule, cultural shock. He has heard, and he has guessed, and he has seen to some extent with his own eyes, there in his native West Indies, the workings of racial prejudice in varying degrees of blatancy and subtlety. Yet nothing of this had prepared him for the monolithic institution of white supremacy he must confront on his entry into the United States. Stokely Carmichael—to cite one instance—was, quite visibly to a fellow West Indian, a man in a state of acute cultural shock during his more or less brief public life in this country.

To this complex of pathology proceeding from that social cause must be attributed some, at least, of the implacable resentment exhibited by West Indians, as a whole, toward the ethnic injustice that poisons so much of American life. It is not the only influence that impels them to political activity, yet it is at all times a paramount factor. Some of their conservative black American critics ask why it is that they did not display the same militancy against colonialism in the West Indies. The simple answer is that they did. But the colonial masters, to confine the matter to the West Indies, were more elusive and often not even present. When West Indian blacks looked around them, they saw themselves in the majority, and they saw blacks like themselves in positions of power and possessing both public and private status. It was far from a perfect disguise, of course, and in any case no one could blink the fact that these elevated blacks were, after all, dressed-up marionettes on an imperial string manipulated from afar by the metropolitan power to subserve the classic ends of colonialism. This much, and more, was quite evident. But the British practiced colonialism, for the most part, as a matador engages a bull.

In the American practice of internal colonialism, white supremacy is the bull and the exploited blacks are the matador. A West Indian, on arriving here, suddenly finds himself transformed from a bull into a matador. The reversal of roles upends his consciousness, and he seeks not only redress for his present hazards as a matador but vindication for his past as a bull.

However, to shift the metaphor back into more prosaic terms, the presence of black West Indians in America has been a catalyst in the black conflict with white supremacy. It would be pure gibberish to claim that without West Indians, apathy and resignation on the part of black Americans would have committed the struggle to the cautious initiatives of black conservatives in the leading strings of white liberals. This would ignore or discount the frequent incidence of black revolt against oppression from the earliest days of slavery to the moment (and well beyond it) when Monroe Trotter denounced Woodrow Wilson face to face at the White House for the white supremacist that the pious-sounding "savior of mankind" really was. This minor scholar with a Southern background was so incensed by Trotter's forthright exposure of the fraudulent character of his professions of democracy that he informed Trotter then and there that he would never in future receive any deputation of which Trotter was a member. Trotter was a Harvard man and a better man than Wilson, but he lacked a Colonel House to manipulate him into the Presidency of the United States, which would have been impossible anyway, because Trotter was black. Lloyd George and Clemenceau saw straight through Wilson at the Peace Conference in Paris in 1919 and used him accordingly. Henry Cabot Lodge finished the job in the United States Senate. William C. Bullitt's vengeful diatribe against Wilson is, obviously, the consequence of a deep personal loathing under cover of an attempt at scientific analysis of the latter through a species of collaboration with Freud. Yet Bullitt's account in his collaboration with Sigmund Freud (*Thomas Woodrow Wilson: 28th President of the United States: A Psychological Study*) is not fundamentally at odds with that aspect of Wilson's character revealed in his encounter with a black man who refused to truckle and genuflect to him.

Their number is legion, these black men crippled and struck down for presuming to stand up like men. Paul Robeson, Adam Clayton Powell, H. Rap Brown, Eldridge Cleaver—the list is endless—have all fallen victim to the same white supremacist vengeance. Granted that

217

each in some way or other did things that should have been left un-
done, the plea that they were only human would have availed them—
if they were white. Being black, their crime was stretched, as a matter
of course, to fit the foreordained punishment.

Eldridge Cleaver, as a writer, and unlike the generality of black
writers (with the exception of Richard Wright), does not whine about
the racial wrongs committed against him and his people. Unlike Baldwin, for example, he will not comfort his tormentors. And he is
sophisticated enough to see that blackness alone cannot be taken to
predict the side of the barricades on which a man will stand in the
moment of truth. There are many whites, decent and sober people,
who will stand with Cleaver against those blacks who put their trust
in accommodation. The Jews tried that tactic in Germany, and look
at what happened to them.

Yet it is necessary to draw a line between accommodation at the
expense of principle and accommodation in furtherance of principle—
a difficult line to draw and often invisible except to the historical eye.
What seems like weak-kneed expediency at a given moment may, on
reflection, turn out to have been the farsighted purpose of an iron
resolve. Perhaps the only valid test of the distinction is William James's
pragmatism: does it work? Or, did it work?

Hindsight tends to elevate Negro "Uncle Toms," at least in some
instances, to the status of cold practitioners of demographic realism.
It is true that in 1750, blacks were 22 per cent of the population of
this country. It is also true that 200 years later they were only 11
per cent of the population. But the latter percentage represented in
terms of absolute numbers 12 million blacks. (This figure relates more
accurately to the decade of the thirties than to that of the forties.
Even then, it is an official figure, which is usually off by 2 or 3 million, at least.) In 1972, blacks (certifiable, recognizable blacks, excluding the countless millions who have either "passed" or are "passing") numbered around 25 million. At their present rate of increase, if
their increasing intransigence does not subject them to decimation or,
more drastic still, a "final solution," by the end of the next generation,
say, a period of about 30 years, they will number between 40 and
50 million. When this stage is reached—if it is reached—the white
supremacist game is up. Maybe the supercautious black leaders have
had this in mind all the time. "Increase and multiply" has been the
immemorial advice of the Southern Negro clergymen to their congre-

218

gations. "Increase and multiply" has sounded from the lips of their Northern Negro counterparts. The wave of European immigration outran for a time the natural increase of blacks in the United States and reduced its proportion relatively to the whole population of the country. But blacks were not submerged in the tide. They rode the surf. The rollers they were waiting for came in the shape of their own fecundity. They contrived a population explosion of their own long before the concept had gained currency as a portent of ecological disaster.

So what is to be done about them? As we have seen, three things, mainly: exterminate them; separate them; or assimilate them. The first is well within the limits of American possibility. The second is already being canvassed by some blacks and some whites. The third is tentatively broached now and again by "nigger lovers" or by those who, despairing of the practicability of the two other approaches to the problem, resign themselves to the last.

Congressman Mendel Rivers of South Carolina, interviewed by *Life* shortly before his death, said that "white southerners are more Nigra than white"—a remarkable view, indeed, coming from such a quarter. And also a remarkably accurate view. Anyone who has resided in the Deep South cannot fail to see the profound affinity, despite all the brutal violence and manifestations of hatred, between the two groups; an affinity as deep as the ties of blood between brothers. Of all human situations on a comparable scale, this centuries-long re-enactment of the perennial drama of Cain and Abel is, surely, the most compelling.

Yet there is an epic guilt that has so far eluded capture by art. It is the racial guilt, not only of the South but also of the whole North American culture. By racial guilt is meant both black and white guilt, both North and South. Victims who resign themselves to oppression are as guilty as their oppressors. The question that always precedes this finding is not why they were oppressed but why did they *need* to be oppressed? It is because he insists on posing this question that Djilas, for instance, is so inconvenient to Tito. A profoundly honest response must, nevertheless, equate the guilt of the victim with that of his oppressor. But Tito apparently does not know this; and neither, it seems, does Djilas. Yet it is the duty of a full human being to pose the question. And Djilas does. But when this question is asked of black men, what can their answer be? Or when asked of German Jews?

Why do men *need* to be oppressed? Is it merely so that a great satirist of the human condition, such as Mark Twain, might make a character (in this instance, Huckleberry Finn) describe an explosion that has occurred and answer, when asked "was anyone hurt?," "No'm. Killed a nigger"? Certainly there must be some profounder reason than this for the compulsion of groups of the human species to interlock themselves in reciprocal bonds of victimization and oppression.

Nor is the answer to be found in "marches," whether on Washington, D.C., or Selma, Alabama. The inherent problem simply is not capable of solution by the pacific technique described by a Roman writer of the classical age as "*Solvitur ambulando.*" Nor, again, will it yield up its secret to blacks and whites in a New York Urban Coalition constituting themselves into a glee club in the wishful, liberal hope that the key will be found with the inscription "*Solvitur cantando.*"

These are the delusions from which well-intentioned people suffer when they cannot bring themselves to deal decisively with the root causes of social ills. This is the way of the Social Democrats, whose excellent intentions paved the way for the Nazi terror in Germany; of the Kerenskyites, Social Democrats of the Russian stripe, whose faltering irresolution gave Lenin his historic opportunity; and of all those who, like Goethe, would choose injustice rather than disorder.

The United States, to draw on John Donne, is not "an island, entire of itself . . . [It is] a part of the main." It follows that the black insurrection against the American society is, on its own negligible scale, a part of the world revolution whose present-day incidents, wherever they occur, have their genealogy, if not their genesis, in the modern historical process. Any occupant of the American Presidency may be George III in the view of Eldridge Cleaver or in that of the endless succession of blacks to whom the vaunted democracy of the United States is a mouthing hypocrisy. Tyranny is nonetheless tyranny because it is imposed upon a minority. It does not derive a special exemption from the fact that it discriminates beneficently in favor of the majority. The odor of sanctity to which it aspires quickly becomes a vile stench in the nostrils of the world.

The present situation and its immediate outlook are vastly confused by the anarchic impulses disseminated by the new technology. For the sake of mankind, said Novalis, science should take one step backward until mankind had succeeded in taking two steps forward. This is a counsel of the utmost wisdom. For the possibilities of geno-

220

cide now within reach of only partly civilized people, such as the Americans (but not only the Americans), can merely inspire pessimism in any detached observer of the human scene. At his present stage of evolution, man is not to be trusted with such dangerous playthings. His moral level is, as yet, only that of an irresponsible two-year-old, a precocious child with a vicious streak.

Blacks must defend themselves against this child and against themselves, for this child is present in them, too. In so far as they are concerned, this child is the American society.

Frederick Douglass once said that "he who is whipped oftenest is whipped easiest." Never, never should blacks forget this—if they wish to survive.

6

IT IS NECESSARY to keep white racism in perspective. It is equally necessary to make the most scrupulous distinction at all times between whiteness, purely as such, and white racism. It is true that the bare fact of whiteness suffices to give rise to a presumption of racism. This can hardly be avoided in the historical circumstances. Nor on the whole does contemporary experience offer instant rebuttal to this presumption. Still, the duty devolving upon an impartial witness continues to be both exacting and inescapable. He must not follow the multitude to do evil. His own racism, if he be black, will give practical expression to his antagonism to white racism, yet it is not likely to provide an antidote. It will only aggravate the disease. This is why the real work of dealing with the problem of racism lies not among blacks but among whites. It is among this latter group that the disease is endemic. It is they, the whites, who are the germ carriers; it is they, in particular the European whites, who are the primary source of contagion.

Few will need to be reminded that the Pilgrims left Europe as that continent was proceeding toward an exchange of the humanism of the Renaissance for the scientism of the Enlightenment. In the specific terms of this development within their country of origin, Great Britain, it meant that they departed from an English society intolerant of religious differences, celebrant of social caste, mercantilist in economic practice, restrictive of intellectual freedom, and divided politically between the upper-class adherents of royal absolutism and the middle-class proponents of parliamentary supremacy. When they went to Holland en route to the New World, Shakespeare was still alive and Louis XIV ruled by divine right in France. A graphic idea of the political temper of the seventeenth century may be gained from the "Royal Catechism" on which Louis XIV was brought up. The author was the Bishop of Vence. A typical passage goes as follows:

You are the handsomest child in the world. . . . You are the visible and authentic image of God. Your Majesty should always remember that you are a Vice-God. [Cited by Brinton, Christopher, and Wolff in A *History of Civilization*.]

Bishop Bossuet did as well for the Dauphin. He wrote the *Politique tirée de l'écriture sainte* (*Political Principles Drawn from Holy Scripture*). Here are some of his scriptural inferences:

Subjects owe the prince complete obedience. . . . The prince is owed the same services as the fatherland. . . . The fatherland must be served as the prince intends. . . . Not even persecution exempts subjects from the obedience they owe the prince. . . . Subjects may oppose to the violence of princes only by respectful remonstrances, without mutiny and without murmur, and by prayers for his conversion.

Well toward the final quarter of the twentieth century, black Americans would be expected to maintain the attitudes prescribed in the foregoing passage.

Nor was this framework of admonitions constructed around the duties of seventeenth-century French subjects alone. It was characteristic of the absolutist demands of the monarchs of that age in Europe. A civil war had to be fought in England, a king dethroned and the institution of monarchy itself briefly terminated, in order to assert the right of the people to participate in their own governance. The political and military conflict in England had been prepared, and was reinforced, by a succession of social theorists who propounded, in the main, the liberation of the individual from the thralldom of the state.

Yet, as has already been pointed out, Christian Europe had applied its religious inspiration to dividing mankind into those who were, like themselves, Christians and those who were not. As these latter mainly were nonwhite, the two categories—non-Christian and nonwhite—

became the negative basis of an ethnic outlook that was the European progenitor of white racism.

The European immigrants into North America, from the first settlers in Virginia and Massachusetts early in the seventeenth century to the latest influx in the twentieth, were bearers of mixed cultural traditions. They ranged from liberal middle-class dissenters (with here a sprinkling of aristocrats and there an admixture of *haute bourgeoisie*) to slum proletariat and peasant serfs. It would not be wholly accurate to denominate them as they have been described, "the scum and refuse of Europe." But it is true that they were extremely indiscriminate in their social composition. J. C. Furnas writes, in *The Americans:*

The absurdities and extravagances of nativism need not altogether obscure the intelligible cultural case against unrestricted immigration. In their *Beyond the Melting Pot* (1963) Nathan Glazer and Daniel Patrick Moynihan, one "the son of a working-class immigrant, the other, the grandson," say: ". . . we would not know how to argue with someone who maintained that something was lost when an original American population was overwhelmed in the central cities by vast numbers of immigrants of different culture, religion, language, and race."

Furnas also cites James K. Hosmer's *Short History of Anglo-Saxon Freedom* as follows:

We have been so over-hospitable in receiving all comers that we are in some danger of losing our character as an Anglo-Saxon land. The Thirteen Colonies were a fairly homogeneous body, with Celtic and Teutonic admixtures too small to affect appreciably the mass about them. . . . [Now] one in every six of us is of foreign birth while one in every three has both parents of foreign birth . . . it is natural for thoughtful men of the original stock to feel somewhat insecure . . . an important reason for a brotherly drawing toward those who, in spite of superficial differences, are yet substantially one with ourselves. Every Anglo-Saxon should hold the leadership of his race to be something which is bound up with the welfare of the world.

This American scholar's views were published in 1890 as hordes of European immigrants swarmed across the Atlantic.

Indeed, the only group that has entered North America since the seventeenth century which was carefully selected was the black African slaves. Only the best were chosen, and only the sturdiest survived the monstrous agony of the Middle Passage and the relentless servitude

224

of the plantations. These blacks comprised a truly elite group of settlers and are the only instance of a selective infusion among the numerous elements of the American people.

The cultural traditions of the main concourse of European immigrants, in so far as they possessed a common denominator, were first of all Christian. On the secular side, they were libertarian; which is to say, the immigrants were either in active revolt against authoritarianism or, at any rate, dreamed of an ideal polity, where individual liberty in social consort with enlightened law represented the highest political value. But their vision was also, in large part, of a transformation of their economic condition. At this point they entered the market place as competitors, either actual or potential, with a vital stake in the promotion of their self-interest. Thus, as European Christians they were committed to the establishment of a white racist kingdom of God on earth; as political creatures, they were hostile to authority and passionately adherent to individual liberty; as the human resources of the economic structure of capitalism, they were the disinherited of the mercantilist system of the Middle Ages but now the heirs of the supplanting system of *laissez faire*, whose testator was the Industrial Revolution. Dispossessed by Colbert, they had been reinstituted as heirs by Adam Smith. But such as they were, in all their prismatic quality, they brought, in their successive waves to North America, much that would uplift and enlighten, much that would transfigure and regenerate, but also much that would disfigure and destroy. Their principal victims would be the North American Indians and the transported black Africans. The former would break under their onslaught; the latter would bend, but not break. The chief ideological weapon in their extensive armory would be the dogma of their racial primacy. They would deploy it to remorseless effect, drawing deeply upon their European tradition of social violence, with which they would suffuse the life of the new country, until to be violent and to be American were one and the same thing.

Three points in particular must be noted. First, these white European immigrants brought to the New World—to North America—not peace but a sword. They brought violence, for that was the common imperative of their social circumstances in their transatlantic origin. The Europe that spewed them out had never known a century of peace in 1,000 years, nor a decade's in a century. The evolution of

Europe into a congeries of nation-states was pock-marked by violence. Brutal incident and concerted force were the usual accompaniments of social change on that continent. Its inhabitants were conditioned to violence as a normal reflex of their neurological structure. They were also indoctrinated with the notion of violence as a functional mode of solving problems and attaining national objectives. War was a commonplace of the evolution of European society. It might occur on a domestic level in the form of internal uprising or *Jacquerie;* it might encompass the limited scope of a pogrom; it might mount to the scale of revolution. It might, on the other hand, transcend national boundaries in order to secure the design and assert the will of one or more states against another or others. Whatever the character or motivation of its specific occurrence, it was as native to the European continent as the Rhine or Tiber, Seine, Tagus, or the North Sea. Violence, war, revolution—these were the natural features of the social and political evolution of Europe. Violence was either military or paramilitary, random or concerted, but it was constant. So was revolution, though this did not always take the form or express the content of violence. In its intellectual aspect, revolution in Europe was often more covert and less continuous. Its essential character was anti-authoritarian. Most of the time, the constraints of orthodoxy bore down quickly and uncompromisingly upon all intellectual novelty. Nothing was so distasteful to the guardians of the ruling beliefs, and so feared by them, as a new idea. No one was more certain of official disapproval, with the virtual certainty of punishment, than the expositor of a deviant idea.

The Catholic church was in some degree to blame for this oppressive tyranny over the European mind, yet the fault lay not wholly with it. Political absolutism was no less jealous of the privileged position of established ideas and, except where its interests were in conflict with those of the church, combined with the latter to enforce the intellectual sovereignty of traditional dogma. It was a revolution of the profoundest consequence when skepticism first insinuated doubt of ruling assumptions, and tentativeness challenged certainty as the mind-set of an intelligent man or woman. It was a revolution of world-shaking import when Francis Bacon's inductive method superseded the Aristotelian categories and when Descartes inaugurated the era of modern science. These developments occurred against a continuously unfolding panorama of social violence and military convulsions. New weapons and new tactics of organized warfare preoccupied the best minds of the succeeding generations. What it all meant in the end was power: the power to dictate the lives of men by acquiring and employing unquestioned authority over their minds.

The Europeans carried their etiological diseases to the North American continent, carried their inculcated neural reflexes of social violence, their propensity to revolution, and their white Christian racism. It was not a prepossessing heritage, to this extent. Yet beyond this, they carried a portion of their ethnic inheritance that offset the grave social liability constituted by the remainder and that went far toward redeeming the whole: they carried with them a conviction of the imperative necessity for individual liberty, whose supreme expression was the unfettered freedom of the mind to inquire, uncoerced by authority, into all things in heaven and on earth.

To this European estate, Frederick Douglass, Booker T. Washington, and W. E. B. Du Bois, being black, were at best contingent legatees; while John Adams, Thomas Jefferson, and Abraham Lincoln, being white, were deemed natural and incontestable heirs. Hence white racism in the United States of America; hence the fear of black revolution in the United States of America.

7

THE THREE CENTURIES of, first, colonization and, thereafter, independent nationhood of America culminated in its belated entry into the First World War. By the end of that conflict the center of world gravity had shifted definitively to the United States. The British Empire, whose decline the German Chancellor Bismarck thought he detected half a century before the First World War, had reached the stage where greatness might still be dissembled despite enfeeblement. Yet the pretense was growing harder to maintain, and within twenty years it would be altogether dissipated by a revived and revanchist Germany. Meanwhile, Germany had been dismantled economically and humiliated politically by the Treaty of Versailles. Senegalese mercenaries of France were deployed as occupation troops in the former kingdom of the Imperial Kaiser to police the spoils of victory. Their presence was also intended to bring home to the Germans the racial meaning of the latter's defeat. The German Emergency League against the Black Horror was founded.

Europe had had a great fall, and all the presidents, prime ministers, and plenipotentiaries could not put it back together again. They tried. Wilson's Fourteen Points and the amphictyonic charade of a League of Nations testified to their efforts. The failure of the attempt indicted their greed, lack of vision, deficiencies of intelligence, and moral obliquity. Lloyd George, Cle-

228

menceau, Orlando, Wilson—these were not inspired prophets calling a new world into being from the ashes of the old. They were
circus performers: jugglers manipulating nation-states, or the designs
of nation-states; trapeze artists swinging, simianlike, from one political expedient to another; tightrope and high-wire walkers teetering
to and fro above the gaping world concourse in a precarious act
known as the balance of power. Behind all their histrionic fervor,
their mouthing subservience to the will of the people, and the vaunting
oratory with which they proclaimed their intention to "make the world
safe for democracy," they were nothing but a gang of nationalistic
hucksters crying their shoddy political wares in the market place of
world power. They spent their time outwitting and outmaneuvering
one another, each trying to gain as much as possible for himself and
his particular bloc of interests at the expense of the others. Apart
from this, two matters were their especial concern: how to suppress
revolution wherever it threatened what they conceived to be their
national interests; and how to continue, extend, and intensify by the
device of colonialism the subjection of the nonwhite groups of mankind for the benefit of the whites.

While President Wilson was enunciating his Fourteen Points in
Paris and professing in the borrowed language of exalted concepts his
reverence for democracy, the administration of his country, of which
he was the chief magistrate, was actively making good its claim to
be regarded as the most racist regime since Andrew Johnson succeeded the white martyr Abraham Lincoln. The Peace Conference of
1919 was a farce counterpointed by Carthaginian tragedy. Wilson must
have noted the failure of the Congress of Vienna to establish a persisting organization to maintain the unsteady balance of power so
tortuously arrived at after the overthrow of Napoleon. He can scarcely
have failed to remark that not half a century had elapsed when some
among the former allies were at each other's throats. Great Britain
and France, then on opposite sides, were now acting in military
concert against Russia, Britain's former partner in the struggle against
Napoleon. Wilson's League of Nations now, at the end of the First
World War, would avoid these bloody versions of musical chairs. It
would substitute moral principle for *Realpolitik*. But it did not. From
the beginning, there had been little doubt as to the essentially racist
character of the new world organization. To cite a few instances: the
inhabitants of the former German territories in Africa were not freed

from colonial thralldom by the League of Nations, but were merely handed over to new European masters; the Arabs in the Middle East were relieved of Turkish domination only to be subjected to British overlordship; India continued in its centuries-old role of colonial vassal of the British Crown. Nor was the position of the sub-Sahara African colonies altered by the establishment of the League of Nations. They and their inhabitants remained chattels of the European powers to be exploited at will for the paramount benefit of the latter. The League of Nations mirrored its principal advocate with merciless accuracy. Wilson's racism, his canting hypocrisy, his lack of political realism in the larger compass of international affairs, and, above all, his profound ignorance of Europe as distinct from his academic knowledge of European history—these were all transparent in the wordy pietism that was so cynically translated by his European colleagues into political unscrupulousness. Sir John Simon's stupidity over Manchuria in 1926 and Sir Samuel Hoare's knavery over Ethiopia ten years later— Mr. Henry Stimson of the United States acting in diffident, uneasy concert in the first instance and M. Pierre Laval cast as evil instigator in the second—were both impartially to be attributed to the machinations of white racism.

The world endured the League of Nations for two decades. The League might have redeemed itself and done much to avert the Second World War had it not squandered its already limited capital of moral authority by its racist betrayal of Ethiopia in that African nation's struggle to defend itself against a European aggressor, Italy. Membership in the League of Nations did not suffice to rid China of the colonial incident of extraterritoriality imposed by the European powers in their partitioning of the country into spheres of influence. The League of Nations was an accomplice of white racism. Its demise at the onset of the Second World War was no cause for lamentation. The world was relieved of a white racist sham, and it was good riddance. It had abandoned Ethiopia to Mussolini with the same supineness with which it contemplated the horrors of the Gran Chaco conflict and the lynching of black Americans. It did make some fuss about the persistence of slavery among the Arabs, but it was tongue-tied about the extermination of Australian aborigines at the hands of the white usurpers of that land. Thus encouraged, white Australia, acting through its courts of law, declared later on, in April, 1971, that the surviving aborigines possessed no "legal title" to their ancient tribal lands. The argument that induced this conclusion is not without a certain usefulness in illustrating the doctrine of legality according to the canons of colonialism and white racism.

The underlying facts also have a distinct charm of their own. The government of Australia entered into a mining agreement with a Swiss-Australian consortium called NABALCO. By this agreement NABALCO undertook to develop an alumina-bauxite project on land traditionally held by aboriginal tribes. The tribes, contesting the legal validity of the project, asserted their title to the land, alleging that "we know we were always there." They adduced as proof of their contention sacred relics and other artifacts. Tribal leaders testified in support of the claimants; so did qualified anthropologists. But the white Australian judge decided against them and in favor of his government, as might have been expected. In his finding, he said, as reported in the New York *Times,* the "so-called doctrine of communal native title had no place in the common law. . . . All land in the area concerned, upon foundation of British colonies, became the property of the Crown." Thereafter, a valid title to the land could be derived only from the Crown. Naturally, the aborigines were unable to meet this criterion. Having always been there, at any rate long before the first boatload of white convicts arrived in Australia to establish the title of the British Crown, the dispossessed aborigines had never thought of obtaining a document of ownership from the white imperial usurpers. Therefore, in the view of the latter, as enunciated of course by their own tribunal, the aborigines could make no valid title to the land.*

The Indians of North America have had much the same sort of experience at the hands of European settlers. Aside from the attempt to exterminate them, or at least to drive them off their ancestral lands, the solemn treaties negotiated between them and the European intruders have in effect amounted to no more than a fraudulent sham. The whites never had the slightest intention of observing the terms of these treaties and, in actual fact, have seldom done so. In the long history of their relations with the Indians, the recorded instances are few indeed when fidelity to the pledged word has chastened the white man's cynical faithlessness or subdued his murderous greed.

The history of the world as a whole during the past 500 years has

---

* On Australia Day this year (1972), the government of that country proclaimed as its policy: "Australian law does not recognize Aboriginal title to land in Australia." The reason asserted is that the "relationship of the Aborigines with the land was not sufficiently economic to amount to a proprietary interest."

been dominated by the conjunction of technology with the ascendancy of the white groups of mankind. The genetic reasons, if any, for the occurrence of the latter phenomenon are obscure; indeed, for the most part, nonexistent. Chance plays a much greater role in these matters than is commonly conceded. Yet, even if there were no such thing as chance, all phenomena being predictable in terms of an infinite series of probabilities, the half-millennium-long predominance of the whites must nevertheless be regarded as simultaneous with the highest progress of the human species in every quantifiable respect. These circumstances cannot be glibly correlated as cause and effect; perhaps they cannot be correlated at all. Their relationship may be simply a matter of coincidence. Certainly, on the North American continent, as elsewhere, material achievements were counterpointed with characteristic frequency by moral squalor. It is impossible to review even the most self-justifying accounts of the irruption of the Europeans into the Western Hemisphere without shuddering at the grisly horrors they perpetrated in the name of their God, for the sake of their greed, and because of their lust for gold.

Still, it is equally impossible not to recognize that amidst all the spiritual and moral degeneracy, a revolution on the immense scale of human possibilities had occurred. That its momentum was derived from the new technology and that its inspiration, at first Christian, would modulate presently into a racist imperative, and that libertarian concern for the individual would be supplanted by totalitarian reverence for the state, even in so-called democratic societies—these, and more, still do not diminish the claim that a virtual transformation of the terms of human existence had been achieved by the white group of mankind apprenticed to the sorcerer's trade of the new technology. Their curiosity, the salient trait of the group, aside from their insatiable greed and monstrous cruelty, was unbounded. From this unequaled inquisitiveness, this unprecedented desire to peer into and to prove all things, came the technological revolution. For ill as well as for good, it released the spirit of the human species and, preeminently, that of the white man. Of all upheavals in the course of the evolution of the species, it has had the profoundest consequences. For this, all mankind is indebted to the white group. But the matter does not end there.

The judge in the Australian case involving the tribal lands of the aborigines observed, *obiter dicta*, by way of "philosophical justification of colonialism": "The whole earth was open to the industry and enterprise of the human race, which had a duty and right to develop the earth's resources. The more advanced peoples were therefore justified in dispossessing, if necessary, the less advanced." A more explicit affirmation of the law of the jungle would be difficult to imagine. Yet while this has always been the brutal rationale of colonialism, it has also played the amoral role of devil's missionary as the motivating spirit behind the intrusion of the white groups of mankind into other cultures.

At the conclusion of the First World War, for the first time since the ascent of the whites to world hegemony, the principle of self-determination was enunciated in a mood of pious preachment, rather than as a conviction of ethical principle, that was typical of the moralizing politics of Woodrow Wilson. It was not, of course, intended to apply to the nonwhite peoples subjected to colonialism. But the outcome of such declarations sometimes goes counter to their informing impulse. In this instance, it was quickly seized upon by the subjugated nonwhites and transformed into a philosophical weapon and, alternatively, a political tactic to secure their liberation. Yet this was not what the whites had in mind. Certainly, as Winston Churchill made clear, it was not his intention or, as far as he should be able to determine this, the intention of the government of Great Britain, where India or any others of His Britannic Majesty's nonwhite dominions beyond the seas were concerned. Nevertheless, the concept of self-determination, once having escaped from the genie's bottle, would not be put back again. More than anything else, this pietistic declaration tolled the bell for colonialism in its traditional form. Thereafter, the white nations engaged in colonial overlordship would adopt a different strategy. They would "grant" political independence, but they would go as far as they possibly could to maintain their economic domination; which is to say, political independence would be a mockery, since these nonwhites would continue to exist in economic servitude.

The point to be made is the fundamental distinction between the respective ways of ancient and modern empires with conquered peoples. In the former case, captives were enslaved and tribute exacted. Perhaps, as in the Roman instance of Julius Caesar, an army of occupation (witness Gaul; witness Britain) was quartered upon the subjugated country, and a bureaucratic administration installed to carry out the business of government. The whole process had almost always a military purpose. There was no racial mystique involved. And this is the precise, though not exhaustive, difference between ancient and modern imperialism, between conquest and its consequences for the conquered in the ancient mode and the modern concept and practice of colonialism. No discussion of racism in the United States can pretend to realism without taking into account its distinctive character as a group phenomenon. There is no intention to suggest that it is unique to the whites in their relations with other groups. It is clear, however, that the whites have developed it into a principle of statecraft and applied it to subvert the self-esteem of non-whites in all instances of intergroup contact. It is at this point, and in this manner, that racism may be regarded as a novel infiltration, engineered by the whites, into the conventions that previously governed the conduct of conquerors toward the conquered. As such, it has proved to be the deadliest and most persistent foe of the political concept of self-determination.

As a direct result, European nations in general and their trans-atlantic counterpart, the United States, are unable to contemplate with composure the existence of free and independent nonwhite nations. On the domestic level, as, for example, within the United States, the subjection of nonwhites further illustrates this disinclination of white racism. There are purists who split hairs whenever the term "colonialism" is extended to cover the treatment accorded to nonwhite minorities within white racist cultures, as, once again, in the case of the black population of the United States, or in that of the Pakistani, African, and West Indian immigrants in Great Britain. The word, "colonialism," these nominalists argue, should be applied only to the relationship between a metropolitan power and its over-seas territories—even thongh, putting aside the geographical considera-tion, the political, economic, and social incidents are virtually indis-tinguishable in the one case from the other.

They are, in a formal sense, correct in their contention that the internal racist tyranny imposed on nonwhites in countries predominantly populated by whites is not, according to classical usage, to be des-cribed as "colonialism." There is a difference. But it is a mere matter of geography. The characteristic incidents remain the same. The prin-ciple of the subjection of nonwhites continues in active operation. The objective of economic exploitation persists unchanged. So does the purpose of political exclusion or enfeeblement. And so does the color-caste position of inferiority of the nonwhites. Nothing is different ex-cept the scene of the circumstances. Precision of language, although

234

an indispensable condition of intellectual accuracy, is sometimes exaggerated in order to obscure substantial injustices. The misuse of this invaluable tool of mental clarity is a pettifogging game played on occasion by scholars and others to whom form can be more important than substance, and the letter more greatly to be esteemed than the spirit.

Until relatively recent times, as recently indeed as in the comparable instance of the abolition of extraterritoriality in China in 1942, no white man would as a rule be brought to justice before the courts of the Southern United States for an offense against a black man. The juridical effect of extraterritoriality in China was much the same, *mutatis mutandis*. No white man—that is, no national of the European states that had partitioned China into their respective spheres of influence—could be brought before a Chinese court for any reason whatsoever. The principle at work in both instances, as well as the practice in China and the American South, was one and the same. Shorn of its trappings of local custom, derived, in the American South, from the institution of slavery and, in the Chinese Treaty Ports, from the consequences of military conquest, two purposes were to be effectuated. One was the exploitation of nonwhites and their territorial resources for the economic benefit of the whites. The other was the racial predominance of the whites. In this regard, the dubious achievement of the white group has been to extend racial differences into divisions of caste, assuming for itself with the aid of technology— and, supremely, the gun—the topmost position at the apex of the pyramid.

The European assailants of the Chinese concept of China as the "Middle Kingdom," with its xenophobic disdain for other peoples, impute racism to the Chinese in much the same way that white Americans impute black racism to blacks who respond in kind to white racism. But dislike of foreigners (the British are much like the Chinese in this respect) and an exaggerated sense of self-importance—as, for instance, in the case of the French—are very different matters from racial prejudice. Great Britain and France are both racist countries. But while there are numerous instances of Chinese disesteem for foreigners and, not infrequently, of their geocentric attitude toward the rest of the world, nothing of this has essentially anything to do with racism. It may have a great deal to do with an inflated sense of cultural superiority, but that is something else. Reviewing the evidence on a world-wide scale leads to a single, inescapable conclusion:

the transmutation of racial differences into an operative principle of caste distinction, eked out by pseudoscience, is the unique achievement of the white segment of mankind. The concept of race is not peculiar to them (the Arabs, for instance, have long espoused and practiced it in their relations with sub-Sahara Africans). But the elevation of their racial difference—their miscalled whiteness—into a mystique of decisive sociological implications is uniquely their achievement.

It is against this background that the phenomenon of white racism must be considered as it occurs in the United States, and within this context that the necessary conclusions are to be formulated; so that the moral contradictions that bedeviled Woodrow Wilson as the luminous Prophet Most High of the League of Nations and as the white racist President of the United States can be more profoundly appreciated. These contradictions have persisted from the very founding of the republic, from Jefferson, Madison, and Washington to the present day. As far as one can see, they are likely to persist for a long time to come. In the deepest and most elemental sense, these contradictions are in fact the United States. For there are many and mutually incompatible Americas. This is a land of multitudinous facets, a land of innumerable diversities, and yet, a land of curious, paradoxical unity. It is not, however, an organic unity, but one of system and function, of which the world of physics, with its opposed yet complementary particles of matter and antimatter, may offer a molecular model. Such a metaphor may also illustrate more graphically the application in practice of the political theory of federalism. Said the historian George Bancroft, in 1866, to a joint session of Congress met to commemorate Abraham Lincoln:

In the fullness of time a republic rose up in the wilderness of America. Thousands of years had passed away before this child of the ages could be born. From whatever there was good in the system of former centuries she drew her nourishment; the wrecks of the past were her warnings. . . .

The fame of this only daughter of freedom went out into all the lands of the earth; from her the human race drew hope.

This declamatory rhetoric was not without a solid core of truth. But it was far from being the whole truth. It adorned, rather than proclaimed, the truth. Earlier, while the United States was lurching toward civil war, Europe was agitated by recurrent conflict, domestic and external. Chartism in England and the Revolution of 1848 in Germany and France were succeeded in the first instance by the Crimean

236

War; and in the second and third by the protracted Prussian struggle with Denmark to incorporate the duchies of Schleswig and Holstein into the German Confederation, and by the French struggle with Austria over Italian territory. Meantime, the socialist theories of Marx, Bakunin, and Proudhon, among others, germinated in the fertile soil of the Industrial Age. The specific gravity of revolutionary ferment was modified by the new ideology, with its principal base in the mass of the urban proletariat and now, as distinct from formerly, only secondarily in the agricultural peasantry. The object of revolution was now, more nakedly than ever, the seizure and redistribution of state power by a violent process of class displacement. Henceforward—and this perhaps is the supreme insight of Marxism—class interests in any given society would be regarded as inherently irreconcilable.

The Schleswig-Holstein question was settled at about the same time as the American Civil War came to an end. The Union was restored in the latter case, and in the former, Bismarck came nearer to his goal of a united Germany. He would rear Germany to the status of a world power and then be dismissed for his pains by William II. Yet by the time of his dismissal from office, Germany would be among the leading industrial nations of the world. The Franco-Prussian War of 1870 was the foundation stone of the German state, and Sedan its epigraph. The Civil War consummated in the instance of the United States a more perfect union, with Appomattox chiseled in letters of blood upon its base. In both cases, the road led to empire. In both cases, the way was illuminated by the world-expanding achievements of the new technology. In both cases, a national culture would evolve whose world impulse was racist. The one would derive its inspiration from the Christian sense of group particularism diffused throughout Europe with the invention of movable type, and subsequently rationalized in modern terms by Houston Stewart Chamberlain, a disciple of Gobineau. The other would also acquire a legacy of Christian particularism from its ancestral European sources, would engage in a sordid rationalization of racial exclusiveness in the form of slavery inflicted upon black Africans, and subsequently would find in Lothrop Stoddard its own counterpart to the racist Englishman turned German, Chamberlain.

Clinton Rossiter wrote, in *The American Quest, 1790–1860:*

The more we learn of the growth of the American economy in the opening decades of the nineteenth century, the more clearly we see that cotton was indeed a king whose influence, if not whose sovereignty, extended to all parts of the country. By concentrating so heavily on cotton, by producing the world's most eagerly devoured commodity at the neglect of other forms of agrarian, commercial, and industrial activity, the South fed the mills of England and New England, speeded the accumulation of capital, lured men west to grow crops to sell to other men in the South too obsessed with cotton to grow such crops for themselves, and stimulated both diversification and flow in every part of the country. Emerson was more shrewd and less amusing than he knew when he asserted: "Cotton thread holds the Union together; unites John C. Calhoun and Abbott Lawrence. Patriotism for holidays and summer evenings, with music and rockets, but cotton thread is the Union."

Cotton was more than that: It provided well over half the value of all exports between 1820 and 1860, and thereby made the position of the United States in the world economy both tenable and profitable. Since the South did the growing and the Northeast most of the financing and managing of the export trade, Southerners got far smaller a share of the profits from cotton than they thought (and we today might also think) they had coming. Even as the South lagged socially, technologically, and culturally behind the rest of the country, and moved politically and emotionally into a hostile posture, it furnished powerful economic support to the American search for modern nationhood. The planters of cotton, unwittingly and even against their collective will, did almost as much as the builders of railroads to nourish the development of a viable economy and growth of an indestructible Union. Once again we must marvel at the capacity of men to make history—especially when it is not the history they think they are making.

This was doubtless quite true, but after 1870, as Hugh Thomas points out in *Cuba: The Pursuit of Freedom, 1762–1969,* the United States outstripped England (which had until then been in the lead) in steel production. From just under 20,000 tons in 1867 it produced well over "500,000 in 1877, and over a million by 1880." And Germany soon was not far behind. The displacement of cotton by steel marked the transition from the Industrial Age to the Age of Technology.

Side by side with these developments in the United States, domestic violence marched apace, punctuated and amplified by foreign wars. After the war against Mexico, there was William Randolph Hearst's war, otherwise known as the Spanish-American War, the second Philippine Insurrection, and the First World War. "The Wages of War," a statistical study of the causes and periodicity of war and peace (cited by the New York *Times*), calculates that between 1815 and 1965, wars were waged throughout the world in all but twenty-four of those 150 years. During this period Europe was engaged in sixty-eight wars. The number is greater, but it appears that Russia was not included as a European country. The authors of the study describe Europe as having been the most "war prone" area.

By 1859, Great Britain had more or less completed its conquest of India with the suppression of the Sepoy Mutiny. It had engaged, meanwhile, in the Crimean War, with France as its ally, against Russia. In concert with other European powers, it had threatened war if the Schleswig-Holstein question were not resolved to its satisfaction. Bismarck—and his master, William I of Prussia—after having fabricated an alliance with Austria to despoil Denmark of the two disputed duchies, then turned on Austria. France undertook military intervention in Italy, also against Austria, rewarding itself with Nice and Savoy, and magnanimously presenting Venice to Italy. Together with these happenings, the internal restructuring of European society continued. The principal agent of change was the new technology, which had brought into being large masses of industrial workers whose unprecedented demands upon the entrenched interests stirred unrest and acted to subvert the foundations of the old order.

But the Reform Bill of 1832 in England was also in some measure the consequence of the Napoleonic era, and the events of 1848 in France and Germany were, similarly, not unrelated to the irruption of that remarkable genius upon the European scene. Above all, however, the social ferment of mid-nineteenth-century Europe traced its origin immediately to the invention of steam power, the mechanical loom, accelerated locomotion, and other mechanical devices, whose effect was scarcely less than the creation of a new world, with European man (and his transatlantic counterpart, the North American) modified by these developments into what, virtually, was a new human species. There was a release of human energy on the part of the white group as vast as an apocalypse. The centuries that had elapsed since the Mongols turned back on the threshold of the conquest of Europe and the Arab penetration was halted at Tours by Charles Martel had produced Renaissance, Reformation, and Counter Reformation, printing and gunpowder, the manumission of the individual (in social theory) from authoritarian constraint imposed alike by church and state, and the supersession of uncritical belief by scientific inquiry.

239

At midpoint in the nineteenth century, new facets of the infinite possibilities of existence had been revealed through those mechanical inventions, which did not so much inaugurate as asseverate the Industrial Age. Behind it all was this titanic explosion of social energy set off by the white element of mankind. There had been similar explosions before in the history of the human species: Egyptians, Assyrians, Persians, Arabs—all in turn had come to the critical flashpoint of their cultures, had ignited, and then illuminated or incinerated other human groups amongst whom they had hurtled in their headlong, flaming, centrifugal incursion. The First Crusade had been an outward and visible sign that the white group had discovered the mutual convertibility of ideology and energy in the myth-encrusted witness of the Christian faith. Other portents were not lacking. The conceptual transition from a Ptolemaic to a Galilean universe, the navigational proof attained by unparalleled daring that the horizon concealed no abyss but was simply a function of the circumference of the earth, the consequent discovery of the New World and other thitherto inaccessible realms, Newton's law of gravitation, Bacon's *Novum Organum,* subsequently refined into the scientific method of Descartes, the revolution in the conduct of war presided over by Napoleon I, the hypothesis of physical evolution through natural selection attributed to Darwin—these—and much else of scarcely less importance—were some of the sparks from that magnificent combustion of curiosity, will, and daring of white mankind. It would radiate outward until, by the twentieth century, earth, sea, and air, though not conquered, had nevertheless been brought into the service of the thought, action, and imagination of the whole species. By then the moon itself had been made to yield up its inviolacy, and the footprints of men—white men—and the impress of their artifacts on the surface of the planet evidenced once again the quasarlike dispersion of the turbulent, questing energies of this human group.

The collective energy that had brought the Arabs to the intellectual concept of zero, their religion to the remote places of the Orient, their armies to France, and their civilization to Spain had declined with the desiccation of those once vast, fertile plains, which were the material basis of their restless, inventive, and ramifying culture. That was an ecological disaster which cost them the larger world hegemony toward whose attainment their group energy drove them almost, as it were, by instinctual, ethnic tropism. Nor was this ecological insensitivity alone the cause of their descent into cultural decay and national impotence. They showed at all times insufficient respect for the sanctity of life, which partly expressed itself in their avid and tenacious regard for the institution of human slavery and led eventually, as it always does, to contempt for the objects of its servile system recoiling upon itself and brutalizing the masters even as it enfeebled them and imbued their slaves with the passion for liberty and a lust for revenge. The great Aztec Empire was brought down less by the military valor or genius of a handful of syphilitic Spaniards than by the internal subversion wrought by disaffected Indian masses resentful of the tyranny of an imperial elite.

After the Civil War in North America had been fought to the successful restoration of the Union and the black slaves had been liberated, the industrial North, with its economic principle of *laissez faire*, was suzerain over the vanquished agrarian South, still shackled to mercantilism. But everywhere throughout the country, the new mechanical inventions were providing the means for the realization of its twin destiny, continental and manifest. Not only was the frontier continually being pushed back, but by 1870 the area of the country had increased by conquest and annexation from 867,980 square miles and a population of 3,929,214 in 1790 to 2,973,965 square miles and a population of 39,818,449. During the War of 1812, the country had satisfied itself of the ability of its own relatively small navy to contest the traditional sea power of England. Just over a decade later, it asserted the Monroe Doctrine and issued a preliminary challenge to Russian sovereignty over Alaska. By 1854, with Russia embroiled in the Crimean War, the Russians themselves saw the handwriting on the wall, and by 1867 Russian America was no more. Alaska formally became United States territory at a nominal purchase price of $7.2 million.

Meanwhile, the internal cohesion of the country was also achieved through linkage by canals, telegraph, and railroads. Clinton Rossiter celebrates the last medium as

the product of an immense outpouring of human energy: a web of more than 30,000 miles of track that had conquered distance, stirred flow, and done more than any other material achievement to create a national economy, and thereby had helped to hold together a country tugged this way and that by strong centrifugal urges.

These, too, were the years of Reconstruction, that brief post–Civil War attempt by the North to introduce into the South what the North itself had never attempted in its own sector of the country: the practice of political democracy shorn of white racism. The country as a whole was going through a convulsive spasm of its continuous revolution. Federalism, as a republican form of self-government, was under constant necessity to prove itself as the highest political wisdom possible in the national circumstances. The decentralization of sovereign power through the medium of states' rights led from time to time to exacerbated debate over such issues as nullification and interposition. Yet, for a country to whose future there was so far no visible prospect of a limiting term, and whose destiny seemed to be one of well-nigh limitless expansion, federalism, with its characteristic blend of elasticity and dynamism, was more congenial to the given actualities, and also less obstructive of competing interests, than a more static system might have been. Where the latter would have congealed mutually adverse interests into irreconcilable opposites, federalism quantified them in terms of the general welfare and reconciled them on the principle of aspiration to a "more perfect union." These were years of volcanic strivings, and not the least eruptive amidst all the thunder of American success was the racial issue. From this there was no surcease, for blacks, although no longer slaves, were in certain respects, by the end of the period of Reconstruction, even worse off than they had been as unfree chattels of a soulless system. White racism continued to be the salient trait of the American society and to give the lie to the latter's professions of human equality under the law.

This was equally the case in Europe, except that such professions were rather more restricted there, allowing of course for France whose attachment to the ideal of equality was hardly less fervent than its devotion to the racist mystique inseparable from colonialism.

John Strachey writes in *The End of Empire*,

From about 1870 onwards, a new wave of imperialism surged out upon the world. Two countries of Western Europe, Britain and France, led the way. But they were avidly imitated. Germany, America and Japan hastened, late but formidable, to share in the partition of the world which was taking place. Even some of the smaller states—Belgium, Holland, Portugal—managed to get or retain a share. Vast but still semifeudal structures such as Austria-Hungary and Russia were effectively stirred.

242

Britain, both because she still just held the lead in industrial development and because she already possessed a nucleus of empire, essentially India (but also the West Indies), held over from the mercantile epoch, took the lion's share in this new wave of imperialism. [British] acquisitions add up to a territory of 4,754,000 square miles with a population estimated in 1902 at 88 millions. It is important to remember that this whole "Colonial Office Empire," as it might be called, was, essentially created only seventy or eighty years ago. Therefore its life span, since it is now in rapid dissolution, will prove to have been under a century.

It must not be thought, however, that the lion's share was the only one. On the contrary, French acquisitions in this period, principally in Africa (but also Indo-China), were territorially impressive (3,500,000 square miles but with only 26 million inhabitants). Belgium got what proved to be the rich prize of the Congo (900,000 square miles, 8½ million inhabitants). Moreover, Germany at length united, and year by year becoming the most formidable industrial power in Europe, began her colonial career in this period. She annexed, in the same 30 years, a million square miles of territory with 13 million inhabitants. Japan, which only started out on her staggeringly successful course of self-modernisation under forced draft in 1867 acquired her first colonies in this period, as a result of her wars with China at the end, and with Russia just after the end, of the century.

The United States of America also gave what appeared to be unmistakable signs of launching herself upon the imperialist course. She cleaned up fragments of the empire of Spain (Cuba, Puerto Rico, the Philippines) and asserted, in a degree varying all the way from the establishment of a virtual protectorate in Panama to a mere reinterpretation of the Monroe Doctrine elsewhere, her general overlordship of the Americas. Finally, during the whole of this period Russia was pushing out her boundaries, eastward and southward over Asia. As usual, her development was a special case peculiar to herself. In particular, her acquisitions were landlocked and contiguous to her metropolitan mass, instead of maritime and scattered over the continents.

This dry catalogue of the territorial acquisitions of the imperial states in the heyday of the new imperialism, i.e., in the forty years from 1870 to 1914, can convey but a faint impression of the overwhelming power of the Western drive towards the conquest of the world. Nor will it give us any clue as to the causes of this explosive phenomenon.

This last is a curious statement coming from a man who was capable of identifying the Proconsul Cromer's motives in Egypt during the period of British suzerainty as "financial," and who could say of

Alfred Milner in South Africa, "What he was concerned with now that the war [the Boer War] was won, was to unite the white races in order to establish a secure white hegemony."

In a word, unwilling as John Strachey was to admit it, the causes of the "explosive phenomenon" of which he speaks—"the overwhelming power of the Western drive towards the conquest of the world"—are manifest in the two case histories he examines: British imperialism in India and in South Africa. They were economic and racist. These two causes operated in a symbiosis whose consequence was colonialism. But what is chiefly remarkable and, given its racist inspiration, also inevitable is that the Western drive was directed toward the subjection of nonwhite peoples. Even Japan, though not a Western nation, but now highly imitative of the West, satisfied its ambition for territorial acquisitions at the expense of China.

The national impulse of the United States toward expansion through the conquest of weaker human groups, whether within or beyond its borders, must be seen as an instance of a larger process of the same kind occurring at the same time on the part of the whole Western world. That this segment of the larger world was white, and that the objects of its aggression were nonwhite, render the racist imperative self-explanatory. That these nonwhites were in possession of valuable resources of immense utility and profit to the activities of the technological era makes equally understandable the economic basis of colonialism. To keep in view the role that racism played in the imperialist drive for foreign conquest and exploitation, it would be useful at this stage to quote from Kavalam M. Panikkar's *Asia and Western Dominance* on the typical attitude of the Dutch in Indonesia as reflected by the following statement of the founder of Batavia in the sixteenth century:

"May not a man in Europe do what he likes with his cattle? Even so, does the master here do with his men, for everywhere, these with all that belongs to them, are as much property of the master, as are the brute beasts in the Netherlands. The law of this land is the will of the king and he is king who is the strongest."

Strachey comments, in *The End of Empire:*

It is to be feared that Dutch policy in Indonesia was founded on this view, faithfully reflected it for many decades, and never became wholly free of it right up to the loss of Indonesia in 1946.

It would, however, be a comment of insufficient application if its meaning were not extended to embrace the characteristic attitude of whites everywhere in contact with other cultures. The language of that sixteenth-century Dutchman echoes times without number in polemic and apologia on the subject of slaveholding in the American South and as justification in the whole theory and practice of white racism. The internal logic of this view prompted the British, holding India in fee as a vast, subcontinental fiefdom of the Imperial Crown, to turn presently to other areas of the world where nonwhite peoples were in possession of lands and resources that promised economic profit and assured strategic bases for the establishment of military and naval power. India was the colonial platform from which Britain launched its nineteenth-century drive for world empire. In the two decades preceding the effort of the United States to impose commercial intercourse upon Japan, Britain succeeded in forcing the cession of Hong Kong by the Chinese as a consequence of the infamous Opium War of 1842, by which this noxious traffic was inflicted on China. By 1859, the Americans, French, and Russians had joined the British in dividing the spoils of Chinese defeat and subjection.

By the time the British came, toward the end of the century, to the annexation of South Africa, the racist principle of colonialism had long since been enunciated and established. The fact that as late as 1905, Lord Alfred Milner, in a speech in Johannesburg, was still articulating it as a fundamental ground of belief simply adds to the cumulative effect of a long series of such declarations. Milner said on that occasion:

When we who call ourselves Imperialists talk of the British Empire, we think of a group of States, all independent in their local concerns, but all united for the defence of their own common interests and the development of a common civilization; united, not in an alliance—for alliances can be made and unmade, and are never more than nominally lasting—but in a permanent organic union. Of such a union the dominions of our Sovereign as they exist today are, we fully admit, only the raw material. Our ideal is still distant, but we deny that it is either visionary or unattainable. And see how such a consummation would solve, and, indeed, can solve, the most difficult and the most persistent of the problems of South Africa; how it would unite its white races as nothing else can. [Cited by Strachey in *The End of Empire*.]

The unity of the white group—not only in South Africa—has

always been a vital element in the grand design of the imperialists. Its natural enemy is nationalism, but whenever it has been possible to restrain this disruptive force, the unity of the white races has prevailed over even the anarchic impulse of the profit motive. In the twentieth-century instance of the American war in Vietnam, the European nations have assisted America in financing the colossal expense of this war by enduring for years a steadily worsening process of inflation in their economies, created in considerable measure by their collusion in America's dumping of billions of overvalued dollars in Europe. Known as Eurodollars, they produced inflation in European economies by artificially increasing to a tremendous magnitude the amount of dollars in circulation there. Germany alone absorbed some 30 billions of these bloated dollars—almost enough, were they converted into gold, to deplete the entire reserves of bullion in the vaults of the United States at Fort Knox. (These Eurodollars were also used by American corporations to acquire control and ownership of European businesses.) When the Germans protested, they were threatened with the withdrawal of American troops from Germany if they attempted to convert their holdings of dollars into gold. Hypersensitive to inflation as a result of their horrendous experiences with devalued currency after the First World War and again after the Second World War, the Germans would not long tolerate in office any national administration that permitted this ghost to walk again. National imperatives here displaced the white racial solidarity that had been expressed by the indirect support (through this financial expedient of a massive American balance-of-payments deficit) that the white nations of Europe had been giving to the United States in its war against a nonwhite people in Asia. But Germany at last precipitated an economic crisis by declining to contain any longer the huge tidal wave of American dollars.

One day later, the chief American representative at the peace talks with North Vietnam in Paris inquired of the representatives of the latter country whether they were "serious" in their bid, which the North Vietnamese had offered time and again, for a cessation of hostilities on terms whose reasonableness was manifest to the whole world, if not to the white American aggressors. This was merely an example of the ability of the world monetary system to bring even so rich and powerful a nation as the United States to heel were it disposed to do so. But the world monetary system is in the control

246

of the white (which is synonymous with the rich) nations, while the nonwhite (synonymous with poor) nations are in the situation of client states who are obliged to come, hat in hand, begging for handouts. It would be absurd to argue that racism alone is here to blame. It is by no means wholly the fault of the whites that nonwhites the world over—with the exception of the Japanese—are either relatively or absolutely impoverished. The final cause inheres in the nonwhites themselves; the whites amorally exploit the cause and rationalize their exploitation on an ex-post-facto basis of racism.

Yet the point must be emphasized that white racism, whatever its economic rationale, is also the expression of a conviction of ethnological superiority that owes much less to reason than to an irrational frenzy on the part of the white group of mankind in general to assert its collective supremacy. This *folie des blancs*—insanity of the whites—has brought unutterable misery to the human species as a whole, but it has also engendered some of its noblest aspirations and most daring triumphs. On balance, however, were there to be a choice between the obliteration of the whites from time and history, on the one hand, and, on the other, the slower, less technocratic, less machine-infatuated, and more moral evolution of the remainder of the human species, it would be the latter that might represent the surer hope for a higher genetic consummation. Yet the limited point to be made here is that racism is a specific group trait of white Western man. Thus American society cannot be evaluated from this point of view except as a particular instance of a general characteristic of the social culture of the whites.

"Two men I honour, and no third," wrote the British racist Thomas Carlyle, in *Sartor Resartus,* during the course of his tortured philosphizing:

First the toilworn Craftsman that with earth-made implement laboriously conquers the Earth, and makes her man's. Venerable to me is the hard Hand; crooked, coarse; wherein notwithstanding lies a cunning virtue, indefeasibly royal, as of the Sceptre of this Planet. Venerable too is the rugged face, all weathertanned, bespoiled, with its rude intelligence; for it is the face of a Man living manlike. O, but the more venerable for thy rudeness, and even because we must pity as well as love thee! Hardly-entreated Brother! For us was thy back so bent, for us were thy straight limbs and fingers so deformed; thou wert our Conscript, on whom the lot fell, and fighting our battles wert so marred. For in thee too lay a God-created form but it was not

to be unfolded; encrusted must it stand with the thick adhesions and deface-
ments of Labour; and thy body like thy soul, was not to know freedom. Yet
toil on, toil on: thou art in thy duty, be out of it who may; thou toilest for
the altogether indispensable, for daily bread.

A second man I honour, and still more highly: Him who is seen toiling
for the spiritually indispensable; not daily bread, but the bread of Life.
Is not he too in his duty; endeavouring towards inward Harmony; revealing
this by act or by word, through his outward endeavours, be they high or
low? Highest of all, when his outward and his inward endeavour are one:
when we can name him Artist; not earthly Craftsman only, but inspired
Thinker, who with heaven-made Implement conquers Heaven for us! If the
poor and humble toil that we have Food, must not the high and glorious toil
for him in return, that he have Light, have Guidance, Freedom, Immortality?
— These two, in all their degrees, I honour: all else is chaff and dust, which
let the wind blow where it listeth.

This Carlylean claptrap is quoted to provide further documenta-
tion of the kinds of values that defined so much of the philosophic
framework of white racism. The types Carlyle celebrates in his maud-
lin effusion are the precise contrary of the "indolent, two-legged cattle"
he denounces in his *Occasional Discourse upon the Nigger Question*.
These latter are "Demerara Niggers," or otherwise individualized as
"Quashee." They are black. But the "rugged face, all weathertanned,
besoiled, with its rude intelligence . . . the face of a Man living
manlike" is, of course, white. Nothing had occurred in the decade and
a half between the publication of *Sartor Resartus* in 1834 and his
Occasional Discourse upon the Nigger Question in 1849 to make
Carlyle more sensible. He became only more emphatically what he
always was: a wordy trafficker in pretentious nonsense. Such as he
was, however, he typified white racism and its pseudomorality with a
fidelity equaled, though not surpassed, by the philosophers of race
intent on finding justification for the enslavement of blacks in the
United States.

Despite Carlyle and his like, it was not that the blacks and other
nonwhites, wherever they were, exhibited an incapacity for toil. That
simply was not the case at all. An Indian or Chinese peasant, a sub-
Sahara herdsman or Egyptian fellah, worked quite as hard as a
Manchester factory hand in the darkest period of the Industrial Age
in Britain. Toil is largely a matter of incentive. It may even be amongst
the eternal virtues. And yet, shorn of incentive, it is no virtue. More-

248

over, the tripod of state systems—economic, political, and social— from which the fortunes of the toilers in these respective countries were suspended, differed from the European (or Western, including the United States) in both quality and degree. The difference in these respects was of a magnitude that spelled, finally, a fundamental distinction between the ethnic experiences and aspirations out of which the contrasted systems, respectively, had evolved. For hundreds of years the British had aimed at parliamentary democracy in varying postures with varying degrees of national intensity—and with varying success—but that, at any rate, was their aim. For hundreds of years the Chinese had aimed at group conformity as an operative principle of large-scale governance, diffused through elaborate hierarchies bound by explicit codes of social behavior. For hundreds of years India had seen in its refinements of caste distinctions the essential meaning of its ethnic destiny. For hundred of years Egypt had been supine in its debasement as the deteriorated descendants of a once ascendant people. But Africa is a special case, to which appropriate consideration must be given.

Not enough is known about the correlation, if any, between climatology and ethnology to enable definitive, let alone conclusive, statements to be made. It remains an unanswered question why, for instance, some groups of mankind have chosen to address themselves to their ecological problems from the standpoint of environmental adaptation and others from that of environmental transcendence. It is not known why the Pygmies of Central Africa have chosen the path of adaptation to the environment, as, similarly, the Eskimos of the Far North of the American continent have done, while the Teutonic tribes set about to manipulate their environment with the clear object of transcending it. Arnold J. Toynbee's theory of challenge and response is inadequate as an explanation of this phenomenon. It also imports into consideration of the matter a scheme of values in which successful response to challenge, in Toynbee's formulation, is an index of group superiority. Other issues arise and are not settled by his Christian ethnocentrism. Why is environmental transcendence necessarily to be more highly esteemed than environmental adaptation? Would the Pygmies of Central Africa have demonstrated a more successful response by, shall we say, importing giant bulldozers, leveling trees and clearing forests, in order to put up air-conditioned dwellings and otherwise engage in the internal and external intercourse of modern nations? The fallacy that betrays Toynbee is a product of his assumption that white European criteria are the decisive standards by which all other human groups must either stand or fall. The concept of challenge and response could not be valid for the notional exploration of the mentality of the Pygmies unless this group were shown to accept that concept for itself as a determinant test on Toynbee's terms. It might be that the idea of challenge and response played no part whatever in their conception of the world and their place in it. Challenge and response, as terms of an environmental dialectic, might simply never have been conceded a place in their scheme of things. It does not seem to have occurred to Toynbee that the coarse materialism of his major synthesis oversimplifies and too narrowly delimits the meaning of life to a European context.

There is a certain racial arrogance about Toynbee, as when, for example, he asserts in *A Study of History* that "the Black races alone have not contributed positively to any civilization—as yet." The palpable absurdity of this statement is in no way diminished by his subsequent, disarming qualification that "it is to be remembered that there are many white peoples that are as innocent of having made any contribution to any civilization as the Blacks themselves." Toynbee is wrong, in fact, whatever his motive in making this assertion about the black races. Greater authorities than he on Africa have exposed the falsity of the statement by revealing the existence of African civilizations of a very high order by any criterion. Whether positively or negatively, directly or indirectly, the contribution of the black races to world civilization is widely recognized by ethnologists and cultural anthropologists who, unlike Toynbee, are guided by accepted canons of scientific investigation rather than overbalanced by hypotheses in support of which they do violence to historiography with a partisan selection from the available evidence. This, however, is the historical method of white racism. The record of the history of the blacks in the United States, as it has been compiled by white historians, is another notorious example.

At all events, the automatism of Toynbee's formula of challenge and response is self-stultifying. Clearly, there are challenges to which a higher social intelligence would make either no response or a negative response. Take the invention of the atomic bomb, for instance. That it had never occurred to the Pygmies to try to fabricate such a device would undoubtedly be construed by white ethnocentrists as part of the evidence attesting to the absence of scientific attainments among the Pygmies. But it might emerge from a less self-infatuated process of group appraisal that a much higher social intelligence is involved in *not* making than in making an atomic bomb. Perhaps the Eskimos should have concerned themselves with blasting the polar icecap by means of their own independent discovery of atomic energy so as to change the climate of their environment and thus reduce their ecological problems to more manageable proportions—in European or white North American terms. Having modified the climate prevailing throughout their habitat, they might in time have found it possible to build split-level homes constructed from the lumber of the newly afforested areas or, preferably, from the standpoint of commerce, imported from the United States. There would also have been changes in their diet, so that they need no longer subsist on the raw flesh of fish and animals. They would be able to barbecue steaks in their back yards, complete with fried onion rings and baked Idaho potatoes. In that way, as with the Pygmies of Central Africa, they could then be considered civilized.

It is not surprising, given his Christian ethos, with its Calvinist inspiration, that at no point whatever does the idea of happiness enter into Toynbee's mechanistic equation of challenge and response. Where these nonwhite peoples are concerned, it is, for him, a demonstration —and no more—of the dynamics of challenge and the statics of re- sponse. Obviously, to anyone but a white Christian European bred to the notion of success as conquest of the physical environment to the point of manipulation without regard for its ecological consequences, the Pygmy or Eskimo ideal of adaptation to the environment is a confession of group inferiority. Yet it gradually becomes clearer and clearer that while in the short run the transcenders of the environment can show spectacular results for their mode of response, in the long run it is the adapters, like the Pygmies and the Eskimos of the Far North, who possess the greater ecological intelligence.

A major element in the cataclysmic tragedy of European irruption into Africa has been the terrible ecological damage inflicted upon the country, so that numerous forms of wildlife are on the verge of ex- tinction, where indeed they have not already been wiped out, and the reciprocal balance between the land and its inhabitants, human and nonhuman, has been shattered. Add to this the encroachers' monstrous record of human enslavement, the wanton destruction of syntheses of communal life patiently evolved through thousands of years of social trial and error, and the wasting blight their pathic cruelty brought upon the future of this group of the human species. When the entire record is evaluated, the only comparison that yields a truly graphic significance is to be obtained from the Spanish incursion into Central America and the Caribbean. That the Africans and vestiges of their hereditary culture survived—as was not the case with the Mayans and Arawaks—is most of all testimony to the defensive struggle waged against the Europeans by the tsetse fly and the *Anopheles* mosquito. To these, more than to anything else, is sub-Sahara Africa—in particular, West Africa—indebted for what it has been able to preserve or salvage from the European slave traders and, thereafter, colonialism.

"*Seule de tous les continents l'Afrique n'a pas d'histoire!*" It is pointless to engage in refutation of this statement, if only because it so plainly refutes itself. The purpose in citing it is merely to lend additional emphasis to the observation that this has long been the general European and white American attitude toward the "Dark Continent." Yet Franz Boas could write:

It seems likely that at times when the European was still satisfied with rude stone tools, the African had invented or adopted the art of smelting iron. Consider for a moment what this invention has meant for the advance of the human race. As long as the hammer, knife, drill, the spade, and the hoe had to be chipped out of stone, or had to be made of shell or hard wood, effective industrial work was not impossible, but difficult. A great progress was made when copper found in large amounts was hammered out into tools and later on shaped by melting; and when bronze was introduced; but the true advancement of industrial life did not begin until the hard iron was discovered. It seems not unlikely that the people who made the marvelous discovery of reducing iron ores by smelting were the African Negroes. Neither ancient Europe, nor ancient western Asia, nor ancient China knew iron, and everything points to its introduction from Africa. At the time of the great African discoveries towards the end of the past century, blacksmiths were found all over Africa from north to south and from east to west. With his simple bellows and a charcoal fire he reduced the ore that is found in many parts of the continent and forged implements of great usefulness and beauty. [Cited by Du Bois in *The World and Africa.*]

Indeed, the evidence of civilized attainments in Africa is so vast and authenticated that only the most irrational white racism is capable of maintaining its denial. A contributor to the *Journal of the Royal Anthropological Institute* (Vol. 43) remarks:

I feel convinced by certain arguments that seem to prove to my satisfaction that we are indebted to the Negro for the very keystone of our modern civilization and that we owe him the discovery of iron.

But how else could the ravaging of Africa be rationalized unless by the allegation that the "Negroes," as the Europeans called them, were savages devoid of history and incapable of civilization? Between 1870 and 1900, Britain alone acquired 4,883,883 square miles of territory in Africa, with more than 75 million inhabitants. From 1899 to 1902 it had fought the Boer War in South Africa for reasons best expressed in the words of John Strachey in *The End of Empire:*

But who can really doubt that the simple issue on which the war was fought was whether or not independent Boer sovereignty was to be cleared out of the way of the British entrepreneurs and investors who wanted to make their fortunes out of mining the diamonds and the gold which, it had been discovered, underlay the fields which the Boers were tilling? For the Boer regimes, while they did not prohibit the exploitation of these precious minerals, did hamper it, refused civil rights and citizenship to the incoming British entrepreneurs and their staffs, taxed them arbitrarily, and generally stood in the way of the full exploitation of what was turning out to be one of the most attractive of all the fields for the overseas investment of the flood of British capital which was being generated at home. Moreover, the mines of Kimberley and the Rand were likely, it was felt, to be immensely profitable, not only because of their diamonds and their gold, but also because there was available on the spot a supply of ultra-cheap labour. This was provided by the "Kaffirs" or native African tribesmen who had been recently subdued and could be made to work for subsistence or less. The question of who should use this labour and benefit from the surpluses which it produced, the British in mining or the Boers in farming, could, it turned out, only be decided by war.

The Boer War created profound social stresses in England, dividing the country with all the sundering passion that the current war in Vietnam has brought into the contemporary life of America. Although, in the instance of the Boer War, white groups were embroiled with each other, nonwhites were also involved as potential sources of cheap labor of invaluable worth to the victors. Cheap labor indeed was so highly prized by the British imperialists that when, after the war, there was for a time a shortage of African labor, the British proconsul, Lord Milner, imported indentured laborers from China. The imperialists resorted to India for the same purpose: as a source of cheap labor to be exported as commercial occasion warranted.

Whether in North America, Central and South America and the Caribbean, Asia, or Africa, the whites have always exploited nonwhites as an abundant supply of inexpensive labor. Their treatment of these human cattle has been consistent in its brutality from the beginning, in the early years of the sixteenth century, up to the present time. The tone of humanitarian commentators on this theme tends in many cases to become shrill with indignation that sometimes is not wholly free from self-righteousness. But as to the objective situation that has compelled their protests, there can be no doubt of its revolting character. No one, surely, needs to be reminded of the barbarities practiced against African blacks in mines and fields and factories by the white interlopers in South Africa at this very day. It was no better earlier in the century, and the First World War, when it broke out in 1914, merely provided another of those recurrent interludes in the record of imperialism when whites turned against one another to fight like jackals and hyenas over the carcasses of exploited peoples. The First World War, although it began in Europe and ended there with the redefinition of local frontiers and the redistribution of political power, extended also to Africa and Asia. On these latter continents, the victorious European nations, given direct military assistance toward the end of the four-year conflict by the United States, divided the spoils amongst themselves. But not alone were the lives and destinies of the subject nonwhite peoples of Asia and Africa recast and redirected by this outcome; the blacks of the United States, too, were decisively affected.

These blacks had been permitted to take a more or less inconspicuous role in the Spanish-American War of 1898. They nevertheless distinguished themselves. Several of them were awarded the Congressional Medal of Honor. But along with this, more than 100 blacks were lynched in the Southern United States. It is noteworthy that also in this year Charles Chestnutt's novel, *The Marrow of Tradition*, was published. It dealt with a theme of perennial concern to blacks in their relations with whites: whether to retaliate against the latter with violence or with love. The situation of the blacks was desperate throughout the country. Lynchings, disfranchisement, the whole gamut of oppression, continued in their terrifying incidence during these years at the end of the nineteenth and the beginning

254

of the twentieth century. Booker T. Washington's granite resolve to be passive in the face of provocation dominated the public attitudes of the blacks in general. Yet here and there were clear signs of coming changes. Though never abating his opposition to Washington's strategy, Du Bois made an abortive attempt to collaborate with him in the work of the Committee of Twelve for the Advancement of the Interests of the Negro Race. This organization had the financial support of Andrew Carnegie. John D. Rockefeller was munificent in his gifts to the General Education Board, among whose objects was the training of blacks to teach at schools in the South. But Washington's racial philosophy came increasingly under attack from other blacks. Monroe Trotter joined with Du Bois in repudiating Washington. Opposition arose as well from other quarters among the blacks. And all the while, the lynchings proceeded, together with the exclusion of the blacks from exercise of the franchise. With one or two exceptions, by 1904 they were effectively deprived of the right to vote in the Southern states. The following year Du Bois organized the Niagara Movement to "protest emphatically and continually against the curtailment of their [the blacks'] political rights."

The chasm between Booker T. Washington and W. E. B. Du Bois could no longer be spanned by conciliation in any form. Matters of fundamental principle were involved. Washington retained the support of the leading white philanthropists of the day and continued to be recognized in official quarters and by the white press as the "accredited" leader of the blacks and their spokesman on all issues. Among the blacks themselves, however, his leadership had suffered a degree of erosion, although his abdication of social equality as a goal to be striven for by blacks reflected accurately enough the temper of the group as a whole in the national circumstances then prevailing. How in all realism could blacks concentrate their energies on social equality in the absence of anything like adequate economic opportunity anywhere in the country, and in the face of their virtual disfranchisement in the South? Conceivably, Washington was wrong to abjure the political struggle. Du Bois, equally, was wrong to attach such pre-eminent value to it. Somewhere between the extremes of abjuration and attachment lay the intelligent degree of political activity for blacks. But in the fury of Du Bois's polemics and the obduracy of Washington's position, so constructive a compromise was unattainable. When Theodore Roosevelt entertained Washington at dinner at the White House, his breach of caste tradition infuriated the white South, but it also conferred the highest seal of official approval upon Booker T. Washington's formula of economic co-operation, social separation, and political abstention. However, Du Bois was acquiring the backing of white Northern liberals in his quest for a counterpoise to what he regarded as the regressive racial theories of Washington. American capitalists on the whole threw their support to Washington, whose allegiance to the black *status quo ante bellum* posed no threat to their energetic acquisitiveness. But adherents of Du Bois's point of view were becoming more numerous as Washington neared the end of his life. Internal developments in the United States also conspired to arouse sectional disaffection among the blacks regarding Booker T. Washington's policy of accommodation.

Monroe Trotter was, next to Du Bois, the most articulate of Washington's black opponents. He was a remarkable man in his own right. A graduate of Harvard College, where he was a classmate of Du Bois, he first engaged in business as a real-estate broker, then took up the cause for full citizenship for blacks in the United States. He founded a newspaper in Boston, *The Guardian,* and devoted its columns to unremitting advocacy of this cause, accompanying it with a sustained and devastating attack on Booker T. Washington and all the latter stood for. In those early years of the twentieth century, Monroe Trotter was fifty years ahead of his black contemporaries in his opposition to white liberal manipulation of the black struggle in America. His position was that the blacks should assume independent leadership and control of their own political organizations. He refused to join Du Bois when the Niagara Movement became the National Association for the Advancement of Colored People. He did not demur to the objective; but he declined to entrust the leadership of the black struggle to whites. It would be half a century before Trotter's stand in this respect became a generally accepted principle among blacks. Trotter's National Equal Rights League never attained the size, standing, or influence of the NAACP. Blacks still were too lacking in group self-confidence, and the racial circumstances of American society were too hostile, for the sure and untroubled accomplishment of Trotter's aim of dispensing with white paternalism. The NAACP, with its circumspect, genteel militancy, was more in accord with the objective realities and with the social temper of its founders. Among such as they, Monroe Trotter was a hawk among fowl. He had neither scope nor place there. But by the time of his death in 1934, he had seen in Marcus Garvey a foreshadowing, however imperfect, of his fundamental design of independent black organization. Had the span of his life been equal to Du Bois's, he would also have seen black fighters for racial justice emerge in his own image. In 1909, however, a year after the Springfield, Illinois, riots, the leadership of black Americans, in so far as it was not embalmed in the possession of Booker T. Washington, was exercised by white liberals. Du Bois was widely respected and deeply influential, yet he had no mass following. Washington, more widely respected than Du Bois, and more deeply influential, continued to enjoy a mass following, although to an eroded degree.

By the time of Washington's death in 1915, the First World War had begun, and he had seen, from the evidence of Woodrow Wilson's distempered racism and the generally depressed condition of the blacks, the short-term failure of his strategy of racial accommodation. He might have consoled himself that the conflict was not yet over and that his Fabian leadership had won for his people, hard-pressed as they were, a vital breathing space. He had gained for them time and space to organize themselves for the climactic struggle that lay ahead. That was his indispensable gift to them. By the opening years of the century his leadership, which, from a military point of view, was intrinsically revolutionary (though in conventional terms he fought no war and counseled none), had ossified into tactical inflexibility. He had nonetheless carried out on behalf of his fellow blacks a masterly retreat in the face of the savage onslaught of the white racist avengers of Southern defeat and humiliation. He had successfully led his people out of a trap whose jaws gaped to seize and rend and destroy them. It is not the test of a revolutionary, or the warrant of revolution, to conform invariably to a traditional pattern. Booker T. Washington was a revolutionary. The time will come when he will be adjudged by general consent among his people the greatest of all black American revolutionaries.

Du Bois endorsed black participation in the entry of the United States into the First World War. That conflict, of course, did not immediately involve this country on an active scale. It was nevertheless in its way an international extension of the violence endemic to the American society. The First World War was preceded by the Chinese Revolution in 1912 and the Balkan War in the same year. Between

1900 and 1915, more than 1,000 blacks were lynched in the United States. Beginning with "increased lynchings in 1915," writes Du Bois in *Dusk of Dawn,*

there came in 1916 lynching, burning and murder. In 1917 came the draft with its discrimination and mob rule; in 1918, the turmoil and discrimination of actual war; and finally in 1919 the worst experience of mob law and race hate that the United States has seen since Reconstruction.

Blacks were refused as volunteers into the armed forces in the period preceding the entry of the United States into the war. When, eventually, in common with others they were drafted, they were trained in segregated units at segregated encampments. While blacks were being drafted for military service, still another in the unending chain of those incidents took place that gave ghastly point to the fact that whether in war or in peace the persecution of the blacks would continue.

A Negro was publicly burned alive in Tennessee under circumstances unusually atrocious. The mobbing and burning were publicly advertised in the press beforehand. Three thousand automobiles brought the audience, including mothers carrying children. Ten gallons of gasoline were poured over the wretch and he was burned alive, while hundreds fought for bits of his body, clothing, and the rope. [*Dusk of Dawn.*]

Incidents of this character were a virtual commonplace of the period. Here is another:

Five Negroes in Lee County, Georgia, were lynched en masse and there came the horrible public burning of Jesse Washington in Waco, Texas, before a mob of thousands of men, women and children. "While a fire was being prepared of boxes, the naked boy was stabbed and the chain put over the tree. He tried to get away, but could not. He reached up to grab the chain and they cut off his fingers. The big man struck the boy on the back of the neck with a knife just as they were pulling him up on the tree. Mr. —— thought that was practically the death blow. He was lowered into the fire several times by means of the chain around his neck. Someone said they would estimate the boy had about twenty-five stab wounds, each one of them death-dealing." [*Dusk of Dawn.*]

This was the work of a mob of white racists. Needless to say, they all went unpunished by the law.

There really is no need to catalogue at undue length the countless horrors perpetrated by American whites against blacks throughout the centuries. Yet the perspectives of black insurrection in the United States must be adequately established so that contemporary effects may be justly attributed to their antecedent causes. For this purpose it is necessary to incur the risk of reiteration of certain themes and events. The deep, intincturing strain of white racist violence in the American society must be mentioned again, and the inordinate degree to which it has been directed against black Americans must be repeated and re-emphasized. The alternative risk is one of implying, by default, a formless void from which black insurrection has emerged much after the fashion of the creation of the world by the God of the Christians according to their sacred scriptures. Yet the essential perspectives would be inadequate if they did not bring into focus the fact that the racist violence that white Americans have visited upon blacks in the United States has its historic counterpart in the racist violence that throughout five centuries Europeans visited upon the nonwhite peoples of Central America and the Caribbean, Asia and Africa, in the guise of colonialism.

"History," said Leibnitz, "is the true demonstration of religion." There is a distinct correlation between the outward thrust of Christian Europe from the period of the First Crusade, the antecedent organization and release of the Europeans' collective energies by their common Christian belief; and the dawn of the technological era at the Renaissance. Gold and ivory, tobacco, sugar and cotton: each in turn, or all together, inspired in these invigorated Europeans a desperate casuistry aimed at reconciling their gluttonous unrestraint with the religious abstinences prescribed by their reputed Saviour. The heathen were beyond the pale of salvation, for they were not heirs of the body and spirit of Christ. The hand of God was readily seen in the geographical chance by which heathen could be thought to be synonymous with nonwhite. The ensuing theory of race was the perfect anesthetic for the European conscience.

By the nineteenth century, while blacks were being oppressed and persecuted in the United States, European states were busily engaged in similar activities against other nonwhite peoples in Asia and Africa. In both cases, the basis of oppression was a mixture of economics and racism, the latter validating the former as a consequence of the "white man's burden," and the former justifying the latter as an endeavor to carry out a "civilizing mission." Between

1870 and 1914, the European nations (including Russia) were suzerain over Asia and Africa, as well as the nonwhite territories of Oceania and the Caribbean. Japan alone among the nonwhite nations could assert an independent status. North, South, and Central America were under white domination. Australia had proclaimed, and was maintaining, a policy of exclusion of nonwhites as permanent settlers in that land. Canada pursued the same course. Wherever one looked about the world, the white groups of the human species were lords and masters of the nonwhite groups. Everywhere, in Tennyson's phrase, was "the grey barbarian lower than the Christian child."

Aside from such poetic reflections upon political actualities, there was a European philosophy of race. Gobineau had written, in *The Inequality of Human Races:*

Such is the lesson of history. It shows us that all civilizations derive from the white race, that none can exist without its help. . . . Almost the whole of the Continent of Europe is inhabited at the present time by groups of which the basis is white, but in which the non-Aryan elements are the most numerous. There is no true civilization, among the European peoples, where the Aryan branch is not predominant. In the above list no negro race is seen as the initiator of a civilization. Only when it is mixed with some other can it even be initiated into one. Similarly, no spontaneous civilization is to be found among the yellow races.

Gobineau's statement specifically referring to the "negro race" both anticipates and amplifies Toynbee's to the same general effect.

Thomas Carlyle, who was born two decades earlier than Gobineau, expounded a similar theory of race in *Occasional Discourse upon the Nigger Question.* In his apoplectic prose, he foamed at the mouth about "Quashee Nigger." This pseudophilosopher speculated with turgid sarcasm on the political equation to be struck in democratic terms between the vote of a "Demerara Nigger and Chancellor Bacon." He was particularly exercised by the abolition of slavery in the West Indies:

I say, if the Black gentleman is born to be a servant, and, in fact, is useful in God's creation only as a servant, then let him hire not by the month, but by a very much longer term. That he be "hired for life," really here is the essence of the position he now holds.

Carlyle refers to the emancipated blacks as "two-legged cattle," and he proceeds:

Not a pumpkin, Quashee, not a square yard of soil, till you agree to do the state so many days of service. . . . You are not "slaves" now; nor do I wish, if it can be avoided, to see you slaves again; but decidedly you will have to be servants to those that are born *wiser* than you, that are born lords of you; servants to the Whites, if they *are* (as what mortal can doubt they are?) born wiser than you.

He is obsessed with what he deems the natural inferiority of the black groups of mankind, and he asks with his habitual petulance: "On the whole, it ought to be rendered possible, ought it not, for White men to live beside Black men, and in some just manner to command black Men?" Perhaps, he evidently thinks, he may be suspected of hatred of blacks.

Do I, then, hate the Negro? No; except when the soul is killed out of him, I decidedly like poor Quashee. . . . With a pennyworth of oil, you can make a handsome glossy thing of Quashee. . . . A swift, supple fellow; a merry-hearted, grinning, dancing, singing, affectionate kind of creature, with a great deal of melody and amenability in his composition. This certainly is a notable fact: The black African, alone of wild-men can live among men civilized.

The last statement puts one in mind of Booker T. Washington's remark that "the Negro seems to be about the only race that has been able to look the white man in the face during the long period of years and live—not only live, but multiply" (*Negro in the South*). It is not the only coincidence to be observed between Carlyle's racial caricatures and Washington's self-criticism. Washington's denigration of his own group may also be construed as racism in reverse. This would, of course, assimilate it even more closely in a negative fashion with Carlyle's positive racism. Ignorance makes ill-assorted bedfellows. For all his occasional lapses into racial obscurantism, Washington was a black revolutionary with a genius for guerrilla warfare carried on with unflagging persistence behind a camouflage of accommodation.

Carlyle, on the other hand, the author of *The French Revolution*, was as benighted a reactionary as ever pretended to enlightenment. "One always rather likes the Nigger," he condescended, in *Shooting Niagara: And After?*,

evidently a poor blockhead with good dispositions, with affections, attachments,—with a turn for Nigger Melodies, and the like;—he is the only Savage of all the coloured races that doesn't die out on sight of the White

Man; but can actually live beside him, and work and increase and be merry. The Almighty Maker has appointed him to be a Servant.

Another Englishman, Anthony Trollope, contemporary with Carlyle, viewed the black man as follows, in *The West Indies and the Spanish Main:*

Physically he is capable of the hardest bodily work, and that probably with less bodily pain than men of any other race; but he is idle, unambitious as to worldly position, sensual, and content with little. Intellectually, he is apparently capable of but little sustained effort; but, singularly enough, here he is ambitious. He burns to be regarded as a scholar, puzzles himself with fine words, addicts himself to religion for the sake of appearance, and delights in aping the little graces of civilization. He despises himself thoroughly, and would probably be content to starve for a month if he could appear as a white man for a day; but yet he delights in signs of respect paid to him, black as he is, and is always thinking of his own dignity. If you want to win his heart for an hour, call him a gentleman; but if you want to reduce him to a despairing obedience, tell him that he is a filthy nigger, assure him that his father and mother had tails like monkeys, and forbid him to think that he can have a soul like a white man. . . . Without a desire for property, man could make no progress. But the negro has no such desire; no desire strong enough to induce him to labour for that which he wants. In order that he may eat today and be clothed tomorrow, he will work a little; as for anything beyond that, he is content to lie in the sun. . . . To recede from civilization and become again savage—as savage as the laws of the community will permit—has been to his taste. I believe that he would altogether retrograde if left to himself. . . . These people are a servile race.

Pronouncements such as this typified the British attitude toward blacks in the nineteenth century, especially during that portion of it when Britain held an enormous area of the world in fee. And, as has already been said, the British racial posture toward blacks was closely paralleled in the corresponding period by the American.

A prominent abolitionist, Dr. Benjamin Rush, furnishes an American instance in point. Rush was a veritable type of the humanist whose liberal idealism went hand in hand with white racism masquerading, in his case, as scientific utterances. He was active in the cause of the emancipation of the blacks; and he was, in fact, president of the Pennsylvania Society for Promoting the Abolition of Slavery. Yet he asserted, in evident earnest, that endemic leprosy was the cause of the

262

"blackness of Negroes." In his essay, "Observations intended to Favor a Supposition that the Black Color (as it is called) of the Negroes is derived from the LEPROSY," cited in *The Poisoned Tongue,* edited by Stanley Feldstein, he offered the following proofs of his high-minded contentions (quoting a Dr. Theiry's "account of the disease of Asturia in Spain," which he translated):

The skin becomes black, thick and greasy. There are neither pustules, nor tubercles, nor scales, nor anything out of the way on the skin. The body is not in the least emaciated. The breathing is a little difficult, and the countenance has some fierceness in it. They exhale perpetually a peculiar and disagreeable smell, which I can compare to nothing but the smell of a mortified limb.

And, Rush remarks, "This smell mentioned by Dr. Theiry continues with a small modification in the native African to this day."

The distinguished abolitionist continues:

The original connection of the black color of the negroes with the leprosy is further suggested by the following fact taken from Bougainville's voyage round the world. He tells us that on an island in the Pacific Ocean which he visited, the inhabitants were composed of negroes and mulattoes. They had thick lips, woolly hair, and were sometimes of a yellowish color. They were short, ugly, ill proportioned, and most of them infected with the leprosy, a circumstance from which he called the island they inhabit, the Isle of Lepers.

He quotes a Dr. Moseley:

They are void of sensibility to a surprizing degree. They sleep sound in every disease, nor does any mental disturbance ever keep them awake. They bear surgical operations much better than white people, and what could be a cause of insupportable pain to a white man, a negro would almost disregard. I have amputated the legs of many negroes, who have held the upper part of the limb themselves.

This great friend of the "negroes" also puts forward his own original opinions:

Lepers are remarkable for having strong venereal desires. This is universal among the negroes, hence their uncommon fruitfulness when they are not depressed by slavery; but even slavery in its worst state does not always subdue the venereal appetite, for after whole days, spent in hard labor in a hot sun in the West Indies, the black men often walk five or six miles to comply with a venereal assignation.

263

Those gallant and ardent West Indians. The learned Dr. Rush proceeds:

The woolly heads of the negroes cannot be accounted for from climate, diet, state of society, or bilious disease . . . it would seem that the leprosy had found its way to the covering of the head, and from the variety of its effects upon the skin, I see no difficulty in admitting that it may as readily have produced wool upon the head of a negro, as matted hair upon the head of the Poles.

He cites a traveler "into the interior parts of Africa," a certain Mr. Hawkins, to the following effect:

The difference of color [in lepers] cannot arise from the intercourse of whites and blacks, for the whites are very rarely among them, and the result of this union is well known to be the yellow color, or mulatto. Many of the natives assert that they are produced by the women being debauched in the woods by the large baboon, ourang-outang, and by that species in particular called the guaga mooroos.

Indeed, Dr. Rush himself reports:

A white woman in North Carolina not only acquired a dark color, but several of the features of a negro, by marrying and living with a black husband. A similar instance of a change in the color and features of a woman in Buck's county in Pennsylvania has been observed and from a similar cause. In both these cases, the women bore children by their black husbands.

At length the doctor inquires:

Is the color of the negroes a disease? Then let science and humanity combine their efforts, and endeavour to discover a remedy for it. Nature has lately unfurled a banner upon this subject. She has begun spontaneous cures of this disease in several black people in this country.

Finally he prescribes:

To encourage attempts to cure this disease of the skin in negroes, let us recollect that by succeeding in them, we shall produce a large portion of happiness in the world. We shall in the first place destroy one of the arguments in favor of enslaving the negroes, for their color has been supposed by the ignorant to mark them as objects of divine judgments, and by the learned to qualify them for labor in hot, and unwholesome climates. . . .

We shall add greatly to *their* happiness, for however well they appear to be satisfied with their color, there are many proofs of their preferring that of white people.

It is quite true that a thriving cosmetics industry has been established (mainly by whites) amongst "Negroes" on the basis of Dr. Rush's last observation.

But if this outstanding abolitionist was a friend of the black people, what of their enemies?

James Henry Hammond, of South Carolina, might serve as an example (and not necessarily the most rabid) of these latter. In an address before the Senate of the United States in 1858, he declared:

In all social systems, there must be a class to do the mean duties, to perform the drudgery of life, that is, a class requiring but a low order of intellect and but little skill. Its requisites are vigor, docility, and fidelity. Such a class you must have, or you would not have that other class which leads progress, refinement, and civilization. It constitutes the very mud-sills of society and of political government; and you might as well attempt to build either the one or the other, except on the mud-sills. Fortunately for the South, she found a race adapted to that purpose to her hand. A race inferior to herself, but eminently qualified in temper, in vigor, in docility, in capacity to stand the climate, to answer all her purposes. We use them for the purpose, and call them slaves. We are old-fashioned at the South yet; it is a word discarded now by ears polite; but I will not characterize that class at the North with that term; but you have it; it is there; it is everywhere; it is eternal. [Feldstein.]

There was a Dr. Samuel Cartwright, of New Orleans, whose *Natural History of the Prognathous Species of Mankind* was published in the year 1857. It was a very influential book. Some of the racist wisdom to be derived from it goes as follows:

The African will starve rather than engage in a regular system of agricultural labor, unless impelled by the stronger will of the white man. When thus impelled, experience proves that he is much happier, during the hours of labor in the sunny fields, than when dozing in his native woods and jungles. He is also eminently qualified for a number of employments, which the instincts of the white man regard as degrading. . . . Every white man, who has not been degraded, had rather be engaged in the most laborious employments, than to serve as a lacquey or body servant to another white man or being like himself. Whereas, there is no office which the negro or mulatto covets more than that of being a body servant to a real gentleman. There is no office which gives him such a high opinion of himself, and it is utterly impossible for him to attach the idea of degradation to it. . . . North or South, free or slave, they are ever at the elbow, behind the table, in hotels and steamboats; ever ready, with brush in hand, to brush the coat or black the shoes, or to perform any menial service which may be required, and to hold out the open palm for the dime. The innate love to act as body servant or lacquey is too strongly developed in the negro race to be concealed. It admirably qualifies them for waiters and house servants, as their strong muscles, hardy frames, and the positive pleasure that labor in a hot sun confers on them, abundantly qualify them for agricultural employment in a hot climate.

Dr. Cartwright comments upon "the weak will" of "negroes," then observes:

The white man has an exaggerated will more than he has use for; because it frequently drives his own muscles beyond their physical capacity of endurance. . . . A man [obviously, a white man] possessing a knowledge of the negro character can govern a hundred, a thousand, or ten thousand of the prognathous race by his will alone.

Another physician, John H. Van Evrie, of Washington, D.C., published in 1853 a book entitled *Negroes and Negro "Slavery": The First an Inferior Race: The Latter Its Normal Condition*. A single quotation will suffice:

In regard to the negro, there can be no doubt, not merely because, by himself, he is a non-producing and non-advancing savage, but because his entire structure, mental and physical, is adapted to juxtaposition. All the other races have a certain specific character to overcome first, or to be understood and properly harmonized, but the negro is a blank, a wilderness, a barren waste, waiting for the husbandman or the Caucasian teacher to develop his real worth, and gifted with his wonderful imitative powers, he not only never resists, but reaching forth his hands for guidance and protection, at once accepts his teacher, and submits himself to his control.

The flood of ignorant and malevolent slander continued unabated and, because of its source, may be thought to have reached high tide in the following extract from one of Thomas Jefferson's effusions on this subject:

The first difference which strikes us is that of colour. Whether the black of the negro resides in the reticular membrane between the skin and scarf-skin, or in the scarf-skin itself; whether it proceeds from the colour of the blood, the colour of the bile, or from that of some other secretion, the difference is fixed in nature, and is as real as if its seat and cause were better known to us. And is this difference of no importance? Is it not the foundation of a greater or less share of beauty in the two races? Are not the fine mixture of red and white, the expressions of every passion by greater or less suffusions of colour in the one, preferable to that eternal

266

monotony which reigns in the countenances, that imoveable veil of black which covers all the emotions of the other race? Add to these, flowing hair, a more elegant symmetry of form, their own judgment in favour of the whites, declared by their preference of them, as uniformly as is the preference of the Oranootan for the black women over those of his own species. [Cited by S. Feldstein in *The Poisoned Tongue*.]

In view of his own mulatto children, Thomas Jefferson himself must have been an "Oranootan."

It was not that there were no contrary expressions of view. Nor should it be concluded that to indict the characteristic white racism of Europe and America is to present a comprehensive summary of those cultures embracing every aspect of their generic life. And it would be the crudest oversimplification, not to speak of capital dishonesty, to ignore the continuous assertion of the supremacy of moral principles within and without the religious orders. The claims of a higher spirituality were put forward unceasingly in all the white Christian cultures in an attempt to persuade men, and even to coerce them, into making their lives a testimonial to the Divine Exemplar.

Martyrs were never wanting from the earliest dawn of the Christian era to its present twilight. Missions proliferated; sects abounded; the Christian witness flooded into every compartment of the life of states and subjects throughout the white cultures and, by zealous extension, into the nonwhite cultures of mankind. John Ball and John Wesley in England, Luther and Calvin on the Continent, Roger Williams and Cotton Mather in North America, all testified with differing degrees of ardor and fanaticism to the perfection of Christ and the perfectibility of man. Nowhere indeed was Christian inspiration lacking throughout the entire era that, religiocentrically, bears its name up to the present day. At the height of the worst excesses of the Spaniards in Central America and the Caribbean, there was a Las Casas to plead the remembrance of Christ in an attempt, however vain, to stay his countrymen from their murderous consummations. And even were heaven to call upon Las Casas to justify the petition to his earthly sovereign—an act fraught with measureless historical consequences, by which he sought to make black Peter pay for Indian Paul—even were this to ensue, Las Casas would earn the mercy of heaven for what, at worst, was an overflowing compassion at the sight of "the tears of the Indians." No one, therefore, even should he be "black as the night from pole to pole," would be warranted in the view that the white cultures of the Christian world were thoroughly and without exception, in the imperishable phrase of Saint Augustine, "*magna latrocinia*"—great banditries.

Yet the most resolute attempt to be objective in assessing the cumulative effect of these cultures upon the rest of mankind would err in the spirit of Dante's "colorless neutrality" if it did not come to an adverse judgment in the matter. The incontestable ground of decision must be that, despite their saints and martyrs, sectaries and missionaries, shrines and suspirations, the white votaries of the Christian confession as a whole have shown too little compassion for the weak. It is not that they have been merciful to one another, but that, dividing mankind into white and nonwhite, they have asserted an ethnic warrant for mercilessness. It is futile to prescribe that men should love one another with the same order of affection that each bestows upon himself. Indeed, having regard to the forbidding incidence of self-hatred among the human species, a drug so potent as mutual love should be dispensed only with the utmost caution. Most people, if allowed in fact to love others as they do themselves, would be nothing less than mass poisoners. Nor would the prospect be any happier if justice were to be substituted for love, and men required simply to be just to one another. For it is trite beyond repetition that one man's justice may be another man's intolerable inequity. There is no nostrum, despite Jesus Christ and Martin Luther King. One must proceed, as in all profoundly complicated questions, on a piecemeal basis, step by slow step, inch by painful inch, by stupendous trial and disastrous error. Justice partakes to a degree of the quality of light: it can be seen, it can be measured, it can even be synthesized; but. unlike light, which responds to physical laws, the distinctive trait of justice is irony.

One may go further, perhaps, and attribute to it as well the character of paradox. Can it be other than paradox that a religion so imbued as Christianity with doctrinal obligations of love, justice, and mercy should in practice deny them with such willful persistence throughout the centuries?

It is the custom of social fantasists to retreat from the distasteful facts of this world into the more agreeable visions of utopias. Men as diverse as Sir Thomas More, Tommaso Campanella, Samuel Butler, and Edward Bellamy have envisaged ideal polities as alternatives to existing actualities. In most cases, the societies they have fabricated are more intimately related to Communist theory than to Christian inspiration. Toward the end of the nineteenth century, when Bellamy's *Looking Backward: 2000–1887* was published (1888), the United States put a gloss upon the Monroe Doctrine by thrusting Spain out of Cuba. The next year it dealt with an insurrection on the part of the Philippine Islands; more than two decades later, it entered the First World War. Bellamy's utopia reflected inversely the condition of American society. The brotherhood he adumbrated was everywhere contradicted by the Hobbesian "war of all against all" that prevailed. Men were the servants of industrialism rather than its masters. Competition had taken pride of place over co-operation as the animating spirit of the life of the country. Bellamy posited the year 2000 as the vantage ground of social transformation from which the year 1887 might be surveyed. He did not foresee the First World War, or he would have recognized it as differing only in scale and immediate causes from the civil commotion marked by insistent violence, which the genius of federalism as a political system alone restrained from anarchy. The Haymarket Riot in Chicago in 1886 was an overture to the appearance of *Looking Backward,* but it was also the postlude of a discordant song whose violent staccato was the birth cry of the American society.

The entry of America into the First World War was a confirmation of the geopolitical fact that its frontier was no longer determined by the irruptions of internal expansion. As it had moved across the Pacific to the Far East, it now traversed the Atlantic to the borders of the heartland of Europe. It was, in a manner of speaking, a sentimental return to an ancestral home, though bloodstained in the event and afterward scarred with chicane and the serpentine convolutions of peacemaking at Versailles. Genuine idealism in the popular sense prompted America's entry into the First World War. There was a widespread belief, held with unquestioning fervor by great masses of Americans, that the world could thereby be "made safe for democracy." The calculators of international finance, at once sordid and sophisticated, did not share this national mood of knight-errantry. From their standpoint, the aim was to make the world safe once more for business, for the uninterrupted pursuit of financial profit. A democratic world would be an arrangement in which big business could not be left unmolested in its traditional view of profit-making as an enterprise of superior importance to human well-being. It could not be left undisturbed in its entrenched custom of regarding men and women (and children, too) as cheap sources of labor, and black men and black women (and black children, too) as cheapest of all. So international finance, in its megalithic role of big business, would have nothing to do with democracy. On the contrary, the financiers would deploy their batallions and maneuver all their forces in Machiavellian formations to defeat it. They succeeded. And the world was made safe for another two decades, not for democracy, but for big business. Although Woodrow Wilson was humiliated and frustrated at the Peace Conference at least as much by his own incompetence as by the machinations of his European colleagues, the Treaty of Versailles marked the displacement of Pax Britannica by Pax Americana. The United States was now the foremost world power. But its black citizens, who had given the full measure of their allegiance to their country in the struggle, continued to be regarded in social theory and treated in social practice as pariahs to be tolerated at the far removes of the society but on no account to be admitted to the main concourse of the national life.

It was at this point that Marcus Garvey emerged on the American scene. Yet, his epiphany would remain obscure in its origins if the immediate circumstances of his emergence were not described, as they will be, with some particularity; and if, too, some indiscursive reference were not made once more to the anterior record of domestic violence, especially against black Americans, which heralded, as indeed it had incubated, his appearance.

Richard Hofstadter and Michael Wallace, in *American Violence: A Documentary History,* subsume its occurrences under a series of headings: political, economic, racial, etc. Chronologically, the volume begins with violence between Pilgrims and Puritans in 1634 and ends with the events surrounding the Democratic Convention at Chicago in 1968 and the assassination of Senator Robert F. Kennedy at Los Angeles in the same year. The intervening three centuries were saturated with blood.

Though Hofstadter and Wallace have furnished only a few instances of violence (and those quite briefly related) in the long struggle against the Indians, enough is suggested to make clear the remorseless savagery of the white onslaught. The massacre of the Sioux Indians at Wounded Knee is replete with all the horror of My Lai in Vietnam. Ranging abroad, General Leonard Wood's slaughter in the Philippines in 1906, by the American troops under his command, of every one of the 600 Moro tribesmen—men, women, and children—

who were surrounded by his troops, surpasses even My Lai in its bestial unrestraint. Wood and his troops were congratulated by President Theodore Roosevelt "upon the brilliant feat of arms wherein you and they upheld the honor of the American flag." Few troubled to ask how any country's honor could be upheld by violating the principles of common humanity. This was a distinction that Theodore Roosevelt himself, in his characteristic confusion of violence with courage, usually failed to make. In this, he was typical of his country and its people. The testimony given by a number of American soldiers at a Congressional investigation (hearings before the Senate Committee on the Philippines) in 1902 closely resembles the contemporary statements of American troops and other military personnel participating in the Vietnam war. Far from being an isolated instance in American history, My Lai was simply another link in the unending chain of brutal outrages committed by Americans both inside and outside the United States. Inside, against Indians and blacks; outside, against nonwhite foreigners. Two circumstances are constant in their recurrence: violence of the most savage character; and its perpetration against nonwhites.

The American society is distinguished, like the South African society, by its pathological racism. Yet it would be wrong and gravely misleading to conclude that this can be taken as an ultimate judgment upon the American society. For there is a good deal more to this highly complex organism than that pronouncement, whatever its accuracy. Marcus Garvey was not a product of American violence. He merely reacted to it.

In the course of the hearings before the Senate Committee on the Philippines, testimony such as the following (cited in *American Violence*) was elicited:

Q. And had you orders to shoot?—*A.* Yes, sir. . . .
Senator Carmack. The orders were given to fire. Go ahead and tell the whole story.
The Witness. After that two old men came out, hand in hand. I should think they were over 50 years old, probably between 50 and 70. They had a white flag. They were shot down. At the other end of the town we heard screams, and there was a woman there; she was burned up, and in her arms was a baby, and on the floor was another child. The baby was at her breast, the one in her arms, and this child on the floor was, I should judge, about 3 years of age. They were burned. . . .

271

The Chairman. What troops were those?

The Witness. M Company, the Twenty-Sixth. . . .

By Senator Dietrich: . . .

Q. Where was this fight or battle where these two old men were killed?—
A. At La Nog. . . .

Q. Did you see these men killed? — A. Yes, sir.

Q. You say that they raised the flag of truce? — A. They had a white flag;
some sort of a piece of white cloth on a bamboo stick. They came out hand
in hand; they had their hands clasped.

Q. Did you shoot at them? — A. No, sir; I did not.

Q. Did you see anybody else shoot at them? — A. Yes, sir.

Q. Who? — A. Well, I saw people shooting in that direction; I don't know
whether they were shooting directly at these people or not.

Senator Beveridge. Could you give the names of those whom you saw shoot?
A. No, sir. I know Sergeant Conway . . . reported to Captain McDonald
that he had killed two more niggers.

To bring the matter up to date in the present instance of the war
in Vietnam, "gooks" should be substituted for "niggers." But whether
"gooks" or "niggers" or "slopes" or "slants," the point of paramount
substance is that these objects of American violence are, in any case,
nonwhite.

To revert to the earlier massacre of the Sioux Indians at Wounded
Knee, there is this account:

The Indians surrendered immediately, raising a white flag. On December
29, 1890, the camp was surrounded. The Indians were disarmed.
Forsyth suspected that the braves were concealing more weapons under
their blankets. They were being inspected when one Indian pulled out a
rifle and it discharged. Some claimed he was placing it on the pile of con-
fiscated weapons and it went off accidentally, others that he deliberately
shot at the troops. Immediately the soldiers fired a volley point blank
into the Indians, and then wholesale fighting began. The artillery had been
trained on the camp and was now discharged amidst the women and
children, and fleeing Indians were shot down. It is estimated that 200 to
250 Indians were killed. General Miles, who has been followed by most
historians, termed it a "massacre," and relieved Forsyth of his command for
"reprehensible" behavior. But Forsyth was restored by the Secretary of
War, who blamed the incident entirely on the Indians, and eighteen
soldiers received Congressional Medals of Honor. The massacre marked the
psychic as well as physical crushing of the Sioux, the end of the Indian
wars, and the completion of the white man's conquest of the Indians.

It is not in order to pile horror upon horror that the earlier instance of the Cheyenne Massacre in 1864 is cited:

The territory from Central Kansas to the Rocky Moutains, between the Platte and Arkansas Rivers, had been the domain of the Southern Cheyenne and Arapaho Indians before the 1850's. The gold rush to Pike's Peak brought many settlers to the territory and put great pressure on the Indian tribes. By 1859 the Indians were compressed into a small circle of territory which straddled a main line of white emigration. In 1861 the Indians were persuaded by government officials to sell that land to the United States and move to a gameless, arid section of the Southeastern Colorado Territory. The Indians claimed they had been cheated and had misunderstood the treaty; in 1864 some tribes in Colorado were goaded into a war and killed many settlers. The Cheyenne, who were then at peace under Chief Black Kettle, gave up their arms and camped where they were promised protection by federal troops against the Colorado militia. These promises were not kept. A contingent of Colorado militia under the command of Colonel J. M. Chivington, a Methodist pastor in civil life, fell upon the unsuspecting camp, refused to acknowledge a white flag of surrender, and slaughtered and mutilated perhaps as many as 450 men, women, and children. The soldiers scalped the dead and dying, then cut out the genitals of the women and stuck them on poles or wore them in their hats. Chivington later remarked that the children had to be killed because "nits make lice."

A local newspaper called this episode "a brilliant feat of arms" and said that the soldiers "had covered themselves with glory." A Congressional Committee, however, said Chivington had "deliberately planned and executed a foul and dastardly massacre which would have disgraced the veriest savage among those who were the victims of his cruelty."

In the same year, 1864, on April 12, in the course of the Civil War, there occurred the Confederate massacre of Negro troops at Fort Pillow, Tennessee. According to the Bergmans:

A Confederate cavalry force under Maj. Nathan B. Forrest, captured the Fort garrisoned by Negro soldiers. Wholesale slaughter followed, and every sort of atrocity took place. Approximately 300 soldiers, many of them wounded, plus women and children, were killed.

Reviewing the whole record of the American pathology of violence, one is tempted to concede the truth of Charles A. Beard's observation concerning the Spanish-American War (in *Contemporary American History, 1877–1913*) that "contrary to their assertions on formal occasions, the American people enjoy war beyond measure, if the plain facts of history are allowed to speak."

But Hofstadter, in *The Progressive Historians*, does not take Beard's hedonistic view of the American obsession with violence. He seeks answers to the questions

why, long before this country had a large, militant organized labor force, it had some of the bitterest and most violent strikes in the history of international labor movements? Why, without organized militarism or an established and influential military caste, have we so loved generals in politics? Why have we entered with such casual impulsiveness into wars with England, Mexico, Spain, and North Vietnam?

He prefaces the foregoing passage by remarking that

certainly American history, even without feudalism and socialism, has been far from bland . . . the story of our early mobs and rebellions; the long, ruthless struggle with the Indian; our filibustering expeditions; our slave insurrections; our burned convents and mobbed abolitionists and lynched Wobblies; our sporadic, furiously militant Homesteads, Pullmans, and Patersons; our race lynchings, race riots, and ghetto riots; our organized gangsterism; our needless wars.

Hofstadter need have sought no further than his own preamble for the answers to the questions he posed. If, as he asserts, we have "entered with such casual impulsiveness into wars with England, Mexico, Spain, and North Vietnam," then this is the logical consequence of, in his own words, "our early mobs and rebellions; the long, ruthless struggle with the Indian; our filibustering expeditions; our slave insurrections; our burned convents and mobbed abolitionists." And these in turn are the cause of our "lynched Wobblies; our sporadic, furiously militant Homesteads, Pullmans, and Patersons; our race lynchings, race riots, and ghetto riots; our organized gangsterism; our needless wars." We are prisoners of our history, incarcerated in a bloody, self-reproducing cycle of interlocking cause and effect. And if the question is asked why, the answer is surely to be located with historical precision in our European heritage of violence as the final arbiter of all issues.

The mores of the American society are those of the European nation-states stripped bare. Like its historic progenitor, the European nation-state, the American society is Christian, violent, and racist. For most of its existence, the history of this society has been dominated by the idea and actuality of frontiers to be superseded, from the Ohio River to the Sea of Tranquillity. For all of its existence, the American society, it must be repeated, has been Christian, violent, and racist. Christianity would seem, at first glance, to be incompatible with violence and racism —that is, if contemplation of Christianity is restricted solely to its ethical content. But if the instrumental record of Christianity is considered— its employment as an ideological agent of military conquest, alternating with its use as a social device for dividing the will of the disinherited, and deflecting their energies from the effective concert of resistance to their despoilers—then all at once the seeming incompatibility vanishes. It is not the formal content of Christianity that has blighted the lives of the nonwhite groups of mankind wherever this creed touched them, but its institutional willingness at all times to come to terms with the world. Given this outlook on the part of the Christian corporation, the Church of Rome, it is not difficult to see how a Faustian bargain could be struck with technology at the inception of the Renaissance, and why such melancholy consequences were thus foreordained.

The liberation of human energies was nothing short of apocalyptic. It resulted from the condensation, into the One God of Christianity, of the profligate dispersion of social energies among many gods, which formed the essence of paganism. "I am the Lord thy God. I am a jealous God. Thou shalt have none other gods but Me." By accepting this formula, Christians came into possession of an eschatology that released them from the scattered religious allegiances of paganism and enabled them to achieve a cohesive unity of mass devotion. As a method of social organization, Christianity far outstripped its rivals. And this was the sense in which, pre-eminently, it was envisioned and employed by the institutional elite, the Christian church, into whose hands it had fallen. The nonwhites (the Mohammedans of the seventh and eighth centuries excepted) with their many gods thus were no match for the Christians with their One God. In fateful succession, forty years after the fall of Constantinople Columbus blundered into the New World. The genie that is History finally liberated European man from the bottle. Thenceforward, to the Americans of the present historical period, there is a clear line of development. In their self-righteous sense of world mission, in their addiction to armed violence, and in their rationale of racism, they are the lineal descendants of the primal loins of European nationalism. Nor is it in any degree surprising that monotheism should once again have proved itself of superior efficacy to polytheism as a principle of social organization. The example of Ikhnaton (Amenhotep IV), who renounced the plural deities of his predecessors and replaced them by a single God, had long since afforded instruction to this effect. Egypt was never better organized and seldom more prosperous in its domestic life and external affairs than when the social energies of its citizens were marshaled to respond in unitary allegiance to a religious conception of One God.

The same phenomenon is to be remarked in the instance of the Arabs whom Mohammed persuaded where possible and coerced where necessary into accepting Allah as the One God. The energizing force of this spiritual decoction carried the Arabs on a wave of military conquest from the Fertile Crescent to France. But the Arab society, unlike the Christian, deduced from its monotheistic inspiration no program for the secular reform of its class structure. Arab feudalism persisted fundamentally unchanged. The dynamic of Christianity was twin-motored: it was imperialistic in its outward drive for foreign conquest propelled by territorial ambition; and it was revolutionary in its transforming effect upon its own domestic society. But the Mohammedan inspiration, while it galvanized the energies of its Arab converts and launched them headlong in military quest of expansion, left largely untouched the class relationships that were the traditional basis of its native society. So that almost two millennia after the Hegira from which the Prophet ascended to power, Arab society, in its tenacious adherence to a primitive class structure, is fossilized at roughly the point of development that Christian society had attained during the Dark Ages.

It is not without a strain of irony that Marxism, with its besetting emphasis on the paramount reality of class conflict, emerged as the dialectical heir of Christianity. And if it be asked what has this to do with the evolution of the American society, the answer is: everything. For classlessness was, surely, the principal strand in the fabric of relationships that interwove to form the frontier society, whose spirit has so deeply pervaded the customary life of America.

Nothing in the nature of a historical tour de force is being attempted by the observation that Davy Crockett had more than a little in common with the Elizabethan adventurers who, in hyperbole suggestive of Crockett's later flights of violent imagery, boasted that they had "singed the beard" of the King of Spain. Consider Crockett in one of his typical outbursts (cited by Boorstin in *The Americans*):

Fellow-Citizens and Humans: These is times that come upon us like a whirlwind, and an airthquake: they are come like a catamount on the full jump! We are called upon to show our grit like a chain lightning agin a pine log, to extarminate, mollify, and calumniate the foe like a nigger put into a holler log and rammed down with a young sapling!

Pierce the heart of the enemy as you would a feller that spit in your face, knocked down your wife, burnt up your houses, and called your dog a skunk! Cram his pesky carcass full of thunder and lightning like a stuffed sassidge and turtle him off with a red hot poker, so that there won't be a piece of him left big enough to give a crow a breakfast, and bite his nose off into the bargain. Split his countenance with a live airthquake, and tarrify him with a rale Injun yell, till he gives up all his pertensions to the clearings this side of Salt Pond, and clears out like a streak of greased lightning chased by the crocodiles of the Mississippi.

Hosses, I am with you! and while the stars of Uncle Sam, and the stripes of his country wave triumphantly in the breeze, whar, whar, whar is the craven, low-lived, chicken-bred, toad-hoppin', red-mouthed, bristle-headed mother's son of ye who will not raise the beacon light of triumph, smouse the citadel of the aggressor, and squeeze ahead for Liberty and Glory! Whoop! h-u-rah, hosses, come along—Crockett's with you—show us the enemy!

There is a startling family resemblance between Crockett and the great heavyweight prizefighter Muhammad Ali, once known as Cassius Clay. They are both, Crockett and Ali, superlatively, Americans. From Crockett to Ali, and before as well as after, violence in America has been elevated to the godhead to sit at the right hand of Money, the Creator of all things. Violence in the American theogony has much the same status and function as Siva in the Hindu hierarchy of deities. Like the latter, American violence is a destroyer. Like the latter, it feeds on carnage. One has only to consider the ungilded record.

In general, Americans are familiar from their history texts with the rebellion against George III, whose causes were compressed into an outcry of "No taxation without representation." There, tyranny was the challenge and revolution the response. To put it otherwise, the American colonists revolted against the denial to them by the British metropolitan power of what they conceived to be justice. The cumulative occasion of 1776 was, in essence, justice denied. The Whisky

Rebellion (1794) and Shays' Rebellion (1786–87) were, similarly, protests against injustice. In these two latter instances, they were no longer directed against a colonial power, for national independence had been won. It was the new federal government of the United States of America that now was the object of civil revolt on the ground of justice denied. One might cull a numerous catalogue of like instances from the vast repository of recorded attempts by the most diverse groups of mankind to redress the balance of secular or religious injustice. The number is as large as that of the myriad attempts to create workable human societies. The French and Russian revolutions have been mentioned as modern instances of popular disaffection; which, however much they might vary in their ideological impulses or dialectical formulations, were always nevertheless, affirmatively, a demand for justice or, negatively, a protest against injustice. In every reach and facet of human affairs there is no dynamic so potent to bring about cataclysm and effect change as the denial of justice.

Injustice is the natural parent of revolution. And revolution may be described as change by convulsion. Everyone knows this and understands it quite well. One of the proudest boasts of a free people is its intolerance of injustice; one of its stoutest claims is the right to correct injustice by persuasion if possible but by violence if necessary. The most luminous pages of American history are those that record the resistance of Americans to injustice. The degree of injustice is a prime factor in precipitating revolt, but the kind of injustice is a factor of even more decisive consequence. A revolution may not be justified because a modicum of injustice attaches to the incidence of taxation as distributed between rich and poor. But it would certainly be justifiable if the poor were taxed for what was deemed "excessive reproduction of children" while the rich were free to procreate without restraint. The precise degree or kind of injustice suffices as a rule to equate it with tyranny. And, as every American knows, resistance to tyranny is obedience to God; with a single important exception copiously illustrated from the pages of American history: when black people decide to obey God by resisting tyranny. At this point, white racism interposes its fiat and declares such resistance intolerable. The necessary conclusion to be drawn is that resistance to tyranny is, in the view of the white sector of the American society, not a prerogative of the blacks. In keeping with its character as an indefeasible right of whites only, blacks are not admitted to its exercise. Nonetheless, un-

278

discouraged and insistent upon their right to what they regard as justice, blacks have continually revolted against the tyranny that has been imposed upon them, internationally, ever since their first contact with whites and, within the American society, ever since they were landed upon the shores of this continent. The one is as well documented as the other. W. E. B. Du Bois has summarized, in *The World and Africa,* the record of black revolt on the international level as follows:

The slave revolts were the beginnings of the revolutionary struggle for the uplift of the laboring masses in the modern world. They have been minimized in extent because of the propaganda in favor of slavery and the feeling that the knowledge of slave revolt would hurt the system. In the eighteenth century there were fifteen such revolts: in Portuguese and Dutch South Africa, in the French colonies, in the British possessions, in Cuba and little islands like St. Lucia. There were pitched battles and treaties between the British and the black Maroons and finally there was a rebellion in Haiti which changed the face of the world and drove England out of the slave trade. A list of these revolts follows:

        1522: Revolt in San Domingo
        1530: Revolt in Mexico
        1550: Revolt in Peru
        1550: Appearance of the Maroons
        1560: Byano Revolt in Central America
        1600: Revolt of Maroons
        1655: Revolt of 1,500 Maroons in Jamaica
        1663: Land given Jamaican Maroons
  1664–1738: Maroons fight British in Jamaica
        1674: Revolt in Barbados
        1679: Revolt in Haiti
  1679–1782: Maroons in Haiti organized
        1691: Revolt in Haiti
        1692: Revolt in Barbados
        1695: Palmares; revolt in Brazil
        1702: Revolt in Barbados
        1711: Negroes fight French in Brazil
  1715–1763: Revolts in Surinam
        1718: Revolt in Haiti
        1719: Revolt in Brazil
        1738: Treaty with Maroons
        1763: Black Caribs revolt
        1779: Haitians help the United States Revolution

1780: French Treaty with Maroons
1791: Dominican revolt
1791–1803: Haitian Revolution
1794: Cuban revolt
1794: Dominican revolt
1795: Maroons rebel
1796: St. Lucia revolt
1816: Barbados revolt
1828–1837: Revolts in Brazil
1840–1845: Haiti helps Bolivar
1844: Cuban revolt
1844–1893: Dominican revolt
1861: Revolt in Jamaica
1895: War in Cuba

These revolts show that the docility of Negro slaves in America is a myth.

Herbert Aptheker, in his *American Negro Slave Revolts,* has performed a similar service, though much more exhaustively, in respect of the incidence of black revolts against slavery. He found "records of approximately two hundred and fifty revolts and conspiracies in the history of American Negro slavery." Nor does this complete the testimony. For blacks have continued to revolt against the perpetuation of American racial injustice despite the abolition of slavery. Their attachment to the principle of resistance to tyranny has been demonstrated by an unremitting pattern of protest, violent and nonviolent, and intermittent outbreaks described as "riots." They are all evidence in one form or another of a continuous state of black revolt, either actual or incipient, and seething beneath the surface of American life up to the present.

This is not to assert that the entire population of 25 millions of identifiable blacks are unceasingly obsessed by the urge to revolt. Not at all. The black middle class certainly is not; and considerable segments of the black lower classes are either too apathetic or too disorganized to focus upon revolt as an instrument of redress for the racial and other forms of injustice to which the American society subjects them. It would be the grossest distortion to pretend that the contrary was the case. The points being made are that the tinder of revolt is always available in abundance in black lower-class communities, and occasionally in black middle-class communities; that there is always a significant nucleus of blacks motivated, as is only natural, by the necessity to revolt; and, finally, that neither tinder nor hands to kindle it are ever lacking among the black inhabitants of the United States. They are the objects of tyranny. That is indubitable. Injustice is meted out to them as a steady and remorseless diet from the slum tenement or rural shack to the grave. Theirs is, accordingly, an undeniable duty of resistance. They fulfill their highest obligation as citizens of a professedly liberty-loving state by engaging in revolt against tyranny—not less when they are called upon to resist it abroad than when they recognize the necessity to do so at home. So doing, they are right to regard themselves as obeying God.

Yet, even if there were no appeal to divine justification, there would still remain the human warrant to maintain oneself at any cost in a condition of freedom undergirded by justice. Thus, should God desert man and exhibit a callous indifference to his plight—as to many blacks and other nonwhites, speaking within the context of racial justice, He seems to do—then, man—American black man; Indochinese yellow man; Angolan black man; South African black man; North American Indian red man; Mexican-American brown man; Arab brown and black man; Rhodesian African black man—all these, and others— black, yellow, red, and brown, subjected to tyranny by white racial injustice—have the right as well as the duty by the inherent law of their being to revolt. They owe the discharge of this duty not only to themselves, but also to that larger human society whose only title to existence is moral decency and whose inveterate enemy is injustice.

Black Americans participated in the First World War—the war to "make the world safe for democracy"—despite the many hobbling obstacles strewn in their path by white American racism. W. E. B. Du Bois, in a famous editorial in *Crisis,* the journal of the National Association for the Advancement of Colored People, called on his fellow blacks to "close ranks." In preponderant majority they did so. But A. Philip Randolph was less enthusiastic about black participation in the war. A magazine—*The Messenger*—which he published in association with Chandler Owen, was the vehicle of his opposition. When "Pro-Germanism Amongst the Negroes" made its appearance in the magazine, Randolph and Owen were prosecuted and, on conviction, sentenced to imprisonment.

As was only to be expected, the blacks in the armed services were accorded the usual admixture of grudging acceptance and relegation in substantial numbers to work in service battalions. Many, however, got the chance of actual combat and acquitted themselves well; in numerous cases with distinction. Then they returned home to their quarter of a world that they had fought to "make . . . safe for democracy."

In 1917, the year the United States entered the war, thirty-eight blacks were lynched in the South, and approximately 100 killed in the race riot that occurred in East St. Louis, Illinois. The following year fifty-eight blacks were lynched. There were more race riots. But the next year, 1919, surpasses those immediately preceding in the sheer volume of racial violence. In a period of six months, seventy-six blacks were lynched and twenty-five race riots took place. This also was the year of the Chicago race riot, where nearly 40 people were killed and more than 500 injured. "In October," according to the Bergmans,

Negro farmers in Elaine, Arkansas, attempted to organize the Progressive Farmers and Household Union to protest the low prices paid for cotton by white planters. Anti-Negro riots broke out and over 200 Negroes were killed; 79 Negroes were indicted and brought to trial on charges of murder and insurrection.

The United States after the First World War was haunted by the fear of Communism. This political ideology was regarded as the major threat to the security of the nation by every postwar administration until Franklin D. Roosevelt and the advent of the Second World War. Fear of Communism furnished a convenient pretext for repression. On the arbitrary orders of Attorney General A. Mitchell Palmer, numbers of immigrants and so-called radicals, running into the hundreds, were arrested and deported. This was the year (1919) of the Boston police strike, the steel strike, and a general strike in Seattle. There was an outbreak of terrorist incidents. The reaction of the national administration was the suppression of civil liberties. The United States had become a society pursued by specters of its own creation. The widespread consciousness of prevalent social injustice recoiled upon the country and precipitated confusions so deep that only a line as thin as a vestige of order preserved it from chaos. America's inability, which was partly the product of its ruling-class unwillingness, to translate its professions of equality into actual social practice bore with especial weight upon the black (and, of course, the Indian) inhabitants of the country. In so far as the Indians were concerned, a New York *Times* book reviewer recently summed up their plight with succinct exactness:

"What have we done that the American people want us to stop?" Sitting Bull asked wearily of an American Army officer. And though neither answered, both knew the answer: "Living" . . . There was nothing the Indians could do, short of committing suicide, that would appease white Americans or stop their relentless and systematic destruction of Indian life.

It is only necessary to substitute Vietnamese for Indians in current circumstances in Indochina in order to recognize that the same impulse is at work, and the same purpose in view, now in Indochina as then against the Indians in North America. In both instances, nonwhite peoples are the victims, and whites the mass murderers.

Thus the American society has been convulsed for most of its existence by the contradiction between its theoretical aspiration to justice and its cynical disregard in practice for its widely trumpeted aspiration. Social injustice and white racism can be collected into a common category as the prime causes of division and malaise in America. Their responsibility for group disaffection, internecine strife, and revolutionary ferment is clear. And equally plain is it that blacks are the chief, though not the sole, sufferers.

Ernest Hemingway, notoriously, took in his life and work a sacramental view of violence. His attitude was that of a reverential celebrant at a high mass. It would be difficult to call to mind another writer of comparable stature who was so obsessed with violence, except Mark Twain. A fundamental distinction between these two great writers in this respect must, however, be noted. Always implicit in the work of Mark Twain is a quality of moral revulsion against violence. It is quite unmistakable. The clinical details he provides are set down with a clear emanation of spiritual distaste, although he does not judge and neither does he moralize. These things occurred, he implies, and he chanced to be present at the scene. They are quite epidemic in their occurrence, so that in the fictional persona of his most celebrated character, Huck Finn, he spends much of his time in flight, psychic no less than physical, from these violent horrors of the growing up of America.

I out with my knife and cut the rope, and away we went!

We didn't touch an oar, and we didn't speak nor whisper, nor hardly even breathe. We went gliding swift along, dead silent, past the tip of the paddle-box, and past the stern; then in a second or two more we was a hundred yards below the wreck, and the darkness soaked her up, every last sign of her, and we was safe, and knowed it.

Surcease from violence is what Twain celebrates, while Hemingway celebrates the violence itself. A typical instance of violence in Twain's experience—it is indifferent which—recorded through his surrogate, Huck Finn,

made me so sick I most fell out of the tree. I ain't a-going to tell *all* that happened—it would make me sick to do that. I wished I hadn't ever come ashore that night to see such things. I ain't ever going to get shut of them— lots of times I dream about them.

Hemingway was an idolater of violence, a seeker after violence. His was a pilgrimage to this Grail, in his art as in his life, for which he searched the world over. Twain, on the other hand, chanced to encounter violence, and encounter it he did with little or no abatement in the long adolescence of American life and society. Archibald MacLeish later on was to declaim, "America was promises. . . ." True enough. But America also was violence. Twain does not shrink from that fact, but neither does he endue it with the mystic quality with which it was enhaloed by Hemingway's repressed Puritan religiosity.

A still more luminous illustration of this theme might be afforded by a comparison of Mark Twain and Henry James. The latter's aestheticism was so offended by the coarse violence of American life and manners that he sought in self-imposed exile in Europe sanctuary for his outraged sensibilities. But Mark Twain endured, in the terms subsequently prescribed by William Faulkner. He also prevailed, if the proof of his prevailing can be taken to have been supplied by Hemingway's judgment that

all modern American literature comes from one book by Mark Twain called *Huckleberry Finn* . . . it's the best book we've had. All American writing comes from that. [Philip Young, *Ernest Hemingway.*]

In the year 1920, Marcus Garvey, a black Jamaican, appeared on the American scene. He landed in New York in March, 1916, after a pilgrimage spread over several years that took him from Jamaica to Costa Rica, Panama, Ecuador, Nicaragua, Honduras, Colombia, Venezuela, Great Britain, and, finally, the United States. He was twenty-eight years of age on his arrival in this country. His wanderings after the original departure from his native land bring to mind those of the Prophet Mohammed before the latter's mission ignited and caught and held the religious imagination of his fellow Arabs in concentric circles of nationalistic fire. Garvey's appeal was a similar mixture of the secular and the religious. Yet in so far as the latter ingredient went, while there was a canonical center represented by his African Orthodox church, and a rubric prescribed by its hierarchy, these were subordinate to his secular ambition, which was the redemption of Africa and the return of the blacks scattered throughout the world to their ancestral homeland, thus terminating the diaspora. That was Garvey's dream. If it cannot be said that he came within waking distance of its realization, it may nevertheless be asserted with unimpeachable accuracy that he shook the whole world awake to the possibility of the release of hundreds of millions of blacks from their psychological, no less than physical, subjugation by whites. And if Garvey failed to accomplish his material designs, he succeeded as though by magic in striking at, and in countless instances striking off, the centuries-old shackles of white racist domination from the consciousness of blacks.

This was Garvey's principal achievement, and it was one of no mean order. Here is where the racist whites, even beyond their physical subjection of blacks, had succeeded in imposing what until Garvey's coming was an unshakable thralldom. They possessed on their own terms and manipulated for their own ends the collective consciousness of the black group of mankind. Of all the feats of mass psychic subjection achieved by one group against another, this on the part of the whites must, surely, rank among the most stupendous. Customarily, great emphasis is placed on the physical or material aspects of white racist supremacy in the world at large. Yet whatever its magnitude and diffusion, it cannot begin to compare with the psychological conquest of blacks by the whites. When everything has been said about Marcus Garvey, all his failings estimated and his foibles justly contemned, this must nevertheless remain true: he, wellnigh singlehanded, in the space of a decade or less liberated the ethnic consciousness of blacks throughout the world. He did not redeem Africa, though even here the effect of his mission is not negligible. But he did more: he opened the gates of the psychological prison in which for centuries white racism had incarcerated the ethnic consciousness of blacks, and bade them, with bombast, no doubt, yet with irresistible conviction: Arise; come forth. And they did. So was the mission of this curious, Cagliostrolike figure accomplished.

He was helped by circumstances that were, objectively, not of his making. The immediate situation in the United States after the end of the First World War was conducive to his mission: in particular, the embitterment of the black soldiers who had discovered in Europe a freedom from racial discrimination wholly alien to their American experience, but who on returning home found that nothing had changed in this respect during their absence. If anything, it was worse. And the evidence was supplemented by an increased incidence of lynchings and a mounting crescendo of race riots. Garvey was a man who had chanced upon the exact conjuncture of his talent and ambition with the circumstances and the hour. No one may say that he failed. Such a mission as he embarked upon is not subject to the common assessment of failure or success. There is only one test to be applied: did the prophet reveal his message? In Garvey's case, the answer is, unhesitantly, yes.

That an unheralded black man, whose intellectual endowments were less a compound of substance than a compost of pretension, should have been the vehicle of this enterprise of black redemption need occasion no surprise. Irony and paradox are the favorite sport of the gods. That he should have made his way from the Caribbean backwater of St. Ann's Bay, Jamaica, to world attention in Harlem is more remarkable as a revolutionary intrusion into the mainland destiny of black Americans than as the private hegira of a prophet with a consuming sense of his personal importance to the redemption of Africa. What is chiefly amazing about the enterprise, considered from this distance, is Garvey's abiding concern with the liberation of Africa as a paramount goal to which the awakening of black Americans was merely a means. He sought, in effect, to make Zionists of black Americans and, indeed, of blacks everywhere. His message was: it is time to end the diaspora, time to return home. His American opponents— notably, W. E. B. Du Bois, Chandler Owen, copublisher of *The Messenger*, Robert S. Abbott, publisher of the Chicago *Defender*, the publicist George S. Schuyler, Alderman George Harris, editor of the New York *News*—felt that the aim of blacks should be leveled at the attainment of full citizenship in the United States, which, rather than Africa, was their true homeland.

In the light of this fundamental divergence of view, it is not without irony that toward the close of his life Du Bois ceased to weep by the waters of the Potomac and ended his days honored and venerated in Africa. He had viewed Garvey's dream as a nightmare threat of disaster for black Americans. Yet, in his own case, it was the means of his personal redemption from ignominy and rejection in the United States. No one opposed Garvey with such inflexible hostility as Du Bois. In the end, no one owed so much to Garvey's vision as this man who had worked with a resolution so inexorable to encompass his downfall.

Like Martin Luther King, Garvey, at the outset of his public career in the United States, was the victim of attempted assassination by a fellow black. Unlike King, in whose case a white assassin was, subsequently, successful, Garvey at his death was not accorded the apotheosis of martyrdom. He died in England in June, 1940, at the age of fifty-three, as the British Empire in its twilit recessional was retreating from Dunkirk, sped on its way by Hitler's legions. The infinite reach of irony provides yet another illustration of the strange revenges that history is capable of contriving. The essential philosophy of the imperial agglomeration that the British had put together under the pretext of a civilizing mission was white racism. From this point of view the only difference between the Nazis and themselves was a difference of degree. The Nazis were an extreme instance of a British racial attitude. It is not known if Garvey in his final moments, as the remnants of the British Expeditionary Force were being ferried across the channel from Dunkirk, was able to relish the grim vindication that time and events had provided for him. He had not sought the downfall of the British Empire, and if he could be adjudged guilty of black racism, it was on grounds that were plainly a reaction compelled by the aggressive tyranny of white racism. But the British Empire was in ruins, and the hand that struck it down was that of a white European racism only more immoderate and amoral than its own.

8

THE YEARS BETWEEN the deportation of Marcus Garvey from the United States in December, 1927, and his imprisonment on charges of mail fraud in February, 1925, were a national prelude of unrest, punctuated by epidemic violence, to the economic depression that further blighted the decade before the outbreak of the Second World War. Racial strife continued unabated. The efforts of organized labor to reduce and contain the power of capital over the lives of the workers frequently erupted in bitter clashes between the two antagonists. The economic process in America had brought unemployed millions of its citizens to penury and the humiliation of soup kitchens. As always, the blacks were much more keenly disadvantaged and much more deeply humiliated in their traditional role as the outcasts of the system. There were few to champion their cause; fewer still to relieve their hunger.

But there were to come two men, black Americans, both patently influenced by the work of Marcus Garvey and both intent on carrying toward completion the task of the psychological liberation of blacks that Garvey, amongst other objectives, had set himself. One was Adam Clayton Powell; the other was Malcolm X.

The qualities that set an individual apart in his or her time and place are not always easily definable. They are often the product of imponderables: the reflection of a mood, the shadow of a nuance. At other times they may be the tangible sign of some chance consistency with a dominant circumstance or, again, of opposition to it. The coin is one and the same. Personal significance is the reverse and inconsequence the obverse side. The currency of reputation is minted in the market place. There, value is determined by demand. But the market place, with its typical unpredictability, also constructs the material context for a mystique. In its own inscrutable way, it sets the stage for the mystique and brings the principal players before the footlights; that is to say, it creates a demand for the mystique. Next, it contrives the means of popular satisfaction. The pivotal questions are threefold; they revolve around: the material setting—the matrix—of the mystique; the personality of the chief actor or actors; and the effect of the drama upon spectators and participants alike.

The facts of Malcolm X's preparation for his leading role in the morality play that culminated in his death in 1965 are widely known and well authenticated. His slum childhood in all the hideous squalor of hopeless poverty; the decay and despair of the life around him; his frustration at school; his irruption into criminal activities: burglary, violence, traffic in prostitution and narcotics, dope addiction; his imprisonment and conversion to the beliefs of the Black Muslims—all these things are public knowledge.

His early life seems indeed to have been spent in a milieu suggestive in all its social horror of Maxim Gorki's *Lower Depths.* There was the probable murder of his father by white men, his mother's mental collapse and her removal to a lunatic asylum, the disintegration of the family, the parceling out of the children, the teacher who counseled him to become a carpenter rather than aim at becoming the lawyer that he wanted to be. Then came his street "hustle" in Harlem, the dives, bars, whores, dope peddlers and addicts, numbers bankers, gunmen, gangsters. Leaving Harlem in fear for his life, he returned to Massachusetts, to the same thing, before going to prison, convicted of burglary. Those seven years of confinement were the turning point for him. He read, he thought, and he became a disciple of Elijah Muhammad, Leader and Teacher of the Black Muslims. The theology of the Black Muslims, in so far as it may thus be described, is something of a miscellany of articles of faith derived from the tenets of Muslim orthodoxy and from a rubric of virulent hatred of white people.

No one of Malcolm X's extraordinary intelligence could have failed to recognize from the outset the building blocks of economic independence, to be achieved by organized self-help; social redemption, to be attained through renewed self-respect; and black racism, as an antidote to the poison of white racism, that were the foundation stones of the religious structure to which he devoted his gifted apostolate. Neither could anyone of his intelligence have failed to recognize as the historical architect of this edifice the long record of racial iniquity that has characterized the American society. A just balance must be struck. The Black Muslims are not the inexplicable products of some blameless void. They are the necessitated outcome of a centuries-long chain of causation. Only by blinking at this fact is it possible to indulge in self-righteous denunciation of their separatist revolt. Only by a corruption of the historical evidence is it possible to avoid indicting white American society for procuring by its own persistent evil an implacable hatred from its outcast depths.

Malcolm X was a man of great charm, affable in private conversation, reasonable in debate across a luncheon table. At Twenty-two West, a restaurant in Harlem where he was often to be seen, he could be engaged in talk in which another's opinion and his dissent left him as smiling, courteous, and hospitable as he had been at the outset of the exchange. He was easy to approach and hard to leave, precisely because he was so *reasonable*. Even when he spoke of "white devils," and he was reminded that there were "black devils," too, he maintained his habitual air of judicial calm. It was not simply because he was skilled in the histrionic arts of the demagogue (indeed, was he a demagogue?); nor was it solely due to his somewhat rigid, Aristotelian sense of logic, nor to his sovereign lucidity, nor, lastly, to his commanding physical presence; though, unquestionably, these all played their especial and determinant roles in his repertoire of persuasion. Without either discounting or unduly distinguishing it, his remarkable voice may be noted—its organlike resonance; the enormous range of its oratorical effects. The manner in which he gave the impression of seeing into, through, and far beyond others may be remarked. The quality of his rhetoric—"so American," as an Englishman once said of it—may be noticed. All these attributes may be listed and yet will not abstract what beyond doubt was his most potent talisman: his utter sincerity. No one ever questioned this in Malcolm X, this luminous outer glow of burning inner conviction.

It would have been so easy to have dubbed him a fanatic. Some did. Yet not so many as might have been supposed; singularly few, indeed, when what he advocated throughout most of his public career is borne in mind. For he "came not to send peace, but a sword." Perhaps the relative infrequency of the charge of fanaticism against him may be ascribed to the stern rectitude of the racial inferences he drew from the premises of American history. People knew, whether they agreed with him or not, that he was speaking the truth. It might be the unappetizing truth, but it was no more and no less than the truth.

You sure ain't ketchin' hell 'cause you're American, 'cause if you were American, you wouldn't ketch no hell. You ain't ketchin' hell 'cause you're white, 'cause if you were white, you wouldn't ketch no hell. You're ketchin' hell 'cause you're black. That's why you're ketchin' hell.

That was a more colloquial passage in the course of one of his speeches. During the same speech, one that he made at Detroit before his apostasy and subsequent murder, he referred to the Bandung Conference. For the first time, he said, black men had succeeded in coming together to make common cause against their enemy, the white man. And they had been able to do so only by resolutely keeping the white man away from Bandung. *They* had excluded *him*.

This theme, the exclusion of the white man, dominated his public utterances. Directed toward black audiences already embittered by the white man's injustice, it cast a powerful spell. The teeming overflow audience of white America shuddered at the implacable oratory. Still another reason for Malcolm X's inordinate powers of persuasion was that, despite the high emotional content of his central topic, he never ranted. He managed at most times to sound eminently judicious, and to speak ex cathedra even when he attributed omniscience to his Leader and Teacher: "Elijah Muhammad says . . ." In the end his superb intelligence got the better of him. He could incant the formulas no longer. But meantime he went up and down the country preaching the Black Muslim gospel that the lowly estate of the "so-called Negroes" in the United States was the logical consequence of the diabolical wickedness of their centuries-old oppressors.

His arguments were clear and explicit, free of beclouding symbolism, replete with concrete illustrations of the points he ceaselessly hammered home. He spoke in simple and direct language, employing a self-evident and irrefutable logic, and drew illuminatingly upon history. He had copied an entire dictionary, word by word, page by page, during his prison term, and the result was palpable in his careful and discriminating diction. If it was not always faultless, it was never pointless. Every syllable mattered; every word justified itself by its function in the expression of his thought. There was no peacocking adornment, no display to tickle the gallery. For him, language was intended to do, not merely to be; that is, to declare, clarify, and convince. And so he chose the simplest words, the pithiest phrases, the most economical means consistent with the possibilities of logical persuasion, to reach the minds of his listeners.

What black, however prosperous, is immune to a lucid recital of the cruel oppression he and his forebears have been obliged to endure in this country? What black, at the very apex of personal success, is unaware that the great mass of his fellow blacks is still enclosed in a nationwide stockade over whose walls few escape? What black, middle-class, stable, and satisfied, does not see in the face of a white man the mirrored image of countless millions of oppressors? Here lay the secret of Malcolm X's profound, if carefully hidden, success with the black middle class. They knew that what he was saying was true, as true as the American dollar, in which, like their white counterparts, they put their deepest trust. Deny him as they might in public, in private they could only accept him. Reject him as they might for the benefit of their white patrons and associates, in the privacy of their homes they could only hope for his success. Success? What success? Did they indeed hope that he would somehow succeed in subverting the established order? Hardly. They were in the main too sensible, too realistic, to indulge themselves in such fanciful nonsense. But they could wish, and they did, that he would go on giving white people hell and, in the end, perhaps, thereby bring them to confront for the first time the suppurating horror of their chronic wickedness.

So despairing, beneath its comfortable veneer, is the outlook of middle-class blacks in this country. Never, of course, would they permit themselves to become identified as protagonists of Malcolm X. Quite the reverse. They were meticulous in uttering reasoned disclaimers of his preachments. Particularly in those quarters—white quarters, of course—where their "I know not the man" might, as they calculated, do them the most good. But when the blinds were drawn and black spoke to black, it was a different story. Then Malcolm X came into his own. As he does right at this moment.

His appeal to the black masses was understandable enough. Nothing more is necessary to elucidate that mystery than a walk through a black ghetto, whether in an urban or a rural setting. Nothing more is necessary than knowledge of the past and awareness of the present. The charge most often made against him, where the black masses were concerned, was not that he misrepresented anything or exaggerated or falsified the facts of their squalid condition, but that he aroused and inflamed them. In other words, what he said was true, but his purpose in saying it was questionable.

When he advocated racial segregation, was he simply reviving a Communist lure of a black belt? Not only the Jewish people have yearned for Jerusalem. But Malcolm X, it is safe to say, intended nothing so visionary, so impracticable, as a black state within the comity of the United States. Certainly not in the light of his subsequent political sophistication. What he was expressing through the rhetoric of racial separatism was an affirmation of the will of blacks to exist on their own terms, unimpeded in their progress, unimpaired in their dignity, unimpeached in their self-esteem as equal co-dwellers in this land, where they are at once the largest as well as the oldest ethnic minority. It was, in its designed rhetorical effect (for he knew as well as anyone the practical limitations of such a demand), an outright repudiation of the American culture. It was no more than that. Yet it could scarcely have been less if he was to be consistent with his contempt for the middle-class black goal of integration. He did not see this goal so much as integration, in James Baldwin's famous phrase, "into a burning house" but as integration into a brothel; just as he saw America as a "prison" for "so-called Negroes." A psychologist might find the attribution of these equivalents of crime and immorality to American life interesting in view of Malcolm X's background. But interesting or not, his background does possess considerable significance in any attempt to analyze the mystique of this remarkable man. He inveighed continually against what he deemed the historic debauchery of black women by white men in America. Time and time again he denounced the racial evils that drove black men like himself into crime and prison.

There was a deep Puritan strain in him. Although he was the child of a black West Indian mother (from the island of Grenada) and a black American father, there was a good deal of the seventeenth century New England divine about him, with his insistent emphasis on exemplary moral conduct through continence and, together with this, his tendency to polarize social questions into stark simplifications of good and evil. Blacks understood these tendencies and responded to them. Despite the prevailing myth, blacks are deeply moral people. Their religious attachment is largely fundamentalist, which is why the literalism of the Baptists has been so influential in shaping their beliefs and traditions.

Malcolm X was a Black Muslim, but far deeper than his adherence to that ethnoreligion was his fundamentalist faith in the power and sanctity of the Word. To hear him discuss the Constitution of the United States was to listen, as it were, to a Talmudic scholar expounding the Book. There was the same enshrinement of the written text, the same intellectual prostration before it, the same ingenuity in glossing it with interpretive refinements of unswerving literalism. To transfer the matter to another historical environment, it may be noted that the social and religious customs of the Africans long depended for their preservation on verbal transmission. To paraphrase C. G. Jung slightly, the memory of the tribe ensured continuity, since it lacked writing as a vehicle for this purpose. But in critical essence, the survival of its heritage was confided to the Word. When blacks were uprooted from their native soil and transplanted in America, they encountered another human group, namely, their white masters, who were as servile to the Word as they. The only difference was that in the case of the blacks the Word was verbal, and in the other it was written. But they and their masters were all fundamentalists. They had little difficulty in accepting the supreme authority of the Christian Bible, since it was only the graphic distillation of a social process that had remained unwritten with them.

Virtually to the end of his life, Malcolm X remained curiously unaware—or seemed to—of two crucial circumstances: the comparatively unevolved state of the human species; and, possibly following from this, the formidable natural obstacles to peaceful social intercourse. Someday someone more enlightened than Malcolm X may give adequate attention to the chemistry of group relations, with results that may be startling no less than revealing. Meanwhile Malcolm X busied himself throughout the land and beyond the seas, fatally oversimplifying these profoundly complicated matters. Yet, in all fairness to him, his was not the role of the social scientist; it was that of the preacher-politician. Nevertheless, he was in the orthodox tradition of black American leadership, which for generations had been exercised by religious rather than lay elements. Malcolm X was, in short, a traditionalist. He invoked the aid of a Supreme Being—Allah—to redress the woes of his fellow believers, and he rendered homage to a high priest—Elijah Muhammad—to whom he conceded the divine office and prerogatives of Prophet. His appeal to black Americans of all classes was, therefore, well within the familiar terms of the established orthodoxy. Moreover, he had sinned, had confessed his sins, and had turned away from his wickedness. Now he preached repentance and salvation.

Compounded with this religiosity was his secular hostility, his condemnation of the white man, the wicked, unregenerate author of the black man's ills. The very language of his chastisements was culled from traditional sources. White people were "devils." They were also "snakes." It was, of course, this established symbol of malignity to which Adam and Eve owed their expulsion from the Garden of Eden. The white serpent had tempted the black Eve and procured her debauchery. This is not the theology of a simpleton, unless one is willing to conclude all Christendom simpleton. It is, on the contrary, a skillful appeal to psychological factors that may be relied upon to evoke with little or no obstruction preconditioned social reflexes. To the extent that it was not deliberately so conceived, it was quite probably unconscious on Malcolm X's part. In either case, its orthodoxy was indisputable. Once this fact has been grasped, Malcolm X's philosophical authority can be traced to its primal source, and its effectiveness calculated in the light of objective actualities quite apart from matters of personal charisma.

"Big Red," born Malcolm Little in a rural town in the Midwest, was an imposing figure, and he was not unconscious of the part this physical factor played in the spell he cast upon all who came into contact with him. But there was something else. He himself alluded to it in his *Autobiography:*

I got so I could feel my audiences' temperaments. I've talked with other public speakers; they agree that this ability is native to any person who has the "mass appeal" gift, who can get through to and move people. It's a psychic radar.

It also explains the gift he possessed in such transcendent degree of getting right inside the guts of every black who heard him. His was a truly Circean spell; to listen was to linger, and to linger was to be transformed. One was never quite the same again.

Where he differed from the New England archetype with a sense of religious mission was in his advocacy of violence as a means to the end of securing social justice. In so doing, he conjured up a grim specter to affright the American society. He spoke of revolution and bloodshed as the indispensable conditions of root change in a society. That was the way, and no other was possible. The perverse iniquity of the white man had brought this about. In one of his speeches he adduced some historical analogies of popular revolutions aimed at redressing deep-seated grievances. All of these mass uprisings, he argued, were based on land. "The land-*less*," as he put it, "against the landlords." The French Revolution, he said, was based on land. So were the American, the Russian, the Chinese. The black revolution, then, would derive from a similar inspiration. This conclusion was both crude and misleading in its half-informed naïveté.

There was, demonstrably, a complex of factors in each of the revolutionary precedents he cited, of which land hunger was only one. The American Revolution, for instance, was plotted and carried out by landlords. The middle-class Frenchmen who fomented and directed the eighteenth-century revolution in their country were, on the whole, less concerned with the redistribution of land than with the abstract rhetoric of the "rights of man." The social theorizing of the Encyclopedists was a sharper spur to the bourgeois revolutionaries than was the feudal concentration of vast estates in the hands of the French nobles. The Russian Revolution was exactly a case in point. It had its origin in the disaffection of the middle class, in particular of the urban middle class, and was at first almost exclusively urban in its objectives. Only later did it expand to embrace the peasantry. But it was bourgeois to begin with, rather than proletarian, as may be said to be the classic case with revolution.

In time Malcolm X did come to recognize this complexity, and when he did, he became an apostate to his Black Muslim faith. His apostasy began, overtly, with his overtures to the black middle class after his return from a pilgrimage to Mecca. Much earlier, however, he had been appealing to all blacks to unite on the basis of what they had in common, which was their hatred of the white man. But he had outlined no program to bring middle-class blacks within the scope of his design. In his post-Mecca phase, he proceeded to do so. And it was precisely at this point of his ideological evolution that he was gunned down. He had seen too late that the key to the solution of the black-white impasse in the United States reposed, as it had always done, in the massive patience, the Archimedean balance, the invincible forbearance, of the black middle class. Once he had scorned and derided them, mocking and vilifying them as "Uncle Toms." Now he courted them. His attitude toward whites exhibited a corresponding change. He had met blue-eyed, white-skinned Moslems in the course of his pilgrimage to Mecca who had been completely egalitarian in their conduct toward him, as well as toward other black pilgrims. He confessed he had been mistaken in the sweeping condemnations of whites, without exceptions, that he had previously indulged in. He began to speak of universal brotherhood. Nevertheless, he did not diminish his hostility to racial prejudice, nor did he give the slightest hint of any inclination to compromise with it. Quite the reverse, in fact. He was mainly instrumental in preparing a petition for presentation to the United Nations charging the United States with crimes against its black citizens.

In his appearances at Orators' Corner on 125th Street at Seventh Avenue in New York City and elsewhere the widened compass of his philosophical concern became increasingly evident. He continued to denounce white people, but no longer all white people. He continued to attack the black middle class for their ingrained habits of self-seeking, as he alleged, and their callous indifference to the plight of their less fortunate fellow blacks. But they were no longer *all*, irredeemably, Uncle Toms; no longer *all*, inveterately, enemies of their oppressed brethren. He had begun to conceive of an Afro-American community from which, naturally, whites were to be excluded; yet, not any longer because they were indiscriminately hated, but simply because they were not black. At the same time he made it clear that he was not precluding the prospect of understanding with white people of demonstrated good will. Indeed, he would welcome it.

By now he had been expelled from the ranks of the Black Muslims. The ostensible reason for his expulsion was a remark he had made with reference to the assassination of the much-lamented President Kennedy. Something about "chickens coming home to roost." It was an ill-advised and, in the tragic circumstances, a vicious comment. He was first suspended from his Black Muslim ministry and silenced "for ninety days." His prompt, unhesitant reaction was to assert his submission to his Leader and Teacher, Elijah Muhammad, and his loyalty to the movement. Then, as the months wore on with no apparent softening of Elijah Muhammad's anger, Malcolm X took a fateful decision. He broke with the Black Muslims. In addition, he denounced Elijah Muhammad. His death followed shortly. This is not to imply that the former event was the cause of the latter, although Malcolm X himself had predicted it. Moreover, the alleged assassins were apprehended, tried, and convicted.

Speculation on this particular point must yield in long-term interest to other probabilities. What would Malcolm X have gone on to accomplish had he lived? Or, at the moment of his death, had he already fulfilled whatever function his genius and character had ordained for him? Certainly his impact on all classes of his contemporaries is at least as great now as it was during his lifetime. It may even be greater, for his martyrdom has already invested his memory with a legendary quality, which is the stuff from whose interweaving of fact and myth immortality is made. His fundamental thinking, which was imbedded in a theology of the wickedness of the white man, is essentially the thinking of most blacks, disguise and conceal it as they may. Nothing so clearly elucidates this fact as the deep, persisting appeal of Malcolm X to all categories of black society in America. He spoke—for them—from the far, hidden recesses of their hearts. Some blacks may have differed from him— and some undoubtedly did—in his assessment of the possibilities of turning the white man away from his racial wickedness. Some were more optimistic than he. But no black in America is unaware of the cruelties perpetrated against him and his like by the dominant white society throughout the centuries, continuing into the present and, as far as they can see, likely to continue well into the future.

There is hardly a black anywhere in this country who somewhere in his body or soul does not bear a wound, a scar, inflicted upon him by the infamy of the dominant white society. There cannot be a black in this country who at some searing instant of immedicable agony has not hated white people. If one black, luckier in this respect than most, has not personally felt the lash and cut of white hostility, then his mother has, his sister, his father, his brother, his cousin, his grandmother, his grandfather—unto the fourteenth and fifteenth generations. Malcolm X knew this and exploited it. In so doing, he had little difficulty achieving direct, intimate, and authentic communication with *all* blacks. They knew at firsthand, in their own bodies and souls, what he was talking about; and they knew that he was telling it "like it is," telling the profound, the historic, as well as the galling, immediate truth, and nothing but the truth.

But did they, as Malcolm X did, yearn for vengeance? Some unquestionably did. But the remarkable fact about black Americans is their extraordinary capacity for love. Blacks are loving people. They appear to have singularly little capacity for sustained hatred. By their collective restraint, in general, they have elevated themselves to guardianship of the moral life of America. At the touch of a friendly hand, the glimpse of a kindly smile, the sound of a cordial voice, they become irradiated. White people know this, and white people have exploited it. Where Malcolm X would have failed, and by the time of his death he had seen the certainty of failure, was here—precisely here—in the rejection by most blacks of the notion of revenge. Despite his monumental accomplishments, Malcolm X had failed, and recognized that he had failed, in his original attempt to put vengeance into the hearts of his fellow blacks. And this, beyond all doubt, is why—pretexts aside—he parted company with the Black Muslims. Whoever guided the hands that fingered the triggers that fired the shots that killed him, Malcolm X can fairly be said to have laid down his life for a cause he came at last to believe in. Toward the end, he had begun to sound like a brown-skinned Savonarola as he castigated the evils of contemporary society. His acquired asceticism, against the preceding background of his self-confessed libertinism, gave him, too, something of the quality of a Pauline figure. And then, a tragic thing happened on the road to Damascus.

He bequeathed a mixed inheritance to his fellow blacks, "so-called Negroes," as he was in the habit of describing them: on the one hand, he gave them a resuscitated awareness of their history, which was surely a useful thing to do; on the other hand, by a too narrow and obsessive emphasis upon the more painful episodes of that history, he may have engendered a certain emotional imbalance among them, an injurious disproportion of judgment. Nevertheless, his influence persists. No black, however fervent or even impassioned his disclaimer, has been unaffected by it. Perhaps there was poetic, if not ethical, justice in the manner of his death. For years he had dedicated his extraordinary gifts to a primeval baying for revenge. His death was in the grim and wasteful spirit of this abysmal evil.

William Bolitho wrote in the course of the Introduction to his luminous series of studies of historical personages *Twelve Against the Gods:*

It is so with all great characters. Their faults are not mud spots, but structural outcroppings, of an indivisible piece with their personality.

This view is also contained in the familiar reflection on qualities possessing, inherently, their own defects. Bolitho's twelve lives have, in the main, four things in common: the course of each life (or chapter of adventures, as he would have described it) is not a straight line, but a parabola; at the high point of its trajectory, the adventurer is seized by vertigo, a momentary dizziness; because of the parabolic quality of each life, it tends at some point along the curve to return to its beginning; typically, the adventurer is trapped by his success. Bolitho was an aphorist of no mean distinction. "It is," he said, "when the pirates count their booty that they become mere thieves."

The application of Bolitho's insights may illumine afresh the career of Adam Clayton Powell. In any event, it will preclude drafting the ready-made, hand-me-down banalities of Greek tragedy into an American seriocomedy. The comic portion of the whole episode centers around Powell's having been cast in the role of a Negro in the macabre farce of racial identity in the United States. In any society where sanity in such matters counted for more than blind bigotry, the precise racial group to which Powell belonged would either be a matter of no consequence or would be established by common-sense canons bearing some visible relationship to the categories of modern science. But in such a, perhaps, utopian state of affairs, Adam Clayton Powell might have been merely the "poor parish priest" he often claimed to be—a handsome, eloquent, fun-loving parish priest, irresistible to the ladies and a bit of a trial to the grave vestrymen and sobersided trustees of his church; but an excellent man at heart, instantly responsive to the joys and sorrows of his flock, and wonderfully consoling in that final hour that awaits us all. Perhaps that is what he would have been elsewhere than in America, and otherwise than as a Negro. But there was this chance conjunction of his having been born in America and thereafter constrained to be Negro. (There seems to be evidence that at least once before the die was cast, he trifled unsuccessfully with another racial identity.)

Adam Clayton Powell's decision to throw in his lot with the Negroes could not have been either a simple choice of ethnic affinity or an easy acceptance of relegation to an inferior caste. By appearance, tastes, and temperament, he was designed for a leading role on the side of the dominant majority in his particular segment of the national *opéra bouffe*. In appearance, he was a white conquistador; his tastes were those of a spoiled only son of devoted, well-to-do parents; his temperament was that of an affectionate child whose willfulness from time to time might betray him into profligacy and errant causes, but whose loyalty to the conventional order and whose eventual return to its fold would never be in doubt. Beyond this, his natural intelligence in all its unusual brilliance could be relied upon to reveal to him, sooner or later, the buttered side of his slice of the world's loaf. So there really was no reason for undue worry about him. And indeed there need not have been—if he did not have to be a Negro. Even then everything would have been all right, and he would have come to no harm, if only he had never left home, never left Harlem, never left the Abyssinian Baptist Church. But as Bolitho observed: "Adventure must start with running away from home." So Adam ran away from home. He ran away, first of all, to the New York City Council. Then, his appetite whetted for further adventure, he ran away to the Congress of the United States; which is a long long way from Harlem, a long, long way from home. At the same time, his superb endowment of mind and will and daring must often have whispered to him in the language of Philip to Alexander: "Seek another kingdom, my son, that may be worthy of thy abilities, for Macedonia is too small for thee."

It is not without point, as a reflection on the American society, that "home" for a black almost invariably conjures up a sense of narrow circumscription. The domestic pasture of a white citizen of the republic always affords a larger grazing area than that parceled out to a black. "Your huddled masses yearning to breathe free" are, inside America, nonwhite. This circumstance derives a particular irony from the fact that the large majority of these nonwhites are not, in the commonly accepted meaning of the term, "immigrants." Emma Lazarus certainly did not have *them* in mind. The point of substance is that no black up to this time can think of the United States as "home" without experiencing a momentary chilling sense of restriction. In the South, a black careless of this condition has usually been disciplined by violence. In the North, the customary methods of punishment have taken subtler forms. Adam Clayton Powell's entire career, public and private, was a constant, impassioned protest against this enshackling confinement. After all, "Don't Fence Me In" is a sentiment by no means alien to the American tradition, except—and this is crucial to the whole complex—when it is asserted by a nonwhite. Powell was, essentially, a frontiersman, a black frontiersman. He found this racial fence galling. What man of spirit would not? In a cant phrase of the modern psychologues, he "reacted" to it.

As to the methods of his reaction, there can be (and there are) differences of opinion. But as to the social validity of his urge to react —to defy, deride, subvert, transcend, these arbitrary limitations imposed upon him as a Negro—no honest man can have any doubt. It is as natural as the urge to escape from prison. This is what America has meant to its black citizens: a prison. Most of them, having broken no laws, transgressed no ordinances, infringed no rules, nevertheless find themselves hemmed in, wherever they turn, by the walls of a sociological prison. Adam Clayton Powell was no exception. In common with other blacks, he had experienced this sense of restriction, suffering enchainment without reason by an all-pervasive, all-powerful racial tyranny. In the ghettos of medieval Europe and their later Eastern European successors, there were actual legal proscriptions decreed or enacted against the Jewish inhabitants. The Jews of the ghettos were expressly restricted in their freedom of movement and explicitly denied the liberty to engage in any but scheduled occupations. All these prohibitions were graven on the tablets of the Christian law. But in the case of the blacks, after their emancipation from slavery in this country over 100 years ago, they acquired, in theory and constitutional intent, full and equal freedom with express legal sanction. But their newly won freedom was largely notional, a thing of pious proclamation rather than actual social transformation; as they soon found out. And as it has continued to the present.

Adam Clayton Powell's attempts to climb over the wall to freedom had, of course, the inevitable result of concentrating the watchful attention of his jailers upon him. All such attempts on the part of blacks in this society have had precisely that consequence. This is not to say that Powell was not sometimes reckless or foolhardy, or worse. He was. Unfortunately; because his own freedom and that of his fellow blacks depended upon his efforts to liberate himself. Since, had he succeeded in making good his escape, a vast concourse of his fellow prisoners would have followed him over the wall. It was, without the slightest question, the prospect of a mass breakthrough in such an event that had the effect of focusing the watch of the prison guard upon him. Solitary confinement in Harlem (or Bimini) would have been punishment sufficient to fit the crime, perhaps—"suspension in limbo," as one newspaper subsequently put it. But his fellow prisoners, with astounding and, from the standpoint of the white jailers, wholly unexpected unanimity, displayed a clear understanding of the reasons for his plight, and a desire as reckless as his own to share the fate he had incurred at the hands of the dominant society. Hitherto safe black leaders, trusties who could be relied upon to keep their fellow prisoners quiet, rallied to his aid. They spoke out on his behalf, confounding the cherished white belief that Powell was a maverick, a rogue steer whom the other black steers would be only too happy to have cut out of the herd.

How had this astonishing situation come about? The answer is quite simple. It was because all these people knew that they were, precisely like Powell, prisoners behind the bars of the American society. They were in some instances trusties, ticket-of-leave men, but they were prisoners nonetheless.

Prison is an unnatural institution, and its inmates are inclined to develop irrational, antisocial traits. It would be only psychological realism to examine the behavior of black Americans against this background. There must otherwise be only an imperfect understanding of what to so many decent, well-intentioned whites seem, in this particular instance, the motiveless aberrancies of Adam Clayton Powell. Most blacks in America suffer from stir fever; Powell not, indeed, more than most but simply more visibly, or more flamboyantly. Yet when all is said and done, this is a matter of individual temperament, and a man ought not to be hanged simply because he prefers the vivid naturalism of Rousseau to the muted impressionism of Monet. At all events, one should neither condone nor condemn out of mere emotionalism and partisanship. The effort to rise above prejudice in any form whatever must always be made. A good deal of Powell's public conduct suggests that, like so many blacks, he had become stir-crazy. Some men are better adapted than others by temperament, better suited by character, to the abnormal conditions of prison life. Some accept their sentence, which in the case of blacks is usually life imprisonment, with philosophic resignation. Others, like the late Malcolm X, foment protest. Yet others, like Adam Clayton Powell, spend their time in a persistent effort to break out. All this is understandable enough. The most pathetic sight in the world is a human being—any human being—behind bars. Watch a vanload of prisoners being driven, enclosed under guard, away from a criminal court. Even a caged animal in a zoo is a saddening spectacle.

So the career of Adam Clayton Powell was that of a human being imprisoned behind sociological bars and desperately, recklessly, defiantly trying to free himself, and trying to free his fellow prisoners, too. For Powell did not attempt merely to free himself. He could have done that quite easily, by keeping his mouth shut, by putting his conscience to sleep. He could have made his way to freedom on his own. Having achieved power, or on his way to the achievement of power, he could have employed a soothing, inoffensive vocabulary. To the service of a purely personal ambition, he could have yoked a habit of contented, undisturbing, ruminating expression that would not have offended his jailers or alarmed them, but instead would have earned him marks for good conduct and the repute of a model prisoner.

Why, then, did he not go his way alone? With his good looks, so indistinguishably white, his quick, resourceful mentality, his eloquence, his personal charm, his assured financial position, why did he not moderate his protest, making it mellifluous rather than inflammatory, consoling rather than challenging, reassuring rather than castigating? Why did he march, instead, up and down 125th Street in Harlem, carrying picket signs demanding jobs for blacks in the jim-crow shops, where they were spending the little money they could wrest from a hostile economy? Why, still earlier, did he organize soup kitchens to feed the starving poor of Harlem, and this at a time when the prospect of a political career of any consequence could scarcely have been conceivable? Why did he hurl himself at one barrier after another that blocked the path of blacks to decent progress: the civil service of New York, the transportation system, the banks—to cite only a few? Was it because he was ambitious to become a civil servant, a teller in a bank, a bus driver, a subway motorman or conductor? Was it for any of these reasons?

Individual blacks will tell you of his generous compassion in time of trouble. One relates how in a season of intense personal grief and misfortune, he received an invitation from Powell, with whom he was only slightly acquainted, to attend a reception for a visiting dignitary at the Abyssinian Baptist Church. This particular black was not a member of Powell's congregation, nor to this day has he the remotest idea of how Powell came to hear of his private calamity. But Powell welcomed him with the utmost kindness, spent a good deal of time away from more important guests talking to him, encouraging and buoying him up with the most sympathetic delicacy and insight. And this story can be multiplied by thousands of similar instances. So why was he not concerned only for himself?

Look for a moment at the facts. In his congregation at the Abyssinian Baptist Church, Powell had the solid nucleus of a political constituency capable of ensuring his return to Congress as long as he lived. There was nothing that that congregation would not do for him. Money? Power? Pre-eminence? There were 10,000 to lay these things at his feet, and to account themselves blessed in so doing. What did he lack? What was it that Adam Clayton Powell wanted and did not have? What was it that even his 10,000—and more—could not give him? In one word, freedom. Freedom within the American society. To have all and yet to lack this, this sole thing supremely beyond price— freedom. Here was the granite irony on which this gifted, generous man shattered himself. How mocking, how derisive, must the chairmanship of an important committee of Congress seem when its holder is everywhere and in every way reminded at the height of his power and authority that he is merely a trusty, rewarded for good behavior or the promise of it, in default of which he can at any time, at the will of his jailers, be stripped of his privileges; which, of course, was exactly how matters turned out. There could have been no other outcome, and no one knew this better than Powell, familiar as he was with the ruthless ways of power: white power, as some people call it.

Why, then, did he not play it safe? Was he, in effect, saying to white people: you rejected me, so I will show you? Was it as narrowly, as meanly personal as that? The motive of private vengeance is human enough, but it is not for that reason commendable. If indeed it were merely private, would he not, for instance, have married a white woman? This is the way some blacks choose to demonstrate both their defiance of and contempt for the unwritten proscriptions imposed upon them. But the closest he came to marrying a white woman was when he took a Puerto Rican to wife. Of his other two wives, one was a light-skinned black American, the other a darkskinned black West Indian. Few white women could have resisted the lure of marriage to this magnificently attractive man, whiter in appearance than numerous whites who pretend to that racial category; devoid, in physical fact, of the least semblance of any Negroid trait. Together with this, he was well-to-do, highly educated, of impressive intellect, beautifully groomed, with polished and courtly manners, a born leader, a clergyman of the most respectable antecedents, and a politician of vast power and influence. Negro or not, many white women in America would have consented to become Adam Clayton Powell's wife for the mere proposing. Why did he spurn them? What significance is to be assigned to this factor in the whole complex of this fascinating man? For fascinating he was. He had only to enter a room for all interest to become riveted upon him and for everyone else to acquire a subordinate importance. But this fascination also bred envy of him, which, of all human vices, is the most dangerous, because it is the most easily aroused and also the most implacable. How white men must have envied Powell!

He must have known this; he could hardly have been unaware of it. So why was he not smarter? Why, then, did he not throw Polycrates' ring into the sea? Why the recklessness, the foolhardiness, tantamount—almost—to a desire for martyrdom?

Anyone deeply nurtured in the New Testament of the Christian Bible, as Powell was, unwittingly acquires a taste for martyrdom. Jesus Christ is the Great Exemplar. It is not without significance that Powell, on being made to stand aside at the reconvening of the Ninetieth Congress, emerged before his supporters on the steps of the Capitol to compare his fate to that of Jesus Christ. The statement he was prevented from making to Congress in his self-defense on that day also contained a reference to the assassination of Julius Caesar, the great Roman soldier and martyr-politician. In each case, martyrdom was the theme of the allusion. One is tempted to incapsulate the whole matter in summary terms and assert that Powell deliberately courted martyrdom; that, being well aware of the risks he was taking, he nevertheless attempted to escape from prison by scaling the wall and was "shot down" by the prison guards while doing so, as, some years later, was alleged in justification of the death of George Jackson.

But the truth is never single-faceted. There were other things, as well. Powell's peccadilloes—his amatory escapades, his flouting of the rules to which all blacks must be obedient if they are to reach and keep some precarious public eminence—may be seen as self-indulgence or as a thumbing of his nose at a social order he had on many occasions openly denounced as hypocritical. There is no question whatever that in the United States a wide disparity exists between the latitude enjoyed by whites for their human frailties and that permitted blacks. As Whitney Young, of the National Urban League, put it with respect to Powell: "In this country you cannot be both black and wrong . . . [but] you can be white and wrong and still make it." Young was talking about the black-white double standard. "If you're white, you're right. If you're black, stand back." By this folk aphorism, blacks have long expressed their awareness of the disjunctive character of American morality. Yet this dual system of moral weights and measures does possess its own internal logic. Prisoners are restricted persons. They cannot reasonably expect to have the same degree of liberty as those who are civilly free. This does not suffice to make the double standard self-validating; it simply indicates the source of its sustenance. Anyone who, like Adam Clayton Powell, managed to get to the top of the wall before being shot down must also have got a disturbingly sharp glimpse of the possibilities of freedom on the other side. He got to the top of the wall and so was able to see, more clearly than any black before him, the Promised Land.

The top of the wall, however, proved to be his Mount Pisgah. As with Moses, his journey would end there. But while the Hebrew leader and patriarch expired in the fullness of his days, the black leader was cut down at the height of his accomplishments. He was Chairman of the House Committee on Education and Labor and, in the opinion of two Presidents, an extraordinarily effective chairman. More than half a hundred major pieces of legislation, involving expenditures amounting to billions of dollars and affecting the welfare of millions of Americans, black and white, were efficiently piloted through Congress under his helmsmanship. No serious question has ever been raised on the score of his unusual abilities. The fact that he was a splendidly gifted man has been conceded by even his most vociferous enemies. This itself was no small concession, for it is not the custom to admit that blacks are uncommonly endowed except as prizefighters, sprinters, baseball or football players, singers, dancers, clowns, comedians, or something of the sort. Powell forced recognition of his abilities and achieved in the process power such as no black, and few whites, have ever wielded. The acquisition of such unprecedented power also brought him much closer than any black had ever been to the whites who traditionally exercise it. He saw them with remorseless clarity, and he came to feel an overwhelming contempt for them. Were these bunglers and hypocrites his masters? Well, he would show them.

There were two paths open to him. One was to demonstrate, as blacks customarily have been obliged to do, his moral superiority to the white leaders. Blacks have always been forced to be morally better than whites: to be better in order to deserve less. They have never been allowed an equal margin for their human frailties. Never have they been able to get out of line without incurring a drastic penalty. Powell knew this as well as any black. The other path was the one he took: that of showing that he was just as human as they, thus refusing the traditional black role of moral exemplar. He would claim, and assume, the full panoply of white American liberties: the privilege to do wrong no less than the duty to do right. *They* went on pleasure trips around the world at the public expense; so would he. *They* engaged in amatory escapades, which the white press, by tacit agreement, concealed from the public; so would he. *They* openly spurned rules and defied the law; so would he.

Powell cannot have been blind to the chance he was taking. What made him think, then, that he, a self-styled black, could get away with it? He had challenged the *Ding an sich*, the very dragon of custom itself. For a while, curiously, and to the immense divertisement of Powell's constituents and his national following, the monster appeared hesitant to do battle. Meanwhile Powell made rings around the reluctant creature, blowing smoke from fragrant cigars into its horrendous visage, jumping on and off its bristling back, pulling its tail, making faces, thumbing his nose at it. For blacks, it was the best entertainment they had had in centuries. With sublime, self-confident daring, he ridiculed the monster. "Audacious black power!" he shouted at it. Then he became overconfident, and the creature got him; as he knew all along it would, if he mocked it long enough. Shortly before he became chairman of the House Committee on Education and Labor, he had spoken of retirement. He had had enough by then. But what is the purpose of a Himalayan peak unless some mortal tests his hardihood against it? The chairmanship was such a peak, and irresistible to Adam Clayton Powell. So he scaled it.

Bolitho's theory of transient vertigo returns to mind, the momentary spell of giddiness that all climbers are familiar with as they plant crampon after crampon, painful step by step, up the mountain face to the uttermost height. It is a rhapsody of the heights, akin to the narcosis of the deep that afflicts divers at the farthest point of their descent. In the one case, there is the urge to hurl oneself down, having, like Icarus, approached too near the sun. In the other, there is an abdication of the will to return to the surface and its supplanting by a rhapsodic urge to drown. Bolitho would have speculated that Adam Clayton Powell's fall was due to vertigo sustained at a considerable height. The great biographer would have been partly right. Nevertheless, it was his weakness as a student of human character that he tended to isolate his subjects (Alexander the Great, Casanova, Columbus, Napoleon I, Cagliostro, Woodrow Wilson, among them) from their social environments. His method was rather that of the entomologist than the ecologist. Yet, human character does not emerge from the void but is the product of an infinitely diverse combination of genetic and environmental circumstances. Bolitho was prone, on the whole, to ignore these factors and to see the subject of his study as a spontaneous act of unconditioned self-creation. Despite its defects, his method enabled him to achieve deep interior penetration, but at the cost of seeming to treat his subjects as laboratory specimens without necessary relation to a specific environment.

Bolitho would also have seen Powell as having attained in the chairmanship the highest point of his trajectory and then as proceeding along the curve of the parabola back to his beginning: the Abyssinian Baptist Church. It is possible, however, that Bolitho's mathematical metaphor is too facile an explanation and too fanciful a prediction. It makes insufficient allowance for the interworkings of the environment, which in Powell's case is of the utmost cogency. It is constituted by a centuries-old conflict between blacks and whites, which, instead of abating, is showing signs of becoming more and more infuriated.

Throughout the course of his public career, Powell had been at the center of this conflict. He was more than a leader; he was a symbolic figure to blacks, a proud and potent talisman in their struggle against white oppression. When he fell, they all gathered around him, protecting him as best they could from the hostile shafts of his enemy—and theirs—the white man; obviously, not each and every individual white man, but generic white man, the categorized white man. That is what blacks feel themselves to have in common, and with excellent reason, as who could deny? Moreover, as they contemplate the society they inhabit, they are bound to recognize its characteristic hostility. They can not help doing so, for this hostility is shown in myriad ways, all vying in remorseless virulence. When they look abroad, they can make out the familiar features of this typical white American attitude exhibited toward nonwhite peoples everywhere in one guise and another. Some time ago a black remarked that on a trip to Germany he had been treated with unvarying courtesy by numerous Germans in all walks of life. He encountered the coarse usages and rude abrasions of racial prejudice for the first time in Germany when he met some white Americans there. Whatever Powell's failings, blacks both here and abroad naturally incline to view him as simply another black victim of the white man's racial enmity.

It is as difficult for blacks to judge Adam Clayton Powell on his merits as it is for whites to judge him without racial prejudice. Well in advance of his appointment by Congress to the committee designated to report on Powell's fitness to be seated, the eventual chairman of that special committee said to the press: "Powell is as irritating as a hangnail—and you may quote me on that." Was such a person likely to be an impartial chairman?

Had Powell been wiser, he would have restrained his craving for effulgence. He would have been a quieter, less assertive Negro. Had he found his need to be flamboyant beyond his power to control, he might perhaps with perfect safety have chosen the stage as his profession. He could also have dwelt in complete immunity and segregated splendor, as do so many clergymen, black and white, in the bosom of his devoted congregation. Instead, he ran away from home, and, as in the case of the Divine Preceptor of Powell's Christian faith, he was set upon a pinnacle of the temple; whereupon the devil said unto him: "If thou be the Son of God, cast thyself down." Christ had the strength of character to resist the devil; Powell did not. He cast himself down.

Since Powell cited Jesus Christ as well as Julius Caesar as precedents for his unhappy fate, it may not be inappropriate to present an obiter dictum from that pre-eminent authority on the state of man, William Shakespeare, with reference to Julius Caesar:

> O! what a fall was there, my countrymen;
> Then I, and you, and all of us fell down.

With a profound sense of intimate transference, the blacks have experienced the bitter significance of those lines. It will be two decades, and perhaps longer, before a black once again occupies in Congress a position comparable to Powell's chairmanship. To speak of, say, Senator Edward Brooke in the same breath as Powell is fatuously to misconceive the relative importance of the two men to blacks. Powell was a black leader at a profound and visceral level of being a black. Powell's career was a product of segregation; Brooke's is an offshoot of integration. In so far as blacks are concerned, and although Brooke is a splendid man, all the king's horses and all the

310

king's men of Madison and Pennsylvania avenues could not remodel him for blacks into a satisfactory likeness of Adam Clayton Powell. What was said over the bier of the late Malcolm X by the celebrated black actor Ossie Davis has been echoed with a unique degree of near unanimity in the wake of the fall of Adam Clayton Powell: "He was our prince—our shining black prince."

Powell was black, as it were, merely by courtesy, although his white appearance, before blacks acquired and asserted their present pride in blackness, actually worked in his favor. Straight hair cascading over his handsome face as he denounced the white man from his pulpit and damned him from the platform, he was a paradoxical figure of compelling persuasion to blacks—paradoxical because few men as white as Powell have been so forthright in their denunciation of white racism; and, for that matter, relatively few black men, either. Blacks are now demanding a more Negroid type of leader, physically speaking, than Powell. Their preference is for an unequivocally black man, other things being equal. This choice simply reflects their new pride in blackness, as well as their growing contempt for everything white. Their loyalty to Powell remains not unaffected, it is true, but undissolved. They remember how, with all his failings, he always stood by them, championing their cause, which often seemed hopeless, when he might have advanced his personal interests by making terms with the enemy. In his hour of disaster, they did not forget.

In the odd and unexpected fashion in which matters of this sort sometimes turn out, Adam Clayton Powell united blacks more solidly behind him in consequence of his fall than he ever did while he was flying high, too high, too near the sun. For they are as one in their recognition of the double standard by which Powell was judged by his white peers, as one in their belief that the moral lynching of Powell only confirmed the implacable vendetta of the white man against blacks, against nonwhite peoples. It may not be true, but blacks certainly think so, and this may, after all, be Adam Clayton Powell's signal triumph: that at last, by his martyrdom and self-sacrifice, he temporarily united blacks, induced them to close their ranks on one issue, and to feel, to think, to speak, to act—as one.

9

It is against the whole of the preceding background that the inspiration of one of the phases of the so-called black revolution must be assessed. The phase here referred to was ushered in by Rosa Parks on a public conveyance in Montgomery, Alabama. If the course of the October Revolution in Russia in 1917 was fatefully determined by Lenin's passage through Germany in a sealed compartment of a railway train, the trend of the imprecisely designated black revolution in the United States was set in a new direction by Rosa Parks's refusal on December 1, 1955, to defer any longer to customary segregation in public transport.

This was yet another instance of the black response to centuries of calculated denial of social justice in America. A society that is at such pains to create outcasts should not be heard to complain too loudly at outbursts of outrage on the part of the pariahs. The mutation of outcasts into outlaws is a phenomenon that any social scientist, even the most gradualist in philosophy, could predict. The general discomposure amongst whites that greets the appearance of organizations like the Black Panthers and the Black Muslims and of individuals such as Eldridge Cleaver, H. Rap Brown, and Fred Hampton is a precise index to the profound unreason at the core of white racism. Even an archetypical American like Paul Robeson—Bunyanesque in so many of his aspects as artist, scholar, and athlete—stimulates, finally, only resentment amongst the whites, because he had the ill grace to occur in a black skin. Muhammad Ali (the former Cassius Clay), who is so reminiscent of Davy Crockett—another archetypical American figure—provokes a similar reaction amongst whites for the same reason. Imagine an American Muhammad Ali in a white skin. He would long since have taken a foremost place in the pantheon of American heroes, and his boasts, self-conceit, cockiness, strength, and skill would all have become legendary, with immortality conferred by unanimous white acclamation. And there would never have been the slightest bother about Vietnam. A folk hero of such mighty proportions would have gone his legendary way untroubled by that trifle. It has happened before. But, always, the hero was white.

It was not so much because Cassius Clay changed his name to Muhammad Ali. Many people in America have changed their names— and continue to do so—for varieties of reasons. European immigrants with names presenting certain phonetic difficulties change their names for the sake of social or business convenience. Jews change their names in order to escape, in some instances, the burden of Jewishness. No widespread concern, let alone protest, is occasioned by these practices. "What's in a name?" is, in general, the usual communal response. Not, however, where the black Davy Crockett is concerned.

The former heavyweight champion of the world was guilty, in the first place, of base ingratitude in his behavior toward whites, who, after all, were prepared to cascade upon him the torrent of adulation with which they attempt in such instances to wash away the guilt of their white racism. But he would not let them. He would not chase after white women, in the fashion of Jack Johnson—another unconciliatory type. So they were unable to shake their heads and make the usual self-preening comment that is also a condemnation: "That nigger is crazy about white women!" He was not humble, like Floyd Paterson, whom, like poor Yorick's skull, they knew well. He was not accommodating, like Joe Louis, who, in one of his more inspired flights of oratory outside the ring, once accused President Franklin D. Roosevelt of "makin' muh people lazy." This statesmanlike observation was directed by the great black prizefighter at certain aspects of the social legislation of the New Deal. No; the black Davy Crockett from Kentucky was none of these things. Even unlike the magnificent Sugar Ray Robinson, he had no considerable entourage of personal assistants to do his sovereign bidding. He neither drank nor smoked, nor was he avid in his pursuit of the "sisters"—those beautiful and alluring black women whose presence invests the entire country with such compelling charm.

And then this ungrateful—well, let us say, so-called Negro takes off and becomes a Black Muslim. Becoming still more uppity, he refuses to co-operate with his draft board. Then he communicates to the world at large, and specifically to the government of the United States, that he has "nothin' 'gainst them Cong." Incredible. What monumental nerve. So he must be taught a lesson. He must be stripped of his title, sent to prison, ruined. They—the blacks—must all be taught a lesson. If Muhammad Ali is allowed to get away with this—this defiance of law and custom—where will it all end? He doesn't want to fight for his country. The country that's been so good to him. The country that let him make money. Become a millionaire. Even though he's a nigger. Do you see what they're like? Those Southern crackers have the right idea. The only good one is a dead one.

So, for a brief moment, in due course, Joe Frazier became an honorary white man. As the Japanese are in South Africa. And now the Chinese, too—all honorary white men.

The case of this runaway black—this Muhammad Ali—was a bad one indeed. He had repudiated not only the white man's religion, but also the white man's name. An example had to be made of him. Loose the dogs on his trail. "Let 'em tear him a spell . . . runaways ain't much account nohow and it makes the rest more afraid to run away when they see how they are sarved." Otherwise, imagine the black youth of this nation following him en masse into the camp of the Black Muslims—rather, into their mosques—and away from the military encampments, the houses of prostitution, the dope dens, the seamy bars, the defoliation, the poison, the torture, the mass murder, and the ecstatic joys of the free-fire zone in Vietnam. Here was this so-called Muhammad Ali giving up a chance to make a fortune in the ring because he just did not have the guts to go out and "search and destroy," kill some gooks, rape some slants, zap a few Cong women and children. And this country, the U.S.A.—LOVE IT OR LEAVE IT—had been so good to him. It goes to show you; it just goes to show you: you can't do anything with them.

It was indeed an intolerable situation. The example of Muhammad Ali entailed the prospect of considerable numbers of blacks bloated up, individually, to the size of Jim Fink, with a collective mind to engage, like Fink and Crockett, in shooting duels (with whites as targets) all over the "home of the brave." So when Muhammad Ali was at length permitted to fight again in the ring and was beaten by his black opponent, Joe Frazier, an astonishing incident of racial transmutation occurred. Joe Frazier, a man of unequivocal blackness, suddenly appeared to be so white that he was invited to address the legislature of his native state. Everything possible was done to make him an honorary white man. He was even received by the President at the White House. For large numbers of white Americans, he had translated into actuality one of the fondest dreams of white racism: he had whipped the ungrateful nigger braggart, the Black Muslim fanatic, the bigmouth who had presumed to scorn money—yes, money! Imagine that—rather than soil his black rump by jumping into the blood bath that his country was so valiantly contriving in Vietnam. This nigger who'd had the gall to give up his good white name and take on some no-good, no-count foreign A-rab name.

The enormity of Muhammad Ali's offense can best be appreciated by the reminder that there are white Americans who regard the acquisition of an Anglo-Saxon surname as one of the most valuable prizes offered by the American society.

The only question worth asking, however, is: why did Muhammad Ali act as he did? The answer is brief and instant: because America is cruelly unjust to him and his fellow blacks; cruelly unjust as a matter of policy; cruelly unjust as a matter of everyday practice. Muhammad Ali acted from a sense of outrage at this long-established and persisting injustice. Rosa Parks acted in the same spirit, and out of the same compulsion; so, earlier, did Nat Turner; and so, later, did Angela Davis—all blacks and all outraged by the relentless denial of rudimentary justice.

The case of Angela Davis is especially instructive. A young black woman of unusual intelligence and uncommon physical attractiveness, a brilliant student of philosophy, an instructor on the staff of the University of California at Los Angeles, a Communist. Dismissed by the Board of Regents for this reason; rehired by the university in consequence of a legal decision annulling the action of the Board. Subsequently accused by the State of California of supplying guns in furtherance of a criminal conspiracy. Became a fugitive from what is euphemistically called justice. Apprehended, imprisoned, denied bail. Remained imprisoned, because unadmitted to bail, for sixteen months. Then was released on inordinately high bail. Her trial has just been concluded with her acquittal by a jury of twelve white men and women.

The verdict, as well as the entire course of the trial, did not vindicate American justice; it merely reflected the intense glare of world-wide interest in which the proceedings were held.

The recital of these facts discloses only the skeleton in a horrifying tragedy enacted by white American racism. Once again, as so often in the past, the principal victim is a black woman. "The system of slavery," writes Herbert Aptheker in *The Colonial Era,* "was brutality personified and while it was torture to the male slaves, its impact upon the female really defies the power of language." The abolition of slavery altered the legal relationship between blacks and whites. But it would be long before the whole sociological complex could be modified; and, from a psychological point of view, longer still until group attitudes, deeply entrenched in the subconscious, might be changed. One of the most salient features of the slave system was the whipping of black women. Both white men and women habitually indulged in this pastime. In the case of white men, it assured their sadistic dominance, with all its sexual motivation, of black women, and it certified their mastery over black men. Where white women were concerned, it provided, in similar sadistic fashion, a means of redress for the resentment they felt against black women for being so attractive and accessible to white men. The whipping of black women, or, to put it another way, the victimization of black women, is a profound and compulsive need of the American psyche. Frederick Olmsted's account of the whipping of a black girl by a white overseer is, in all its sadosexual horror (the girl having been made to strip naked before being beaten), symbolic of the pathology that has invested the relations of white American males, in particular, with black women from the slave period to the present day.

To understand the recent plight of Angela Davis, all legal technicalities aside, it is necessary first of all to understand the psychological compulsion white American males feel to whip black women. This is as true of the Founding Fathers as of an earlier ornament of American society, William Byrd, of Virginia. Many of them whipped black women: the civilized Thomas Jefferson no less than the courtly Mr. Byrd. A look at Byrd's diary for the years 1709–1712, cited by Herbert Aptheker, is instructive:

2/8/09: Jenny and Eugene were whipped
4/17/09: Anaka was whipped.

5/13/09: Mrs. Byrd whips the nurse.

5/23/09: Moll was whipped.

9/3/09: "I beat Jenny . . ."

9/16/09: Jenny was whipped.

9/19/09: "I beat Anama . . ."

11/30/09: Eugene and Jenny were whipped.

7/15/10: "My wife against my will caused little Jenny to be burned with a hot iron . . ."

8/22/10: "I had a severe quarrel with little Jenny and beat her too much for which I was sorry."

10/9/10: Byrd whips three slave women.

1/22/11: "A slave pretends to be sick. I put a branding-iron on the place he complained of and put the bit on him."

2/2/11: "My wife and little Jenny had a great quarrel in which my wife got the worst but at last by the help of the family Jenny was overcome and soundly whipped."

3/20/11: He beats a Negro woman.

4/30/11: He has two male slaves beaten.

5/1/11: "I cause Prue to be whipped severely . . ."

8/4/11: "I was indisposed with beating of Prue, and tired . . ."

9/26/11: "I had several people whipped . . ."

9/28/11: Eugene was whipped.

12/13/11: His wife whips a slave while a guest is present.

2/5/12: His wife causes several slaves to be whipped.

3/2/12: His wife beats Jenny with the tongs.

3/3/12: Billy is beaten.

4/9/12: His wife causes Molly to be whipped.

5/22/12: His wife beats Prue very violently; he whips Anama severely.

6/6/12: He found Prue with a candle by daylight, for which "I gave her a salute with my foot."

6/30/12: Three women and one man are beaten.

7/30/12: Molly and Jenny whipped.

9/3/12: His wife "gave Prue a great whipping."

This psychotic urge to whip blacks has by now been encoded in the genetic structure of white Americans with such a power of command as to be in large numbers of instances quite irresistible, so that the problem of justice for blacks in the American society is a psycholegal matter. Such was Angela Davis's predicament. As a black woman in the power of a white-dominated society, she had to be whipped. Either she submitted to being whipped or, with the "help of the family" (the white newspaper press, radio and television, and the officers and institutions of the law), she would be "overcome" and subjected to the severest penalties. The sadosexual compulsions of the white segment of the American society toward blacks made dishonest nonsense of the claim that it was possible for Angela Davis to receive justice as a matter of course in American courts, dominated, as they are, by a deeply rooted scheme of social values in which blacks have long been the traditional objects of punishment. Unless world opinion was marshalled in her support and the American legal system itself placed on trial, as in fact occurred in this instance, Angela Davis would have received the racist "justice" so often meted out to blacks in this country. President Nixon had already presumed her guilty in advance of her trial. Without black women to whip, American society will have lost a vital wellspring of its collective energy, as well as an important source of group catharsis. And so also in the case of black men. Vast as their material contribution is to the building of America, their psychic usefulness is greater still. They have carried out the role of tribal scapegoats, passive, vegetative figures, whose cardinal function is sacrificial. In this way they appease and propitiate evil powers of malign intent against the tribe by being put to death and, through the same ritual, also serve to provide rational explanations for irrational occurrences.

It would be a facile parallel, and misleading, to try to set side by side the Jewish experience in European society and the black experience in American society. The historical parameters are dissimilar, for one thing. For another, the substantive circumstances differ too widely. The Jews of Europe were proscribed; the blacks of America were enslaved. Liberalization of the Jews' status was the prelude to the Jewish holocaust in Europe. Emancipation of the blacks may be the prelude to their extermination in America, since now they are no longer valuable property but only troublesome freedmen; which is to say that, as a group, they have rejected their sociological role of scapegoat. Here, precisely, is the entire content and significance of the so-called black revolution in the United States. It is in refusing any longer to be scapegoats that blacks like Angela Davis and George Jackson acquire the character and warrant the description of revolutionaries. The means they choose of repudiating the role of scapegoat reflect certain political necessities of the American society.

This is, after all, an existential question. As a black woman, Angela Davis is confronted with a narrow range of choices within which she must act to change the course of American history. Essentially, the

318

methods she might adopt (this being synonymous with choice) would be either legal or extralegal. They would be legal if she went along with the manner in which the Constitution has been tortured in order to supply a specious foundation of right for the traditional denial of justice to blacks; extralegal (or, if it be preferred, illegal) if she respected the Constitution as the fundamental law of the land and, according it a literal obedience, drew from its plainly explicit terms plainly explicit meaning. In the latter event, she would naturally object to being whipped as black women were whipped before they learned to read and have continued to be whipped even now that they can read. She would try to defend herself in accordance with the organic law's sanctioning of the inherent right of self-defense. And because she is a woman of extraordinary intelligence regardless of skin color, of uncompromising will, and of resolute principle, she would naturally attempt a task prescribed for her by the magnitude of her abilities: she would attempt to change the course of American history. No longer should black women submit to being whipped by white men and white women.

So Angela Davis resisted. She fought back. Any act of resistance in a reactionary society is an act of revolution. Anyone who fights back in such a society is a revolutionary. It is necessary to distinguish dissent, which typically expresses itself as a function of middle-class values whose prime criterion is respectability, from resistance, which typically expresses itself as a principle of self-defense whose eventual aim is the overthrow of the individual or group resisted. Dissent is compatible, and often congenial, with conservatism. Resistance connotes the existence of tyranny. Dissent is a parliamentary (or extra-parliamentary) tactic employed by social democrats. Resistance embraces the strategy of revolution. Angela Davis is a member of the resistance to tyranny in America. That she is a Communist is beside the point. But exactly in point is the fact that she belongs to the resistance. This is much more important—for black people—than her Communism. It is quite conceivable that a white Communist may be an enemy of the black resistance in America. A black Communist, too, may be regimented into opposition to the black resistance. So for black people in America it is a good deal more useful to be a member of the resistance, whether white or black, than to be a Communist. As it happens, Angela Davis is both a black Communist and a member of the resistance.

What is this resistance? It is not in any sense an organized movement toward agreed and corporate ends. Rather, it is fluid and amorphous, an emanation of the spirit of all those people in America, white as well as black, who do not merely dissent from tyranny but oppose it, work against it, think against it, dream against it, hate it, and would destroy it. In so far as black people are concerned, tyranny in America takes, for the most part, the form of racial injustice. Angela Davis is a victim of this tyranny. One supposes that few would be found to argue a passive acceptance of tyranny in all circumstances; perhaps fewer still to argue that a tyranny that blights the lives of millions of blacks should not be opposed. One is left, therefore, with the residual question of the appropriate choice of methods. One of the salient characteristics of tyranny is its insistence on dictating the emotional responses of those whom it oppresses, of prescribing their reactions, and of certifying or discrediting the nature of their struggle for redress. Tyranny is always the advocate and tribunal of its own cause. Angela Davis must, accordingly, be judged by the very tyranny that she opposes. Her judges and their judgment seat are the instrumentalities of the tyrant. This is what reduces justice for black people in America to a mockery. Together with this, there is the psychotic disease of racial prejudice, with which the preponderant mass of white Americans are afflicted. The police, the courts, the prisons are all focal points of this infection. It is unreasonable to expect that from a society so deeply permeated by racial hatred and contempt for blacks there should emerge a system of justice entirely free of this taint; and also administrators and functionaries of the system above the reproach of racial bias. A racist society naturally spawns racist individuals in all capacities. Who has ever heard of a cobra giving birth to a nightingale? Organisms reproduce themselves in their own image.

From the beginning, in her Alabama childhood, Angela Davis knew that being born black in America was the sign that America was her mortal enemy. Not everything in her formative and adolescent years reinforced this augury; there were contradictions. Racism in America is not all of a piece, a monolith. Instead, it is in the nature of an architectural design replete with secret passageways and unexpected recesses, concealed rooms and hidden staircases, here straightforward exteriors and there dissembling façades, hospitable chambers side by side with chambers of horrors, civilized amenity intertwined with primal animosity. To alter the metaphor: nothing so misleads concerning the real character of white racism as the assumption that it is a sort of monocellular organism. Quite the contrary. It is a creature of the utmost complexity. The same man or woman may be perfectly intelligent about any number of things, but abysmally stupid in his or her white racism. The same environment may be delightfully permissive in many ways, but arbitrarily restrictive in accordance with the canons of white racism. In most white men there either lurks or looms a white racist, and in most white women, too, in the United States of America, and many other places on this planet.

The central social fact of Angela Davis's life—the central social fact of the life of every black person in America—is white racism. This was hammered into her at every turn. It was and is an essential element of her existence. There were moments when the hammering was less unrelenting, occasions when the hammer was sheathed in velvet, interludes when the hammer descended lightly instead of pounding, pounding, pounding, as it usually did. There were such exceptional times and such marginal circumstances. Yet the substantive reality remained constant. No one of Angela Davis's acute sensitivity and brilliant intelligence could have been content, in the face of this actuality, to behave as blacks in America are expected to do in this situation; that is, to fabricate cheerful illusions about the nature of white racism; to behave as if, provided only you were a good nigger, white racism would be kind to you. Many blacks are expert at this charade. Some make fine careers out of it. But Angela Davis said no to this; she refused; she would have none of it. Hence her recent predicament. Instead of engaging in the agreeable black middle-class pretense that all you need is some ambition, common sense, and stamina and the American dream will come true for you, too, she applied her splendid intellectual endowments to historical analysis—a dangerous thing for a black American to do; but also, for any self-respecting black whose intellectual curiosity is the measure of her self-respect, a thing necessary and inescapable. To fall in with Marx and Hegel, as Angela Davis did, is naturally to fall out with American society, although Hegel did have some good things to say about North America. In the Introduction to his *Philosophy of History* he wrote:

America is therefore the land of the future, where, in the ages that lie before us, the burden of the world's history shall reveal itself—perhaps in a contest between North and South America. It is a land of desire for all those who are weary of the historical lumber-room of old Europe. Napoleon is reported to have said: "Cette vieille Europe m'ennuie." It is for America to abandon the ground on which hitherto the history of the world has developed itself.

It is curious, though not altogether unexpected, that Jean-François Revel (*Without Marx or Jesus*) takes much the same view of America as "the land of the future." But the "revolution of values," which he considers America pre-eminently to be capable of, seems to have rather less to do with Hegel than with Nietzsche's "revaluation of all values."

However, Hegel and Marx were important influences in the development of Angela Davis's world outlook. Discussing Hegel's postulate of the triadic movement of world history, Bertrand Russell observed:

It was an interesting thesis, giving unity and meaning to the revolutions of human affairs. Like other historical theories, it required, if it was to be made plausible, some distortions of fact and considerable ignorance. Hegel, like Marx and Spengler after him, possessed both these qualifications.

The trinity of intellectual influences crucial to the formation of Angela Davis's cast of mind may be completed by adding the name of Herbert Marcuse. Marcuse assumed for a while the mantle of presiding sage to the intellectual element of the youthful revolt against the governing values of the American society. He was then on his way to advanced age, but, in Hegel's phrase, "the owl of Minerva spreads its wings only with the falling of the dusk." Marcuse's brilliant pupil mirrored the master's own mind and reflected his insights with that *Doppelgänger* likeness at once so flattering and so reassuring to the dispensers of learning. He came to consider her the best pupil he had had in thirty years of teaching. She may well have been.

There can be little doubt that Angela Davis is a black woman of formidable brilliance. For this reason, it is more than likely that her intellectual contributions to Marcuse were in sum at least as much as his to her. With brilliant students who possess original and creative intellects, teachers are largely unnecessary. In such cases, they usually do more harm than good. They obstruct the natural path of the student's development and deflect him from his insights. Where they should be learning from the student, they waste his time and theirs attempting to teach; the distinctive intellectual quality of a student of this order is a gift of knowing, while teachers are bent on encumbering him with what they absurdly esteem as "knowledge." The usefulness of a teacher, from the standpoint of imparting information, is confined as a rule to students endowed with the ability to regurgitate copiously after ingesting greedily. The selective and discriminate intelligence requires no teacher, as such; a guide, perhaps, a companion; but not a pedagogue. The intellectual harm done by teachers far exceeds any good they may do. Fine intellects are daily corrupted and fruitful insights frustrated by their officious interference. Marcuse does not seem to have placed Angela Davis at this disadvantage. She was his pupil, but she is not his product. Centuries of the black experience in America culminated in Angela Davis. Had Marcuse never entered her life, she would nevertheless have found her way to Marx and Hegel in the course of her intellectual pilgrimage to her own historical synthesis. Marcuse pointed out some landmarks, indicated signposts here and there, but Angela Davis already knew her destination. For her, the journey's end would be a realizable vision—even if for the moment no more than a vision—of fundamental change in the American scheme of values according to which Sunday-school children, provided only that they were black, might be bombed and murdered in a church in Birmingham, Alabama, without occasioning much more than ripples of protest on the surface of a centuries-deep indifference in the very heart of the dominant white society. Angela Davis knew at firsthand of this murderous outrage. If she knew that alone, and nothing more, it would be enough. She would need no further knowledge to warrant her quest by any route for the weapon with which to put an end to the life of the monster.

The search for the Minotaur in a Cretan maze is an allegory not wholly inapplicable to Angela Davis's crusade against white racism. No one, except the monster itself, stands on scruples about the manner in which the hideous beast is to be dispatched. In the mythology of Western culture, much is made of those heroes who do battle with monsters. St. George and the dragon is among the most celebrated, as well as recurrent, of these legendary stories. There have so far been no suggestions from any quarter of Western culture, or outside it, for that matter, that St. George was unduly harsh to the dragon. The methods he employed against the horrible creature have never been questioned. At no time has any objection been lodged on the score of the means he selected for the end he envisioned. He slew the dragon. Good show! The same with Theseus. He slew the Minotaur, a monster with a well-cultivated taste for youths and maidens. Everybody has been quite happy about that ever since. There was not the slightest quibble about the methods he used.

These monsters are mythic crystallizations of evil. Their slayers are created in the same way, out of the tribal *mythos,* as personifications of good. Their storied battles are the stuff of morality plays that tell of the polar dualisms of human existence. In their outcome, when the hero wins, they give reason for celebration and are transmitted to posterity because they affirm the transcendent character of the human will as a weapon with which to subdue the hostile forces of the universe. They represent hope as an antidote to despair, the triumph of good over evil, and life over death.

The empirical sources of myths are in nearly all cases impossible to trace. Largely, they are matters of speculation. Attempts to excavate whatever substrata of facts lie beneath them usually encounter universal concepts rather than discover particular origins. The actual circumstances prior to their condensation into myth vanish into primal obscurity. What is not in doubt, however, is the social commencement, where the originating cause is quite certainly to be derived from an incident or complex of incidents within the experience of a given human group, prehistorical and, as likely as not, primordial. By oral transmission from generation to generation over millennia, incident becomes symbol, story accretes into myth. At this point the crucial elements, in so far as they individuate the social experience that is the subject of the story, are abstracted. They then undergo metamorphosis from human particulars into human universals. A heroic deed is transmuted into the generalized concept of courage; a social outrage, with its attendant horror, into the metaphor of a monster. The incapsulation of human experience into myth and symbol exhibits the imagination at its perennial task of preserving whatever in the given circustances is common to all mankind by translating it from its particular setting into universal significance. In the sense that the poet is a maker, he achieves the highest consummation of his art by mythmaking. For there he attunes his lyre to the recital of the climactic experiences of human existence. When he sings of monsters, he may weave his melody out of a symbolism abstracted from immemorial actuality, yet his inspiration is not obliged to impose this limit upon itself. He may abjure myth and, adopting the creative impulse of current incident, devote his minstrelsy to the saga of black Americans in their unceasing struggle against the monster white racism. He may sing of Angela Davis and of George Jackson.

No one reproaches Theseus for having slain the Cretan Minotaur; or St. George, the dragon. Neither does anyone call into question the methods employed by these heroes. But Angela Davis and George Jackson, together with other black American revolutionaries, are expected to observe every nicety of means in their efforts to destroy the monster white racism. Instead of their being regarded as bene-factors of the American society, they are considered its internal ene-mies. A curious irony this, when the monster basks in the admiring tolerance of so much of the society, while those who would end the life of the monster are hunted down and, when caught, shut away and not infrequently murdered. This is perhaps the most eloquent, as it is by all odds the most persuasive, testimony concerning the real nature of this society. The evidence it reveals is to the effect that this society cares less for those who would rid it of the monster than it does for the monster itself. The conclusion can scarcely be avoided that there must be something monstrous about such a society.

The murder by bombing of Sunday-school children in Birming-ham, as well as an unending series of similar atrocities, had already intimated this conclusion to Angela Davis. She did not need Marcuse or Marx or Hegel to formulate it for her. Their intellectual perspec-tives were valuable, but her own experience was decisive. Neverthe-less, it is probably the case that they provided a framework of refer-ence from which she could draw a larger sum of meanings to illuminate her experience. In considering the behavior of white men in a racist society, she could read in Hegel's *Philosophy of Right*:

Man is therefore evil by a conjunction between his natural or undeveloped character and his reflection into himself; and therefore evil belongs neither to nature as such by itself—unless nature were supposed to be the natural character of the will which rests in its particular content—nor to introverted reflection by itself, i.e. cognition in general, unless this were to maintain itself in that opposition to the universal.

With this facet of evil, its necessity, there is inevitably combined the fact that this same evil is condemned to be that which of necessity ought not to be, i.e. the fact that evil ought to be annulled. It is not that there ought never to be a diremption of any sort in the will—on the contrary, it is just this level of diremption which distinguishes man from the unreason-ing animal; the point is that the will should not rest at that level and cling to the particular as if that and not the universal were the essential thing; it should overcome the diremption as a nullity. Further, as to this necessity of evil, it is subjectivity, as infinite self-reflection, which is present in and confronted by this opposition of universal and particular; if it rests in this opposition, i.e. if it is evil, then it is *eo ipso* independent, regarding itself as isolated, and is itself this self-will. Therefore if the individual subject as such does evil, the evil is purely and simply his own responsibility.

If it were supposed that Angela Davis's native American simplicity had been corrupted by acquaintance with this German proponent of the Absolute, the objection to this facile supposition must surely be the bourgeois respectability of Hegel's ethical system. His middle-class servility to the Prussian state (which, however, at one time, earlier in his life, he despised) was consistent with his philosophic reverence of the state as a political entity. Orthodox Communists profess a similar attitude toward the state. They indeed go further toward outright deification of the state than Hegel ever did. For Hegel, the Absolute is the Whole. For orthodox Communists, however, the state is the Near Absolute, and only the complete realization of socialism will cause it to "wither away." While rejecting theism, the orthodox Communists have constructed a theology in which socialism is the counterpart of heaven. The only difference—and an important one indeed—is that the attainment of perfect classlessness will ensure the materialist paradise here on earth. The Christian promise of the capitalist theology is restricted to supersensible satisfactions in an unknown realm after death. But the principal concern of this distinction here is its affirmation of a dialectical absolute in the form of perfect socialism. This is the orthodox Communist version of Hegel's concept of the Whole as Absolute. Perfect socialism, or complete classlessness, is the Whole. This may be translated into a theory of a suprastate; at which point it is likely to be discovered that there has simply been an exchange of Christian for Marxist eschatology. Yet there can be no denying the usefulness of the Marxist canon as a mediate tool of historical analysis. In Angela Davis's hands, it laid bare with materialist precision the inherent mercilessness of white American racism. Marcuse may have supplied the tool for Angela Davis, may have demonstrated the course of its construction from Plato through Hegel to Marx; but her own intellect did the rest. Quite apart from Marcuse, it was the American society itself that gave to Angela Davis that body of black experience, historical as well as contemporary, from which she could deduce the justness of Hegel's description, when applied to white racism, as "this final, most abstruse, form of evil, whereby evil is perverted into good and good into evil."

For the benefit of anyone who somersaults to the conclusion that Marx and Hegel were philosophic yokefellows, and that as a disciple of the one, Angela Davis was inescapably a disciple of the other, the following passage from Marx's preface to the second edition of Capital is cited:

My dialectic method is not only different from the Hegelian, but is its direct opposite. To Hegel, the life-process of the human brain, i.e., the process of thinking, which, under the name of "the Idea", he even transforms into an independent subject, is the demiurge of the real world, and the real world is only the external, phenomenal form of "the Idea." With me, on the contrary, the ideal is nothing else than the material world reflected by the human mind, and translated into forms of thought.

The mystifying side of Hegelian dialectic I criticized nearly thirty years ago, at a time when it was still the fashion.

It was possible for Angela Davis to construct a synthesis out of the philosophic elements common to Marx and Hegel. One of those elements that could have been crucial to her synthesis lay ready to hand in Marx's statement that "philosophers have only *interpreted* the world in various ways, but the real task is to *alter* it" (*Theses on Feuerbach*). The world she would attempt to alter was the bourgeois world of white racism in America. And she would be aware, undoubtedly, of the concluding paragraph, next but one, of the *Communist Manifesto*:

The Communists disdain to conceal their views and aims. They openly declare that their ends can be attained only by the forcible overthrow of all existing social conditions. Let the ruling classes tremble at a Communist revolution. The proletarians have nothing to lose but their chains. They have a world to win.

Yet all this would be ludicrous fantasy on Angela Davis's part were her revolt groundless; that is to say, if the objective conditions of the American society contradicted her point of view and were themselves the factual proof of the perversity of her activities. But if your childhood acquaintances in your hometown are murdered in church by white racists (who go unpunished), and if your life and that of your parents and their parents as far back, almost, as the beginning of the society, have been shorn of human value by these white racists, if you inhale terror from the very air around you, and if any incautious step you take may betray you to humiliation and violence, if your racial identity alone, the mere color of your skin, is sufficient to brand you as a pariah, then what are you to do? And if you are Angela Davis, endowed with a brilliant mind and a close and comprehensive knowledge of the centuries of iniquities that continue to be heaped upon you and your like, and if you are aware that the rate of improvement in this state of affairs is dictated solely by your ability to extort concessions through instilling fear of a bloody alternative, and that any rational course of action can be pursued only with the slenderest chance of success against the entrenched unreason of an irrational society, then what are you to do?

Hegel observes, in his *Philosophy of Right*:

Theft, cowardice, murder, and so forth, as actions, i.e. as achievements of a subjective will, have the immediate character of being satisfactions of such a will and therefore of being something positive. In order to make the action a good one, it is only a question of recognizing this positive aspect of the action as my intention, and this then becomes the essential aspect in virtue of which the action is made good, simply because I recognize it as the good in my intention. Theft in order to do good to the poor, theft or flight from battle for the sake of fulfilling one's duty to care for one's life or one's family (a poor family perhaps into the bargain), murder out of hate or revenge (i.e. in order to satisfy one's sense of one's own rights or of right in general, or one's sense of another's wickedness, of wrong done by him to oneself or to others or to the world or the nation at large, by extirpating this wicked individual who is wickedness incarnate, and thereby contributing at least one's quota to the project of uprooting the bad)—all these actions are made well intentioned and therefore good by this method of taking account of the positive aspect of their content. . . .

To this context there also belongs the notorious maxim: "The end justifies the means." In itself and prima facie this expression is trivial and pointless. Quite so, one may retort in terms equally general, a just end of course justifies the means, while an unjust end does not. The phrase: "If the end is right, so is the means" is a tautology, since the means is precisely that which is nothing in itself but is for the sake of something else, and therein, i.e. in the end, has its purpose and worth—provided of course it be truly a means.

But when someone says that the end justifies the means, his purport is not confined to this bare tautology; he understands by the words something more specific, namely that to use as means to a good end something which in itself is simply not a means at all, to violate something in itself sacrosanct, in short to commit a crime as a means to a good end, is permissible and even one's bounden duty.

It would not have been necessary for Angela Davis to read this in order to discard the moralisms fabricated by ruling classes for the purpose of training subject classes into submissiveness. She might have come to the point of view enunciated by Hegel purely on her own, simply by observing the nature of the society of which she was herself a product. She possessed the clarity and strength of mind for the task, and there was abundant incentive in her personal experiences to urge her on to it.

There would be, after all, no conceivable warrant for the presence of black revolutionaries in the United States if the racial circumstances of life in this country were decent and equitable. No one would be found to argue that such conditions should either be ideal or, failing this, regarded as a basis for revolution. Nobody, and certainly no black man or woman, maintains this position. What gives rise to extremism among blacks is the extreme inequity of the country toward them. Their extremism, such as it is, is an equivalent response to the extreme hostility shown them by the society as a whole. Here is where it all begins: at this point where white racism demands that blacks be considered inferior to whites and therefore subjected to unequal treatment. This is racial tyranny. Neither Angela Davis nor any other black needs to be reminded that "resistance to tyranny is obedience to God." They resist, as well they should. And since the tyranny they resist is completely unscrupulous in its methods of oppression, there does not seem to be any practical reason why they should be fastidious in their choice of the means of resistance. It is as if one were grappling with an enemy who is armed with a knife. There is another knife within reach. One tries to get hold of it so as to be equally armed. Whereupon the enemy, while carefully retaining his knife, and at the same time doing his utmost to inflict a fatal wound with it, lectures one about the immorality of using a knife against him and the unlawfulness of such an action. This leads inevitably to the opinion, held by many blacks, that the besetting aim of white racism is to keep blacks at a disadvantage in perpetuity.

The question of gun control becomes important only when blacks acquire—and use—guns against whites. So long as whites had more or less the monopoly of using them against blacks, there was little or no agitation for gun control. So long as only blacks—and other non-whites—were in the main the victims of the traffic in heroin and other addictive drugs, there was nothing more than a muted outcry. And this came, partly strangled with the passive connivance of the white governing class, from within the black communities. But as soon as white youths began to fall victim to the traffic, and especially when this became the case with white middle-class youths in the suburban areas, sternness and indignation informed the public attitude of the white racists.

So when Angela Davis takes account of all these circumstances, when she contemplates the whole course of the racial situation in the United States, and considers historic outrages and contemporary atrocities, the murder of innocents, the mutilation of men, and the violation of women—all black—all black—all black—from Africa to Attica, how can she be expected to feel, what can she be expected to think, what can she be reasonably expected to do?

Society shifts the onus, in the well-known manner of white racism, to Angela Davis. Legal devices are employed in order to put on her the burden of defense. Law and order; but never—never—justice. Law and order is for the subject classes; justice, for those who rule. In any case, on a realistic basis, justice is simply the right of the stronger.

In the sixteenth year of the Peloponnesian War, the Athenians sent ambassadors to the Melians, against whom they had initiated hostilities. This embassy, cited in Thucydides' *The Peloponnesian War,* addressed itself to the Melians as follows:

For ourselves, we shall not trouble you with specious pretences—either of how we have a right to our empire because we overthrew the Mede, or are now attacking you because of wrong that you have done us—and make a long speech which would not be believed; and in return we hope that you, instead of thinking to influence us by saying that you did not join the Lacedaemonians, although their colonists, or that you have done us no wrong, will aim at what is feasible, holding in view the real sentiments of us both; since you know as well as we do that right, as the world goes, is only in question between equals in power, while the strong do what they can and the weak suffer what they must.

This is perfectly straightforward and, as an expression of *Real-politik* or *machtpolitik* (one and the same thing), unsurpassed. It could not seriously be supposed by any sane person that justice, in the sense of the impartial apportionment of right and wrong, was possible in a world inherently unequal, let alone in a country characteristically racist. The real objection is to the "specious pretences" of which the Athenian ambassadors spoke, and which Hegel, in his *Philosophy of Right,* refers to as "hypocrisy." He wrote:

In every end of a self-conscious subject, there is a *positive* aspect necessarily present because the end is what is purposed in an actual concrete action. This aspect he knows how to elicit and emphasize, and he may then proceed to regard it as a duty or a fine intention. By so interpreting it, he is enabled to pass off his action as good in the eyes both of himself and others, despite the fact that, owing to his reflective character and his knowledge of the universal aspect of the will, he is aware of the contrast between this aspect and the essentially *negative* content of his action. To impose in this way on others is hypocrisy; while to impose on oneself is a stage beyond hypocrisy, a stage at which subjectivity claims to be absolute. . . .

Evil and doing evil with a bad conscience, however, is not quite hypocrisy. Into hypocrisy there enters in addition the formal character of falsity, first the falsity of holding up evil as good in the eyes of others, of setting oneself up to all appearances as good, conscientious, pious, and so on—conduct which in these circumstances is only a trick to deceive others.

This is the typical conduct of white racism, but Angela Davis was not deceived. Indeed, her actual offense against the American society consisted of her very refusal to be deceived, or, at any rate, to *appear* to be deceived; a masquerade that blacks, traditionally, are expected to engage in with stereotypic grins, slurred, slack-mouthed speech, and a comical shuffle toward the watermelon patch. When they refuse to play their customary roles in this masquerade, they become candidates for Soledad or San Quentin or Attica. Refusal to play these roles takes numerous forms. One example is nonconformism within the law. When, however, nonconformism is directed against custom, as in certain areas of the South, the consequences for the nonconforming individual may be quite as severe as infringement of the law. In some places, custom commands greater veneration than the law, again as in various parts of the South. There, racial custom is often reverenced with more zeal than in any other section of the country. Birmingham is an illuminating instance.

Herbert Marcuse, in elucidating Hegel's political philosophy in *Reason and Revolution,* makes the following point:

Modern society does not unite individuals so that they can carry on autonomous yet concerted activities for the good of all. . . . The attainment of a positive freedom requires that the individual leave the monadic sphere of the private interest and settle himself in the essence of the will, which aims not at some particular end but at freedom as such. The will of the individual must become a will to general freedom. It can become such, however, only if he has actually become free. Only the will of the man who is himself free aims at positive freedom. Hegel puts this conclusion into the cryptic formula that "freedom wills freedom," or, "the free will . . . wills the free will." The formula contains concrete historical life in what seems to be an abstract philosophical pattern. It is not any individual, but the free individual who "wishes freedom". Freedom in its true form can be recognized and willed only by an individual who *is* free. Man cannot know freedom without possessing it; he must be free in order to become free. Freedom is not simply a status he has, but an action he undertakes as a self-conscious subject. So long as he knows no freedom, he cannot attain it by himself; his lack of freedom is such that he might even voluntarily choose or acquiesce in his own bondage. In that case, he has no interest in freedom, and his liberation must come about against his will. In other words, the act of liberating is taken out of the hands of individuals who themselves, because of their fettered status, cannot choose it as their own course.

Historically, freedom and blackness are irreconcilable in the United States. Between these polar antitheses Angela Davis became acquainted with Hegel, Marx, and Marcuse but did not become free. However, she did not "voluntarily choose or acquiesce in [her] own bondage." On the contrary, freedom has remained, in the most tragic personal sense, her prime obsession. Not revolution, but freedom. Yet, to listen to her accusers, one would suppose it to be the other way around: that her actual objective was not freedom but revolution. Angela Davis would be arrayed like a martyr, rather than arraigned as an alleged criminal, if society once permitted her true aim to be disclosed. So would many other blacks now vilified as violent revolutionaries. Call these people, and all such as they, freedom fighters, even though they are not white Hungarians in revolt against the Soviet Union, but blacks in revolt against the United States. Not revolutionaries, but freedom fighters, for this has been the historic character of blacks in America from the beginning. To make the worse appear the better cause, and also to put itself in a good light, the American society suppresses the character of the goal blacks fight to gain, namely, freedom, by calling them revolutionaries, with all the bourgeois, capitalistic reproach that the term implies. In addition, by so doing, the society assumes the role of the accuser and places blacks in the position of the accused. Above all, it escapes the necessity to examine itself, which, if it were honestly to do, would result at once in a complete reversal of the roles of accused and accuser.

An honest society, when, in the name of the "people," it accuses blacks of offenses that, superficially, are infractions of the law of the country, but that in a fundamental sense are political because of the oppressive nature of white racism—an honest society would make frank disclosure of its own historic and contemporary shortcomings and candidly assume, to an equitable degree, responsibility for legal consequences of which it is the sociological cause. But the American society will never do that; it will simply continue, as long as it is allowed to do so, to invert cause and consequence, standing them on their heads, and acting the part of the righteous society whose blameless conduct has mystifyingly produced a national community of black delinquents.

A columnist for the New York *Post*, a white millionaire, with all the advantages in his own early life of wealth, careful nurture, expensive schooling, and every good thing that money could buy, details in one of his periodic pieces for that newspaper a list of George Jackson's delinquencies in and out of prison. Assuming the accuracy of the list, where, might we ask this columnist, is that list of racial delinquencies of the United States that were directly contributory to George Jackson's, and between which there is a clear causal connection?

The New York *Times* has indulged itself in the same pastime. Therefore, the same questions may be put to the New York *Times*. What is its view of the racial record of the United States, and does there occur to this newspaper the fact that a distinct correlation of cause and effect exists between that racial record and the delinquencies of the late George Jackson?

George Jackson may be held to be not wholly without fault. It would be no compliment to his powerful and acute intelligence to do so. There is no point in providing romantic justifications for failures of social intelligence on the part of any individual, black or white. The concern here is with accurate historical analysis.

There is a custom in the United States according to which blacks are rewarded for having been "the first" to breach in some approved fashion a wall that formerly enclosed a preserve of opportunity exclusive to white racists. Such blacks are accorded patronizing notice in one form or another. On occasion they are given useful jobs for which, in some instances, they are quite unsuitable. The talents that enabled them to be "first" in desegregating a white racist university are not necessarily the same as would enable them to be foremost as— shall we say—investment bankers. Yet this practice does represent an attempt by white racism to maintain the traditional distinction between niggers to be whipped and niggers to be fondled. The latter are "trusted" as the house nigger in the slave period was trusted: the "first of his race" to sleep outside the door of the master's bedchamber.

But the practice is not invariable. Some of these "firsts" preserve in their subsequent careers the militancy that impelled them in the particular instance to act as they did. Others settle for the token jobs they are offered. Thereafter their militancy resumes its natural color of opportunism. The problem they confront in most cases is that of being black militants when the hand that is feeding them is white. The problem is aggravated when the white hand is unusually generous or uncommonly distinguished. How can a black be militant and at the same time work for the Ford Foundation or the Rockefeller Foundation? How can a black be militant and at the same time work for the New York *Times?* That is the problem: how, in the first place, to reconcile racial militancy with economic necessity, and, in the next, to reconcile economic necessity with racial self-respect. It is a problem that most militants find insoluble. Yet there are militants whose high level of professional competence at a given job, combined with their intelligent management of their militancy, does enable them to achieve the reconciliation of racial self-respect with economic necessity. The former is not sacrificed to the latter.

In the case of Angela Davis, this problem did not arise. She was not a "first" in the accepted and approved sense. So there were no rewards for her. Only persecution and obloquy. The critical faculties that she brought to bear upon the American society, especially with regard to its treatment of its black citizenry, were not conferred upon her by Marcuse or bequeathed to her by Marx and Hegel. They were her own innate endowment, although Marcuse may have stimulated her employment of them; he is a social critic of vast acuity. Nor can he have communicated to his pupil any uncritical worship of Hegel, for he writes, in *Reason and Revolution:*

The fault with Hegel lies much deeper than in his glorification of the Prussian monarchy. He is guilty not so much of being servile as of betraying his highest philosophical ideas. His political doctrine surrenders society to nature, freedom to necessity, reason to caprice. And in so doing, it mirrors the destiny of the social order that falls, while in pursuit of its freedom, into a state of nature far below reason.

Marcuse imports his critical dispassion into the more commodious sphere of national behavior, as well. In this specific example, he considers the use of language as propaganda. He writes in *Negations:*

However the administered language is rigidly discriminating: a specific vocabulary of hate, resentment, and defamation is reserved for opposition to the aggressive policies and for the enemy. The pattern constantly repeats itself. Thus, when students demonstrate against the war, it is a "mob" swelled by "bearded advocates of sexual freedom", by unwashed juveniles, and by "hoodlums and street urchins" who "tramp" the streets, while the counterdemonstrations consist of citizens who gather. In Vietnam, "typical criminal communist violence" is perpetrated against American "strategic operations." The Reds have the impertinence to launch "a sneak attack" (presumably they are supposed to announce it beforehand and to deploy in the open); they are "evading a death trap" (presumably they should have stayed in). The Vietcong attack American barracks "in the dead of night" and kill American boys (presumably, Americans only attack in broad daylight, don't disturb the sleep of the enemy, and don't kill Vietnamese boys). The massacre of hundred [of] thousands of Communists (in Indonesia) is called "impressive"—a comparable "killing rate" suffered by the other side would hardly have been honored with such an adjective. To the Chinese, the presence of American troops in East Asia is a threat to their "ideology," while presumably the presence of Chinese troops in Central or South America would be a real, and not only ideological, threat to the United States.

The loaded language proceeds according to the Orwellian recipe of the identity of opposites: in the mouth of the enemy, peace means war, and defence is attack, while on the righteous side, escalation is restraint, and saturation bombing prepares for peace. Organized in this discriminatory fashion, language designates *a priori* the enemy as evil in his entirety and in all his actions and intentions.

This inversion of language for political ends was also one of the late Aldous Huxley's preoccupations. In an essay, "Words and Behaviour," he wrote:

The most shocking fact about war is that its victims and its instruments are individual human beings, and that these individual human beings are condemned by the monstrous conventions of politics to murder or be murdered in quarrels not their own, to inflict upon the innocent and, innocent themselves of any crime against their enemies, to suffer cruelties of every kind.

The language of strategy and politics is designed, so far as it is possible, to conceal this fact, to make it appear as though wars were not fought by individuals drilled to murder one another in cold blood and without provocation, but either by impersonal and therefore wholly non-moral and impassible forces, or else by personified abstractions.

Standing language on its head is a semantic stunt in which the white racists of the American society delight to indulge themselves. Thus, they speak of the "black problem" when, of course, this really means the "white problem"; of "law and order" when this really means "continued oppression of blacks"; of "black violence" when this really means "white lawlessness." These are illustrations of Marcuse's reference to the "Orwellian recipe of the identity of opposites."

Angela Davis already knew of this formula of linguistic perversion at firsthand. For her, it was not an academic exercise in the analysis of language but a pattern of social realism designed to cause her, the black victim, to appear as the transgressor. She did not need Marcuse to reveal this to her; or Marx, or Hegel. The only illumination necessary was her own experience at the hands of the American society. If she required confirmation of her own experience, she needed only to look around her and into the immense well of black experience in America, centuries deep. It would be obscurantist to attribute her Communism to the water she drew from this well. The intellectual elements of the Communist persuasion have appealed to brilliant minds before Angela Davis's. Its emotional content, too, has not been lacking in charm for political visionaries of the most diverse origins. Were Angela Davis a white Anglo-Saxon Protestant of irreproachable New England antecedents, she might still have been a Communist. The grounds of her allegiance could simply have been philosophical. She might have found its schematic rigidities congenial to her temper. Hers would not have been the first instance of a gifted intellect bewitched by dogma. Thomas Aquinas had long preceded her in this direction. The categories of a priori reasoning have often ravished otherwise superb intellects. "The world," lamented George Santayana, "is full of conscript minds; only they are in different armies. And nobody is fighting to be free, but each to make his own conscription universal." The pre-eminent mind holds fast to the conviction of final tentativeness as the terminal process of critical inquiry, all knowledge being hypothetical, and knowing, itself, in a cognitive sense, being indeterminate—a concept whose philosophical expression is best defined by Heisenberg's principle of uncertainty in physics. Probability is all.

It is one thing, however, to prescribe the ideal intellectual temper but quite another to engage in active combat against white racism. Calculating the number of angels capable of dancing upon the point of a needle is a different order of personal commitment from confronting the usages of tyranny with the intention of wiping them out. "This is it," Marcuse wrote in *Negations*.

The woman, the land is here on earth, to be found here on earth, living and dying, female for male, distinguished, particular, tension to be renewed, Romeo's and Don Juan's, self and another, yours or mine, fulfillment in alienation. No Eucharist, no crucifixion, no resurrection, no mysticism. To find this woman, to free this land: *hic Rhodus, hic salta!* And don't jump into Nothing. Waking up from sleep, finding the way out of the cave is work within the cave; slow, painful work with and *against* the prisoners in the cave. Everywhere, even in your own land which is not yet found, not yet free, there are those who do this work, who risk their lives for it—they fight the real fight, the political fight. . . . The political fight is the fight for the whole: not the mystical whole, but the very unmystical, antagonistic whole of our life and that of our children—the only life that is.

This is the life that white American racism would deny and Angela Davis would affirm. Never the twain shall meet. While, as now, white racism is in the ascendant, Angela Davis—"to free this land" (if one may adapt the terms of Marcuse's vision)—sacrifices her freedom, does the work, risks her life for it, and fights "the real fight, the political fight." And since the ascendancy of white racism means the supremacy of sociopaths, then black women and black men will continue to be whipped in one form or another. Even when they may have transgressed the law, their plight still is not merely that of wrongdoers. Theirs is a psycholegal situation where the law must be redressed, but, no less important, the sadistic demands of white racism must not go unsatisfied.

Angela Davis must therefore be whipped, and so must George Jackson, in a measure far exceeding the sum and nature of their transgressions, just as William Byrd of Virginia and his wife once whipped "Jenny and Eugene," their black slaves.

William H. Grier and Price M. Cobbs, in their book *Black Rage*, remark:

Black men and women have this complex of problems in large measure because they have always been regarded by white Americans as sexual objects, exotic people living close to instinct and primitivism. The fascination black people have for white people in the sexual area can hardly be exaggerated, and this factor alone makes a major contribution to the charged quality of racial relationships in this country.

To speak of black revolution in America, a convulsion of which blacks like Angela Davis and George Jackson are regarded in some quarters as the harbingers, is to speak of a highly complicated set of circumstances as much sociopathological as political and economic. It is not difficult to see that George Jackson was much more an object of hatred from the standpoint of the dominant white society than a subject for rehabilitation. This major segment of the society was at all times less concerned with helping Jackson than with punishing him. What made Jackson's case one of unusual desperation was, as with Angela Davis, his uncommon intellect. Such an attribute in the black slums of America must be attended by uncommon good fortune if its possessor is to avoid becoming a black version of the white sociopaths who relegated him to the slums in the first instance and are determined to keep him there. The grim choice presented to black slum dwellers in general is confinement either there—in the slums—or in jail. The search of the blacks for a way out of this hideous dilemma is precisely the case for revolution in America.

By revolution is meant, first, a fundamental transformation of American values on the subject of race; second, the accomplishment of this transformation by peaceful and constructive methods, wherever possible; and third, the intelligent application of whatever methods are elsewhere necessary. The indiscriminate employment of force in a blind and vengeful frenzy can only be self-destructive and will only procure wasteful bloodshed and needless chaos. However, these are nice distinctions which it would be unrealistic to suppose capable of recommending themselves to blacks rotting in the slums that so largely constitute their heritage in America. To counsel patience and restraint to these blacks in such circumstances is to proffer advice of unattainable perfection. When, as is only natural, they exhibit impatience and unrestraint, the ingrained habit of society is to punish them savagely. This is a reaction compounded in considerable part of hatred and fear. Hated as they are by whites, blacks are also feared as a result of the very hatred visited upon them. So long as they remain the passive or apathetic objects of this hatred, they give no reason to arouse latent fear. But the moment they show the least sign of sloughing off their drugged or diseased indifference, they are regarded as dangerous animals to be closely confined or, breaking loose, shot at sight.

The causes of their breaking loose, which are the conditions of the slums, are more often than not disregarded or otherwise taken insufficiently into account. Yet these conditions are a prime breeding ground of revolution in America. But there are other breeding grounds. The lives of Angela Davis and George Jackson did not intersect in the slums. Angela Davis is the product of a well-to-do, middle-class background. The intersection of her life with Jackson's occurred at the point of racial injustice. This is the common focus of white racism in America. It is the point of radiation of white racism into all levels and aspects of black life in the country. Racial injustice joined together the lives of Angela Davis and George Jackson, as it has the lives of all black Americans regardless of their origin or subsequent circumstances. Racial injustice is the greatest unifying force in black life in America.

If, because of her economic situation, Angela Davis exemplifies the black intellectual revolt against white racism, then George Jackson, for the same reason, illustrated, by his life and its tragic course and culmination, the black proletarian revolt. Gifted with a first-rate intellect, the Chicago slums in which he spent some of his formative years might not alone have been effective, horrible as they were, in denying him scope and incentive for the constructive development and useful expression of his talents. But in alliance with white racism, the slums corrupted his childhood and drove him into juvenile delinquency. *Optima corrupta pessima:* the best, when corrupted, becomes the worst. This is in no sense to imply that Jackson was "bad." But it is certainly to suggest that the perversion of his brilliant intelligence into antisocial courses during his childhood and adolescence was clearly the consequence of slum conditions in combination with white racism. What else, might one ask, drives so many black youths to drug addiction and other forms of behavior labeled "criminal"? What else but the deadly alliance between white racism and the black slums. If it were singly a matter of slum housing and its attendant social and economic conditions, if there were no such leprous thing as white racism, then the twisted growth of George Jackson would have been an aberration traceable to some inherent defect. Gifted men—and

George Jackson was a gifted man—have often achieved the constructive expression of their endowments despite disfavoring odds of slum conditions. As hideous and appalling as the slums are in all their stunting wretchedness, they alone would be insufficient to explain fully or justify completely the human being called George Jackson. Neither are the slums adequate justification for the behavior of the innumerable thousands of blacks who have resorted to antisocial solutions of the problems confronting them. But once white racism is brought into the picture and its role evaluated, then George Jackson and those numberless thousands of blacks become perfectly understandable.

White racism is the difference. Its presence aggravates every social ill. Although it cannot be argued that white racism is always and everywhere the sole cause of black slums, its contributory role, even when not decisive, is nonetheless definite. Wherever the two circumstances exist together, there is either cause or correlation to connect them. This is especially the case in a white racist society. Black slums may be created by black societies. One has only to look at the black countries of the world to discover the grim truth of this proposition. Similarly, white slums may be created by white societies. Once again, the evidence is readily apparent from the barest inspection of white societies. But where black slums exist in white societies, not only are they created by those societies, but the incidents of their existence are also invested with a peculiar character. The circumstances of slum living, already horrifying, become more monstrous still because of the injection into them of factors commonly recognizable as the characteristics of white racism. These consist, in part, of the transmission to the black group of slumdwellers of a conviction of their own inferiority based on their blackness. To this is added the fact that they are slum dwellers. And the one is used to reinforce the other. The blackness explains the slum dwelling, and the slum dwelling is seen as the natural consequence of the blackness. The conjunction of blackness and slum dwelling comes to be regarded as producing its own undesirable spawn: crime, shiftlessness, unemployability, aberrant social conduct. Hence the need for police intervention, judicial punishment, and jails. Hence the fact that the blacks are a minority of less than 15 per cent of the American population, but a majority in some instances of more than 70 per cent of the population of American jails. This is the work of white racism. It is an important element in the case for revolution in the United States.

However, one must draw a necessary distinction between white Americans and white racism. Not all white Americans are white racists. While it is true to say that as a whole the American society is racist, it does not follow that all whites are racists. In this connection, the task of black Americans is to winnow out the chaff from the wheat. And an exceedingly difficult task it is, calling for extraordinary patience and intelligence. This is an important element in the case against revolution in the United States. As a rule, it is inadvisable to throw out the baby with the bath water.

At the same time, however, a black upheaval has been taking place in this country, and its occurrence is manifested in many ways, palpable and impalpable. This is plain once acknowledgment is made of the process initiated by segments of the black group aiming at violent or nonviolent displacement of white ruling-class values. This is the course that a significant number of blacks are embarked upon, and the goal toward which their current struggle is directed.

Amidst all the fever and menace of violence, perhaps the most revolutionary of all developments is the attitude of blacks toward themselves and, its corollary, their attitude toward whites. The first is expressed by the slogan "Black is beautiful"; the second, "White is right."

With the minting of the slogan "Black is beautiful," white aesthetic norms, which for centuries had dominated black standards of self-evaluation, were overthrown. This phase of the cultural despotism imposed by whites upon blacks came to an end. It was not simply that black physical traits suddenly became desirable and, to that extent, white physical traits were rejected. The process of aesthetic subversion went much deeper than that. The total effect was that whites, as a whole, were extruded, nonviolently, from their traditional class position. Their whiteness deteriorated from a social advantage to a disadvantage. It was no longer desirable to be white. On the contrary, the further physical traits receded from whiteness, the more valuable they became. The consequence is that "whitey," as a racial epithet, is more vile now than "nigger."

Two blacks in the modern era were mainly responsible for this development: Marcus Garvey and Malcolm X. Two blacks in the current period have been dramatically representative of this transformation of racial values: Angela Davis and George Jackson. The luxuriant hair growth in which Jackson is alleged to have secreted a gun and the great Ethiopian nimbus of hair that aureoles Angela Davis's lovely face are the symbols of this transformation. Something of the predicament of black women before this aesthetic revolution may be gleaned from *Black Rage:*

At the time of this writing [*circa* 1968] the overwhelming majority of Negro women have their hair "fixed" by some method, including the use of a hot comb. The hair is oiled and the heated comb is applied. Usually there is some incidental burning of the scalp. The ordeal itself is long and tiresome, involving hours spent waiting while the overworked beautician moves from customer to customer. To look "presentable" the woman must have her hair pressed every week, or at least every two weeks. Thus the black woman is never free of the painful reminder that she must be transformed from her natural state to some other state in order to appear presentable to her fellow men. . . . As if this were not sufficient, there is one final degradation associated with hair. Passionate love-making is a vigorous business and touseled hair is to be expected, but if a woman perspires too freely, her pressed hair becomes kinky and must be straightened. And thus even in the triumphant bed of Eros she is reminded that what should be her crowning glory is in fact a crown of shame.

It seems remarkable that it should have taken such a long time for black women and black men to achieve the reversal of aesthetic values earlier referred to. Why did it not happen sooner? The answer is in the complete dominance of the black psyche hitherto exercised by white racism. No conquest so conclusive has ever been recorded. It was not absolute only because of the unpredictable appearance from time to time of individuals like Nat Turner, Denmark Vesey, Marcus Garvey, Malcolm X, Angela Davis, and George Jackson. For some reason, or none at all, these individuals, and such as they, have kept reappearing in one persona or another throughout the entire course of black history in America. They, well-nigh singlehanded, each in his generation, rescued the black psyche from total enslavement by white racism. Standing alone against the course of events, they intervened with ideas in some instances and with action in others. But always implicit in their intervention, directing and sustaining it, was their conviction of the truth, unquestionable as they saw it, that blacks were at least the equals and at best the superiors of all whites. This attitude is also racism. Yet in the given circumstances, it had a positive value of revolutionary magnitude. The black psyche languished in abject servitude from which only the messianic force of some ideological extremism could arouse it. To fight the extremism of white racism with the extremism of black racism is not, ethically, ideal. It can be observed, however, that it has much the same pragmatic effect as employing fire to quench fire. Were white racism amenable to reason, black racism would be intolerable. But taking white racism as it is, black racism is understandable.

Still, it must not be thought that the reformation of black hair styles and, in general, the new cosmetic self-respect of black women are to be taken as illustrative of black racism. These developments are simply part of the continuing process of redeeming black aesthetic norms from the centuries-long domination of white racist standards. As a phase of that cultural activity, they are vital to the emancipation of the black psyche. The Emancipation Proclamation of 1863 freed the bodies of slaves, but their collective psyche remained in thralldom. In assessing the measure and meaning of figures like Marcus Garvey, Malcolm X, Angela Davis, and George Jackson, this realization on their part glows like hot steel, incandescent at the heart of their thought, ablaze in the motivation of their work. Since black Americans tend to be theological in their thinking, it might be said, as a more intimate revelation of their fundamental plight, that they are engaged in a struggle to repossess their souls. So whatever the light in which Malcolm X and George Jackson may appear to white racists, or whatever the depth of the shade, to blacks as a whole they are essentially redeemers; misguided, perhaps, in many ways, but nonetheless inspired by a mission of the utmost consequence to blacks; that is, the deliverance of their people from the clutches of white racism. And so with Angela Davis; so, too, with Marcus Garvey, in the reflective aftermath of the years since his apostleship, when the message he brought has, if anything, deepened in its relevancy and quickened in its urgency.

Whites—and in particular white racists—cannot evaluate blacks like these by any standard common to themselves and to black Americans; which is why they shout for "law and order," invoking the sanctions of this formula to dissemble their own lawlessness. George Jackson's prison record and the recital of his delinquencies must be considered against the background of the racial character of the American society. Only then will the true significance of the man and his circumstances emerge. Merely to recount his infractions of the law without apportioning the correlative, if not causal, guilt of society is to suggest that Jackson carried on his existence in a sociological vacuum. And this would be manifestly absurd. To what extent is a white racist society responsible for the derelictions of its oppressed black minority? That is the question. But no white racist will face it. He clamors instead for the easy way out of his own malfeasances. He shouts, "Law and order!" And then he shoots. The pattern is the same whether in Sharpeville in South Africa or in Attica, New York.

The really singular feature of the black uprising is, then, its retort to white racist might by plucking, red-hot, from the crucible of the centuries of tyranny the aesthetic challenge: "Black is beautiful." No aspect of the black uprising has had such genuinely revolutionary consequences. Neither bullets nor barricades, nor even ballots. Almost overnight (although in fact it was a principal feature of Garvey's racial propaganda), this slogan transformed a large and vital area of the attitude of black people in America toward themselves. They applied now, for the first time in hundreds of years, aesthetic standards that were a rejection of those set up on self-serving grounds by the white racists. The hair of their womenfolk in all its natural, unstraightened beauty, their facial characteristics in all their ethnic variety, their speech, food, and group style of life became the proud symbols of a separate and profoundly conscious identity.

Until that moment, "White was right." As the ruling class in the society, the whites possessed the dominant power by which the concept of right was validated. They were the exemplars from whose standards the blacks had taken their own.

"If you're white, you're right. If you're black, stand back." So the blacks stood back, as they were bidden by local law and national custom, and slavishly imitated the whites. To be "free, white, and twenty-one" was the passport to the American paradise at the summit of the world. The whites made the conventions, made the laws, and made whatever money there was to be made. And there was plenty of it. The blacks were outcasts and, at the slightest sign of discontent with their pariah status, might be treated as outlaws. White was right because whites had the power. White power was the pragmatic key with which the ethical code could be deciphered. The system of law itself was simply an organic function of white power. It was a white man's country, and, despite its considerable black minority, in effect it remained so until the intermittent tremors of black disquiet attained with Marcus Garvey and Malcolm X the force of an eruption. That the United States is, conceptually, no longer a white man's country can be attributed to the resistance to this idea on the part of many black men and women throughout the centuries. In the twentieth century, due recognition must be given in this connection to the work of Booker T. Washington, W. E. B. Du Bois, Paul Robeson, Monroe Trotter, Martin Luther King, Adam Clayton Powell, and many others. But, pre-eminently, and in particular from a psychological point of view, it was the work of Marcus Garvey and Malcolm X. They were the supreme architects.

The power to dictate the terms of the life of a society, to prescribe its mores, enunciate its laws, and declare its customs; the power to determine which groups within the society are to be privileged and which disadvantaged; the power to arrogate superior status to oneself and to impose inferior status upon another; the power to admit to and to exclude from the market place, the schools, the places of worship and of public enjoyment, the places of repose, of healing, of habitation; the power to reverse in the collective minds of a subordinate group those values by which, in normal circumstances, good is identified as good and evil as evil; the power, accordingly, to twist the mentality of an oppressed group into affirming evil as good and good as evil; the power not only to bind their black bodies but also to shackle their black souls; the power to make them hate and despise themselves for being black, while envying and fawning upon others for being white; the power to make them crawl so that in numberless instances they lose the will to walk upright again; the power to subhumanize and, at last, dehumanize; the power to take away a man's humanity—this, this is white power. It is what is meant when whites, surveying themselves in the mirror obsequiously held up to them by their society, react with smug racist pleasure to their image and whisper or confide, announce or declaim: "White is right." This is what Angela Davis and George Jackson, Eldridge Cleaver and Huey Newton, Muhammad Ali and the Black Muslims, Roy Wilkins and Whitney Young, the NAACP and the National Urban League, and all and each and every black man and woman with a shred of self-respect, whatever the divergences between their respective methods, are committed to fighting with every breath they draw: white power; and its evil genius, white racism. That is the common enemy. That is what all blacks are fighting, Black Mississippi sharecroppers and Wall Street black stockbrokers alike.

Yet, despite the massive and protracted violence directed against them by the American society, blacks as a whole have shown little disposition to resort to countervailing violence as a means of resistance. It would be easy to point to the numerous, if sporadic, instances of armed revolt by small groups of blacks and take those as evidence of a general will to violence amongst the black community. That would be easy but quite wrong. There is no such widespread inclination on the part of the black people of the country, taken all together. Quite the reverse. They may in actual, unsensational fact be described as remarkably restrained in the face of daily provocation for hundreds of years. Their profound conservatism, combined with their religious convictions, has undoubtedly contributed much to this attitude. Above all, however, is their love of America. *They,* rather than the white racists, are the true patriots.

But patriotism does not imply a supine acceptance of tyranny. On the contrary, it is sometimes necessary to struggle to save one's country from internal enemies masquerading as superpatriots. Such a struggle can take many forms. The repudiation of white racist values by black Americans is one example. They have sought to supplant those values by appeals to their African heritage. Some have resumed semblances of African dress. An interest in African languages has been revived. These developments are not symptoms of black repudiation of America, but of black rejection of white racism. They do not represent an attempt to replace American values by African values. Rather, they are an effort to transform American values, in so far as they are racist, by asserting the values of that older civilization in which black Americans had their origin. They are, in a manner of speaking, a recourse to ancient principles. And since it is clear that white racist values subserve, in particular, the special interests of the white ruling class, the black struggle is, in its essence, directed against that group. This being the case, it is not difficult to understand the clamor for "law and order." This demand has always been the protective incantation of a ruling class, especially when its position is threatened by an upheaval on the part of those whom it has disinherited and subjected as a condition of its acquiring and maintaining power.

Thus, when a white millionaire columnist in a New York City newspaper spreads out the record of George Jackson's transgressions but omits to note that the gravest transgressions of all were committed by the society of which Jackson was a black member; when he nowhere mentions poverty as a factor that is contributory, at least, if not directly causal, and that this poverty was contrived against Jackson and millions of others, black and white, by this society; then he is guilty at once of sociological inaccuracy and moral blindness. And when the New York *Times* headlines the news of Jackson's death at the hands of his captors in a United States prison with a description of him as an "enigma," it, similarly, is guilty at once of moral blindness and sociological inaccuracy. It was not Jackson but the American society to which the term "enigma" should have been applied. Surely, a society is an enigma when, as the richest the world has ever known, it creates poverty amidst its overflowing abundance and imposes it, with all its distorting and diseasing potentialities, upon those, like Jackson, whom it despises because of their race, and others, like poor whites whom it despises because of their class. What is a society that dooms gifted people like Angela Davis and George Jackson to persecution and frustration, if not an enigma? There was a logic about the life and death of George Jackson that was wholly necessitated by the ingredients of the personal tragedy that the society had so perversely constructed for him. Where the society itself is concerned, no such logic exists, except the logic of sociopathology, the logic of a sick society infected by the disease of white racial superiority. "We hold these truths to be self-evident, that all men are created equal. . . ." If this is a self-evident truth, then what is the society in which Angela Davis was imprisoned and George Jackson was killed in murky circumstances in the jail where he was held? What is this society in the light of that "self-evident truth"? An enigma? No. A lie.

It must be made entirely clear what is intended by "black revolution"; in particular, what is meant in this context by "revolution." There is need here for something in the nature of a special definition, since, aside from the pronouncements and activities of marginal groups of blacks, from whom the great mass of the black population stands tactically aloof, there is no revolutionary upsurge in the classic sense among the generality of black Americans.

It is not that the large majority of blacks in the country are quiescent, uncaring, or apathetic, divided in their counsels or fearful of consequences. They remain, instead, convinced, despite much incitement to the contrary on the one side, and overweening provocation on the other, that the way of endurance is in the long march the better way out of the wilderness and into the Promised Land. So while there are revolutionary conditions and revolutionary fervor in the black slums of America, there are no barricades in the streets. Blacks still manage to sing, still manage to dance, still manage to laugh. Not all blacks. Not all, by any means. And because cataclysmic movements, like large-scale revolutions, can be produced by small cadres, disciplined and committed, the prospect of black revolution in the United States cannot be completely written off. It might happen, but it is unlikely.

An intensification of white racist oppression is far likelier and, indeed, is already occurring. Where this may lead, one may foretell. There can be a "final solution" for blacks in this country. The prisons of the United States even now are concentration camps for blacks, preponderantly, and other social misfits. The increase in black militancy has been accompanied by an increase in the severity of official repression. Upheavals in the jails are some of the symptoms of reaction to these parallel developments. Whether this will prove to be the stone thrown in the lake, with its consequence of an ever-widening series of concentric circles until the concentrated masses of urban blacks are gassed and machine-gunned in their thousands by police action supported by state and federal troops abetted by armed helicopters overhead and auxiliary tanks on the ground in the black ghettos—whether this will come to pass, one may dread to contemplate but hardly dare to leave out of account in the light of the white racist lust for extermination of the hated blacks.

"Until Attica," wrote Harriet van Horne in the New York *Post* of September 24, 1971, "I had no true measure of how thoroughly the Negro is despised by our white racist society. . . . And until Attica I never imagined how much fear and vindictiveness resided in the vaunted warm American heart." Harriet van Horne (possibly because she is white) was merely belated in her appreciation of these actualities. Had she been black, enlightenment would have descended upon her much sooner.

But while there is no generalized black revolution, as such, in the United States, and neither is there likely to be, the same statement cannot be made with equal accuracy of either the actuality or the prospect of widespread repression of blacks. For one thing, this repression has already been in existence for three and one-half centuries. It is, as ever, an actuality with blacks. The only question at this point is whether it will become a more painful actuality. A not inconsiderable number of black Americans do not find it difficult, in view of the demonstrated nature of white racism, to visualize their extermination as an objective of American bigots. It would be idle and misleading to assert that some do not arm themselves with guns and other weapons to be used in their self-defense in that event. There may be underground activity among groups of blacks, as there is among groups of whites, of a character that may perhaps be described with fairness as revolutionary. Considering the intensity with which, as a rule, black people in this country are repressed, it would be surprising if there were not some such activity going on among them at least in marginal areas. By activity is meant preparation for revolution in the classical sense. But on the other hand there is sufficient surface activity of a clear and determinate quality to deflect speculation and allow concentration on existent facts. The revolutionary reversal by blacks of white racist values, which until now had dominated their consciousness and distorted their self-images, twisted their aesthetic standards and degraded their self-esteem, is the real black revolution that is taking place in America: this subversion and overthrow of the psychological regime of white racism that once forced blacks to loathe themselves by making them appear hateful to themselves in their own eyes. This, above all, is what is meant by black revolution.

That there should be a revolution by blacks in this sense toward the indicated goal of total overthrow of white racist norms, no decent-minded person would be found to deny. That there should be bloodshed, none but the bestial would wish. Yet, wishfulness should not be confused with probability.

In the most precise sense, however, what the black people of the United States are, as a whole, engaging in is not revolution but resistance. The blacks of the United States constitute a resistance movement. That is their actual character today, as it has been for three and one-half centuries. The entire substance and pattern of black life in America acquire coherence and consistency and become explicable across the vast range of sociological design and absence of design, narrative and nuance, when its fundamental dynamic is recognized as resistance. This is the key to the whole black experience in the United States in its infinite complexity: black resistance, everywhere and at all times from the beginning of the blacks' connection with this country up to the present time. A black slave, a black sharecropper, a black laborer, a black lawyer—whoever he or she may be —each and all alike are members of the black resistance.

Those who come to the surface are labeled by American tyranny, in consonance with Orwell's identity of opposites, as revolutionaries; unless they are supremely clever men, like Roy Wilkins or Whitney Young, who are able to combine in themselves at one and the same time, and to execute with superb pragmatic skill, the functions of their membership in the black resistance, those of black revolutionaries, and those of constructive black moderates, without ever allowing the enemy—American tyranny—to identify them as revolutionaries. This is where Booker T. Washington succeeded and W. E. B. Du Bois failed; where Whitney Young succeeded and Paul Robeson failed; where Martin Luther King succeeded and Adam Clayton Powell failed. Yet even when the enemy has entrapped and labeled them revolutionaries because they have been too rash, foolhardy, or greatly daring, they have nevertheless remained brilliantly accomplished members of the black resistance. All of them. All heroes of the black resistance in the United States. Ralph Bunche, Ralph Ellison, James Weldon Johnson, Langston Hughes, James Baldwin, Charles Chesnutt, John Killens, Julian Mayfield, Walter White, Richard Wright—they all have transcendently in common membership in the black resistance, whatever their substantive vocations or modes of personal expression. There they are at one with Nat Turner and Sojourner Truth, Harriet Tubman and Denmark Vesey, David Walker, Samuel Ward, Henry Highland Garnet, and William Wells Brown. There—at the ultimate confluence of the myriad tributaries of black resistance in America. There—with Marcus Garvey and Malcolm X, Eldridge Cleaver, LeRoi Jones (Imamu Amiri Baraka), Huey Newton and Bobby Seale, H. Rap Brown and Stokely Carmichael, George Jackson and that spiritual descendant of Sojourner Truth and Harriet Tubman—Angela Davis.

The distinction between revolution and resistance may be put in a concrete image by citing the parallel careers of Frederick Douglass and John Brown. The former, through all the mutations of his political circumstances, was a member of the black resistance. The latter (white, as it chanced) was a revolutionary. There was more than a touch of John Brown in Paul Robeson, though their lives ran different courses and came to widely divergent ends.

Revolutionary incidents, in so far as they occur amongst the black people of this country, are simply the spume on the crest of the wave of black resistance, silent, massive, and centuries-deep in the fathomless historical depths. What white racist America has to reckon with is not black revolution, but black resistance. There is some visible consciousness of this fact on the part of white racism, overt signs of its awareness of its relative helplessness against black resistance in the eagerness with which it pins the label "revolutionary" on anyone it possibly can while never speaking of the more formidable reality of black resistance. White racism can deal with black revolution, as it usually has, with guns and gas, troops and tanks, white police and black informers. But black resistance—with its guerrillalike impalpabilities, its multitudinous disguises, its dissembling camouflage, avoidance of confrontation, retreats and evasions, seeming apathy and surface quiet, laughter and acquiescence, prayer and submission; and beneath all of this a massive resolve, carved out of granite, to endure, to endure, and always to endure, until enduring gives birth to prevailing—is another matter. A resolve on the part of the blacks that is not passivity but a preference for the snaillike processes of the long view, not inaction but protest and political movement scaled and timed with a precise sensitivity to the art of the possible; a fundamentalist vision of America, as in literal truth, for the good of its own soul, obligated in spirit to live up to the letter of its founding principles; a conviction that this land is their land, their birthright won in blood, chains, work, and immeasurable woe; their heritage to conserve rather than to destroy; their America not to be ravaged by revolution but to be made whole by their steadfast refusal to accept a lesser part of the promise of the land as their portion; their America for love of whom they have borne the whips and scorns of the centuries without ever, in all their mass, lashing out in concerted retaliation against their tormentors—this, this is the black resistance in America.

One of its historical facets was the unwillingness, manifested by sloth and inefficiency, with which the captive black slaves carried out their allotted tasks on the plantations. J. C. Furnas, in his *Goodbye to Uncle Tom*, writes of "the overseer's hourly petty contact with malingering, fornication, illness, squabbles and the perpetual drag of a chronic, spontaneous slowdown for which the whip was the only convenient recourse."

Resistance in this form was virtual sabotage, and it was widespread among the slaves.

The overseer of a great James River plantation readily told a Scottish traveler "that he was constantly obliged to use the lash, both to the men and women; that some he whipped four or five times a week, some only twice or thrice a month; that all attempts to make them work regularly by advice or kindness were unavailing . . . many who . . . appeared attached to the family, would not work without occasional hints from the cowhide."

Thus arose the legend of laziness and shiftlessness among the blacks as dominant ethnic traits, while the truth of the matter was that the shirking and malingering were elements of black resistance, as were the smiling and shuffling and the simulated mental dullness. The white racist comparative "As dumb as a nigger" could actually mean, and often did, "As shrewd a resistance fighter as a black man."

From all the evidence, it is clear that the preoccupation of the main body of blacks in America is not with revolution but with resistance. A marginal number of blacks talk and write of revolution and may even actively prepare for revolution. In so doing, they go counter to the established historical tradition of blacks in this country. Neither do they represent the present character or reflect the current activities of the preponderant mass of blacks, who continue to be, as for centuries they have been, a solid and, for the most part, silent network of resistance to white racist oppression.

It is in contrast with this unspeaking though not inarticulate mass that the forthright declarations of blacks like Angela Davis and George Jackson acquire such saliency. In one of his letters from prison, George Jackson wrote as follows to his mother:

Have you ever wondered how you and I and all our kind lost their identity so fast? The last blacks were brought into this country only seventy-five to eighty years ago, three generations at most. This is too short a time for us to have lost as much as we have. No other people have completely been divorced from their own as we have in such a short period. I don't even know my name. [*Soledad Brother.*]

This namelessness of blacks, except for what Malcolm X used to refer to as "the slavemaster's name," has goaded them into a search for their ancestral beginnings in Africa. This quest is partly expressed by their adoption, in some instances, of African names. The Black Muslims, scorning Christian surnames that were merely the evidence of former slave status, substituted the letter *X* while somewhat inconsistently in many cases retaining Christian first names. Other black nationalists are more thoroughgoing in this respect. LeRoi Jones, for example, has become Imamu Amiri Baraka. The fusion of Arab and sub-Sahara influences is to some extent the outcome of Moslem

352

religious inspiration. Mainly, however, it represents the symbolic rejection by alienated blacks of American culture.

Though an enthusiastic, yet not uncritical, admirer of Malcolm X, George Jackson—despite his lament "I don't even know my name" —was concerned less with his nominal description than with his fundamental identity. He was a subtler and profounder thinker than Malcolm X, with a more accurate mastery of the intellectual tools of historical analysis. But Malcolm X was incomparably his superior in the formulation of ideas for presentation with a view to persuasion. Jackson was aware of his problems of social address in general. He wrote in a letter dated May 25, 1970:

Love's labor—I understand these things, much better than most, always have, but I never could present it in the proper light before. Presentation was the problem. People kept mistaking it for animality or criminality, and then, less sensibly still, un-Amerikan.

Like Malcolm X, Jackson overestimated the possibilities of black revolution in the United States and overlooked, at the same time, the tremendous actuality of black resistance. He misconceived the true characters of his parents and other blacks of their generation, who, in fact, were more revolutionary than he, though less vocal about it. His father possessed the genuine stuff of which revolutionaries are made: self-disciplined, unexcitable, coolheaded, and enduring. By comparison, Jackson was a romantic anarchist of considerable intellectual gifts. He was never able to realize how successfully the blacks have conspired to survive, which is the first duty of a revolutionary. Toward the end of his tormented, but by no means fruitless, life, he achieved in a letter to Angela Davis an unconscious vision of his father and mother and of untold numbers of other blacks:

We belong among the righteous of the world. We are the most powerful. We are in the best position to do the people's work. To win will involve taking a chance, crawling on the belly, naming, numbering, infiltrating, giving up meaningless small comforts, readjusting some values.

In all these processes his mother and father had been engaged all their lives, but he never understood that. He spent a good deal of time preaching to them from his standpoint without taking the trouble to listen to them. As a would-be revolutionary, he had more to learn from them than he ever realized. And because he neglected this part of his self-education, the black resistance in America lost a potential leader of extraordinary brilliance, and he himself remained a black anarchist less resolved to win than eager to dramatize the ritual sacrifice of his life to white racism. He was able to recognize this tendency in other blacks, but he was blind to it in himself. So he could write:

I almost got sucked into some more foolishness yesterday. All the blacks tilting at windmills again. Mindless, emotional, childish abandon, without a thought of winning. Just an attempt to prove their manhood to themselves, to any who may be watching. The result, further humiliation . . . There is so much that could be done, right now. . . . But I won't talk about those things right here. I will say that it should never be easy for them to destroy us. If you start with Malcolm X and count *all* of the brothers who have died or been captured since, you will find that not even one of them was really *prepared* for a fight. No imagination or fighting style was evident in any one of the incidents. But each one that died professed to know the nature of our enemies. . . . It's very contradictory for a man to teach about the murder in corporate capitalism, to isolate and expose the murderers behind it, to instruct that these madmen are completely without stops, are licentious—totally depraved—and then not make adequate preparations to defend himself from the madman's attack. Either they don't really believe their own spiel or they harbor some sort of subconscious death wish.

He was aware of these things; he knew their value as techniques of individual as well as group defense against an oppressor. But he was incapable by temperament of adapting them to the necessities of his personal situation or to those of the black people, as a whole, in the United States. Beyond this, his fundamental error lay in misconceiving the character of the black response demanded by the objective conditions of the racial struggle in this country. He interpreted these conditions as revolutionary, and he advocated a revolutionary response. He was wrong. Resistance was the correct response; for the conditions he was considering, as well as experiencing, were so profoundly intricate a complex of class, caste, and race that to prescribe revolution, with all its crass and brutal oversimplification, was merely to prescribe chaos. That was a recipe natural to anarchism. And George Jackson was an anarchist.

His parents were right. He was wrong. Yet his mistake does not falsify his brilliant analysis of the motive forces of the American society and his profound penetration of its essential character. He saw it plainly, and he saw it whole. It was in his prescription for dealing

354

with it that he came to grief. A finer theoretician than Eldridge Cleaver, and with a more incisive intellect, he came in the end to espouse much the same sort of revolutionary solutions that Cleaver proposed. This conjunction between two such different orders of intellect was facilitated by their common experience at the hands of white racism. A touch of white racism makes all blacks kin.

There is no intention to deny the giant sweep of Cleaver's mind, his tempestuous passion against injustice, or the precision of his historical analysis. And, considering the quality of his experiences at the hands of white American racism, it would be impertinent for anyone to offer him counsels of perfection concerning the nature of his emotional reactions. But thinking—clear, cold thinking, informed and guided by an unrelenting realism—this is a different matter. One has the right as well as the duty to disagree with this superb black fighter whose will to combat can be saluted, whose devotion to the task of achieving and affirming black manhood can be supported, whose triumphant survival of the horrors of the concentration camps that are American prisons can be celebrated, and whose admiring and loyal regard for decent-minded people, black and white, can be shared. Neither is it for want of respect for his powerful intellect, nor want of recognition of his absolute commitment to the cause of racial justice, nor want of deference to his towering stature as a revolutionary leader that one may dissent from his proposed solutions for the unspeakable state of affairs created by white racism.

Having to choose between revolution as advocated by Eldridge Cleaver and resistance as in the tradition of black Americans for centuries past, I choose resistance. Between Eldridge Cleaver and Roy Wilkins, I choose Roy Wilkins; between John Brown and Frederick Douglass, I choose Frederick Douglass; and because in this respect there was no profound antithesis between Booker T. Washington and W. E. B. Du Bois, I choose them as against Eldridge Cleaver and Huey Newton. The respect I accord Huey Newton, however, is not less than that for Eldridge Cleaver: they are both superlative freedom fighters.

Blacks may choose as I have done because of our conviction that white racism will prosper through black revolution but will perish against black resistance. We are of one mind that white racism must die, even if we are of many minds as to the means of its death. The best way to ensure the triumph of white racism is to oppose it with a blind commitment to violence or with a fatuous commitment to nonviolence, without a supremely intelligent regard for the precise nature of the objective circumstances. Emotion is a valuable resource and mainspring of intelligence, but intelligence—lucid, detached, dispassionate—must be the dominant weapon in the armory of all, blacks and whites alike, who would overthrow white racism. An unbalancing emotionalism, however understandable, is of all weapons the least effective and potentially the most self-destructive.

It is illuminating to compare the intellectual processes of George Jackson and Eldridge Cleaver during their confinement in United States prisons.

Jackson writes:

The textbooks on criminology like to advance the idea that prisoners are mentally defective. There is only the merest suggestion that the system itself is at fault. Penologists regard prisons as asylums. Most policy is formulated in a bureau that operates under the heading Department of Corrections. But what can we say about these asylums since *none* of the inmates are ever cured. Since in every instance they are sent out of the prison more damaged physically and mentally than when they entered. Because that is the reality. Do you continue to investigate the inmate? Where does administrative responsibility begin? . . . The blacks are fast losing the last of their restraints. Growing numbers of blacks are openly passed over when paroles are considered. They have become aware that their only hope lies in resistance. They have learned that resistance is actually possible. The holds are beginning to slip away. Very few men imprisoned for economic crimes or even crimes of passion against the oppressor feel that they are really guilty. Most of today's black convicts have come to understand that they are the most abused victims of an unrighteous order.

Eldridge Cleaver in *Soul on Ice* takes essentially the same view. He writes:

One thing that the judges, policemen, and administrators of prisons seem never to have understood, and for which they certainly do not make any allowances, is that Negro convicts, basically, rather than see themselves as criminals and perpetrators of misdeeds, look upon themselves as prisoners of war, the victims of a vicious, dog-eat-dog social system that is so heinous as to cancel out their own malefactions: in the jungle there is no right or wrong.

Rather than owing and paying a debt to society, Negro prisoners feel that they are being abused, that their imprisonment is simply another form of the oppression which they have known all their lives. Negro inmates feel that they are being robbed, that it is "society" that owes them, that should be paying them, a debt.

America's penology does not take this into account. . . . It is only a matter of time until the question of the prisoner's debt to society versus society's debt to the prisoner is injected forcefully into national and state politics, into the civil and human rights struggle, and into the consciousness of the body politic. It is an explosive issue which goes to the very root of America's system of justice, the structure of criminal law, the prevailing beliefs and attitudes toward the convicted felon. While it is easier to make out a case for black convicts, the same principles apply to white and Mexican-American convicts as well. They too are victimized, albeit a little more subtly, by "society". When black convicts start demanding a new dispensation and definition of justice, naturally the white and Mexican-American convicts will demand equality of treatment.

The two foregoing passages, placed side by side, define lines of thought that converge into a measured indictment of American society and the penal system. "Up until now," says Jackson,

the prospect of parole has kept us from confronting our captors with any real determination. But now with the living conditions deteriorating, and with the sure knowledge that we are slated for destruction, we have been transformed into an implacable army of liberation. . . . Some people are going to get killed out of this situation that is growing.

Those were fateful, prophetic words. However, Jackson continues:

These prisons have always borne a certain resemblance to Dachau and Buchenwald, places for the bad niggers, Mexicans, and poor whites. But the last ten years have brought an increase in the percentage of blacks for crimes than can *clearly* be traced to political-economic causes. There are still some blacks here who consider themselves criminals—but not many. Believe me, my friend, with the time and incentive that these brothers have to read, study, and think, you will find no class or category more aware, more embittered, desperate, or dedicated to the ultimate remedy—revolution.

The parallel circumstances of Cleaver's prison experiences were set down by him in the section "On Becoming" in his *Soul on Ice.*

In Soledad state prison, I fell in with a group of young blacks who, like myself, were in vociferous rebellion against what we perceived as a continuation of slavery on a higher plane. We cursed everything American— including baseball and hot dogs. All respect we may have had for politi-

357

cians, preachers, lawyers, governors, Presidents, senators, congressmen was utterly destroyed as we watched them temporizing and compromising over right and wrong, over legality and illegality, over constitutionality and unconstitutionality. We knew that in the end what they were clashing over was us, what to do with the blacks, and whether or not to start treating us as human beings. I despised all of them.

Both Jackson and Cleaver identified the status of blacks within the United States as colonialism. Cleaver, in fact, prefaced one of his pieces with the following quotation from Kwame Nkrumah: "I distinguished between two colonialisms, between a domestic one, and an external one. Capitalism at home is domestic colonialism."

For Jackson, too, capitalism was the archvillain:

The capitalist Eden fits my description of hell. To destroy it will require cooperation and communion between our related parts; communion between colony and colony, nation and nation. The common bond will be the desire to humble the oppressor, the need to destroy capitalist man and his terrible, ugly machine. If there were any differences or grievances between us in the black colonies and the peoples of other colonies across the country, around the world, we should be willing to forget them in the desperate need for coordination against Amerikan fascism. . . . Capitalism must be destroyed, and after it is destroyed, if we find that we still have problems, we'll work them out.

But since colonialism is merely the political tool of capitalism, Jackson asserts:

The people of the U.S. are held in the throes of a form of colonialism. Control of their subsistence and nearly every aspect of the circumstances surrounding their existence has passed into the hands of a clearly distinct and alienated oligarchy [the capitalist ruling class] . . . our principal enemy must be isolated and identified as capitalism. The slaver was and is the factory owner, the businessman of capitalist Amerika, the man responsible for employment, wages, prices, control of the nation's institutions and culture. It was the capitalist infrastructure of Europe and the U.S. which was responsible for the rape of Africa and Asia. Capitalism murdered those 30 million in the Congo.

There are no significant differences between Jackson and Cleaver in their analysis of the political and economic imperatives of capitalism and its social expression as white racism. Both regard capitalism and colonialism as two sides of the same coin. Divergences began to make their appearance in the nature of the counteraction each proposed as the remedy for the ills they diagnosed. They speak often of the attainment and affirmation of "black manhood" as a sovereign element of the projected cure. Cleaver, indeed, declaims at one point: "We shall have our manhood. We shall have it or the earth will be leveled by our attempts to gain it." Given the white racist circumstances of American life, they believe that black manhood can be won only by black revolution. But while with Cleaver this belief seems hardly to have undergone any modification, with Jackson it did. Not that Jackson believed no longer in the efficacy of black revolution, but his belief was eventually qualified by a primary concern with preparation and a paramount concern with winning. To express it differently, Jackson progressed beyond polemic to the "clinical approach, the analytical technique of treating our problems," after having "struggled mightily with myself these last couple of years in an attempt to erase all emotion." On the other hand, Cleaver seems not yet to have arrived at this point. He is capable of magnificent, fulgurating rhetoric, moving in its molten passion.

I know my duty. Having been spared my life, I don't want it. I give it back to our struggle. Eldridge Cleaver died in that house on 28th Street, with Little Bobby, and what's left is force: fuel for the fire that will rage across the face of this racist country and either purge it of its evil or turn it into ashes. I say this for Little Bobby, for Eldridge Cleaver who died that night, for every black man, woman, and child who ever died here in Babylon, and I say it to racist America, that if every voice of dissent is silenced by your guns, by your courts, by your gas chambers, by your money, you will know, that as long as the ghost of Eldridge Cleaver is afoot, you have an ENEMY in your midst. [*Post-Prison Writings and Speeches.*]

The tragic sadness is what white racist America has made of highly gifted black men like George Jackson and Eldridge Cleaver and countless other blacks of a comparable order of intellectual endowment; the cruel, melancholy waste of so much of the vital resources of a society, its people. It would be the silliest effrontery to presume to lecture anyone like Eldridge Cleaver on the subject of his emotions in the face of the monstrous horrors he has experienced at the hands of white racism in America—not at the hands of white people in their generality, but at the hands of white racism. Yet it would be a wondrous accrual of leadership for the cause of the blacks in this country were he, like George Jackson, to aim at the mastery of his emotions while abandoning not the slightest particle of hatred of white racism. The redemption of blacks in America is an objective infinitely more important than the memory and redress of one's personal sufferings. Black manhood is not invariably a prize to be wrested from violent conflict and revolution, but often to be gained by invincible endurance, unsleeping vigilance, tireless preparation, calm calculation, and instinctive awareness of the decisive moment. That is to say, the moment when the tide of white racism at insolent high-water mark, in irresistible flood, begins to ebb, imperceptibly at first, imperiously in its violent slap and wash, back to sea to be swallowed up by the yawning reach and illimitable waste of history. It is necessary to understand that resistance is not only reaction, and revolution is not merely initiative. To prefer revolution to resistance for reasons that have more to do with personal temperament than with the objective situation would simply "throw us," in George Jackson's words, "into a fight where we would be outnumbered 1 to 14 (counting the blacks who would fight with/for the other side) in a race war. War on the honky, it's just another mystification."

Therefore, to measure the needs of the black struggle in the United States by the single imperative of winning—which means not heroics, not rhetoric, not posturing, not unnecessary bloodletting, but out-thinking, outwitting, outwaiting the enemy—this is the strategy of resistance. It has so far secured the survival of the black people of the United States, and it remains their best hope of ultimate triumph over white racism. Revolution, in the sense of seizing the tactical initiative at whatever cost in black lives, even to the point of their wholesale suppression and near extermination, can only raise, with renewed intensity and deepened relevance, the question posed by George Jackson:

Who is the black working for, who does he love when he screams "Honky"? . . . The blanket indictment of the white race has done nothing but perplex us, inhibit us. . . . It doesn't explain the black pig; there were six on the Hampton-Clark kill. It doesn't explain the black paratroopers (just more pigs) who put down the great Detroit riot, and it doesn't explain the pseudo-bourgeois who can be found almost everywhere in the halls of government working for white supremacy, fascism, and capitalism. It leaves the average brother confused. In Detroit they just didn't know what to do when they encountered the black paratroopers. They were so stunned when they saw those black fools shooting at them that they probably never will listen to another black voice regardless of what it's saying.

360

The problem is, then, not only white racism, but also black treachery, black venality, and black stupidity. These ingredients of the problem have coexisted from the outset. There is also the problem of black naïveté, from which both Jackson and Cleaver have suffered, the latter to a larger, more credulous extent than the former. They speak of the "Third World" as if this were an actuality instead of an aspiration, a concrete fact instead of a political concept. Moreover (and Cleaver in this respect more so than Jackson) they envision nationalistic entities, such as sovereign states, acting in any circumstances—or some at least—without a paramount and even exclusive regard for their own self-interest. Naïveté can scarcely be carried much further than that. As a result, they are inclined to make wildly fanciful assessments of the political motives of the Peoples' Republic of China, for example, where the black liberation struggle is concerned. Their lack of sophistication in such matters seduces them into embracing the assumption that China's international role will be determined by ideology rather than pragmatism, and that China will be actuated on behalf of black people by idealism instead of realism. These are fundamental errors of fatal consequence. Cleaver is chagrined by the thaw (or, at any rate, the heightening of the temperature of the ice) in Chinese-American relations and gloomily summarizes this development as having "thrown the revolutionary movement into 'disarray'." No one ambitious to be a revolutionary leader can afford to be so innocent. The pre-eminent interest of the Peoples' Republic of China is itself. Secondarily, perhaps, and only if useful in the promotion of Chinese national interests, its concern may be broadened on purely pragmatic grounds to encompass giving aid to the black struggle for freedom anywhere. A figure like Eldridge Cleaver, who must be respected despite his political naïveté, is not diminished in his symbolic stature because his ardor for black freedom and equality betrays him—momentarily, one hopes—into confusing ideology with pragmatism. He and George Jackson and Angela Davis belong in the company of the black elect.

However they may describe themselves, or be described by their admirers and detractors, they are all alike—each and every one of them—freedom fighters, black freedom fighters.

THE SINGLE FEATURE that more than any other typifies the American society is, to repeat, its endemic racial injustice. But it would be misleading to isolate this circumstance from its European origin. In its racial outlook the United States is the spawn of Christian Europe. And if racism within Europe itself has seemed less overt, less obsessive, less omnipresent than in the United States, it is only because of the much lower ratio of blacks. The problem of racial injustice is to a degree a problem of proximity. The British were able to maintain a lofty pretense of racial tolerance as long as the Indians, Pakistanis, and other species of Asians, and Africans and West Indians kept their distance. But when they emigrated in a massive influx to Britain and actually came to amount to something like 2 per cent of a thitherto lily-white population, Enoch Powell was obliged to come to the rescue. "If you want a nigger neighbor, vote Labor." Mississippi couldn't do much better than that along those lines.

All of this invests the case for black separatism in the United States with an arguable claim for dispassionate consideration. It need not be either recommended or reprobated, but it ought at least to be examined. It may be illuminating to consider it in the light of the persistent denial, throughout three and one-half centuries, of racial justice; the psychological aspect of physical proximity as a factor making for ethnic friction; and as an alternative to the revolutionary activities rendered justifiable by moral outrage on the part of black Americans. When people lose the capacity to be outraged and the will to remedy, even by violence, the causes of their outrage, then it is all up with them. Here, in this conjunction between moral occasion and the will to action, lies our best hope of redemption. A creature in chains—any creature whatsoever—redeems itself by an attempt, however foredoomed, however futile, to strike off the chains. The sin against the Holy Ghost of the theologians is the sin against freedom. To be free—that is, to command impartial justice as one's inalienable right—is the supreme meaning of civilized existence. Yet by justice is not implied the formulations of jurisprudence; rather, the implicit recognition within a human group of the right of each and all of its members to be regarded as ends in themselves, and never to be contemplated, instrumentally, as means.

The difference between whites and blacks in the American society is that the former can be seen as ends in themselves. To be white, simply as such, is an end in itself, while blacks are mere means. That was the fundamental significance of black slavery: blacks were chattels—or economic means. Its social implications, subtending the arc of history from past to present to future, continue to bedevil the descendants of the slaves, who, though freed, yet never acquired freedom. The pivotal lesson of the black experience in America is that it would have been better from every point of view had the black slaves been able to fight for and conquer their freedom instead of having it given to them in the form of emancipation by whites whose contempt for them was, if anything, increased by the very act of benevolence. The coexistence of these contradictory attitudes, white benevolence and, at one and the same time, white contempt for the black objects of benevolence, is a well-documented trait of even the most high-minded white liberalism. It is not a characteristic of mankind in general to be unduly respectful of the subjects of charity. As an alternative, accordingly, to ceaseless racial friction that is the consequence of physical proximity, some blacks propose separatism. The suggestion contains several advantages. One of the most obvious is the chance it could give blacks to recoup, in relative isolation, the immense psychological losses in self-esteem they have sustained through the sort of contact they have had with whites. It is clear that, as against this, the argument is tenable that the same end may be achieved by maintaining contact—which is to say, proximity—on social levels less destructive of the black sense of self-worth than in the past.

This is of course the case, in essence, of what is commonly called integration. All experience thus far has indicated, however, the unlikelihood of anything coming into practical effect that is so reasonable as the latter alternative. The nature of prejudice precludes reason. It is far more likely that racial proximity will, over the short run at least, as in the Southern United States, provide opportunity for arbitrary violence and other forms of oppression with which black Americans are already too familiar. If the Northern experience has differed somewhat from that of the South in this regard, it has been more in degree than in kind, the result in dominant part of the fact that the blacks are more widely dispersed in the North and are, in general, in lesser physical proximity to whites. It must be acknowledged, however, that separatism as envisioned by the Black Muslims, to take this instance, aims at a more or less complete severance of relations with whites. For this reason it is hopelessly unrealistic. Integration, as envisioned by middle-class blacks and white liberal theorists, aims at a more or less complete assimilation of blacks into the social and institutional life of the country and their absorption into the national scheme of values. In short, an assisted passage from subculture or counterculture to the culture of the mainstream. For this reason it, too, is hopelessly unrealistic. In its very reasonableness it takes too scant account of the intractable nature of prejudice. The social separatism espoused by Booker T. Washington still remains the approach least calculated to produce convulsions in the American society. That this should be so gives some idea of the glacial pace of sociological change in the United States of America.

As well, however, it takes into realistic account the obstacles that the proponents of integration are intent on underestimating, and the protagonists of separatism determined to overemphasize. Somewhere between these two extremes lies Booker T. Washington's midstream of social separation islanded by co-operation. It may indeed be no more than a matter of emphasis. One of the most self-defeating characteristics of the propaganda of integration is the massive weight placed upon the avowed need of blacks for proximity to white people. Much can be accomplished simply by not talking about doing it. This has proved a difficult lesson for the black middle class and their white liberal supporters to learn, which, of course, is quite understandable. The first cannot avoid proclaiming their highest ambition; the second are unable to repress their pride at making its attainment possible. Together, they constitute the greatest hindrance to the natural processes of human intercourse in the American society. It is as clear as anything can be that the clamorous advocacy of integration frustrates the task of racial conciliation. This is not to say that integration is inherently undesirable, nor is it to suggest that integration is not now, as for generations past, an established sociological fact. But it is to assert that the sheer orgy of talk about integration undoes its historic actuality and inhibits its present employment in the conciliation of the American society. People as a whole are much likelier to accept what they may consider a distasteful situation if they are encouraged to believe that they are doing so of their own unconstrained choice than if, to the contrary, they are forced to experience every disagreeable sensation of either swallowing an unpalatable object whole or choking on it.

To the extent, therefore, that integration as a social objective may be desirable, and to the extent that it has not already been accomplished, it should be brought about only by careful sociological planning and, above all, extracted from political controversy. Nothing has so cursed the whole issue of race in the American society and blighted all hope of its intelligent and just resolution as its reduction to the status of a political question. Yet the case for separatism, such as it is, cannot be met simply by dismissing it as a counsel of disaffection and despair. The matter must be examined on its merits. If the supreme ideal of American society is a harmonious synthesis of mutually diverse elements, it would seem to matter less whether integration or separatism were chosen as the doctrinaire means to the desired end than that the vital inner balances of society should be organized and preserved by an instrumental device rooted in sociological pragmatism. The grand design of a harmonious and balanced society might best be attained by flexibility in the service of the over-arching ideal. Bearing steadily in mind the interests of the society as a whole, it should be possible to regard integration and separatism, not as mutually exclusive concepts, but as sociological approaches with varying degrees of adaptability to the major end of a unitary society constructed by pragmatic methods from a teeming diversity of human elements: in other words, integration should be the approach where, demonstrably, it will work; and separatism where, again demonstrably, it also will work. Even the possibility of establishing separate states for national minorities should not be discounted without due consideration. The lesson of the Soviet Russian experience in this regard might be worthy of study from the standpoint of its applicability as a solution to similar problems of the United States. American society should, ideally, evolve along lines of intelligent organic development rather than be circumscribed and handicapped in its growth by a mistaken reverence for the fossilized forms of the past. Neither integration nor separatism should be imposed upon the society, whatever the sources of their inspiration. Each should be permitted to make its way at its own pace in accordance with the prevailing features of the sociological terrain, and always with a scrupulous regard to the major synthesis of a civilized society whose governing aspiration is individual liberty. Integration and separatism can be warranted only by their ability to reconcile themselves with this principle.

The Black Muslims share their espousal of separatism with other black groups whose actuating spirit is secular rather than religious. However they may differ in their methods, they are all imbued with the determination to withdraw from the American society. Some of them demand a separate state; others declare their resolve to return to Africa. The demand for a separate state was sponsored by American Communist propaganda in the interval between the two World Wars. With American participation in the second of these wars and the political seduction of Earl Browder, a Communist leader, by President Franklin D. Roosevelt, this drive for black separatism, which was always a negligible movement, came to a virtual halt until it was once more set in motion by the Black Muslims after the war. The Back to Africa Movement did not begin with Marcus Garvey; he merely infused it with new life and brought it to world attention. African colonization societies had long been a feature of the black struggle to escape white racism in America. There was little novelty about this form of the struggle except that Garvey succeeded, beyond all probability, in employing it for the first time in its checkered career with devastating psychological effectiveness. He did so by attaching the impetus of the struggle to a dynamic rebirth of pride in blackness. Within a short time of his messiahship, there were comparatively few blacks anywhere in the world—and certainly none within the large centers of what we call civilization—who had not heard of this extraordinary black man who, in a profound psychological sense, had raised up the black masses of America from the dead. This was the work of that black immigrant from Jamaica. And he did it not indeed singlehanded but yet in the face of much opposition, open and concealed, from many blacks themselves and, above all, from whites apprehensive of the racial consequences that might ensue from the charismatic leadership of this black West Indian.

If it is true that a single moment is given to each and every man or woman, witting or unwitting, at some arbitrary point of their life to make the crucial decision that will thereafter determine its unalterable course, then Garvey's choice of emigration to the United States may well prove in retrospect to have been one of the pivotal episodes in the history of group relations between whites and blacks all over the world. For Garvey's influence did not end, nor indeed had it begun, with his work in the Uinted States. It extended to other parts of the world, particularly to those colonial areas where the overlordship of whites was accepted as an incident of existence as natural and inevitable as the rising and setting of the sun. Garvey and what he represented penetrated deep into those subjugated areas. The partial liberation of Africa and the West Indies from colonial subjection owes at least as much to Marcus Garvey as to the emergence of Soviet Russia as a world power. This is not to say that the Communist state redeemed blacks from colonial servitude in those areas of the world by any direct exercise of its power, but it is unequivocally to assert that the uprearing of this political monolith upon the world scene introduced a competitive factor that forced traditional colonialism to terminate or reduce its dominance and at the very lowest amend or camouflage its forms. Within the United States, the effect of Garveyism was deeper ethnic cohesion among blacks—a situation much abhorred by white racism—a heightened aesthetic sense of self-approval, and an awakened awareness of the possibilities of black organization for political ends. These developments were all inimical to the designs of white racism where blacks were concerned, and Garvey and his movement paid the price in due course. The Black Panthers at a later date underwent, and are still undergoing, a similar experience.

Garveyism was a revolutionary movement, necessitated as a response to white racism in its characteristic pursuit of racial injustice. The Black Panthers also are a revolutionary movement, similarly necessitated by the denial of social justice to blacks that is typical of white racism.

Black revolution in the United States, in the fragmentary degree in which it has usually existed, has never been anything but a last-ditch effort at self-defense against white racism by those blacks who have, with unquestionable justification, lost faith in orderly constitutional process. Yet it does not disparage them to remark that they are not the only black revolutionaries, defining revolution once more in its broadcast connotation as concerted action, with or without violence, to alter, subvert, or destroy the established power of an oppressive state. Bear in mind as well the identity and meaning of the state as a political abstraction of the general will, which the class in possession and control manipulates to secure its own paramount position and to promote its own monopolistic interests. The inevitable result of this class pre-emption and exercise of the state power is injustice to the excluded classes of the society.

In a racist society, class injustice is aggravated by racial injustice. The determinant issue is always the tolerable degree of injustice, since justice in human terms is, on any pragmatic basis, an unattainable social ideal. It is when injustice exceeds its tolerable limits that the class in power must recognize the need to reform itself or to accept the imposition of reform. When it fails to do so, it will have created by its default the necessity for revolution, which, then, it can confront only by tyranny. The position of blacks in the United States has long exceeded the tolerable limits of injustice. Their situation possesses a chronic quality that drives some blacks to revolutionary activity and others, no less disaffected but more prudent, to propagate reform. This distinction between revolution and reform is, from the angle of evaluation of black activism, less a matter of substance than of method. Yet in suggesting that all blacks, considering the intolerable degree of white racist injustice in America, are of necessity revolutionaries, one puts forward the suggestion with certain reservations. It might indeed be more appropriate to observe that all blacks ought to be revolutionaries. Yet, there does linger the need to preserve this statement from too dogmatic assertion. At the same time, there is undoubted warrant for the position that there are many more black revolutionaries in the United States than are enumerated by reference to the membership lists of the Black Panthers, the Blackstone Rangers, or the entire roster of the multiple groups of black Americans who

368

despair, with lavish justification, of anything like a reasonable degree of social justice ever emerging from the pathology of white racism.

Whitney Young, for instance, did not so much embody the prospect of hope in the willingness or ability of white racism to reform itself as he personified the resolve of a revolutionary to use the means at hand to secure desired ends without risking the destruction of the troops under his command. This is what, more than anything else, distinguished him from his fellow revolutionaries Huey Newton, Bobby Seale, Eldridge Cleaver, Stokely Carmichael, LeRoi Jones, Ron Karenga, and others. He was far more skillful a revolutionary than they. He knew far more accurately the size and disposition of the counter-revolutionary forces, far more intimately the personalities in command of them, far more clearly their tactical and strategic objectives. Young once declared in New Orleans that he would resort to violence if he thought he had a chance of winning. But he knew he had no such chance. So, like a good revolutionary, he had conformed his tactics to the necessities of the situation. Whitney Young operated behind the enemy lines; so does Roy Wilkins; so did Ralph Bunche; so did Adam Clayton Powell—until he grew too careless and was made to suffer the penalty of his rashness; so once did Paul Robeson—until the constant strain of dissembling and disguise overcame a temperament better adapted to crashing through opposing linebackers, bringing down the walls of Jericho with trumpet blasts of noble resonance, and, like the Emperor Jones, defying the enemy to vanquish him with anything less than a silver bullet. There was also Walter White, who, in literal fact, posing as a white man, investigated lynchings of blacks in the South at the certain risk of being lynched himself if he were discovered. Others were W. E. B. Du Bois, Monroe Trotter, A. Philip Randolph, Booker T. Washington, Frederick Douglass; historic revolutionaries such as Harriet Tubman and Sojourner Truth, who infiltrated the enemy camp to rescue captive slaves; and many besides, nameless perhaps, but also revolutionaries in both spirit and intent, whatever the nature of the tactics they have judged it expedient, in the light of particular circumstances, to adopt.

No one who considers the public performance of Whitney Young can do so without achieving a clear realization of the qualities that go to make a successful revolutionary in the United States. At once forceful and urbane, uncompromising of principle yet flexible toward details, resolute and disciplined, tough-spirited and enduring, Young

369

was in his too brief lifetime a revolutionary of such consummate adroitness that he accomplished with his death the singular feat of reducing LeRoi Jones as well as Henry Ford II to sorrowing regret. It does not fall to the lot of just any ordinary man to achieve so dramatic a juxtapdodal of antipdodal public figures. Whitney Young was a product of the capitalist system of the United States, and he was not in revolt against capitalism. He was a bourgeois revolutionary, and his struggle was against white racism. The two phenomena, capitalism and white racism, are often found together in intimate association. In the United States, they are even causally connected. Yet one may not invariably infer a causal connection between them.

Communism can also coexist with white racism—as numbers of African students and other blacks have claimed to discover in the course of their sojourn in Communist countries. Whitney Young saw clearly this asymmetry of political cause and racial effect. Thus he did not fall into the dialectical error, so common among those to whom passion is more important than perception, of confusing an economic system with a moral aberration. Young was not without his failings. An occasional tendency to rely overmuch upon the politics of persuasion where, as in the case of the Nixon administration, only the calculated concert of black political power would suffice was an example. Yet a black who could say, as he did, that he would resort to violence if he were convinced that he had a chance of winning, emphatically proclaims himself a revolutionary—by other means. The difference between Whitney Young—as also with Roy Wilkins—and the more vociferous revolutionaries lies exactly here: in this paramount concern of Wilkins and Young with the pragmatic principle of effectiveness, in contrast with the predilection of the other types for noisy threats of self-destructive action. Thus Eldridge Cleaver recently announced from Algeria to the world at large his intention to return to the United States in order to engage there in urban guerrilla activity. One is moved to wonder if Cleaver had ever come across the statement of the archrevolutionary Lenin that "to tie one's hands in advance, to say openly to the enemy, who is better armed than we, that we will fight him, and when we will fight him, is folly, not revolutionary." Much as one can deplore the need to cite the following lines from *The Jungle Book* by the poet laureate of white racism, Rudyard Kipling, they are clearly descriptive of the verbal posturings of some black revolutionaries:

> By the rubbish in our wake
> And the noble noise we make,
> Be sure—be sure—we're going to do
> Some splendid things.

This is not the stuff of which successful revolutions are made. The granite resolve of a Roy Wilkins, however flexible he may be in the tactics he employs, his obdurate persistence, his inexhaustible patience, his coolheaded assessment of the means available for the ends in view, his supreme self-discipline—these are the traits of a genuine revolutionary. To brand Wilkins, as some do, an Uncle Tom is simply to mistake futile motion for effective action. Wilkins scorns the former and believes in the latter. Many of these self-styled "revolutionaries" are incapable of making this rudimentary distinction. It is not necessary to agree with everything that Wilkins does or says in order to see him truly for what, in fact, he is: a dedicated black revolutionary operating behind the enemy lines. It will be of the utmost importance for this generation, as well as coming generations, of blacks to guard against seduction by demagogues into violent courses disastrous in their immediate effect and irreparable in their consequences. Blacks as a whole have displayed, historically, unwavering steadiness in the face of unimaginable provocation. Given the racist character of the United States, with its overmastering impulse to violence, the blacks by their collective restraint and their calm absorption of the stresses imposed upon them have become, so to speak, the balance wheel of American society. This extraordinary group temper might be thought to betoken a love of the United States of America so profound that, even in this way, they would die for it.

The late Martin Luther King was attuned to this element in the group ethos of his fellow blacks with such exquisite sensitivity that he had no difficulty in exploiting it in the service of his own conviction of the moral efficacy of nonviolence. But as a disciple of Christ committed to a doctrine of love, and as a disciple of Gandhi committed to a doctrine of nonviolence and civil disobedience, he combined in himself, despite the moral excellence of his intentions and the social value of his objectives, a trinity of aspirations whose pursuit in the violent arena of American life and society bore all the fateful promise of consigning meek, defenseless black Christians to the bloodthirsty beasts of white racism. For if a man loves himself no better than to submit unresistingly to arbitrary violence being practiced upon him because of his skin color, then there is, surely, a real question whether such a man should not be prevented from loving his neighbor as himself. The only love worth having on the basis proposed by Christ—loving one's neighbor as oneself—is the love of someone who has a superlative love for himself or herself. Christ's injunction may be applied in such a case with a substantial prospect of the recipient's being invested with a love whose quality is equal in every respect to the splendid self-love of the giver.

But a pathological love that is a product of masochistic urges is hardly worth having. The most successful saints in the hagiography of the Roman Catholic church were remarkable for their self-love, which, in their progress to sainthood, they projected outward upon others even, as in the case of Saint Francis of Assisi, to licking the sores of beggars. No one can love another well without first loving himself at least as well. It is this quality of self-love in which Martin Luther King and his first preceptor, Jesus Christ, were so strangely deficient. And it was this deficiency that enabled King, perhaps unwittingly, to contrive, by the advocacy and practice of a philosophy so unsuited to the actualities of American life, the possibility of a holocaust for his fellow blacks. Paradoxically, therefore, King stands not with Whitney Young and Roy Wilkins among those black revolutionaries contemporary with him, but with Eldridge Cleaver, Stokely Carmichael, and others who, lacking as King was in self-love, would express this inadequacy by leading their fellow blacks to mass destruction at the eager, able, and bloodstained hands of white racism. Revolution is not an exercise in recklessness, whether in a Christian, Gandhiian, or Che Guevaran spirit. It is an arduous commitment to cold calculation, calm judgment, clear foresight, and resolute and intelligent action. Impassioned utterances are merely the froth on the tidal wave of revolution, which itself is a movement of the main that flows slowly, irresistibly, up from the silent deep.

The point to be given pre-eminent consideration in determining the wisdom or unwisdom of Martin Luther King's ethical system in its application to American realities is, the question in the formulation of William James, does it work? The answer clearly is: No; it does not. In applying John Dewey's instrumentalism, whose central principle was the social efficacy of a given process, again the answer clearly is: No; King's ethical system, within the context of American actualities, was inefficacious. This is not, as is evident, an adverse criticism of King on moral grounds. That he was a moral man, in the highest meaning of that concept, there can be not the slightest doubt. But was he also wise? Was he perhaps a visionary dangerous to his fellow blacks because he conceived of violence and nonviolence as absolute categories mutually repugnant to each other? Was it in him an intellectual defect of sinister import for his fellow blacks that he could think of violence and nonviolence only as Aristotelian opposites in a closed logical system from which religious intensity had excluded social reality? Before King sought to commit his fellow blacks to acceptance of the ethical system he propounded, should he not have made certain of its acceptance by white racist America? For what he was attempting was nothing less than the construction of a new system of values that went directly counter, in practice if not in theory, to the entrenched customs of this predominant segment of American society.

For violence he would have substituted nonviolence. It was an admirable apostleship of ethical conversion. That is hardly in question. But what was dubious about the whole enterprise was the specific direction he gave to it. It was not the blacks whom, in the main, he should have tried to render harmless as doves. In the vast majority of instances, they were already in that state. It was the whites, the prospective commandants of the concentration camps and caretakers of the crematoria, toward whom he should have principally channeled his ethical fervor. They were the ones who stood in need of conversion from hatred to love. The blacks had consistently demonstrated their wondrous capacity for love through centuries of hatred from the whites. So it was not they, his fellow blacks, who should have been the object of his mission: not they whom he should have chiefly called upon to cultivate and exhibit a quality of whose possession they had already given overwhelming historical proof. It was the whites to whom he should have preached, as Paul to the Gentiles. When one wishes to make converts to Christianity, one preaches to the heathen. When one wishes to make converts to nonviolence, one preaches to the violent.

King's was, therefore, objectively, a misdirected apostleship. He did not waste his gifts, yet he substantially misused them, preaching to the converted. The result was, from the standpoint of black Americans, much as if a shepherd had spent his time exhorting his sheep to be meek, loving, and unresisting to the ravenous wolves lying in wait to devour them. Viewed from this angle, there was a certain defeatism about Martin Luther King: it was as though he despaired of the will and the capacity of blacks to defend themselves; so he decided that the best thing he could do for them was to counsel and prepare them to die without a struggle. Considering the generic racism of the white Western culture, no Nobel Peace Prize was ever more fittingly awarded than to Martin Luther King. Moreover, so apparently deep-rooted was King's fear of the whites, and so convinced was he of the futility of any attempt to mollify them, that the possibility of addressing his missionary zeal directly to them never occurred to him. He devoted himself to preparing his fellow blacks to die as unblemished Christian martyrs, whose compensations in the hereafter would be all the greater because they had also followed Mahatma Gandhi. King's capitalist mentality was here calculatingly at work. He was, so to say, arranging a scheme of deferred spiritual benefits, in the manner of the earthly corporate models, for his fellow blacks. Yet, as King well knew, Gandhi was no advocate of absolute nonviolence. Why, then, did King enjoin this ultimate degree of inhibition upon his fellow blacks? His rewards—at the hands of the whites —were manifold and generous. But his fellow blacks, how were they benefited? How was their position in the American society enhanced? King's death, when it came, was brought by a white messenger. This circumstance lent ironic point to the paradox of a gifted black apostle who was in possession of the right message, but who addressed it to the wrong quarter. It was in the very form and spirit of an old slave tradition. The black preachers on slave plantations addressed themselves, with their message of Christian love and humility, even unto death, to their fellow blacks. Massa and Missy might attend the service, listen, but never really hear what was being said. Nevertheless, Preacher was a good Christian black fellow. Treat him kindly.

There is a further distinction to be made between Martin Luther King and such other blacks, for example, as Roy Wilkins and Whitney Young. Here, a fundamental principle of strategic import is involved. King's objective—the triumph of Christian love through nonviolence— plainly envisaged, though to be sure it did not explicitly invoke, the possibility of a holocaust for blacks in the United States. While such a possibility can never, surely, have been wholly absent from the minds of Wilkins and Young, and even though neither has ever advocated violence, yet neither has counseled what King so passionately

374

recommended: the abdication of the right of self-defense. This is the great dividing line between, on the one side, Young and Wilkins and, on the other, Martin Luther King. At no time whatever did either Wilkins or Young enjoin upon their fellow blacks the abandonment of their inherent and lawful right of self-defense. But Martin Luther King did. Still, King was a revolutionary, although in a purely moral universe of thought and action. His kingdom, like that of his Divine Preceptor, was not of this world. This made him a figure of incalculable danger to the prospect of the physical survival of his fellow blacks in white racist America.

Nevertheless, his concern with the issue of social justice was at all times profoundly impassioned, whatever the unrealism of his methods. He saw as clearly as anyone how the magnificent moral promise of America had been blighted by white racism. But whereas the spectacle of this shriveled and aborted promise inspired in him not anger but sorrow, there were other blacks whose concern with social justice was no less impassioned than King's, and in whom it inspired hatred and contempt.

No surprise will be occasioned by the fact that few elements of the American society gave Martin Luther King such fervent support as that constituted by the Jewish minority. Their traditional attachment to the ideal of social justice would alone have necessitated it. This brings to mind the social phenomenon that has come to be called black anti-Semitism, which is a tiny rivulet of the giant watercourse of Western anti-Semitism, whose headwaters are located in the historic fastnesses of remote centuries. Black anti-Semitism, in so far as it exists, is derived directly from white anti-Semitism. It is a Christian prejudice with which the converted blacks have been infected. The primal source of black anti-Semitism is the white Christian Bible. And the misleading legend of the crucifixion of Jesus Christ is its religious sanction. There are secular aspects of the matter, as well. In the case of the Jewish people, these are mainly economic. Such cultural differences as there are between the Jews of the United States and the rest of the population, on nonreligious levels, tend to reinforce anti-Semitism. None, however, is so decisive in this regard as the effect of competition in the market place.

Yet the central point to be made here is the clear connection between white racism and black anti-Semitism. Insistence upon the fact that white racism is a world-wide phenomenon must not be allowed to diminish—as it were, by diffusion—its significance as a trait of the American society; nor in this manner must its role as the irrational agent of black antisocial impulses be obscured. White racism has flourished because whites as an ethnic group have, on the whole, been its beneficiaries. It is only when the cost of white racism, whether social, economic, or political, has become disproportionate to the advantages derived from it that the whites have been induced or constrained to make racial concessions; or, as specifically in the case of the American society, only when the society itself threatens to be sundered within and so rendered an easy prey to its enemies without have such concessions been unwillingly contemplated and grudgingly put into effect. That was the meaning of President Franklin D. Roosevelt's Executive Order No. 8802 and, in the messianic terms in which he was inclined to view political questions, the meaning of Henry Wallace's nineteenth-century humanism parading in the guise of a twentieth-century program for "sixty million jobs." Those were the days when the white liberal intellectuals of the New Deal set the national tone of social reform and took beneath their wing the still-fledgling aspirations of the blacks for freedom and equality in America.

There were few so prominent amongst these liberal intellectuals as a number of brilliant and gifted Jews whose passion for social justice put at the disposal of black organizations a white leadership of extraordinary effectiveness in their struggle for civil rights. This leadership operated on all levels of the black struggle and in all of its political manifestations. Neither was it confined to the exertion of influence in the councils of government but extended along an unofficial course coterminous with the whole sweep and seethe of black Americans for their rights and liberties. Without the active support and inspiration of the Jews, the struggle for black civil rights would have been a feeble thing indeed. This is not to belittle or discount the titanic efforts of Booker T. Washington, W. E. B. Du Bois, Monroe Trotter, James Weldon Johnson, Paul Robeson, Walter White, and many others. But it is right to emphasize the indispensable role of Jews in that continuing struggle. It was Jewish money that kept alive the National Association for the Advancement of Colored People, and Jewish money that nourished the National Urban League. It was Jewish money and Jewish brains that mounted and sustained the defense of the Scottsboro boys; Jewish money and brains and blood that gave vital momentum to the Congress of Racial Equality and the Student Nonviolent Coordinating Committee and kindred if not associated organizations; Jewish concern, in all its ethical passion, for a just society that carried the conflict over the place of black people in America to its present crucial, yet not hopeless, phase. Therefore, what have blacks against the Jews today, and why?

To select a purely local issue, it is alleged that they have "dominated" the New York City school system. To be sure, the majority of the teachers in the system are Jewish and so, consequently, is the United Federation of Teachers. But the Superintendent of Schools is not a Jew, nor has this position ever been held by a Jew. On the Board of Education itself Jews are in a minority. And so are they a minority on the principal policy-making levels of the system. Moreover, if the argument blacks make is, substantially, that Jews should not be so numerous in the system as they are, then with what alternative means of earning their livelihood are blacks prepared to provide them? For they have the right, precisely as blacks assert it on their own behalf, to work at whatever they choose within the law and the possibilities of the national economy. But this is not the point blacks really want to make, this groundless allegation of Jewish "dominance" of the school system. What they actually wish to say, and evidently do not know quite how to say it, is this: the people who have kept Jews out of executive positions in banks and public utilities, and have reduced their participation in steel and oil and, generally, in heavy industry to a marginal degree, are the very people who bear the historic responsibility for the deplorable condition of the black minority in America. This has been the case from slavery to the present quasi-serfdom from which only a relatively few blacks so far have managed to escape. Was it the Jews who enslaved blacks, lynched them, raped their womenfolk, castrated their menfolk, despoiled their children for more than a dozen generations of the hope or prospect of a decent life? Is it the Jews who continue still to do so? Then why are blacks so intent on transposing cause and effect, obsessed with symptoms, ignoring history, and befouling themselves in a search for scapegoats? The answer, in three or four words, is: the black class conflict.

The leadership of the black struggle for equal opportunity in America has been at issue between the traditional brokers of black powerlessness, the Negro clergy, the NAACP, the National Urban League, on the one side; and on the other, the black lower classes. While the class position of the Negro clergy has been ambiguous, the NAACP and the National Urban League are regarded by the lower classes as organizations held in leading strings by white people and directed to the improvement of the status of middle-class blacks. Integration has become a term of reproach. Only the "Negro bou'g'ies"— contemptuous slang for the black middle-class—now aspire to integration. Whites are repudiated, white norms rejected. Again, why? And once more in a word or two, the answer: black nationalism. This development among black Americans was for a long time incubated in their brutal mistreatment by the white Americans. Marcus Garvey, Elijah Muhammad, and his apostate disciple Malcolm X simply released the chickens from the coop. The pressure of Russian power and imperial ambition, the rise of China, and the deliverance of Africa from white colonialism (this in particular) all combined in their own ways to strengthen the resolve of black Americans to seek, secure, and assert their own collective identity.

The white people with whom blacks have mixed most freely of all are the Jews. These are the whites to whom blacks have been closest. When the process of rejection on the part of the blacks set in, the Jews were the nearest at hand, within reach, as it were, and they felt accordingly the rudest brunt of the thrust. They were the group nearest to the blacks on all levels of the urban sectors of American society; nearest in the ghettos as small shopkeepers, merchants, landlords, teachers, and social workers; nearest in the professions as doctors, lawyers; nearest in the civil service. They were nearest not only because of the sociological circumstances of American life but of their own volition. They themselves, more sympathetic than other groups to the plight of the blacks, had drawn closer to help them. When black rage and despair at chronic mistreatment at the hands of the American society became at length uncontrollable, the blacks struck out blindly at those whites nearest them, and these happened to be the Jews. In a sense, then, it may be said that the Jewish people are paying a penalty for being white but also for their compassionate closeness to the downtrodden blacks. The very fact of their closeness to the blacks resulted in their individual failings becoming more visible to the latter and therefore more resented by them. Of all domestic upheavals, family quarrels tend to be the most recriminatory. For many years in urban life in America, the middle-class Jew has been big brother to the middle-class black. When the black felt himself coming of age, he no longer wished to be quite so dependent upon big brother as he had been; he no longer wished to be so closely advised and guided. With the onset of maturity he wished to be independent, to be free of the need to consult big brother before taking any important step, to stride out on his own. But striding out on his own meant encroaching on preserves that big brother had staked out for himself; meant, as it always does, rivalry, competition with big brother. This is the middle-class side of the coin. The lower-class side is less reassuring. Whether people are Jews or Gentiles, black or white, self-interest tends to preside over their calculations. A Gentile merchant is not less likely to be predatory than a Jewish merchant; a black landlord not less likely to be oppressive than a white. The persona, merchant or landlord, inclines to be unvarying in its typical behavior.

To saddle one particular group of people with the stigmata of a generic type is, of course, a common form of prejudice. The category "Jewish" landlord or "Jewish" merchant is tendentious, a fixed image from which only undesirable social consequences can ensue. That it is prevalent among poverty-stricken blacks (and poverty-stricken whites) is a proof, if anything, of the backwardness of a society that, in the midst of unparalleled affluence, permits such degrading ignorance to exist. Yet it is no more prevalent among destitute blacks (and destitute whites) than it is among well-to-do whites. The fact of the matter is that anti-Semitism is a disease of Western civilization, one of the gravest, for which no remedy has yet been found. To speak of black anti-Semitism as though one were attempting to isolate it as an unrelated phenomenon peculiar to blacks is dangerously to misconceive one of the most menacing impulses in the American society and in the Western world at large. It would be as if one were to speak of black racism without specific and countervailing reference to its historic ancestor and contemporary bedfellow, white racism.

In general, blacks tend to see Jews in racial rather than religious terms. Religion, in this view, accentuates but does not define Jewish identity. Many blacks are inclined to regard all Jews as belonging to the dispersed nation of Jewry, of which the newly founded state of Israel is the reconstituted center. They consider Israel an imposition by white colonialism upon weak Arab countries. As the prominent black author Harold Cruse has written:

The emergence of Israel as a world-power-in-minuscule meant that the Jewish question in America was no longer purely a domestic minority problem. A great proportion of American Jews began to function as an organic part of a distant nation-state.

Black Americans have become aware of the discrimination practiced in Israel against Yemenite and other nonwhite Jews. Some of them are inclined to view it as evidence of the essentially racist character of world Jewry. They assess the Jewish tradition of group exclusiveness not as cultural integrity but as further proof of what they conceive to be the ethnocentric quality of Jewish life. In many cases, they favor the Arabs as against the Israelis, regarding the latter as European interlopers and as "Middle East murderers of colored people."

There is, however, a deliberate political strategy behind these anti-Semitic developments among black people. They are not the chance outcome of haphazard conflict. The spokesmen of the black middle class have as a rule been elevated to leadership by Jewish approval, if not selection, maintained in their positions by Jewish support, and advanced in their careers under Jewish guidance. Black organizations such as the NAACP and the National Urban League were for a long time under Jewish tutelage. They also received support and guidance from leading members of the white Anglo-Saxon establishment. But the interest of these latter, while often expressed in generous bene-factions of money, sympathy, time, and labor, was not precisely the same as that of the Jews. The WASPs were, characteristically, more aloof, though not invariably less munificent, and their social impulse was to keep the blacks in their places. The Jews, on the other hand, wished to reform, where it was not possible to revolutionize, the historic position of the blacks. It has been argued that self-interest, perhaps, was not altogether absent from the Jewish impulse: that while they were invaluable, they were not altruistic; that their own in-secure place in the American society was a factor of calculable import in their devotion to the improvement of the status of the blacks; that the better off the blacks were, the more secure they, the Jews, would be. Unable for historic reasons to rely on the religious tolerance of white Gentiles, they sought in the blacks an ally whom they would raise up and strengthen against the day when, as so often in their tragic experience, they should confront the stony, livid face of Christian persecution. But those blacks who attribute these motives to the Jews overlook the age-old Jewish tradition of social justice. The Jews have never been insensitive to the moral content of the life of any society of which they have been a part. The inescapable fact is that if black people in America are able now, for the first time, to pose a formidable threat to the white Anglo-Saxon establishment, this is due in considerable measure to the tutelage and friendship of the Jews. The blacks themselves have not cried out with greater fervor than have Jews on their behalf: "Let my people go!" It is therefore irony of the most leaden sort that the Jewish people should now find themselves the collective butt of abuse and hostility from numbers of blacks.

This development would be inexplicable but for two things: anti-Semitism, which, although much less overt than formerly, continues to be a commonplace of American life; and the black class struggle. The second point explains much about the present conflict, and it also has a specific relevancy. The black middle class, composed of a comparatively small number of well-to-do "Negroes" (for they are not regarded by the adversary class as genuine blacks), is locked in remorseless conflict with the black lower middle class and the black lower classes, in general. The latter accuse the black middle class of habitual betrayal of the interests of black people, as a whole, in order to promote their own class interest and their individual careers. They regard the black middle class—the "Negro bou'g'ies"—with more loathing even than they do their white oppressors, if possible. For them the "Negro bou'g'ies" are the enemy to be fought and destroyed quite as much as the whites. The black middle class has been the chief beneficiary of Anglo-Saxon patronage and Jewish philanthropy. Some of the spokesmen of the black middle class—the traditional "Negro leaders"—have operated, perhaps unconsciously in some instances, as favored slaves entrusted with the duties of plantation overseers. It is not so much that they have wished to act in such a capacity as that white power has enforced this role upon them. And whether for their people's sake or from ambition for personal advancement or from a combination of such motives, they have typically engaged in compromises.

In the view of the new generation of black militants, these compromises have had the effect of suppressing the large majority of blacks—the "lower classes"—and restricting them within humiliating patterns of white charity and condescension. They say, in fact, that from their standpoint, there has been no progress. Furthermore, as they allege, these "so-called Negro leaders" are kept in their positions and aided and abetted in their injurious activities against their own black people by the support of the Jews. According to this argument, the Jews are therefore as fiercely to be assailed as the "black traitors" themselves. So "Down with the Jews!" they shout in various extremist formulas. "Anti-Semitism!" retort the Jews. Yet these black militants are much more hostile to the traditional "Negro" leaders and organizations than they are to the Jews. And their antagonism to the Jews derives in large part from what they regard as the unholy alliance between Jews and "Negro traitors" to the true interests of the black people. They see Jews as protecting these "traitors" and using their power and influence to advance them wherever possible. Thus they conclude, logically enough, that anyone fighting on the side of their class enemy is fighting against them. But their real objective is the overthrow of the traditional "Negro" leadership. Their quarrel with the Jewish people is merely incidental and arises, on this level, from their hostility to the coalition in which Jews have participated with these, allegedly, discredited "Negro" leaders.

It may be that the Jewish people should become more familiar with the real aims of these black militants. Perhaps they would then recognize that they are not the target. For what these black militants are, in effect, saying to them, in the obscene verbiage of anti-Semitism, is: "You are aiding and abetting these 'Negro' traitors, who are the enemies of the black people. Stop it!" It cannot be easy, of course, for the Jews to abandon their old friends, especially when the latter are under such relentless attack, but it might be well if they were to try to make some new friends among the present—and future— black militants. The incidence of anti-Semitic outbursts would decrease measurably. Nor would it perhaps be unwise on the part of Jews to remove themselves from an exposed position in a black class struggle in which they are caught, strategically, in the middle. The black middle class has social ambitions that upper-class Jewish patronage unwittingly fosters. The black lower classes are only too painfully aware that their own cockroach-tainted food and rat-infested dwellings are part of the price they pay for the privilege bestowed on the black middle class of dining on Park Avenue. The remedy for anti-Semitism in this black class struggle is for the Jewish people to seek and secure the friendship and trust of the black lower classes and their leaders; especially since, despite all the extremist venom, their anti-Semitism is actually more apparent than real.

Black anti-Semitism is in no sense ideological; it is a by-product, although deeply disturbing, of the black class struggle. The root of the trouble between blacks and Jews is that the former, on many levels, expect more large-mindedness and greater generosity of Jews than of any other group within the American society. This attitude can be generalized over a large representation of black people. Yet it is necessary to retain careful sight of reactions conditioned by the various levels on which they occur. On that level where poverty-stricken blacks confront Jewish merchants and landlords, genuine hatred is possible, and does in fact exist, against the Jew who is thought to be an exploiter and a bloodsucker, and this attitude does tend to spread across the whole group of Jewish people like ink spilled on blotting paper. There lies the real danger of black anti-Semitism: there, in the lower depths among the dispossessed. There is where black children catch the disease of anti-Semitism, there in those horrible, festering, rotting slums. Something must be done on this level, and done quickly, for time is running out.

Among the black middle class, with increasing affluence and some slight degree of acceptance on the part of the WASPs, if and when this should occur, a rise in the subtler forms of anti-Semitism such as are endemic in white Gentile circles must be expected. At the present time there is no serious problem of anti-Semitism on this black-middle-class level, for the black middle class continues to be the principal beneficiary of the Jewish social conscience. But it would be unrealistic of Jews not to foresee the possibility of bites to be inflicted on the feeding hand. This, however, is always likely to be a matter of individual ingratitude rather than of group hostility in the form of collective anti-Semitism among the "black *bourgeoisie*." Yet anti-Semitism in America is rampant among the white Gentile middle class. It is a Christian vice and the black Christian middle class is unlikely to be wholly exempt from it. Its present members are not immune as it is. Anti-Semitism does exist, although on a small scale, among the black middle class, and mainly in the form of envy. No one should forget, however, that of all diseases of the human spirit, envy is the deadliest and also the most contagious.

Nor are these prejudices to be found solely in the practices of Gentiles, black and white. There is, among Jews, deep racial prejudice against blacks. Jewish antiblackness was in existence long before the recent outbreak of black anti-Semitism. Indeed, Jewish antiblackness is itself a major cause of black anti-Semitism. For not by any means have all Jews been large-minded and generous-spirited in their attitude toward blacks. Many Jews are as hostile to blacks on racial grounds as any bigoted white Gentiles. Especially on the Jewish lower-middle-class level, though not exclusively there, some have been utterly disgraceful in their dealings with black people. On this stratum of Jewish society, hostility to the advance of black people is both active and overt. It is at this point that the racial conflict in urban housing arises. Here, too, is where the acerbities of competition for jobs grow more intense, and where the order of social precedence comes most sharply under attack. It is, in particular, in this sector of the Jewish community that many Jews have been as racist as some Gentiles in their treatment of the black people. Precisely here is Jewish white racism most evident. But these are individual shortcomings, and they should not be employed to vilify an entire group of people. The Jewish record, although magnificent, is not stainless. Yet where there are blemishes (and it is important to stress this), they have arisen, not out of the body of Jewish religious teachings and ethical precepts, but in direct opposition to them.

Nor is it fair to demand perfection of the Jewish people in their dealings with blacks when blacks themselves are incapable of it in their own dealings with one another. Blacks victimize members of their own group who chance to be lighter-skinned than the rest. It is a form of cannibalism. The darker-skinned blacks attempt to justify themselves by pointing to the former superior status within the black group that the lighter-skinned enjoyed in virtue of their nearer approximation to whiteness. They cite the wrongs inflicted by the lighter-skinned on the darker-skinned by snobbery and condescension. The darker-skinned had remained, in effect, field hands while the lighter-skinned continued to be house servants in the possession of privileges bestowed upon them by Missy and Massa. So, today, with the tables turned, the darker-skinned blacks exact their revenge. Some among them spit at the approach of light-skinned blacks on the streets of Harlem. Wherever possible, dark-skinned blacks exclude light-skinned blacks from the opportunities now at last being made available to the group as a whole. "Half-white nigger" is only one, and by no means the most contemptuous, of the epithets directed against light-skinned by dark-skinned blacks. Cannibalism (for this is what it is in a sublimated form) is no more admirable now, when dark-skinned blacks practice it, than it was when light-skinned blacks engaged in it. Yet it is the spokesmen of these dark-skinned blacks constituting, in the main, the black lower classes (the light-skinned blacks in general were, *ipso facto,* middle class) who in so many instances attack the Jewish people as though they themselves and those they represent were above reproach. It is these people who would rather have inexperienced dark-skinned black incompetents running their community affairs than any light-skinned black, however qualified and able. And yet at the same time they create a continuous din about the prejudice they suffer because they are black. Indeed, they should never cease to cry out while this evil exists, but they must also cleanse themselves.

Black anti-Semitism is, then, to some extent a phenomenon of specific social contact and experience. Where such contact has on the whole been beneficent, as in the case of the Jewish people and the black middle class, anti-Semitism has largely been absent, or, if present, then in the discreetly muted form of material envy. Where such contact has in the main taken place in the slums, between the black lower classes and the Jewish people, between, for instance, Jewish landlords and black tenants, Jewish merchants and black customers, or Jewish welfare workers and blacks on relief, it has had the effect of arousing latent anti-Semitism.

The blacks of America are, predominantly, religious fundamentalists, according uncritical acceptance of the Christian Bible, which, in its pivotal account of the life and death of the founder of the Christian faith, has created a tragic, millennia-long climate of prejudice and hostility against the Jewish people. Christian fundamentalists are, therefore, deeply infected with anti-Semitism. When to this is added, as in the case of urban blacks, the hideous squalor of the slums in which they are condemned to disease, decay, and death, the further rapacity of some landlords and merchants renders their already appalling situation unbearable. When some of these merchants and landlords can be identified as Jewish, the belief of these black fundamentalists in the Biblical account of the crucifixion of Christ distills with terrifying effect the poison of anti-Semitism. And when, finally, the whole complex of circumstances is turned to political account by ambitious extremists, the scapegoat is neither far to seek nor hard to find. He is there: the white entrepreneur in the black ghetto, who may or may not be a Jew, but who will nevertheless so be regarded *pour encourager les autres.*

For the rest, the great majority of blacks—as, most likely, the great majority of whites—do not actively engage in anti-Semitism and do not as a rule indulge in anti-Semitic utterances, but they tolerate them in the latter instance by their silence, and in the former connive at them by their passivity. Where black people exclusively are concerned, the ingredients of anti-Semitism, in so far as they are not already derived from the Christian Bible, are there in the reek and filth of the slums that they are forced to inhabit. The slums not only breed disease, they also create opportunities for demagogues to batten upon the frustrations, hatreds, and despairs that envenom the unfortunate human beings who rot there. To these manifestations on the part of blacks, the Jewish people have reacted with convulsive intensity. But their reaction, which has virtually been unanimous within their community, overlooks a point of pragmatic and perhaps decisive importance. The lower-class blacks to whom, on the whole, these displays of anti-Semitism are confined, have seldom been the beneficiaries of Jewish philanthropic concern. It is the middle-class blacks who have enjoyed this good fortune. The lower-class blacks have, on the contrary, been nearly as much neglected and contemned by the otherwise generous-hearted Jews as by the Gentiles. There is little reason for the lower-class black to make any distinction between white Jews and white Gentiles on this score. The middle-class black has a duty of gratitude in this respect, for he owes much to the charitable interest of the Jews. But the lower-class black may fairly say, although with no unassailable accuracy, that he owes nothing to the Jews; that, in fact, he knows them only as his exploiter.

And it is precisely amongst the black lower class that the outbreak of anti-Semitism has occurred, to which the Jewish people in the mass have reacted with such extreme shock. Black anti-Semitism, like Jewish antiblackness, is a vile thing in any event, but were it the black middle class that had been guilty of these leprous utterances, this large-scale reaction on the part of the Jewish people would have been more understandable. Yet this does not make the anti-Semitic statements of some of these spokesmen of the black lower classes any less nauseating. The brute fact is that the much-vaunted historic alliance between the blacks and Jews was always, at best, a working arrangement between the Jewish middle class and the black middle class under the aegis of the white Anglo-Saxon establishment, between whom and the mendicant black middle class the Jews acted as a *cordon sanitaire.* Middle-class Jews had little, if anything, to do with the lower-class blacks, who were seldom the direct objects of their social beneficence.

The emergence of Africa from colonialism and the political independence being gained increasingly by colored countries are a spur to black nationalism in America. The establishment of the state of Israel has had the same effect upon the Jewish community. Nationalism can be harmless enough when it is restrained within decent bounds. Its inherent dangers usually arise out of its tendency to emotional excesses. It is not difficult in all the tragic circumstances to respect the impulse of self-preservation that constrains, on the part of the Jewish people, the swift outcry of "anti-Semitism." Yet it would perhaps be more effective in many cases if they were to proportion this impulse to the actualities of the existing situation. It should not be resorted to in order to place them, as it were, beyond merited criticism. They will have to decide between being Jews and being white, where blacks are concerned. White Christians confront the same problem. A feeling has developed among some blacks—not all of them by any means extremists—that by trying as resourcefully as they can to make the most of both worlds, Jews merely succeed in demonstrating that there is no necessary contradiction between being a Jew and being a white racist, that, in fact, it is possible for the two to achieve a cynical coexistence.

If the movement toward black separatism is offensive to some whites (and, philosophically, it is just as sterile and backward as the opposite concept of integration), then the onus is not wholly on blacks to modify this trend, but to an even greater extent upon whites to mend their social manners. It must be said, however, that of the white groups within the American society, Jews least of all have given blacks reason to complain on this score. Nevertheless, it is necessary to note a habit among some Jews that can be infuriating. This is the practice of behaving toward blacks as, in the main, other whites do, but when taxed with this fact, of retreating into their Jewishness and crying "anti-Semitism." In short, they engage in a sort of shell game. The pea is never there, and the cry of "anti-Semitism" becomes tainted with confidence trickery. Thus some blacks tend to regard Jews as addicted to the exploitation of their whiteness for the power and privilege it confers, and of their Jewishness as a defense against just criticism. There are blacks who resort, by a similar device, to outcries of "racial prejudice," although, in American circumstances, it would be hard to find any large number of occasions on which such an outcry by blacks was wholly unwarranted. This provides one of the most cogent reasons for the plausibility of the propaganda of black separatism. At the present time in America, it is impossible for blacks to associate with whites on anything like a footing of social equality in the overwhelming generality of cases. The determination by most whites to assert their self-styled "racial superiority" at all costs against blacks is so compelling that their personal convictions of egalitarianism, where these exist, are hardly proof against it. This makes social relations with many whites disagreeable and gives rise to distaste amongst blacks for the company of human beings who take so ludicrous a view of themselves. It is boredom with white people, rather than hostility, that has caused many blacks to decide to have as little as possible to do with them. It is tedious in the extreme to have to do with people whose chief pride as human beings is contained in unscientific notions about the alleged ethnic "pre-eminence" to which they are entitled by their skin color.

In the sphere of international relations, anti-Semitism amongst black Americans—to the extent to which it exists—may reinforce such tendencies on the part of African nations already infected with this social attitude. That would be a colossal misfortune for everyone concerned. As contact between black Americans and black Africans grows closer, however, the contagion of black anti-Semitism is likely to spread by carriage to and fro amongst them unless it is checked and brought under effective control or altogether eliminated, if possible. Of the European nations, West Germany, most of all, can be relied upon to put down anti-Semitism with implacable resolve; although, of course, other white nations—for example, Holland and the Scandinavian countries—will be no less resolute, as their past conclusively suggests. But none will have so compelling a motive as West Germany. For some considerable time to come, the policy of the West German Federal Republic toward Israel will be determined by the necessity to compensate the Jews for the frightfulness of the Nazi period and its abhorrent consequences. The only policy that West Germany will be capable of in relation to Israel and world-wide Jewry is one of atonement. Whatever the merits of Israel's position in any circumstances, West Germany will be unable to be impartial. Because of the past, the position of West Germany is bound to be: Israel—

right or wrong; and this with a simple automatism that, ironically, is as immoral in its own way as the Hitlerian excesses of the past.

Clearly, this cannot be the approach to redeem the moral status of a people and redress their collective conscience for evil once committed in their name. To attach them to a policy that is no less unethical in its consequences (however righteous in its motivation) is to condemn them to repeat the past, if only now in a different form.

Unless the growing racial opposition in the world at large is controlled or conciliated, the moral helplessness of West Germany in its "special relationship" with Israel will measurably reinforce the growth of white racism and render more intractable the deep-rooted hostility between blacks and whites, and whites and other nonwhites. Hitler may have largely succeeded in his diabolical attempt to exterminate the Jews of Europe. Yet, in so doing, he also succeeded in binding the corpse of European Jewry, inextricably, to the surviving, mutilated body of West Germany.

11

THE RELATIONSHIP of a legal system to the community in which it functions is, ideally, the result of a long process of organic growth. The system should not have been grafted upon the community, but incubated within it to become a vital part of its living tissue. The Anglo-Saxon system of jurisprudence may be cited as an example of such a development, and so indeed the corpus of Roman law. In each of these instances the legal system evolved out of custom and group responses to given situations; in each, what came into existence was the product of communal necessity as it enforced its demands in moments of crisis or in less exigent circumstances of council and deliberation. Both in form and substance, such systems of law are reflections of the total experience of a group, its history, its ideals. Most clearly of all, they chart and identify the character and consequence of the conflict of classes within the group, for it is from such internal struggles that much of the body of any indigenous jurisprudence emerges, although the influence of external intervention is often considerable and sometimes, in fact, decisive. One has only to note the impact of the Norman Conquest upon the development of English law. If a general proposition were to be formulated as an expression of how legal systems evolve within communities, external conquest and the internal class struggle would be its operative terms. Yet it would be too sweeping a view unless other factors, less dramatic or intrusive, were also remarked. The civil accommodations of a society, its at-

390

tempts to realize its broader aspirations or simply to settle for the sake of the general convenience or advantage practical issues of commonplace affairs also play their part in generating a native jurisprudence. On balance, the test of its truly indigenous quality is to be met on the basis of whether or not it reflects the whole cumulative experience of the community within which it functions.

Taking the former British West Indies as an example, the presence throughout much of that territory of the Anglo-Saxon system of jurisprudence will be remarked at once. The actual sociological circumstances are well known. People of African descent make up the preponderant mass of the area's population. But at no time whatever have African law and tribal custom been allowed a role in the legal system introduced wholesale by Britain simultaneously with its conquest of these islands. (Exceptionally, the Code Napoléon has enjoyed parallel standing as a governing judicature in the island of St. Lucia.) The colonial power established the Anglo-Saxon body of laws and maintained it without regard to communal necessities as those were modified by the changing composition of the inhabitants of that part of the Caribbean. If in the first instance there was a certain logic or social pragmatism about this, since the British settlers who colonized there regulated their relations amongst themselves by these juridical canons, that show of reasonableness vanished with the importation of African slaves. From that point onward, the same processes of logic and social pragmatism required at least a supplemental introduction of African jurisprudence in the form of tribal law wherever possible. The British imperial power made no such attempt. The plight of the enslaved Africans was worsened—assuming that to have been possible—by a catastrophic bewilderment resulting from the loss of the entire network of guides by which their social intercourse had been regulated. They had been removed from a society where the minutest details of their personal and group lives were carefully prescribed into one whose salient characteristic was its compression of slave law into a single canon of bestial repression.

This, too, was the experience of the black slaves on the North American mainland. Here, as well, the British settlers brought with them a common law generated by their Anglo-Saxon system of jurisprudence; and here, as well, the entire corpus of the law governing the enslaved Africans was concentrated with the most callous insensitivity into a sole commandment of brutal exploitation.

It is this historical circumstance, and all that went with it, which, together with the whole course of other events past and present, is now implied when one speaks of the "black experience" in the Western Hemisphere. And if it be granted, as indeed it must, that a binding system of laws should mirror the gross collective experience of a community, then it is clear that the Anglo-Saxon body of law, which, in fundamentals, remains extant in the United States, can only present a distorted image of the group experience of its black population.

To transfix a specific point of distortion: the sociological history and present legal actuality surrounding the position of blacks in America combine, in so far as this group of people is concerned, to give the lie to the juridical presumption of innocence in the Anglo-Saxon system.

The black experience in America, past and present, is irrefutable proof of the cynicism of this presumption.

Long, long before the appearance of the Black Panthers, and for centuries before the birth of Angela Davis, to be black in America was always to be guilty—of being black. Whatever else any black may or may not have been innocent of has always been, as a rule, of minor substance alongside the major fact of blackness, imputing, by its own existence, guilt. So arbitrary has been the disregard of normal legal processes from police to judiciary in matters involving blacks in America that the inevitable consequence is a chronic miscarriage of justice procured by racist abortions of law.

Two modern instances antedating contemporary black victims of American injustice are Angelo Herndon, railroaded into a Georgia chain gang, and the infamous case of the Scottsboro boys. There are so many others that to recite them all in their vast legion would simply achieve an infinite catalogue of racial iniquity. The two instances illuminate by restricted, though representative, selection. They locate, in the racist principle of black caste inferiority within the compass of American society, at least one of the reasons why law has been subverted in its civilizing function as a servant of an enlightened popular will into a corrupt and despotic master. They indicate why the administration of justice has fallen so widely into disrepute, and the judiciary in so many instances become an object of increasing contempt. Moreover, they suggest something of the nature of the distortions that afflict a society when the fundamental principles of its existence are betrayed by the contradictory character of its practices.

To deny justice to any group in a society is to render the whole society a legitimate arena for revolution. When the rationale for injustice is an assertion of racial prejudice, the only question is how much of the society should be preserved and how much destroyed? It is, then, no longer a matter of maintaining the society intact in deference to its original principles. It will have become a task of moral regeneration and institutional reconstruction to be carried out by those to whom, as previously suggested, it is more important to be human than to be white.

If the judiciary is to fulfill its paramount role as an arbiter of internal conflict, it will be obliged to assume this task of regeneration and reconstruction as a function of more important social consequence than the legalistic determination of guilt or innocence, the investiture or divestiture of rights, the location of wrongs, and the parceling out of indemnities. In short, the judiciary is faced with transforming its traditional attitude toward the problems of society by revolutionizing its basic assumption that property takes precedence over people. The inarticulate axiom of the Anglo-Saxon system of law is an implicit statement that human rights and the rights of property exist together in an indissoluble bond; and that any conflict arising between them is, imperatively, to be resolved in favor of property. The mental outlook of judges operating within this system derives its perspectives and warrants its determinations by conscious reference to that axiom. Like the polestar to a navigator, it is their direction finder amidst the navigational complexities of the law. The dictum that "possession is nine-tenths of the law" is not simply a happy phrase of innocent consequence. Embodied in its epigrammatic elegance is a grim restatement of the historic resolve of Anglo-Saxon jurisprudence to subordinate the rights of human beings to the claims of property.

Anyone who conceives it to have been a symptom of the workings of chance, and nothing more, that the land law of England remained virtually unchanged for 600 years is insufficiently acquainted with the class tyranny, based on property, that defines so large an area of English law from the statute *Quia Emptores* to the passage of the Law of Property Act of 1925, several centuries later. Nor will it have escaped the notice of students of this jurisprudence that human beings acquired greater social importance as ruling-class assertions of the primacy of property were reduced in their capacity to govern relations between men. If the genius of the Tudor dynasty in England was manifested, in the main, by its readiness to preside over the inception of the social movement from a framework of hereditary status to free contract, it is also necessary to concede that in the result it did not abolish or even attenuate the supremacy of property. What in fact it did accomplish was simply the substitution of a new form of property for the old until then regnant over the lives of men. It was their peerless insight into the historical process in England that enabled the Tudors to recognize that the national destiny awaited at that precise juncture translation from a paramount concern with purely domestic issues to engagement in the maritime incertitudes of expansion overseas; and that the country would be unable to pursue its destiny, let alone realize it, if the tremendous social energies imprisoned by the feudal tradition of status were not released and augmented by the still larger concourse of energies at the disposal of the innovation of contract. For this, a new class had to be called into being to redress the inadequacy of the old. In the new commercial entrepreneurs, of whom the Cecils were at once the prototypes, as they were subsequently the paladins, the Tudors found the nucleus of a middle class whose demands upon the future exceeded in passion and superseded in organizational efficiency the allegiance of the old ruling class to a feudal past. Yet, while an effective transfer of the class repository of the state power was accomplished, property nevertheless remained undisturbed and indeed unchallenged as the primary producer of wealth, which, in turn, determined the ability to bargain with true freedom and the prospect of fair advantage in the new arena of contract.

In the end, therefore, status had not actually been abolished. It had not even been enfeebled. The dress was tailored to a new mode, but the material was the same. Status derived no longer solely or mainly from the ownership or possession of land. It flowed now as copiously from successful trade and commercial enterprise. But the notion of contract had ended the monopoly formerly exercised by land as a creator and preserver of status. This had consequences that were no less than revolutionary, though centuries would elapse before the lives of men, in their class relations, could bear incontrovertible witness to that fact. Yet Bosworth Field produced for the social structure of England consequences that were in no sense less momentous than those resulting from the middle-class inspired attack in 1789 on the entrenched feudalism of the French aristocracy or the similar event in Russia in 1917. The war waged by the Union against the Confederacy in the United States in 1861 until Appomattox also had, as one of its incidental results, an effect similar to that of Bosworth Field in that it weakened the grip on the defeated South of the feudal concept of status and inaugurated its displacement by the notion of contract, in so far at least as a substantial number of the inhabitants of the region, namely, manumitted black slaves, were concerned. A general proposition may be formulated to the effect that as a society moves from a presiding concept of status to one of contract, the primacy of property as a determinant of the relations between human beings is diminished. It cannot however be asserted with equal truth that it is displaced. What it does accomplish with more immediate effect is the removal of a decisive quantum of power from one class to another within the society.

But the innovation of contract as a governing principle of human relations does not in any case work social magic. Care must be exercised to forestall such an illusion. The objective situation must be considered with scrupulous regard. Thus it is at once evident that the paramountcy of the notion of contract in the social ideology of the United States has been inadequate to secure in practice that equality which is among the fundamental professions of the Declaration of Independence. And while the racial situation of black Americans is an obvious illustration of the practical inefficacy of this profession, there are other instances in point. For the most part, they may be traced to the inherent incapacity of a moral assertion, an enunciation of principle, to ensure its own supremacy. Always must it depend upon power of a more tangible character to render it relevant and provide it with jurisdictions where its writs may run. Clearly, there can be no equality in the arena of contract between parties of unequal bargaining capacity. Moreover, since wealth does continue to confer status—even if land or its ownership or possession now no longer operates exclusively or chiefly, as it once did, to produce this result—status remains a function or perquisite of wealth. And the prime constituent of wealth is property.

But whether incapsulated in a social theory and institutions of status or crystallized in a concept and practice of contract, property persists in its immemorial role in certain societies as the ruling principle of human relations. Within such societies property ordains the subserviency of the judiciary as an instrument to perpetuate its sovereignty over all human relations. The law administered by judges is a network of regulations designed to this end. Judges are, accordingly, agents of a system whose central principle is the supremacy of property. They have no concern with justice in the abstract, and in so far as they may be said to deal with concrete questions of justice, they do so as functionaries within a social order where property is the major end to be subserved. Judges are therefore acolytes of property. Their assumptions, ratiocinations, decisions, all take their content from the need to give precedence to the claims of property, which is the institutional basis of the administration of justice. Litigants propose; property disposes. And since property has a reciprocal relationship with power, the one interchangeably procreating the other, the social synthesis thus constructed is the source of definition from which justice derives its content.

At this point, inescapably, one or another of the multiple guises in which the alliance between property and power reveals itself must be dealt with. There is no difficulty in recognizing the lineaments of this alliance in the features of the judiciary. Power as property, or property as power—both alike, indifferently, are the spawning ground of the administrators of the law. And the law is, in turn, the rules promulgated by property-as-power for its own self-preservation, for the law is the expression of the dominant interests in a society whose ruling principle is the supremacy of property. The supremacy of law is a mere fiction. So is the impartiality of the judiciary. Judges, who are the servitors of a system in which property is sovereign, can only perform in character: they are obliged to exercise their functions on a class basis, whose intrinsic allegiance is, of necessity, to that sovereign, namely, property, by which the class was created. Within the system of Anglo-Saxon law, judges owe their existence to property-as-power. They are in any case minions of power, and since power is the prerogative of that class which is in major control of the resources of the society, judges, in their collective capacity as a judiciary, are the institutional tools of the dominant social class. They are as a whole helpless in the situation in which they find themselves. They may interpret the law, but they are governed by rules of interpretation that are responses to the claims of the governing class (the largest holders of property) for the protection of its interests.

Nowhere is this seen so clearly as in the rules of criminal law, by which judges are constrained to inflict savage reprisals upon those who impermissibly invade the rights of property. One may with greater impunity desecrate a church than rob a bank. The penalty in the former case is much less severe than in the latter. On the civil side, perhaps nothing else so illuminates the inherent inequality of class positions in a property-dominated society as the measure of damages applied to the calculation of injury to the reputation of a rich man as contrasted with a poor man. The quantum of indemnity arrived at in the latter instance will inevitably reflect the lower-class position by comparison with the former. What is expressed by this illustration is the class power of property to command not only adequate but even excessive redress for any alleged wrong. Judges obey the behests of power. Their own powers are, transparently, derived from the governing institution of property-as-power, precisely as fragments derive from a larger nucleus.

Juries and the police are adjuncts to the judicial process; that is, they are auxiliary arms of property-as-power. Originally, in the early legal history of England, juries were impaneled on a principle of composition that drew its warrant from the likelihood of their residence in the same neighborhood as an accused person, making them the best assessors of the facts alleged against him. A man's peers, it was thought, were the proper evaluators of his guilt or innocence. The custom told a good deal about the sociological structure of England. Feudalism regulated the lives of the inhabitants of the country, which was divided into small social units. There were no large cities as we know them today. A journey of a few miles took an inordinate length of time as a rule, and communications seemed to impede rather than expedite the passage of information from one place to another. People were isolated within tiny administrative units, with certain exceptions, and everyone knew everyone else within those units: their habits, dispositions, and occasions. They were born, reared, carried on their lives, and eventually died under what in literal fact was the national pattern of mutually supervised existence from the cradle to the grave. In those sociological circumstances, the rationale of the jury system had substantial logic and an undoubted practical effectiveness on its side. The institutions of a society, at their most efficient, are organic improvisations based upon convenience or dictated by necessity. The jury system, in keeping with the then contemporary feudal structure of English society, was designed and administered on a class basis. A "jury of one's peers" was not an empty phrase. Nothing makes this plainer than the fact that well into the twentieth century a member of the English aristocracy could be tried only by a jury composed of his fellow aristocrats. But the important point to be borne in mind is the essential character of the jury system as a sociological attempt, in its English origin, to invest a legal innovation with the principle of the feudal differentiation of classes.

The jury system has evolved through the centuries, but it cannot as yet be said that its traditional class character has vanished. Blue-ribbon juries in the United States are evidence to this effect. There is further evidence. "Twelve good men and true" are not infallibly discovered by reference to an indiscriminate roster of voters at political elections. All sorts of undesirables cast ballots at such elections and, as a result, in some places are recruited for possible service as jurors. This process is not rendered acceptable simply by labeling it democratic. Moreover, one of the effects of poverty is that it disfranchises the poor by making them apathetic to the exercise of the right of suffrage. Deprived by their poverty of the incentive to register as voters or otherwise coerced and intimidated, as in parts of the South, into abdicating their right to do so, their names are not inscribed on voting lists from which in some instances jurors are summoned.

The poor (that is to say, the propertyless) have therefore in general been ill-represented on juries. Those who are not poor (not necessarily the rich or even the well-to-do), having greater incentive—because greater hope—to reform or remove their social or economic ills through participation in the political process, have tended to make certain that they vote. Thus they have found their way onto juries, whether by this route or some other, as a consequence of their lesser degree of alienage, if nothing more, from the possession or ownership of property. On the whole, accordingly, the poor are judged by the not-so-poor, the well-to-do, and the rich. Their civil liability is established or denied, their guilt or innocence in criminal proceedings determined, not by their peers or, necessarily, by "twelve good men and true," but by their economic betters—their class superiors in a society stratified by fundamental belief and practice into propertied and unpropertied. This has worked much mischief in the case of the blacks, who comprise, proportionately, the largest segment of those who are poor in the United States; yet, not only among them.

There are other observations to be made about the jury system. One of the most obvious is that, from an institutional point of view, it has grown obsolete. Scientific developments, especially in the field of human psychology, have made clear the inadequacy of a procedure whereby twelve individuals are scrambled together and saddled with an obligation that they possess no trained competence to discharge. Like every other body of men and women, they are not immune to sentiment and not exempt from bias, conscious or unconscious, in issues whose highest resolution depends on inviolable impartiality. Judges themselves are not impartial. They cannot be, since they are products of a society that has trained and selected them to secure the sovereignty of property. They sit where they do as representatives of a system whose major premise consists of an assertion of its own unassailable righteousness. They affect to dispense justice. But the fact is, they cannot. What they do is defend the system they pledged themselves to uphold as a condition of their taking office. That is, in unrefined realism, the meaning of their undertaking to uphold the law. For, as has been said, the law is simply the body of rules formulated from time to time by those who possess the controlling power in a given society. The "majesty" of the law is pure humbug. And the pretense to administer justice is on the same level. The entire process is of much the same character as rolling loaded dice in a crooked gambling joint. The loaded dice are in the hands of the rich; the judges are the croupiers. And the game they play is property-as-power.

The rich treat "justice" as a commodity that they are able to purchase through the processes of the courts. Where the rich are concerned, the mythological figure of justice peers beneath the blindfold that otherwise, in the case of the poor, is firmly in place. Where the rich are concerned, justice counterpoises the scales in their favor with the weights of property. "The law, in its impartial majesty," said Anatole France, "forbids the rich as well as the poor to sleep beneath bridges." This is an expression, at once felicitous and ironic, of the impartiality of law in a society whose central magistracy reposes in the possession or ownership of property. The function of juries, therefore, as ancillary instruments of the law, is less to arrive at verdicts of civil liability and criminal culpability, or their converse, than to lend color to the affectation on the part of society that justice is the object of the elaborate ritual of legal inquiry. Actually, of course, it is nothing of the sort. What is sought is the convenience of society, which further defines itself as a class interest attached to that segment of the whole which, at the given moment, is in effective possession of the power of the society. In every circumstance, it is the values of such a class that the courts and the law are designed to foster and maintain. And though the identity of the class may change from time to time, the object is always the same. It is not an inherent evil of the capitalistic system any more than it is an intrinsic vice of socialism.

Every judge and every juror—in fact, all who participate in the processes of the courts of law as elements of the official arm—is an embodiment of class biases. To the extent that the participants have benefited from the sovereignty of law in the society of property-as-power, to that extent will they in general be biased in favor of its perpetuation. To the extent that they have been disadvantaged, to that extent will they in general be biased against its perpetuation. It is obvious that judges as a whole belong to the former class. The same assertion cannot be made with equal warrant in the case of jurors. These are recruited in many instances from diverse levels of society, both possessors and dispossessed. A general proposition is informulable in this case. Yet this is not quite the main point; which is that, regardless of their condition, what the society requires of jurors as participants in the judicial and ancillary or adjunctive processes of the courts of law is that they maintain at all events the values of the system that sponsors the pageant of justice. Implicit in this requirement is the social attitude that it is better for 1,000 innocent men and women to be wrongfully punished than for the slightest injury to be done to the established order.

The recent spate of conspiracy trials illustrates this point. One such in particular may be briefly cited. Thirteen black men and women, members of an organization known as the Black Panthers, were each, after a trial lasting eight months, acquitted on all of twelve counts alleging conspiracy to commit various unlawful acts. The trial had been marked by accusations of bias on the part of the presiding judge. These accusations were made by the lawyers for the defense. At least one of the jurors also felt so strongly that the judge was biased that he had to be restrained by his fellow jurors from interrupting the trial with an open denunciation of the judge. Yet if it were true that the judge was biased, it would have also been true that he was not only expressing his personal hostility to the defendants and what they represented as a threat to the established order, but the hostility as well of much of white society toward them. The defendants were present in that court, charged as they were, because they questioned the values of a society contemptuous of them and inconsiderate of their welfare. The judge was present in that court, sitting where he did, because he accepted the values of a society respectful of him and considerate of his welfare. He and the persons toward whom he was sworn to administer justice were in direct class conflict, with interests in antipodal opposition. The justice he was sworn to administer was, in actuality, nothing more than the maintenance of the interests of that class whose panoplied agent he was, and whose values he embodied in all the regalia of his judicial trappings.

Judges are class functionaries and nothing else. They derive their position and their powers from the dominant class in society, and their values, which are identical with those of that class, or, at any rate, not markedly dissimilar from them, are the cumulative consequence of their experience and ambition. They derive their "just powers" from the consent of the governing class, "just" being defined, automatically, as the interests of that class. The function of a judge is to act as the guardian of those interests. In so doing, he sets his judicial seal upon the values that are the rationalization of those interests.

Little was therefore to be expected in the way of class sympathy between the judge in the case of the Black Panthers and the defendants. Their mutual hostility was perfectly natural. This is the major circumstance that the rules of legal decorum, the class demand of respect for the judge, and the reverential attitude imposed on citizens in a courtroom are intended to conceal. At all costs, regardless of class actualities, the pretense must be upheld that justice is being done. The value of this fiction to the dominant class in the society is obvious. They make the rules, and they manipulate them in the macabre game they call justice, in which they try to ensure that they will be the only winners.

The verdict of acquittal arrived at by the jury in the case of the Black Panthers did not vindicate the legal system. On the contrary, it was a condemnation of that system which, after all, had spent something in the vicinity of $1 million and an inordinate length of time, involving in some instances prolonged detention of the defendants before trial, in a concerted effort to procure their conviction on nebulous charges of conspiracy. Neither, specifically, was it a vindication of the jury system. Where that was concerned, it simply indicated that the prosecution had not succeeded in picking the right jury.

When, in the South, blacks were put on trial (and all the defendants in the case of the Black Panthers were blacks, though their counsel with one exception were whites), there used never to be any make-believe that the composition of the jury must appear to guarantee an impartial trial. A conviction was the unconcealed objective, so whites only were placed in the jury box. In the North, although the objective was the same, traditional hypocrisy required that the appearance of fairness be maintained whatever the substantial injustice to be perpetrated. Five of the jurors in the trial of the Black Panthers were blacks.

The British, with their typical flair for social illusions, have implanted the core of their system of administering justice in the maxim that "Justice must not only be done, but must be seen to be done." The British are not here enunciating a juridical ideal so much as they are recommending a principle of illusion. The law is a conjuror's art, they are saying, and its practice an act of legerdemain. The important thing is not whether the magician does in fact produce a rabbit from his hat, but that he *appear* to do so. There is the delight of prestidigitation, where skillful illusion is as much to be admired on the stage as in the courts of law—themselves a species of theater. Besides, so long as justice, like religion, was the province of the learned classes, who, in turn, were the beneficiaries of the patronage dispensed by the propertied class in power, other aids to illusion were also brought into service. As the magician engages in mumbo jumbo, articulating gibberish—hey, presto!—in order to add the distractions of the ear to the deflections of the eye, so did the learned acolytes of the law employ the ancient Latin tongue. The habiliments of judges and lawyers, the recondite sound of obscure or unknown verbal usages, and the tortuous mazes, the labyrinthine procedures, in which justice was at length to be sought—all conspired to restrict the search to those, the propertied classes, who had contrived its inaccessibility.

In such circumstances, Justice might coerce, might intimidate, and might awe, yet never—or, certainly, seldom—redress. But the illusion was maintained. The interest of the dominant class in the society demanded no less. If justice were indeed to be done, and not—illusively—seen to be done, the result would be a social revolution. Much depends therefore on the adroitness of the illusionists. Their skillfulness or lack of it is the difference between mass upheaval and the preservation of law and order. The unskillful illusionists of the Weimar Republic gave Hitler his opportunity. He came to power, as his counterparts—whatever their democratic costume—are accustomed to do, in the name of "law and order." He declared:

The streets of our country are in turmoil. The universities are filled with students rebelling and rioting. Communists are seeking to destroy our coun-

402

try. Russia is threatening us with her might. And the Republic is in danger. Yes, danger from within and without. We need law and order . . . without law and order our nation cannot survive. [Cited by Justice William O. Douglas, U.S. Supreme Court, in *Points of Rebellion*.]

This is the typical diatribe of social reactionaries. It is immediately obvious that theirs is not a concern with justice, but with law and order to the exclusion of justice; with law and order related to justice as appearance is to substance. The reactionaries always manipulate the appearance of law and order so as to withhold the substance that is justice. And since justice must mean, inescapably, the distribution of equity in social practice so that no individual or group shall be advantaged or disadvantaged by partiality or bias on any ground whatsoever, law is usually invoked to frustrate justice in any society dominated by class interest. The ensuing turmoil then warrants the next step, which is the invocation of order.

In certain societies, notably the United States, the illusion of doing justice is rendered more difficult of accomplishment by the blatant fact of racial prejudice against blacks. The pretense has indeed been so difficult to maintain that it was virtually abandoned in some parts of the United States. Where some semblance of it was preserved, it produced the ironical effect of emphasizing the substantial absence of anything in the nature of justice available to blacks. Among whites, class interests or sectional politics might operate, and habitually did, to deny justice. The blacks were also disadvantaged in this respect by the intervention of class interests. And since they occupied the lowest class in the society, they were, as a category, the most disadvantaged of all. Their situation, undesirable as it already was, became greatly worsened by the supremacy of white racism as a social principle of American life. Justice was therefore inaccessible to them from the dual standpoint of class and of race. White groups, such as Jews and Roman Catholics, also discovered in their religious affiliations a social bar to justice in addition to particular class exclusions. Yet these never approached even remotely within the American society the wholesale crippling effect they inflicted upon the black group. At this point cultural prejudice became racism. Religious bias, which is characteristic of all societies, was subordinated in point of social pathology to racism, which is characteristic in particular of white Christian Europe and its cisatlantic transplant the United States of America, its Oceanic outpost of Australia, and its enclaves of South Africa and Rhodesia, as well as of Canada. In so far as the

United States is concerned, this development has had, and continues to have, profound and pervasive social consequences for blacks. Its effect upon the jury system is seen in the tragic farce to which, from the standpoint of black Americans, white racism has further reduced this legal institution, artificially kept alive by class interest long after its original justification of feudal convenience had vanished.

In a society so completely in the thrall of class interest and so deeply infected by white racism, the impossibility of impaneling an impartial jury is plain to anyone who is devoted to the ideal of justice rather than to the idolatry of law and order. If justice delayed is justice denied, it is at least as axiomatic that the ideal of law and order immoderately emphasized is repression malevolently contrived and revolution fomented.

Revolution in this context means the attempt, concerted or unconcerted, to procure, peaceably or by violence, changes within a society leading to the redistribution, either wholly or in significant part, of the total components of power—social, economic, and political—among the various classes of the society. In this process, the dynamic of the movement receives its impulse from a class conception of social justice, to which the body and administration of law are integral. In the case of black Americans, this dynamic draws as well upon another source of social energy: the pathology of white racism. This is merely another way of expressing what already is quite obvious: the most unsettling factor in the American society is white racism; it is more than anything else an instigator of revolution. In so far as there is a black revolution in progress (and this, to repeat, is a debatable assumption), it is incited by white racism. Without white racism there would be no so-called black revolution. Black discontent there would be, conceivably, on the order of white disaffection in the region of the Appalachians; black protest on the order of the Jewish demand for top executive positions in American banking and the steel industry; black ethnocentrism, even in the belated form in which it has appeared, on the order of Gaelic-American or Polish-American or Italian-American organizations; black monopolies on the order of the Anglo-Saxon hegemony over some aspects of American life. Black modes and values would then be directly imposed, instead of, as at present, infiltrated through vernacular channels. Such values would also generate their own importance, warranting themselves, instead of deriving that importance intermediately from white acceptance.

Such a revolution has far more relevancy to the administration of justice than might at first appear. Questions of guilt and innocence are issues of fact that reflect the values of a society. The disposition to find the one or the other in specific instances is motivated by acceptance or rejection of those values. In a society where the values of white racism and the claims of class interest are central, guilt and innocence as questions of fact tend to be determined by the tenets of white racism and the allegiances of class. The net effect of any trial in such circumstances can only be an assertion of these values against a transgressor or transgressors. Since blacks inherently—and visibly—sin against these values by being black, there is, quite clearly, what may be described as an implicit tendency on the part of the society as a whole to find them guilty in any case. This tendency is expressed within the context of legal institutions by the hostility of the judiciary, the inordinate bias of prosecuting attorneys, the brutal antagonism of police, and the inclination of juries, wherever whites are in the majority, to convict rather than acquit black defendants regardless of the evidence. In addition to whatever else they may be charged with, black defendants are always, *ipso facto*, guilty at least of being black.

Together with its institutional obsolescence, therefore, as a fossil survivor of a feudal past, the jury system in its present form and function is a legal instrument for the assertion of the racist values of the United States. And this is so even when blacks themselves are members of juries. In most cases they have accepted the generic scheme of values, despite their rejection of white racism. Moreover, no jury is enclosed in a vacuum during the progress of a trial. The injunction against reading newspapers, once deemed an adequate precaution, must now extend to listening to the radio and viewing television. It is altogether inadequate nowadays, in view of the crude or subtle but nevertheless all-pervasive envelopment of the general attention by the media of communications.

To eliminate as far as possible the insidious influence of these media upon juries, and to neutralize the effects of their prior indoctrination with the social values of white racism, juries should be comprised of panels of individuals especially trained for the purpose. Their function should be expressly designed as a professional adjunct to the work of the judiciary. They should be trained in the expert and impartial assessment of evidence, their numbers reduced to panels of from three to five, and, preferably, they should be lawyers working in the capacity of public ombudsmen. A valuable social use would thus be found for the existing superfluity of lawyers (relatively, that is, to the economic resources of the litigants who hire their services). They would then become auxiliary judges, tendering advice to the court on questions of law, and having the power of final determination of issues of fact. But first and foremost, they would be subjected to rigorous psychological tests, as a condition of their employment, to assure their freedom from racism. And they would be servants of the people rather than agents of that official abstraction of the popular will known as the state.

This distinction between people and state is of the utmost practical consequence. Prosecutions are instituted in the name of the people that are, actually, measures taken by the class in power to maintain its predominant position in society. This class (or group) assumes the prerogatives and carries out the functions of the state. The interests of such a class (or group) in the guise of the state often conflict with those of the people. It is manifestly in the interest of the people of the United States, as a whole, to disengage this country from the Vietnam war. Opposed to this, however, is the interest of the state—meaning, partly, what President Eisenhower once called the military-industrial complex—in prolonging the role of the country in this gruesome and unprofitable adventure. The state in its war-making function incorporates the military-industrial complex. And, as much controversy between the executive and the legislature has indicated, the state sometimes engages in activities that are not simply at variance with the popular will embodied in elected representatives, but in outright defiance of it. Similarly, there is ground for the belief that a national referendum held to ascertain the general view of the usefulness of conspiracy trials based on suspicion of motives arising out of political dissent would disclose preponderant sentiment against the practice. It would be in the interest of the people to end the recourse to political repression in the form of conspiracy trials. These trials are an effective instrument in the hands of the state for intimidating its critics and putting down opposition. So the people are not likely to be consulted as to the desirability of the practice; they are only likely to continue to be victimized by it—until by one means or another they succeed in changing the composition of the state. If they are able to do so peaceably, the process is called, in general, reform through constitutional pro-

406

cedures; if by violence, it is called revolution. Yet it would be an oversimplification to distinguish reform from revolution by the single test of whether or not violence was employed as the fulcrum of change. These general observations are necessary in order to disentangle the people, as a sovereign entity, from the state, its plenipotentiary. The two concepts are often confused. Sometimes they are also fused on obscure principles of pretended legitimacy. But only in metaphysical speculations on the nature of the state is it ever identified with the people. In political actuality, the state is most accurately described as an ungrateful parasite. It battens on the people and at the same time despises and misuses them.

There has grown up, accordingly, a class of supercitizens in the United States, operating through superbureaucratic institutions, which, taken together, is the logical end of the process that breeds from the people a state to coerce and contemn them. Nothing is at once so remarkable and so characteristic of the United States (aside from white racism) as the contempt of elected officials for the people who elected them, or the arrogance with which a citizen, elevated by some exercise of the popular will, direct or indirect, to high or low office, thereafter treats the source of his elevation—namely, the people. To watch the President of the United States—any President of the United States—in his metamorphosis from political candidate, beguiling and cajoling, to elected officeholder, condescending and disdaining, is to witness an exercise of the most calculated cynicism in the "degradation of the democratic dogma."

The whole apparatus of the state needs to be divested of the authoritarian character by which it supersedes its origin as an instrument of the sovereign will of the people and arrogates to itself, contemptuously, powers that in the spirit and intent of their exercise usurp that sovereignty.

No one observing the performance of the judiciary and the police in their respective duties would suspect for a moment that these functionaries were, after all, employees of the citizen-taxpayers upon whose suffrage and labor depended their offices and emoluments. One would be hard put to reject the suspicion that they owed their positions to some extraterrestrial power from whom they had received a mandate to be contemptuous of citizens, in general, and of those less privileged, in particular; especially, of course, the blacks. All echelons of the civil magistracy, from the office of the Presidency

407

downward, should be realigned with the equalitarian ideals of democracy. There can be no room for supercitizens or suprainstitutionalism. The President must become an equal citizen; so must the members of the judiciary, and the police. The aspiration of public service should not be office but citizenship. Only thus can the true balance be kept between public ambition and respect for people who are, after all, individual embodiments of the sole meaning that the state can ever possess, which is, to be the servant, and not the master, of the people.

The antithesis in social actuality between law and justice is a direct outcome of an inverted relationship between the state and the people, by which the latter are regarded as achieving their highest consummation as citizens when they conform with exemplary obedience to the former's commands. It is in fact nothing short of remarkable with what tenacity the English jurist John Austin's theory of command as the prerogative of property in the form of the state has survived well into current usages. Neither should the disrepute into which Locke's notion has fallen—that of a consensual relationship between state and citizens, derived from the postulate of a social contract—go unremarked. Our lives as citizens of the modern polity of the United States are dominated by the Austinian concept, which is to be distinguished from authoritarianism only by the pious sanctimony in which it is couched.

Law as command leads, inevitably, to the servility of the citizen, from which he can be redeemed only by the concept of law as consent. But it must be a genuine consent. The democratic fiction that merely procures the appearance of consent is a fertile source of the mutual exclusiveness of law and justice. Authoritarianism is often indebted for its existence to the artificial shams of democracy. One of the most flagrant of such shams is the charade of substituting law and order for justice as the grand design of human society. When this is the case, then revolution, whether violent or nonviolent, is summoned up from the discontents and despairs of society.

Property is, to repeat, in general invested with a conceptual sovereignty in the theory and practice of Anglo-Saxon law. The American body of this jurisprudence was illuminated by an observation of William H. Rehnquist (now a Supreme Court Justice), reported to have been made during the 1952 term of the Supreme Court, when he was a law clerk to Justice Robert H. Jackson. A memorandum

408

written by him on the issue of public-school segregation contained the following statement: "To those who would argue that 'personal' rights are more sacrosanct than 'property' rights, the short answer is that the Constitution makes no such distinction." The Madisonian view, as stated in *The Federalist*, Number 54, is not substantially at variance with that of Rehnquist.

Government is instituted no less for protection of the property, than of the persons of individuals. . . . In the Federal Constitution . . . the rights of property are committed into the same hands with the personal rights.

Nothing so elucidates the notional sovereignty of property as the governing norm of Anglo-Saxon jurisprudence, however, as the history of the right to vote. Well into the nineteenth century in England property qualifications were attached to the electoral franchise. The ownership of property was the decisive test of a man's eligibility to vote. As regards the British position during the period when *The Federalist* was being produced, Madison had this to say:

It was shewn in the last paper, that the real representation in the British House of Commons very little exceeds the proportion of one for every thirty thousand inhabitants. Besides a variety of powerful causes, not existing here, and which favor in that country, the pretensions of rank and wealth, no person is eligible as a representative of a county, unless he possess real estate of the clear value of six hundred pounds sterling per year; nor of a city or borough, unless he possess a like estate of half that annual value. To this qualification on the part of the county representatives, is added another on the part of the country electors, which restrains the right of suffrage to persons having a freehold estate of the annual value of more than twenty pounds sterling according to the present rate of money.

The organic law of the United States formulated in the Constitution was a conservative instrument in many respects. It abandoned to the individual states the decision as to universal manhood suffrage for the inhabitants of the country. Slaves, of course, and women were not considered to be within the terms of this question. They could not vote. But the former were enumerated for the purpose of establishing the population base in the apportionment of representation, and so were the latter. But neither could exercise the right of suffrage, the latter because of the disadvantage of sex and the former because of the prohibition of servitude. The progressive amelioration of the position of women in this regard culminated in their general enfranchisement in 1920 by the Nineteenth Amendment to the Constitution. But even after their emancipation in 1865, the voting rights of the blacks, men and women alike, remained severely circumscribed. Poll taxes, fraudulent exclusion, coercion, intimidation, and murderous force were, and continue to be, although now in a reduced degree, among the incidents of that circumscription.

A certain piquancy inheres in the position of women. As early as 1694, in *A Serious Proposal to the Ladies,* Mary Astell lamented the position of women in English society. A century later, Mary Wollstonecraft produced her *Vindication of the Rights of Woman.* "Let us consider women in the grand light of human creatures, who in common with men, are placed on this earth to unfold their faculties." Almost 200 years later, her exhortation echoes with intensified shrillness and desperation, even though in the interim, by dint of the exertions of the suffragettes and other precursors of the Women's Liberation Movement, women have been emancipated to the degree that they may hold property in their own right, make contracts, be elected to public office, sit in legislatures, enter and practice professions, and exercise the right to vote. The Civil War was in progress in America when, in 1861, there appeared in England John Stuart Mill's celebrated work *On the Subjection of Women.* But it was two generations before, in England, the Representation of the People Act (1918) and, in the United States, the Nineteenth Amendment to the Constitution (1920) bestowed the franchise on women.

Essentially the position of women throughout most of the course of Anglo-Saxon jurisprudence might be summarized in Blackstone's observation that "the husband and wife are one, and that one is the husband." As an expression of their social inferiority, that observation is, in essence, no less applicable to the extramarital situation of women. Males in the human society of many cultures have occupied much the same position as males in the cultures of the lower primates: they are dominant. An even more enlightening parallel may be constructed between the position of women and that of slaves. The common element in both cases is the concept of property. For most practical purposes in Anglo-Saxon jurisprudence, women were their husbands' chattels (or, being unmarried, the chattels of the social order) until well toward the end of the nineteenth century in Great Britain. The situation in the United States after the Revolutionary War and the promulgation of the Constitution differed rather in degree than in kind, although, to be sure, the modification of the

410

common law by statutory enactment in the states of the Union during the succeeding years progressively equalized the position of women in relation to property and contract. Yet, whatever the legal enhancements, the social attitudes of males toward women remained largely unmodified. Males continued to regard women as partaking, in effect, of the nature of property to which incidents of ownership were attached in various guises. On the whole, men viewed women as objects of individual or corporate disposition by the male sex. Slaves were viewed similarly. Both women and slaves were property. But there was this difference: while slaves were mere chattels, women were conceded to possess personality. Comparative modulations occurred with the passage of time and legislation, so that the position of women in America now is, roughly speaking, assimilable to that of blacks: the decisive connection between the two groups being the existence of enabling legislation enacted in their interest side by side with the existence of disabling sociological circumstances accumulated and enforced by custom.

It must be remarked that to be regarded as property in the United States is not necessarily a stigma denoting inferiority. The Fourteenth Amendment to the Constitution expressly equates property with life and liberty in the protection to be accorded by due process of law.

James Madison, in *The Federalist*, Number 10, reflects upon the salient position of property as follows:

Those who hold, and those who are without property, have ever formed distinct interests in society. Those who are creditors, and those who are debtors, fall under a like discrimination. A landed interest, a manufacturing interest, a mercantile interest, a monied interest, with many lesser interests, grow up of necessity in civilized nations, and divide them into different classes, actuated by different sentiments and views. The regulation of these various and interfering interests forms the principal task of modern Legislation, and involves the spirit of party and faction in the necessary and ordinary operations of Government.

Since the Constitution is the basic law of the United States, it would be well to bear in mind the actual character of the federal government which it originated. Richard Hofstadter, in *The Progressive Historians*, cites the following quotation from Woodrow Wilson's *Division and Reunion*:

The federal government was not by intention a democratic government. In plan and structure it had been meant to check the sweep and power of

411

popular majorities. . . . The government had, in fact, been originated and organized upon the initiative and primarily in the interest of the mercantile and wealthy classes. . . . It had been urged to adoption by a minority, under the concerted and aggressive leadership of able men representing a ruling class . . . a strong and intelligent class possessed of unity and informed by a conscious solidarity of material interest.

In other words, property.

Hofstadter is also the source of the citation of *Pollock* v. *Farmers' Loan and Trust Co.,* c. 1890, in which a federal income tax was declared by the Supreme Court to be invalid. The judgment of the Court, delivered by Chief Justice Melville Fuller, decided that an operative clause of the Constitution, when interpreted in harmony with the spirit of the Founding Fathers, led to the inference that it was "manifestly designed . . . to prevent an attack upon accumulated property by mere force of numbers." The antipopulist attitude of the Court accurately reflected a like posture on the part of the Founding Fathers. It also revealed their obsessive preoccupation with the rights of property. According to Charles A. Beard, in *An Economic Interpretation of the Constitution of the United States,* of the members of the Constitutional Convention,

the overwhelming majority, "at least five-sixths," were directly and personally interested in the outcome of their labors, being economic beneficiaries of the adoption of the Constitution . . . forty of the fifty-five who attended had public securities, twenty-four of them in amounts over $5,000, and . . . fourteen had personalty invested in lands for speculation, twenty-four had money loaned at interest, eleven were investors in mercantile, manufacturing, or shipping businesses, and fifteen were owners of slaves.

James Madison's formulation, stated previously, that "those who hold, and those who are without property, have ever formed distinct interests in society" is restated by Charles A. Beard in the following language:

Different degrees and kinds of property inevitably exist in modern society; party doctrines and "principles" originate in the sentiments and views which the possession of various kinds of property creates in the minds of the possessors; class and group divisions based on property lie at the basis of modern government; and politics and constitutional law are inevitably a reflex of these contending interests.

From these premises Beard moves to the conclusion that the Constitution was essentially an economic document based upon the

412

concept that the fundamental private rights of property are anterior to government and morally beyond the reach of popular majorities. It is difficult to envisage a more explicit statement of the supremacy of property.

Beard's thesis is susceptible to certain qualifications on the basis of the evolution of the capitalist system. Property now does not mean exactly what it did at the time of the Constitutional Convention. Then it was a relatively simple matter to separate the propertied from the propertyless. But the subsequent development of capitalism has diffused property in one form and another into a vast miscellany of individual ownership, and the true distinction between the former economic categories is now, quite largely, one of degree rather than of kind. It is precisely the question of degree, however, that is crucial. The answer that it generates defines the hierarchy of the rich, the well-to-do, and the poor. And in so doing, it restates the supremacy of property. The ownership and control of property, in all its varying magnitudes from high to middling to low to zero is a prime determinant of access to the privileges and perquisites of the society. The door is widest at the summit and narrows proportionally along the descent. At the lowest point, where the black poor and the white poor squirm and huddle, there is barely a crack; although, in view of the pervasive racist character of the society, even here the door opens more easily to the weight of white than of black pressure. Indeed, for much of the time black pressure at this bottommost level is unavailing.

The capitalist system, in its American evolution, has extended the franchise of property on a scale so vast, so diversified, and so undiscriminating as to render Marx's theory of economic determinism, with its primitive hypothesis of unconditional class warfare, if not wholly invalid, then, at any rate, infirm in its relevancy to the conditions of the American society. Class warfare is a conspicuous fact of life in the United States. Yet it is not, as Marx postulated, a stark conflict between the possessors and the dispossessed. Rather, is it, in significant part, a conflict—an internal conflict—among the possessors: between those who have a great deal and those who, not having quite so much, want more. The struggle, really, is between those shareholders of the great corporations who occupy higher and lower levels of ownership; so that class warfare in the United States is, as a rule, waged not between the haves and the have-nots, but between the haves. The greatest revolutionary pressure in this country is exerted by the white middle class against the white upper class. By comparison, the revo-

413

lutionary pressure that bubbles up from the white poor is trivial. And if the black poor were not, in addition to their poverty, further disaffected by the racial hostility directed against them, the revolutionary pressure that seeps up from them would be still more negligible.

American capitalism is an aberrant development completely unforeseen by Marx. The terms of its evolution and the national circumstances it has constructed are altogether unique. American capitalism must therefore be viewed in its own context, and the peculiar conditions underlying its unparalleled growth contemplated without preconception. Only in this way can the appropriate dialectical instruments be fashioned for its analysis. A society in which the ownership of property is so widely distributed, and where access to the ownership of property is in general beset by no undue hindrances—such a society does not conform to the outlines of the classical breeding grounds of revolution. This does not mean that revolution is therefore either impossible or undesirable. It only means that revolution in these circumstances would proceed from nonclassical causes.

Thus the supremacy of property in America is not, solely as such, an agent of revolution. It is a sociological condition that engenders certain habits of mind, certain kinds of group initiatives and reflexes, certain conformations of collective temper, identities of purpose, similarities of ambition, common ways of looking at things. But, above all, it brings into being a tribal deity to be worshiped, as well as its secular corollary: a paramount economic allegiance to be maintained; and, however it may differ in its political expression, a social loyalty to be subserved.

The economic motivations of the Constitution of the United States, and its antipopulist objectives, cannot now be otherwise than perfectly clear. The basic law of the land has effectively predetermined the quality of its own interpretation. It has also prescribed to a considerable degree the readily demonstrable fact that its interpreters are in the generality of instances subscribers to its orthodoxy. To put it shortly, they are committed by their political affiliations, economic beliefs, and social philosophy to the necessity of upholding the supremacy of property. The presence of anyone hostile to the claims of property on any judicial bench in the United States is unthinkable. This is the cardinal circumstance that invests judges with the professional character of functionaries of property. And since any attempt to view the whole body of law in detachment from its economic impulses and objectives merely condemns itself by its own unreality, the law must be seen for what, in fact, it is: a complex of rules intended to protect and promote the interests of property, which, in turn, is the progenitor of power. If, in Maoist terms, power emerges from the barrel of a gun, then in a capitalist democracy such as the United States it can nevertheless be seen to issue from the ownership and control of property.

Those who do not own property in America or own only some vestigial fraction of it are poor whites and poor blacks. If impulses toward revolution were to exist in the case of the poor whites, they would be more or less classical in their nature. But were they to exist in the instance of the poor blacks, and in so far as they may indeed exist, they must be considered as deviating from classical precedent because of the incidence of racial prejudice. Given, accordingly, a state system in which property is sovereign, and in which social acceptance measurably depends on possession of property and allegiance to the concept of the sovereignty of property, racial prejudice operates in two ways: blackness is regarded as a bar to the acquisition of property on equal terms with whites; and it is treated as a disqualification for the privilege of professing allegiance to the concept of property as sovereign.

"In every society . . ." observed V. L. Parrington in an essay, "Economics and Criticism," "property is sovereign." The inferior caste position of blacks in the American society is a substantial barrier to their participation in the democratic exercise of that sovereignty. One of the most graphic illustrations of their large-scale exclusion is provided by the excessive difficulty they experience in gaining "access to the judicial system," or, having gained it, in securing its unprejudiced scrutiny of their claims. "If you don't have either personal or economic resources, you don't have access to the judicial system," Richard Falk, Professor of International Law at Princeton University, has concluded. The poverty of the large preponderance of blacks, and of a significant number of whites, effectively excludes them from the remedial functions of the judicial system. In the case of the blacks, as has already been pointed out, racial prejudice enlarges the area of their exclusion.

And yet, blacks in general are unattracted to Communism. This is because they equate communism with repression, while the purpose of their struggle in the United States is to win freedom. They also identify Communism with revolution, and since their objective is freedom, they are careful not to confuse the one with the other. Moreover, they are aware that the really dangerous menace to America is white racism, and that the most insidious enemies of this country are its white racists. So they resist the one and the other, as they have done for three and one-half centuries. Their resistance, at its most sophisticated, is expressed in the work of blacks like Roy Wilkins, Ralph Bunche, and Whitney Young. Theirs—these latter's—may, however, be a mistaken emphasis on integration, as it certainly is an erroneous view of the historical fact of this process.

Within the racial caste structure of the American society, as has already been indicated, the integration of blacks has long since occurred. What the present-day proponents of "integration," therefore, are actually clamoring for is something quite different. They are really demanding a fundamental change in the racial caste structure, whereby blacks will no longer occupy the position of "untouchables." By integration they mean, not the assimilation of blacks into the life and values of the society, for this has already taken place, but a change in their caste level from inferiors to equals; which is to ask, in terms, for the radical reshaping of the American society as a whole. The use of the term "integration" is, accordingly, as misleading as it is offensive to the dignity, and destructive of the self-respect, of blacks.

The opposite clamor, for separatism, is just as stultifying. Except as a psychological expedient of a temporary nature, it is utterly pointless. The path between these two extremes is both open and obvious. It is the path of selective co-operation. The climate of the racial caste struggle in the United States would be transformed overnight if only the vociferous clamor for integration were replaced by the quiet pragmatism of co-operation. Clearly, this does not mean unconditional co-operation over the entire range of issues or any at all. What it is intended to suggest is agreement to abandon the childish nonsense of integration by substituting for it a mature program of intelligent action for the good of America; to discard the contemptible rubbish of crying to be with "them" and, equally, the impractical folly of not wanting to be with "them" in any circumstances. The highest wisdom ever bestowed on blacks in America remains Booker T. Washington's: "In all things that are purely social we can be as separate as the fingers, yet one as the hand in all things essential to mutual progress." But while accepting his counsel in this respect, his advice to refrain

416

from political activity must of course be rejected. The historical circumstances have changed. The wisdom of his counsel for selective co-operation continues to be unimpeachable. His advice against political activity is now untenable.

If racial admixture between blacks and whites is to become sociologically respectable and accepted in the United States, then it will do so through intelligently conceived processes of social education, of which the law is an integral part. But this will be the task of enlightened social scientists; it cannot be confided to the parrot cries of politicians or the irresponsible incitements of demagogues.

Black studies at American universities even now are playing a seminal role in generating a new birth of self-respect among black students. And for the first time, in many instances, white students have discovered that blacks are not a people without a past, an outcast group that occurs somewhere outside of history and beyond the pale of useful knowledge. This discovery conduces to a heightening of esteem on their side for the blacks, for theirs is an increasing awareness that black history is not encompassed solely by enslavement and its aftermath on the North American continent. If one of the functions of a university is to attempt the cure of ignorance for the sake of some higher enlightenment, then the argument for black studies, hitherto a wasteland of racist neglect and distortion, is plainly irresistible. A distinguished economist, Sir Arthur Lewis, argued, astonishingly, in an article in the New York *Times Magazine,* against the critical importance of black studies for black students. Indeed, he expressed the hope that "the majority of black students . . . will reject any suggestion that black studies must be the major focus of their programs." His argument, as a whole, laid bare his inadequate appreciation of the sociological reasons for the insistence of large numbers of intelligent blacks on the institution of these studies. Had his acquaintance with the black experience in America been deeper or, better still, derived painfully at firsthand, his article would have done greater justice to his theme.

The need for black studies proceeds from the same order of urgency that dictated the student sit-ins in the South and other incidents of the general complex of black protest and demand. They are all interrelated, and their common bond is precisely the black experience in America. Black studies are invaluable sources, in their own terms, of the diversified cultural information necessary to the

417

harmonious balance of a pluralistic society. Whites acquire from them quite as much enlightenment as blacks. Where blacks specifically are concerned, these studies have the additional value of revealing a historical past that not only illuminates the present, but, even more, redresses their self-image and imbues them with a consciousness of their cultural worth that white racism has been so intent on destroying. The benefit of black studies, then, is shared by both whites and blacks, with a priceless psychological enhancement accruing in the case of the latter. Lewis did not quite grasp this second point. If the racial history of the United States were otherwise than it is, then black studies, with their present emphasis, would be pointless. But in the light of that historical record and its current extension into the attitudes and practices of white racists, black studies are essential; for blacks, uniquely, have always occupied a psychosocial position in America. And to understand the need for black studies, one must also be capable of understanding the psychological reasons underlying the plight of Angela Davis—to cite again this victim of racist pathology. Aside from its sheer educational value, the psychic redress sought by blacks in the institution of black studies is the obverse side of a historical coin of which the reverse is the psychic compulsion of white racists to maintain them in a state of subjection by force and fraud. One ingredient among many manifested by this compulsion is the psychotic need to punish blacks. And in a society in which white males have been accustomed to whipping black women, Angela Davis is a symbolic figure whose recent predicament is a diagnosis of the psychopathology of white racism. The black studies, whose value Lewis questioned, make this quite clear.

Nor did the sit-ins in the South which did so much to stimulate student protest around the world against the persistent betrayal of the brightest hopes of mankind from generation to generation by cynical, selfish, and shortsighted men, spring full-grown from purely contemporary circumstances. Their antecedents were centuries old, and they themselves were the progeny of American history. But since the inscription of this record has largely been the work of white racism, and history thereby perverted by falsehood and bias, objective truth demands the institution of black studies. As a point of departure, which is pretty much where as a racial group blacks are at the present time, it is quite as important for blacks to understand themselves in terms of their own historical origin and development as to understand the white man's technology. Their mastery of the white man's technology will be all the more thorough when, in addition, they know who they are and how they have come to be where they are. Their ability to compete on level terms in the white man's world will also be enhanced.

The really acute danger is not, as Lewis conceives it, a possibility that the majority of black students might be tempted to make black studies "the major focus of their programs." The eminent economist underrates the hardheaded realism and practical common sense of black Americans. The true danger is, instead, that, without the necessary corrective emphasis provided for American history by these studies, black students will continue to depreciate themselves and the ethnic group to which they belong, while white students will go on viewing them in the debased terms that American racism has made traditional. Then, no amount of what Lewis regards as "success" in the white man's world will, ultimately, be of the slighest use. His black 11 per cent at the top and his black 11 per cent in the middle of the economic pyramid will remain, as in the numerous instances of successful blacks today, just a bunch of niggers. And the condition of the large mass of blacks wallowing in economic squalor and racial contempt at the base of the pyramid will once again underscore the futility of all proposals for the creation of a black elite, whether such proposals are put forward by a black West Indian economist, Sir Arthur Lewis, or a black American sociologist, Dr. W. E. B. Du Bois.

The transformation of the historic condition of blacks in America must come, if at all, neither through black elitism nor black revolution, neither through integration nor separation. It must come by way of selective co-operation between blacks and whites on constructive terms conceived in pragmatism and carried out with common sense for the sake of a grand objective to which the spirit and intent of white racism are alien, and all that is doctrinaire and divisive is foreign: the grand objective of making good in our time the still-unfulfilled promise of America on behalf of the peoples of the world.

A few points remain to be noted concerning the American society, which, in its present and also its historical form, is so concrete an example of Thomas Jefferson's "elective despotism." Much of the current life of the society crystallizes around two major problems, one external and the other domestic. The first involves the imperial role of the United States in world affairs; the second involves the resolution of the internal conflict engendered by deep-rooted social contradictions. At the heart of the external problem is an intractable opposition between the national self-interest and the irrational promptings of white racism. This generates a deviant species of colonialism on the part of the United States that differs from the classical type in point of its relative disinterest in territorial acquisitions. The core of the internal problem coalesces around the inability of white racism to come to equitable terms with the legitimate demands of black Americans. Neither the external nor the internal problem is exclusively racist in character. Yet the fact that this aspect dominates the whole is beyond all question.

No one is so naïve as to suppose that any white population anywhere would be subjected by the United States to the inhumanity of atomic bombing that was visited upon the Japanese people. No one is so innocent as to believe that any but a nonwhite people would be constrained to suffer as the Vietnamese do at the hands of the United States.

It is all of a piece with the official resolve of this country to use nuclear weapons against the Chinese in the event of hostilities with the People's Republic of China. Nor, indeed, can the tender solicitude of the United States for the safety of whites marooned in the former Belgian Congo during a civil embroilment there have escaped the notice of any observer of the world scene. What was clearly visible in that situation was the superior value set by the United States upon white lives as contrasted with black; which is to say, once more in plainly explicit terms, that the world outlook of the United States is predominantly racist in character, and that this outlook threatens the very safety of the republic, because its irrational imperatives tend to subordinate the national interests to the suicidal caprices of white racism.

In no quarter of the life of the republic is the menace to its security more imminent than in the no man's land of domestic relations, where black despair is deepened by white injustice. President Lyndon Johnson's Civil Rights Act of 1964 (which, with certain textual differences, re-enacts the Civil Rights Act of 1875) must, of course, be viewed amongst other things as an attempt at constructive redress of a racial state of affairs in which an Alabama sheriff's employment of vicious trained dogs against blacks engaged in civil protest is another side of the matter; one may even say, the historic side of the matter. For dogs have typically been employed against blacks in the United States, whether to hunt them down when they attempted to escape from slavery or to subject them to various kinds of racist terror and constraint. Black women have similarly been used against black men, and indeed continue so to be used. A formal device for this purpose is the appointment of black women to fill posts of public responsibility in preference to black men equally qualified. The justification usually offered is that white men find it easier to work with black women than with black men. No doubt. Grier and Cobbs, in *Black Rage*, have some interesting observations to make on this point:

The relationship which has the longest history and the most complex psychological structure is the relationship between the white man and the black woman. From the very first introduction of black slaves into America, black women have been used sexually by their white owners. In contrast to the male slaves they had a threefold use—their labor was economically valuable, their bodies had a marketable value as sexual objects, and their potential as breeders of additional slaves was also a source of wealth to their owners. . . .

In her relationship with a white man, the black woman can partake of his power and masculinity and can for once free herself of her degraded self-perception. . . . In any event, in the United States, the psychological truth is that when a white man chooses a black woman, both in his own eyes and in the eyes of his confrères, he has chosen a depreciated sexual object rather than a highly valued one. . . . The social value set on each of the partners reverses their roles, making him the highly valued object whom the woman has been fortunate enough to obtain.

In this way, black women continue to be a species of property disposed of by white men at a higher commercial rate than black men.

Epilogue

PROPHECY, it has been said, is of all forms of error the most dangerous. But the risk must be incurred, for the right to ascertain the past and assess the present carries with it the responsibility to descry the future. This is by no means the same thing as determining the course of events. The distinction is necessary. A central paradox of human affairs continues to be the mutual exclusiveness of prevision and the possibility of sculpturing the form or choosing the content of the vision. The condition upon which the prophetic mantle is assumed is, invariably, vision divested of influence. Only the wilderness can assure a foreteller of a setting congenial to the exercise of his responsibility. The isolation it provides ensures the impotence it prescribes.

One must begin, then, by discarding the sentimental claptrap of the "American dream." No such figment has ever existed anywhere except in the imagination of hordes of immigrants gluttonous for material success. The freedom they have sought has been, in the main, the freedom to make money. Selective immigration, instead of the indiscriminate ingestion of masses of people, provided only that they were white, would have produced a finer America. The quality of American life has been debased by this racist blunder, and its promise blighted. Emma Lazarus's cloying sentimentality was as false as the cast-iron posturing of the Statue of Liberty.

The racial position of the blacks in the United States has been

422

much complicated by the influx of European immigrants. These Europeans, on coming to the United States, discover, in the vast majority of cases, that for the first time in their lives they no longer constitute the lowest social stratum. For the first time there are actually people below them. And the magic wand that has thus raised them up is white American racism. Out of gratitude for their social elevation, and also pleasure at having at long last another human group to look down upon as inferiors, they rapidly become ardent racists. From then onward, black Americans confront new European additions to the already swollen ranks of white American bigots. Making every allowance for the valuable work performed on behalf of black freedom and equality by numbers of such immigrants, the conclusion is unimpeachable that, as a whole, nevertheless, had European immigrants not been permitted to come here in such tidal proportions, blacks and whites in this country would long since have achieved much larger gains of mutual tolerance and respect.

European immigration to the United States has been a millstone around the necks of black Americans. Each successive boatload or planeload of whites has simply worsened the racial plight of the blacks. No matter which of the cardinal points of Europe has been their place of origin, these European immigrants, with relatively few exceptions, have been ethnic obstacles to communal progress between blacks and whites in America. In the southern United States, where European immigration has penetrated much less deeply than in the North, the racial problem is proceeding at a more enlightened pace toward constructive solutions; and this despite the sanguinary violence that has characterized the history of the two racial groups in the South. The Southern population has been burdened with a much lower degree of European immigration than the North. Blacks and whites in the South together constitute the oldest settled population in the country with the least degree of new influxes of European immigrants. And while violence has occurred there on a massive scale of revolting horror, and continues, although with some diminution of scale and intensity, the underlying problem has always been confronted with stark honesty and without the racial hypocrisy that is so typical of the North, which teems with masses of European immigrants. In their febrile haste to become as rabid white racists as any, these stepsons of the wild jackass have done great harm to the cause of freedom and equality for blacks in America.

All human groups, everywhere in the world, will sooner or later have to confront with fastidious and resolute intelligence the necessity to be more sensitive to the quality of their composition than, as at present, reckless of their proliferation. A preliminary step must be the jettisoning of the delusion of race. Whiteness as a criterion of ethnic acceptability must be replaced in America by a revolutionary insistence upon the sheer human excellence of the individual. America, having betrayed itself and denied its promise by the superstitious error that is race, must redeem itself and, in theological terms, achieve salvation by means of the scientific enlightenment that rejects the fallacy of race. But the road to this goal will be drenched with blood. Until it is exorcised of the spirit of racial particularism by grim internal catastrophe, America, in its ethnic ideology and practice, will follow a path similar, though not necessarily identical, to that taken by the Nazis toward Jews and nonwhites, and pursued at the present time by the white South Africans and Rhodesians against the black inhabitants of those lands. To the extent to which a conspiracy, whether unconscious or deliberate, may be said to exist on the part of the leaders of the white groups of mankind to maintain nonwhite groups in subjection, America must be recognized as foremost amongst the conspirators. Yet this does not conclusively augur the American future. Amidst the gloom and overcast are linings of uncertain alloy, but here and there it is even now possible to assay a streak of silver.

Perhaps the most hopeful of these signs is the wakeful conscience of America on the subject of race. The wakefulness of the country on moral issues in general remains the chief source of its probable regeneration. But this prospect should not be taken for granted. Much will have to be done, and not merely professed, if revolution, to the extent that it impends, or resistance, to the degree that it exists, is to be channeled into constructive courses. For apathy and indifference, rather than active moral evil, can yet constitute the chief hindrances to peaceful change.

The America here being forecast will be a confederation, as distinct from a federal arrangement, of political entities, each with its own autonomous institutions subject only to the overriding authority of the confederation in matters touching the common welfare. The decentralization of government will be accomplished under pressure of the plain circumstance that America is otherwise ungovernable.

Of those matters involving the common welfare, racial prejudice will be recognized among them as deeply injurious to the general weal and therefore impermissible either in concept or in practice.

Individual or group poverty will be treated similarly. So will religious fanaticism in all its forms, including organized particularism such as sectarian allegiances in which belief is more highly esteemed than inquiry, or where it is more important for purposes of social accreditation to be Roman Catholic than human, Baptist than human, Lutheran than human, Jewish than human, Episcopalian than human.

Marriage will be divested of its character of a "divine institution" and come to be regarded for what it is: a social arrangement to ensure the protection and care of children, to facilitate the orderly devolution of property, and as an economic device to assure the well-being of dependent women. Yet since the number of such women grows less and less, and the institutional reason for their existence more and more unacceptable, marriage in its present form in America will gradually be replaced by a civil arrangement much more difficult to contract than to dissolve. Inasmuch as the state will assume a larger role in the rearing of children than at present, parental authority will undergo further erosion, and a principal rationale for traditional marriage will be subverted and set on the road to final rejection.

Not long before these observations were set down, the Archbishop of Canterbury addressed a letter to the London *Times* calling for legislation to prohibit the exposure by actors in public theaters of what he vulgarly referred to as their "private parts." He joined a company of eminent Englishmen, among them Lord Salisbury and the Dean of Manchester, who have exercised themselves in that newspaper on the "morality" of a playful charade of small-boy eroticism entitled *Oh! Calcutta!* The Archbishop busied himself in that enterprise, under righteous cover of Christian ideals, at a time when two-thirds of the world either starves or is so ill-fed as scarcely to be in better case; when a monstrous war has been waged for more than ten years by a foreign white invader in Indochina, decimating the inhabitants of that land, despoiling their natural resources, maiming and burning alive their children, ravaging, poisoning, murdering, obliterating. The Archbishop has yet to speak a single word in condemnation of the country that has unleashed this fiendish horror upon a weaker state that dares to oppose its will. As one of the principal leaders of the Christian world community, the Archbishop has yet to call into public question the morality of a country that, possessing 6 per cent of the world's population, consumes 40 per cent of its resources. The Archbishop is silent on these matters. He concerns himself instead with other people's "private parts." Why is the Archbishop's penis more private than his nose? What iniquity inheres in the human organs of generation that the Archbishop and others like him have not implanted there with their moralizing?

His Holiness the Pope, the ecclesiastical head of the world community of Roman Catholics, inveighs against the "sinfulness" of nudity, yet does not dare to condemn a powerful Christian country that with napalm bombs flays alive yellow-skinned people, and with toxic gases deforms their unborn children—nonwhite children. On such a matter and in the face of the mightiest power on earth, the representative of the Prince of Peace is silent. Instead he chooses to use the moral trappings of his office to berate people who decide to worship God in the nude. As if God would concern Herself with the question whether or not due reverence to Her could be expressed only if the worshipers wore clothes. God probably does not wear even so much as a fig leaf. And if His Holiness were to set eyes on God, he would very likely regard Her as a "naked savage" to be converted to Christianity, rendered ashamed of Her body, and taught to worship the golden calf. Of course, if God were so deficient in taste as to manifest Herself as black, His Holiness would consider Her state deplorable and present Her at once with the historic choice between Christian baptism (with its twin accompaniments, political subjection and economic exploitation) and bloody extermination without benefit of clergy. If She manifested Herself as a "white savage," then His Holiness, supported with ecumenical fervor by his Protestant colleague, the Archbishop of Canterbury, would address an urgent appeal to the cultural anthropologists of the world to handle Her with the utmost scientific care and classify Her as a possible survivor of one of the Ten Lost Tribes of Israel. For the Christian church in the modern era has been and, on the whole, remains a powerful world-wide institution of white racism. It is the single most persuasive reason why black people desiring liberty must renounce the Christian church and all its works. No other agency of the white segment of mankind has worked with such steadfast zeal to ensure that in the kingdom of God throughout eternity white folks, as in the words of the black poet Countee Cullen (from his poem "Epitaph for a Lady I Know"):

426

> . . . lies late and snores
> While poor black cherubs rise at seven
> To do celestial chores.

Here, in this great poet's lyricism, is implicit the mass and main of the Christian church's achievement for the black people of the world: their social and political subjection and their economic exploitation, but, worst of all, their psychological enslavement. It has all been done in the name of religious piety.

Alexis de Tocqueville, remarking on the contrasts between the age of Louis XVI and the state of affairs that succeeded Napoleon and the Terror, observed: "When great revolutions are successful, they eradicate the causes that produced them; their very achievements make them inexplicable."

So if the question is what causes has the black revolution—in the fragmentary form of insurrection—succeeded in eradicating, the answer must be: few, very few.

But if the question is what causes will the black revolution—such as it may be—succeed in eradicating, the answer must be that this will depend upon the white counterrevolution. In this way, one restates the fundamental problem of the American society: white racism. No large degree of progress in race relations will be achieved in America unless the white majority permits it. Theirs is the power to effect change, to eradicate causes: the causes of massive, centuries-old black resistance and marginal insurrection. It is not even, essentially, a matter that hinges upon co-operation between whites and blacks. Acting entirely on their own, and without the slightest consultation with the blacks, white America tomorrow, the day after, or next year, next decade, next generation, can put an end, just as soon as it pleases, to oppression of the blacks. So that the question the future poses is not so much what the blacks will do, as what the whites will do. The contending parties will be black powerlessness and white power.

On the face of it, the conclusion would seem to be foregone. When was power ever vanquished by its opposite? As has been said, not without historical warrant, God is usually on the side of the big battalions. Stalin placed his own pragmatic point upon this dictum with his celebrated inquiry: "How many divisions has the Pope?" In purely military terms, the answer of course, as Stalin well knew, was: "The Swiss Guard"; which, in the context of that discussion, was merely a synonym for powerlessness. Transposing this anecdote into the terms of black resistance in America, it is immediately obvious that the blacks are in the military situation ascribed by Stalin to the Pope. The blacks are completely unequipped and almost completely untrained, unorganized, and unprepared for military action. The whites have all, or virtually all, the divisions. Nor will they be so lacking in self-interest as to sit idly on their hands while the blacks arm themselves or in any sense become a military threat to their supremacy. Therefore, in any future conflict between blacks and whites in America involving the use of arms and the deployment of military organization, the blacks will be heavily defeated. But serious theorists of black revolution do not contemplate any such assault upon the white racist line in America. Nothing would give the white racists so profound a sense of self-fulfillment as their successful entrapment of the blacks in a holocaust contrived by the blacks' own rashness and confusion of rhetoric with reality.

The essentials of successful revolution are secrecy, organization, and surprise. And the training of a true revolutionary is through years of quiet, exhaustive, and implacable concentration on the single goal of revolution. Words and their communication are a necessary part of a revolutionary's weaponry. To such a person, words are armed men, each superbly trained to strike at the chosen moment with deadly effect.

Far better, however, than revolution in the United States would be the voluntary release of the blacks from white racist oppression. For mankind at large, this would be the crucial step toward world redemption through enlightened fulfillment of the flickering, though not yet wholly extinguished, promise of America.

It is appropriate at this point to cite these words of W. E. B. Du Bois from *Black Reconstruction:*

One is astonished in the study of history at the recurrence of the idea that evil must be forgotten, distorted, skimmed over. We must not remember that Daniel Webster got drunk but only remember that he was a splendid constitutional lawyer. We must forget that George Washington was a slave owner, or that Thomas Jefferson had mulatto children, or that Alexander Hamilton had Negro blood, and simply remember the things we regard as creditable and inspiring. The difficulty, of course, with this philosophy is that history loses its value as an incentive and example; it paints perfect men and noble nations, but it does not tell the truth. . . .

428

I write then in a field devastated by passion and belief. Naturally, as a Negro, I cannot do this writing without believing in the essential humanity of Negroes, in their ability to be educated, to do the work of the modern world, to take their place as equal citizens with others. I cannot for a moment subscribe to that bizarre doctrine of race that makes most men inferior to the few. But, too, as a student of science, I want to be fair, objective and judicial; to let no searing of the memory by intolerable insult and cruelty make me fail to sympathize with human frailties and contradiction, in the eternal paradox of good and evil. But armed and warned by all this, and fortified by a long study of the facts, I stand at the end of this writing, literally aghast at what American historians have done to this field. . . .

In propaganda against the Negro since emancipation in this land, we face one of the most stupendous efforts the world ever saw to discredit human beings, an effort involving universities, history, science, social life and religion.

If America is to achieve its full promise on behalf of humanity, a special responsibility will devolve upon its white population. The whites of the world are among the most gifted of all the groups of mankind. Historical accident or the stray chance of circumstance cannot explain their present ascendancy. The only just and rational explanation is to be found either in their possession of superior endowments or in their superior use of equal endowments. If the former, there is no reason to suppose its indefinite continuance; as in all human affairs, following the pattern of nature itself, decline and decay will sooner or later set in. If the latter, it may be regarded as a function of specific will that ultimately is subject to the same governing law of decline and decay. There is no sanctuary for permanence; there is only the timeless persistence of change. Many Himalayan ranges that once soared sovereign above the flight of eagles now form part of the ocean floor.

The supreme opportunity of the white group at this point of human evolution consists in putting its magnificent attributes of will and courage, imagination and foresight, ingenuity and resourcefulness, at the service of all mankind. The challenge to the whites is that they resolve to act as trustees of humanity. So far their attainments in the realm of matter are incomparable. Yet there is a higher destiny within their reach that racism, unless it is cast out, will render unattainable and at length contrive their utter degradation.

Within a local compass, black Americans—despite all present and historic discontents—must summon up the faith to speak for America. This does not mean an end to luminous and balanced criticism, passionate and uncompromising repulsion, of hostile usages and unjust institutions. But it does mean belief in the fulfillment, by translation from theory into practice, of the social creed that is uniquely America's: a just society, with abundance freely and equally accessible to all. Whatever the limitations of current circumstances and the hobbling remembrance of the past, black Americans must acquire the will and courage, imagination and foresight, faith and resolution, to become spokesmen of the finer impulses of this land, and prophets of their high and enduring realization. Black Americans must rise above the past and transcend the present so as to command the future. The way is neither through revolution nor love. In the profoundly mixed actualities of American life, the one can only be a bloody and engulfing mire for hotheads; the other an ever-receding mirage for those to whom raptures of fine feeling are more congenial than the austerities of stern thinking.

The hope for redemption of the promise of America reposes in the wondrous persistence of the ideal of personal freedom. For blacks, above all, this grail must always retain a special sanctity and be pursued with unyielding tenacity.

On a planet largely inhabited by people who are not white, America possesses in its black citizens a great and increasing resource for statesmanlike conciliation of the besetting issue of racial differences the world over. The blessings of history are often bestowed in impenetrable disguises.

430

Selected
Bibliography

Aptheker, Herbert. *American Negro Slave Revolts*. New York: International Publishers Co., New World Paperbacks, 1969.

————. *The Colonial Era*. New York: International Publishers Co., New World Paperbacks, 1966.

Arendt, Hannah. *The Origins of Totalitarianism*. New York: Harcourt, Brace & World, 1966.

Astell, Mary. *A Serious Proposal to the Ladies*. London: 1694.

Bancroft, Frederic C. *Slave-Trading in the Old South*. Baltimore: J. H. Furst Co., 1931.

Beard, Charles A. *Contemporary American History, 1877–1913*. New York: Macmillan Co., 1914.

————. *An Economic Interpretation of the Constitution of the United States*. New York: Macmillan Co., 1935.

Becker, Carl. *The Declaration of Independence: A Study in the History of Political Ideas*. New York: Alfred A. Knopf, 1942.

Bellamy, Edward. *Looking Backward: 2000–1887*. 1888.

Bergman, Peter M., and Bergman, Mort N. *The Chronological History of the Negro in America*. New York: Harper & Row, 1969.

Blackstone, William. *Commentaries on the Law of England*. 4 vols. London: 1765–1769.

Bolitho, William. *Twelve Against the Gods*. New York: Simon & Schuster, 1929.

Boorstin, Daniel J. *The National Experience*. The Americans, vol. 2. New York: Random House, 1965.

Brinton, Crane, and others. *Prehistory to 1715. A History of Civilization*, vol. 1. Englewood Cliffs, N.J.: Prentice-Hall, 1955.

Burke, Edmund. *Reflections on the Revolution in France*. London: 1790.

Carlyle, Thomas. *Occasional Discourse upon the Nigger Question*. London: 1849.

————. *Sartor Resartus*. London: 1834.

————. *Shooting Niagara: And After?* London: 1867.

Cartwright, Samuel. *Natural History of the Prognathous Species of Mankind*. 1857.

Cash, Wilbur J. *The Mind of the South*. New York: Alfred A. Knopf, 1941.

Chesnutt, Charles. *The Marrow of Tradition*. 1901.

Cleaver, Eldridge. *Post-Prison Writings and Speeches*. Edited by Robert Scheer. New York: Random House, 1969.

————. *Soul on Ice*. New York: McGraw-Hill Book Co., 1968.

Coon, Carleton S., and others. *Races*. Springfield, Ill.: Charles C. Thomas, 1950.

Darlington, C. D. *The Evolution of Man and Society*. New York: Simon & Schuster, 1969.

Debray, Régis. *Revolution in the Revolution?* Translated by Bobbye Ortiz. New York: Grove Press, 1967.

Douglass, Frederick. *The Life and Times of Frederick Douglass*. New York: Macmillan Co., Collier Books, 1962.

Du Bois, W. E. B. *The Autobiography of W. E. Burghardt Du Bois*. Edited by Herbert Aptheker. New York: International Publishers Co., New World Paperbacks, 1969.

————. *Black Reconstruction in America, 1860–1880*. Cleveland and New York: World Publishing Co., Meridian Books, 1964.

————. *Dusk of Dawn*. New York: Schocken Books, 1968.

————. Introduction to *The Suppression of the African Slave-Trade to the United States of America, 1638–1870*, by A. Norman Klein. New York: Schocken Books, 1969.

————. *The World and Africa*. New York: International Publishers Co., 1965.

Faulkner, William. *The Sound and the Fury*. New York: Random House, 1966.

Feldstein, Stanley. *The Poisoned Tongue: A Documentary History of American Racism and Prejudice*. New York: William Morrow & Co., 1972.

Fischer, Louis. *The Life of Lenin*. New York: Harper & Row, 1964.

Franklin, John Hope. *From Slavery to Freedom: A History of Negro Americans*. New York: Alfred A. Knopf, 1967.

Freud, Sigmund, and Bullitt, William C. *Thomas Woodrow Wilson: 28th President of the United States: A Psychological Study*. Boston: Houghton Mifflin Co., 1967.

432

Frobenius, Leo. *Histoire de la civilisation africaine.*

Furnas, J. C. *The Americans: A Social History of the United States, 1587–1914.* New York: G. P. Putnam's Sons, 1969.

———. *Goodbye to Uncle Tom.* New York: William Sloane Associates, 1956.

Gaston, Paul M. *The New South Creed.* New York: Alfred A. Knopf, 1970.

Genovese, Eugene D. *The Political Economy of Slavery.* New York: Random House, Pantheon Books, 1965.

Glazer, Nathan, and Moynihan, Daniel P. *Beyond the Melting Pot.* Cambridge, Mass.: M.I.T. Press, 1970.

Gobineau, Joseph Arthur, comte de. *Essai sur l'inégalité des races humaines.* 1854.

Goodell, William. *The American Slave Code in Theory and Practice.* New York: 1853.

Grier, William H., and Cobbs, Price M. *Black Rage.* New York: Basic Books, 1968.

Hammond, James H. *Letters on Slavery: 1845.*

Harris, John. *Dawn in Darkest Africa.* Portland, Oregon: International Scholarly Book Service, 1968.

Hill, Lawrence F. *Diplomatic Relations Between the United States and Brazil.* Durham, N.C.: Duke University Press, 1932.

Hofstadter, Richard. *The Progressive Historians.* New York: Alfred A. Knopf, 1968.

Hofstadter, Richard, and Wallace, Michael, eds. *American Violence: A Documentary History.* New York: Alfred A. Knopf, 1970.

Huxley, Aldous. *Collected Essays of Aldous Huxley.* New York: Harper & Row, 1971.

Jackson, George. Introduction to *Soledad Brother: The Prison Letters of George Jackson,* by Jean Genet. New York: Bantam Books, 1970.

Jefferson, Thomas. *Notes on the State of Virginia.* Chapel Hill, N.C.: University of North Carolina Press, 1967.

Jones, Howard Mumford. *O Strange New World: American Culture: The Formative Years.* New York: Viking Press, 1967.

Las Casas, Bartolomé. *The Tears of the Indians.* London: Nath. Brook, 1656.

Lewis, Bernard. *Race and Color in Islam.* New York: Harper & Row, Torchbooks, 1971.

McPherson, James M. *The Negro's Civil War.* New York: Random House, Pantheon Books, 1965.

Malcolm X. *The Autobiography of Malcolm X.* Translated by Alex Haley. New York: Grove Press, 1965.

Marcuse, Herbert. *Negations.* Boston: Beacon Press, 1969.

———. *Reason and Revolution.* Boston: Beacon Press, 1960.

Marx, Karl. *Theses on Feuerbach.*

Mill, John Stuart. *On the Subjection of Women.* London: 1869.

Morison, Samuel Eliot. *The Oxford History of the American People.* New York: Oxford University Press, 1965.

Olmsted, Frederick. *The Cotton Kingdom.* Edited by Arthur M. Schlesinger. New York: Alfred A. Knopf, 1953.

Panikkar, Kavalam M. *Asia and Western Dominance.* London: George Allen & Unwin, 1953.

Phillips, Ulrich B. *American Negro Slavery.* Baton Rouge: Louisiana State University Press, 1966.

———. *The Slave Economy of the Old South.* Edited by Eugene D. Genovese. Baton Rouge: Louisiana State University Press, Louisiana Paperbacks, 1968.

Pike, James S. *The Prostrate State: South Carolina Under Negro Government.* New York: 1874.

Revel, Jean-François. *Without Marx or Jesus.* Translated by Jack Bernard. New York: Doubleday & Co., 1971.

Rossiter, Clinton. *The American Quest 1790–1860.* New York: Harcourt, Brace Jovanovich, 1971.

Rush, Benjamin. "Observations intended to Favor a Supposition that the Black Color (as it is called) of the Negroes is derived from the Leprosy."

Russell, Bertrand. *A History of Western Philosophy.* New York: Simon & Schuster, 1945.

Schoelcher, Victor. *Esclavage et colonisation.*

Sewall, Samuel. *The Selling of Joseph.* 1700.

Smith, Adam. *An Inquiry into the Nature and Causes of the Wealth of Nations.* London: 1776.

Stampp, Kenneth M. *The Peculiar Institution.* New York: Alfred A. Knopf, 1956.

Strachey, John. *The End of Empire.* New York: Random House, 1960.

Tannenbaum, Frank. *Slave and Citizen: The Negro in the Americas.* New York: Random House, Vintage Books, 1963.

Tawney, R. H. *Religion and the Rise of Capitalism.* New York: New American Library, 1954.

Thomas, Hugh. *Cuba: The Pursuit of Freedom, 1762–1969.* New York: Harper & Row, 1971.

Tocqueville, Alexis de. *Democracy in America.* Edited by J. P. Mayer and Max Lerner. Translated by George Lawrence. New York: Harper & Row, 1966.

———. *The Old Regime and the French Revolution.* Translated by Stuart Gilbert. New York: Doubleday & Co., Anchor Books, 1955.

Toynbee, Arnold J. *A Study of History*. Abridgment of vols. 1–6. Edited by D. C. Somervell. New York and London: Oxford University Press, 1947.

Trollope, Anthony. *The West Indies and the Spanish Main*. London: 1859.

Van Evrie, John H. *Negroes and Negro "Slavery": The First an Inferior Race: The Latter Its Normal Condition*. 1853.

Vassa, Gustavus. *The Interesting Narrative of the Life of Oloudah Equiano, or Gustavus Vassa*. 1789.

Walsh, R. *Notices of Brazil*. Boston: 1831.

Washington, Booker T. *Up from Slavery*. 1901.

Washington, Booker T., and Du Bois, W. E. B. Introduction to *The Negro in the South*, by Herbert Aptheker. New York: Citadel Press, 1970.

Williams, Eric. *Capitalism and Slavery*. New York: G. P. Putnam's Sons, Capricorn Books, 1966.

Wollstonecraft, Mary. *Vindication of the Rights of Woman*. London: 1792.